EARLY CHILDHOOD EDUCATION: A PERCEPTUAL MODELS CURRICULUM

EARLY CHILDHOOD EDUCATION: A PERCEPTUAL MODELS CURRICULUM

Doris Pronin Fromberg
Hofstra University

John Wiley & Sons
New York / Santa Barbara / London / Sydney / Toronto

Library of Congress Cataloging in Publication Data:

Fromberg, Doris Pronin, 1937–
  Early childhood education.

  Bibliography: p.
  Includes index.
  1. Education, Preschool—Curricula. I. Title.

LB1140.2.F75   372.1′9   76-45390
ISBN 0-471-28286-3

Printed in the United States of America

10 9 8 7 6 5 4 3 2 1

To Mel, Eden, Deborah

PREFACE

Perceptual models—such as the whole is more than the sum of its parts, indirect progress, and cyclical change—are processes that represent interacting elements. Perceptual models can be perceived through varied experiences in varied forms and they cut across existing academic subjects. In this sense, perceptual models are a framework for an integrated early childhood curriculum.

Much of this book for prospective teachers and teachers of young children between three and eight years of age defines and describes perceptual models, the practical activities in which they are represented, and the settings that support learning. Specific teacher practices as well as specific examples of children's behavior and how interaction between teacher and child occurs are included. Activities and practices are presented in terms of what children may experience directly.

Rather than a statement about either theory or practice, this is a book about varied practices that are welded by a common framework. They are practices that reflect young children's developmental possibilities.

The early childhood years are a uniquely potent time in which flexible thinking, fresh associations, and playful, exploratory outlooks are rich promises to the future. These processes are strengths that teachers must nurture because they support new forms, creative insights, and new orderings of the world.

A downpour of money on early childhood education has not proven to be enough, by itself, to bring about a change in the human experience of all children. It takes more than money or time alone. It takes approaches and perspectives that can be flexible and responsive to children in a changing world.

Beyond today, teachers need to be able to assist children's education next year and twenty-five years from now. Socialization, the roles of men and women, of minority groups, of poor people, of citizens, and of workers are evolving into new forms. Technology creates new literacies as varied as those in mathematics, radio astronomy, film, and the other arts. Perceptual models serve as a way to help young children develop the resources that they will need in order to deal with change.

Perceptual models serve to unify the diverse ways and tools that children can use to learn. These tools and ways of knowing more about the world have been developed throughout history and have been contributed by scientists, social scientists, artists, linguists, philosophers, craftsmen, and others.

However, in these rapidly changing times, and for a long time past, accumulated knowledge has been uncontainable in any finite form. In addition, there are ways of knowing and perceiving that are beyond the funded conceptions of existing scholars. Processes that serve changing and new orderings of the world should be supported.

Therefore, when teachers use the synoptically ordered framework proposed here, it minimizes a consideration of isolated science methods or social studies methods or artistic methods. Rather, an interdisciplinary study of tools is a purpose in this book. For example, the study of the physical world might tie science with values, with aesthetics, with mathematics, and with linguistics. *I see the interplay of varied methods of inquiry on concrete data as a way to seek beyond the cultural limitations of knowledge. Since young children are not limited by adult subject matter divisions, their flexibility is a potent force to be nurtured.*

Activities that involve the use of tools, broadly defined, form the medium through which perceptual models are acquired. Perceptual models create a sense of connectedness, blending "interdisciplinary" interrelations. *The relations themselves become the basic elements for planning.* In this sense, perceptual models are a unique syntax of experience.

A primary reason to employ perceptual models in early education is that such planning emphasizes the natural connectedness of experience. The teacher soaks the young child's environment with perceptual models that are repeatedly embedded in the variant forms of different activities. When teachers plan in this way, children may be helped to maintain their openness to unique, individual possibilities for ordering the world.

Another reason to employ perceptual models in early education is that such planning supports the young child's developing capacity for imagery. The teacher who plans in this way appreciates the *potency of the young child's perceptual modes of understanding.* Learning is supported through interdevelopmental functions. This activity orientation recognizes that *cognitive, aesthetic, psychomotor, and social development are intertwined.*

Teachers need better ways to decide what is worth their personal investment of time and energy with children. There is a need to change the process and politics by which decisions for activities are made and implemented by children, teachers, administrators, and communities.

This book considers these pressures and processes. It is about, and of, adult–child dialogue. It is such dialogue that matters.

Doris Pronin Fromberg

CONTENTS

6   THE FRANCHISED TEACHER'S WAYS OF WORKING: STIMULATING INDEPENDENT EXPRESSION THROUGH DIALOGUE AND THE ARTS

EARLY CHILDHOOD EDUCATION: A PERCEPTUAL MODELS CURRICULUM

CHAPTER 1
PERCEPTUAL MODELS AS AN ALTERNATIVE PLANNING STRATEGY

This book is addressed to those who are becoming teachers of young children and to those teachers who wish to consider ways of influencing children's interdisciplinary use of tools. Since there are many proliferating programs, each generation of teachers is faced with decisions concerning what children need to learn, how to teach, when to teach, and whom to teach. The exploration of alternative ways to decide these issues becomes clearer when a teacher has some consistent reasons for deciding and acting.

In the preface, perceptual models were introduced as a way to help children experience connectedness and varied possibilities for ordering their worlds. In this chapter, since institutionalized schooling is a reality, an image of the child who functions in this setting is presented. Then, a discussion of the role of the teacher will precede an advance look at the contents of successive chapters.

CONNECTEDNESS IN CHILDREN'S LIVES

This book attempts to represent a particular theoretical position rather than an eclectic approach. Since a teacher's style is more effective when he or she has a greater range of, and power to decide between, alternative means, those that are consistent with the perceptual models position are presented.

Usually, teachers have been expected to accept many theories of learning and curriculum development while using standardized methods and materials—a kind of verbal duplicity. This book suggests the alternative of moving from a unifying framework that presupposes a diversity of tools and materials. Substantial ideas should be attainable by a variety of means. In this setting, the socialization curriculum or the textbook curriculum is eclipsed by

THE CHILDREN CAN SEE HOW MANY BLOCKS WILL BALANCE THEIR FROG'S WEIGHT.

children's broader use of resources and tools with the help of a franchised teacher.

A related purpose of this book is to build a picture of activity for your children that moves beyond "one-shot deals" toward a longer range view of developing connected activities. Since activities in themselves are not connectable, the teacher's franchise consists of selection, display, and juxtaposition of activities and materials. In turn, the children's franchise consists of potential receptivity, selective perception, and intentional participation.

I assume that education is not solely the communication of information, or a custodial enterprise. Rather, education is an interactive process of active participants: teachers and learners. Perceptual models are recommended as a framework for developing activities through which such interactive learning can proceed. Learning in this sense represents a unique fingerprint in time for each group engaged in activities.

When children have tools and engage in activities with tools, they have the opportunity to make new connections, an intrinsically pleasurable experience. The traditional distinction is obliterated between schooling as work, an alienated pastime, and play as rewarding. Children can acquire information as a means toward making new connections rather than acquiring information as an end in itself.

As one may instinctively feel—and numerous authors have noted—some of the most significant learning takes place without direct, premeditated teaching (Brown and Bellugi, 1964; Church, 1961; Holt, 1967; Navarra, 1955 . . .). Therefore, teaching involves the creation of possibilities for "significant" encounters. Play, as opposed to escapist, aggressive, or competitive sports, may be defined as personal involvement, a possibly nurturant, "significant" encounter (Ellul, 1965; Lorenz, 1970).

The issue of alienated as opposed to nonalienated, significant activity is paralleled by the distinction between labor and work (Marcuse, 1970). The *purpose* of the activity—how it functions within its societal setting—defines its significance. Through significant activity, humans can be in a nonalienated relation to their work that has its own purpose and direct meaning in their lives. This then is when "work" becomes "playful."

Volumes have been written about play and it would stretch too far afield to pursue the subject here. For present purposes, the main concern is to see that schools have become bound by historical conceptions into a pinching framework. In traditional Western thinking, aesthetic, direct, playful, sensorial, and sensuous experience has been ranked as "lower," less valuable, than rational processes (Northrop, 1946). Yet both direct and indirect learning are realities.

It is not my purpose to reverse the hierarchy but to entertain a balanced relation and valuing of the significance in these dimensions.

Otherwise, without "being" (engaging in direct activity), "becoming" and "nothingness" are linked together in an isolated, undermining relation to the individual person. For the young child, to be is to become, but to become without being is to invite nothingness. (This theme is expanded in Chapter 3.) For young children, constructing their substantive, meaningful knowing of the world takes place through being direct participants in this world. Such substantive, direct action becomes the criterion for significance.

SCHOOLING AS A REALITY

Looking ahead to the activities and proposals, it is possible to be struck with the notion that the existing concept of schooling is obsolete. In many instances it is. At the very least, it is artificial to toss twenty-five to thirty-five children and one adult into a finite box of space for three to six hours each day. Schools have therefore evolved a regimen for training children away from their natural flow of action and exploration to on-cue responses to institutional demands. Teachers have often been teaching schooling in the name of educating.

CHILDREN ARE CHOOSERS

Before young children arrive at school and after they depart, they show themselves to be incredibly able learners. They have made choices from among alternate possible materials and activities that exist in their homes and outdoors. While one child studies every different insect on the way home from school, another notices and classifies motorized vehicles, still another prefers an extended observation of a demolished building site, yet another counts the racks of clothing that men are pushing past him in his crowded garment center neighborhood, and one child is engrossed in sharing wishes with a friend. With a range of real and imaginable choices, most children appear quite able to select a relevant pastime.

CHILDREN ARE DYNAMIC

Each of these children manages to find the *time and energy* to pursue a self-selected choice. You would hardly propose that a child be scheduled to finish insects at the end of this street and begin the study of vehicular traffic on the next street. You could observe the homeward-bound student of insects watching, touching, and collecting for a week or two or longer. He may well be the child who finds stories about birds interesting, who can enjoy watching tadpoles develop in a pond or aquarium, and who learns which seeds to put out for local birds. His *rhythm of activity* is his alone.

When people say that young children have short attention spans, then one must ask, "To what?" Children who feel involved and active in their work are children whose attention span is not a matter of debate or concern. Children whose own rhythm is interrupted, who are required to change frequently from one activity to another, are children whose self-direction is undermined and whose attention span is, at best, polite. If they are honest, they are distracted, and at worst, destructive.

Pacing is related to the power of each child to feel responsible for his or her selection of activity. When the teacher provides for long blocks of times, scholarship is similarly supported. Children extend their attention span when they find meaning in their occupations. Meaning involves a changing commitment. Meaning moves a concrete situation beyond itself. Therefore, beyond looking at choices of activities to offer children, teachers need to consider a child's perceptions of those options that are worth his or her investment of time and energy.

CHILDREN ARE EXPERIENCED

Imagine yourself to be a five-year-old child. You were born sixty-two months ago and spend your time at home with your mother, your older sister, your father, babysitters, grandparents. . . . You find dog toys and pictures in the supermarket and notice the giant inflated banana hanging over the produce counters. When you look up, you see the unpainted undersides of shelves.

New flowers in spring thrill you and you feel that you will never forgive the gardener who must have destroyed the crocuses. Just thinking of him makes you furious. You spend hours building farms and zoos with your miniature animals, blocks, and boxes around the house. There are always mother and father and baby animals. You try to capture birds with your jacket and bring a bowl of milk to the stray dog near your house.

You dread having to kiss all of the uncles goodbye at family gatherings. When thunder wakens you at night you feel your heart beat faster as you race to your parents' bed. That's one good thing about thunder.

You walk to your neighbor's house to see if he can play ball with you but he tells you he cannot come over because he cannot bear to part with his best friend who is visiting. You ask your mother to play with you because you feel so lonely and there's nothing to do. It feels good when your mother tells you what a great checkers player you have become.

You feel puzzled to see your older sister's face contort with disgust when she takes the spoon you have handled. More usually, she wants to take what you have long before you want to give it to her. You will hate Harold all your life for pushing you on the steps and reopening your scraped knee. You will miss your friend Stanley if his family moves away. He taught you to count to one hundred when you were only four years old and shared your horror when the doll baby's paint came off in the water. You play card games together and he taught you how to stack the deck in his favor. You talk about favorite television shows together and race to your mothers because the commercial tells you to tell your mother to go right out and buy IT. You can sing every commercial you hear and ride your two-wheeler without training wheels.

Mosquitos think you are sweeter than grownups. You have been on an airplane for vacation and you played with the goat family, saw all those cats in the old place full of rocks, and rode horses in the mountains. Sometimes you walked such a long time that you wished your father would carry you. Catching waves at the beach is fun but it is easier to swim in a pool.

You feel guilty when you eat more candy than your mother said you could have. You don't quite understand why your mother's not wanting to send the dentist on vacation is a reason not to eat candy. You watch the older children going on the school bus every day. You have had a nursery school car pool but when you start kindergarten you can go on the bus with the big kids. Then you can learn to read more things.

EXPERIENCE IS COGNITIVE, AESTHETIC, PSYCHOMOTOR, AND SOCIAL

Young children's experiencing of the world is at once cognitive, aesthetic, psychomotor, and social. Their entire attention is devoted to solving a problem. They stand ready to repeat a skill again and again, and feel satisfied and supported in their activity. Each child needs a different amount of time to satisfy his or her repetition of mastery—whether the task is tying shoe laces, riding a bicycle, pouring liquids, writing one's name, or fixing a puzzle.

Much of children's understanding about how things work is tied to their physical involvement, their feelings of competence, and their immediate appreciation of the moment itself. When you walk with a young child you can see and hear and appreciate what might otherwise be a lost world of novelties.

Therefore, anybody who proposes to work with a young child needs to be aware that the medium of work is physical and that the child's direct involvement is the basis for his motivation. The child's means become the vehicle for carrying the school's purposes most effectively. In short, early education serves best when children are not alienated from tasks but are enticed by them.

Nevertheless, one may find little disagreement with the notion that education ultimately implies education of the mind. The most loving teacher who is inept at relevant planning and assessing development inflicts situations in which children may experience academic failure. Such subjective failure can hardly find commensurate compensation.

CHALLENGES FOR YOUNG CHILDREN

Skillful teachers, at any time, manage to consider children's affective and social development. Yet all the "warmth" and social sensitivity of a skilled teacher are unable to shelter a child from the self-appraisal afforded by an intellectual failure. The skilled teacher, then, would need to translate the human fund of knowledge (Dewey, 1933) into activities that children can perceive as hopeful or successful, and in which children may see themselves as competent actors.

Two elements here merit elaboration. First, translating the human fund of knowledge for the younger child is a more complex task since representation requires a much more concrete rendering. Second, significant success is most satisfying when it represents the fulfillment of some perceived challenge. Challenge, in this sense, involves both a risk and a perceivable chance for success.

In this interaction with consenting children, it is essential not to disenfranchise the teacher who may have "at least" as equal a right to initiate substantive activities as does the four- or five- or six-year-old child for whom she is responsible. Moreover, wedding the operations of what is taught with how it is taught is probably more important than either operation.

At the same time, using the language of this "wedding" involves traditional notions of "substance" and "form," the eternal split between Eastern and Western thought. Dewey (1934) proposes that an "act itself is exactly *what* it is because of *how* it is done. In the act there is no distinction, but perfect integration of manner and content, form and substance" (p. 109). In effect, the organization within a group, the quality of interaction between teacher, activities, and materials, and children with children and the teacher, the nature of dialogue between them, all serve to influence and become part of what participants learn.

I propose that teachers begin with those activities that can challenge children on their own terms in ways that simultaneously involve cognitive, aesthetic, psychomotor, and social dimensions. These dimensions can be artificially isolated but are indissoluble in reality.

BALANCING NATURE AND REALITY

There is a tradition among some Native American potters to offer a token of seed grain to the earth in exchange for removing raw clay. This group of human beings has taken from the earth only what was essential to life. At a deep level, they were able to appreciate the kind of balance in nature that technological society dimly acknowledges at a veritable crossroads with crisis.

While it is hardly novel to remark that the process of education reflects the society in which it exists, teachers need to be vigilant about the conditions created in early education by the very complexity of society. Specialism seems to grow weed-like not only in industry but in the continuing pendulum swings of early education. When teachers move between emphasizing "either–or" programs while chorusing the "whole child" they remove from children's natures more than is essential.

Rather, park the cars that keep you abreast of the newest slogan and program and hike a bit, appreciating what is taking place all around you. Help children encounter a beautiful today. Dignify the early childhood years with recognition of their own integrity. Teachers must support the present potency and richness of young children's perceptual possibilities; in this book, I propose to relate the potent imagery patterns of young children's natural development with an alternative for early education that retains the natural balance of which the Native American potters are so conscious.

Perceptual models will be explored as an alternate way to seek answers to the question of what might be the substance of learning in early education. This approach includes responding to a question that is broader than what children *can* learn; it involves what children can learn that leaves them the kind of balanced nature that is a human right.

As you meet children each day, you are faced with the issue of how you value the kinds of human beings sanctioned by society. If on the one hand you say that each life is important, that the social contract ought to work, that each person needs to be protected and nurtured within it, and on the other hand it is said that the early years are pivotal in development, then teachers must begin quite early to build solutions to the world's problems.

If you say that people must operate within the given system of law in which they reside, then at what point, and how, does one person decide when that is not possible!? All the glitter of the German university tradition did not illuminate these issues for German jurists during the Nazi regime. There is a need to look at ways to develop self-propelled decision-makers.

Teachers need to seek alternate, more appropriately contemporary ways to approach decision making in the education of young children. Clearly, the Victorian boxes of subject matter need to be replaced rather than renovated yet again. This clarity is reinforced by daily encounters with new forms of literacy that are nonlinear.

For example, you understand clearly when a film cuts from the picture of a man walking through a door to his body rolling down a hill that there was intervening action. You fill in the gap because you are literate in the medium. For a person in his first exposure to this medium, the cutting might be viewed as magical or humorous (Wright, 1954). The visual arts field is another domain in which literacy is continually redefined, with abstract art giving way to "pop" art and pop art giving way to "concept" art.

Steiner (1970), who has written literary criticism, writes of "The Retreat from the Word" to a new literacy of mathematical symbols that are no longer translatable into words. While advanced mathematics is outside young children's competence, it is reflected in their society's pressures. In contrast, film literacy is acquired before nursery school for most children by means of television. While new literacies in society serve to shape schools, and need to be considered, educators must seek answers to the question of balancing children's natural capacities with the realities of their experiences.

LOOKING AHEAD

When teachers decide what to teach, they do so with a larger picture of which children to involve or what specific kinds of issues would attract them. In addition, they have some simultaneous concern for where and when to offer the activity. These elements are frequently not separable. Much coordinated activity occurs intuitively with boundary-crushing strength required for teacher self-awareness to occur.

Therefore, beyond disembodied one-shot activities–things-to-do with children, I propose to try to have the teacher's thinking emerge by moving through a teacher's process of organizing time, place, persons, and actions. In this way, it may be possible to see one level at which continuity operates in the classroom. Therefore, Chapter 2 addresses the look of learning in early education. When we look together at "how" it is done, there is a common basis for deciding the pivotal question of what children might learn in that setting.

Chapter 3 serves as the theoretical core of the book. It considers conceptual development, priorities, and an extended definition of perceptual models.

Chapter 4 deals with alternative strategies for planning a range of activities and the possibilities for connectedness. The sciences, social sciences, arts, and skills are integrated. The blending of concepts, perceptual models, activities, and tools is specified by examples of practical applications.

Chapter 5 is broadly defined and isolates the particular tool of language because it is the primary synoptic tool of society. Syntax model games, decoding games, and other techniques for teaching reading are presented alongside a language-experience orientation.

Chapter 6 discusses the franchised teacher's ways of working: specifically stimulating independent expression through dialogue and the arts. Intervention techniques, some special learning needs, and art, music, literature, and the place of aesthetics in early education are considered. Residual issues of continuity and sequence as well as assessment are presented.

Chapter 7 deals with the rights and responsibilities of teachers and children, problems of social behavior, and patterns of coping. Methods for anticipating and remedying social interaction problems are presented. The teacher as a stimulator of social life through alternative actions is the main topic. Cooperative Mathematics is discussed and mathematical activities are detailed. In addition, the integration of other substantive and social concerns is described.

Chapter 8 brings together the existentialist and Piagetian frameworks that have formed the theory underlying this book. Critical consciousness, values, and political development are related to work with young children. In conclusion, relationships with parents and some prospects for future consideration are discussed.

CHAPTER 2
THE LOOK OF
LEARNING IN
EARLY EDUCATION

This chapter is an attempt to share the writer's image of what learning in early education looks like and feels like. As we proceed together through a synthesized "visit," we can see the incarnation of a particular organization. After looking at alternative possible structures and some common characteristics that distinguish open educational settings, we will consider how a teacher and a group of children plan together. This part is followed by a look at how the beginning days of the relationship between children and their teachers contribute to the development of what we have looked at together. Since this chapter emphasizes structural elements, I propose a way to view the relation of structure and substance for further use. First, a few words about the larger school society.

Regardless how artificial schooling as we now know it may be, it is a real constraint within which teachers operate. Especially in the early years, there has been a pressure placed upon teachers and children to use this time as an introduction to the "real" thing. It is part of the general layman's view of knowledge-as-memory of factual data. It is also part of a profound "objectification" of young children that is related to the notion that schooling needs to prepare children for first grade or fourth grade or whatever grade. Sometimes it seems that the deepest chasm existed between kindergarten and first grade, that over the span of one summer, a differently adapted form of life was expected to have evolved.

If we look at the teacher next year, contrasted with the child today, as the basis for deciding what to teach, it becomes too easy to lose sight of whether or not we may be willing to value the image of the next year toward which children are being deflected.

CHILDREN TRY TO INCLUDE RED BLOCKS IN THE RED HOOP, AND BLUE AND RED BLOCKS WITHIN THE INTERSECTING HOOPS.

All too often, children are moved toward an isolated focus on isolated skills, alienated from their own lives—disembodied as it were. Verbalized fact-stating and memory-cramming, the single-minded and simple-minded attention to detail, obscures the real nature of long-range learning and undermines true scholarship that is more globally structured. After all is said and done, little remains of the bits of information. What remain forever are the residual feelings and attitudes that ultimately dictate how one will behave and receive experience in one's life. This view concurs with Whitehead (1929) that wisdom lies in the use of knowledge. And use implies action. If you think back to the most satisfying residues of your own early education, you are likely to find active participation (sometimes painful, sometimes pleasurable, sometimes simply actively stimulating), serving as a window back in time.

Teachers should attempt to adapt education to young children's real possibilities. Children simply do not develop in the straight lines in which adults think.

In a similar vein, when driving in older, European cities, the shortest distance between two points is a curve. Movement in a straight line clashes with the aesthetic of the city and its necessary system of one-way routings in narrow streets. One type of hairbrush has its bristles set into a rubber foundation. As one brushes one's hair, the bristles adjust to the skull as springs on a bed or shock absorbers on a car.

Increasingly, and slowly, schools have been bending and adjusting to fit children's ways of growing. Children's development meanders in undulating curves and children are permitted to bounce against the curves of their education. When schools, without self-consciousness, sculpt this elasticity, then schools can absorb many children who might otherwise be classified as "special" cases. In this way schools can bend with the slower developing children as well as with those children who require extended challenges. Development is viewed and assessed, not from the vantage point of segregated normative statistics, but from a study of each child in relation to himself and his society.

One cannot conceive such activity in a one-dimensional manner but rather as a Max Ernst painting that explodes one's perception into an infinity of simultaneous experiencing.

IDEALS CAN BECOME REAL

Consider the case of a school that services a low-income housing project and dilapidated, privately owned houses, all set in an industrial complex. There is less open green space and more industrial soot and noise than in most other parts of this city. Rubbish is strewn over empty lots of land. Burned out and partially boarded up structures stand. Many heavy trucks use the area for through traffic. Transportation to the swinging life of the downtown city's museums, theaters, zoos, and parks means two fares and an hour's travelling.

Entry into the aged school building leaves one with wonder at what possible macabre extensions of the outdoors would be found indoors. A nagging rain and overcast sky emphasize the atmosphere, blending well. When the sun shines, it is an affront, lighting up chipped bricks, cracked sections of pavements, grime-sculpted corners, and corrosion-speckled corrugated tin panels.

Many of the children wear handed-down, faded, unironed clothing from which they change into "play" clothes after school. One boy's sweater and head are covered with red lint. Several children have running sores around their mouths, some on their hands. Many heads of hair were washed, perhaps a month before. One is hard put to evoke the memory of a scruffier-looking lot of children.

When you enter the ancient building, designated a "priority" school, you are greeted by a dimly lit section of hall from which can be heard sounds of many children, as if at a park. The passage opens into a corridor painted in varied colors. Through the doors, you can see what appears to be a well-equipped series of nursery and kindergarten rooms, with children working in small groups or alone.

NURSERY

Peering into a nursery room reveals many activities in progress. Easel painting, water measuring at the sink, table-top building toys, drawing with crayons, and looking at picture books in a rug-enclosed area are located at one side of the room. The furniture subdivides the space into smaller areas reserved for these quiet activities.

On the other side of the room is a wonderland full of the sound of children's voices and activity. A teacher is bent over the sand table, talking with five children. Beyond this is an area where wooden blocks are in use. In a dramatics corner and dressup area, children are busily occupied talking and using the materials. A few children are roaming and observing.

The teacher moves away from the sand table and approaches two children who had been roaming. The children agree when she suggests a collage activity. She helps them carry scissors, paste, and textured materials to a table in the less active section of the room. The children help themselves to materials from four shoe boxes, each of which holds materials with a different texture. The teacher cuts some cloth and tissue paper as directed by one child who cannot manage to cut them by himself. She shows him some ways to tear, fold, bunch, crush, and twist other materials so that he could work independently.

After she helps them sort misplaced materials, she walks toward the dressup area. On her way, she stops to admire one child's perseverance with a puzzle and another child's combination of colors at the easel. She stops to ask a child who seems nearly finished with a crayon drawing what he is planning to do next. Satisfied with his response, she reaches the dressup area and is swept up in the purchase of groceries with imaginary money and a price structure that sells apples at a dollar and cereal at a nickel.

She maintains this busy, calm pace for the better part of two hours. Four twenty-minute time samplings reveal a median of five different child contacts each minute. The children appear comfortable, reasonably happy, mostly constructively involved.

The children's comprehension vocabulary is extremely limited. The syntax of many of the three- and four-year-olds is limited to one- and two-word sentences. The faculty is aware that the children's syntax and vocabulary are restricted. The teacher is working on plans for increased verbal contacts with children through syntax model games that are discussed in Chapter 5. In addition, as she circulates from one area to another, she speaks to the children, appreciating, encouraging, questioning, and suggesting.

When she judges that the children can be expected to work independently for a few minutes, she seats herself beside three children who were dumping a mass of objects into the sides of the balance scale. She suggests a guessing game if they could sort the objects that include bottle caps, pine cones, wood cubes, pebbles, rubber washers, spools, and red beans. Since her assessment is correct (and she is quick to note that this is not universally true) that the dumping and giggling activity is a message for her that the children need some stimulation, the children eagerly begin to sort the materials into a set of empty coffee cans covered with colored contact paper. When they are ready, they work together, at first guessing which items would be heavier or lighter in weight and then testing their hypotheses by using the balance scale. Occasional surprises, such as a large appearing pine cone that weighs less than a small metal bottle cap, leads to the discussion of possible reasons. The children offer alternative interpretations ranging through "because" to magic, foul play, and "It feels different."

The teacher notices which child would soon be ready for the next step, counting how many pine cones balance a bottle cap, as well as that child who needs help with sorting objects in the first place. During the year she will arrange for children to sort, classify, and compare according to color, size, shape, texture, weight, space, time, resilience, odor, change, movement, and composition.

KINDERGARTEN

The room for five-year-olds appears similarly furnished but more sophisticated. Most furniture and materials are clearly labelled in lowercase letters.

One area, enclosed on three sides by shelves, contains mathematics-related materials. There is a balance scale with labelled boxes of beads, pine cones, sand, buttons, cotton balls, beans, discs, and other items. There are Cuisenaire rods and Dienes multibase arithmetic blocks. There are also rulers and transparent measuring cups of varying sizes and shapes in a tub on a shelf.

The sociodramatic area contains a hospital section and a store-puppet stage frame. Boxes, shelves, and pegboard enclose an area containing a woodworking bench, carpentry tools, and pine lumber in a basket.

Three children sit at a table setting up electric circuits with wires and clamps leading to different kinds of switches, lights, and buzzers. Nearby, two others are changing newspapers in a guinea pig's cage. Set nearby is an aquarium full of tadpoles at various stages of development while a salamander adds color to the terrarium.

Two children are weaving jersey loops at yet another table while still another child writes her name with a pencil at the top of a crayon drawing. She uses a teacher-made name card as a model.

A child who had made his own picture book with felt-tipped colored pens dictates narrative as the teacher records his comments beside each picture. Then she helps another child begin a two-sided sewing card, obtains additional gummed paper for a collage maker, adjusts wire for a hanging mobile construction, and hangs a child's finished twelve-by-eighteen-inch painting on a bulletin board that contains an unoccupied white oaktag frame.

When she sees that everybody seems reasonably occupied and could be expected to continue for a while, she sits with four children, the balance scale, some standard weights, and a blindfold. The weights, while all the same size, are marked differently according to their densities. The teacher explains that she is isolating the weight from its appearance and tries to help the children begin to develop seriation skills, ordering first two, then three, then five weights.

She further explains to the visitor that she plans parallel activities with other materials. These children had had prior experiences with sorting, by touch, the lengths of wooden Cuisenaire rods placed in bags. Cuisenaire rods consist of ten varicolored hardwood lengths in a series whereby the smallest (a white rod) is one-half the length of the second smallest red rod that is one-fifth the length of the largest orange rod, and so forth. Another way to say it is that two white rods are equal to the length of a red rod and ten white rods are equal in length to an orange rod. With a bare pause for breath, you can now see that five red rods are equal in length to an orange rod and so forth.

They had also used Lavatelli's (1970) seriation pictures. These pictures are on ten identical cards with picture size as the only variable. Two series of ten pictures, one of a child wearing rain clothing and one of an umbrella, are then matched, using one-to-one correspondence after the pictures are seriated.

However, the teacher continues to note that the published materials are teaching conveniences. The children have many seriation experiences in their everyday lives such as comparing sizes of food items, toys, sticks, houses, and people. In addition, the teacher had also constructed series of cylinders using discarded paper rolls, plastic containers, lids, and buttons.

Further, children's understandings of seriation vary and are related to the Piagetian (Piaget, 1947; 1953) concept of decentering, a process through which a young child learns to see more than his own perspective. Part of this development comes with practice and the *dissonance* between first glance observations, concrete referents, and additional experiences.

This understanding parallels children's social development quite as much as it relates to their dealings with objects. Taking turns and learning to share require cognitive abilities. When adults ask a young child to wait his turn, something that some adults at checkout counters, ticket queues, and airline counters have trouble doing, they are asking him to decenter himself, to recognize that the other fellow has rights, feelings, and needs. Yet from a child's earliest days he is expected to be sociable in this cognitively demanding way. The youngest children have little concept of the other person's experiencing of wants. At best, the teacher helps children with necessary language, acceptance of their feelings if not their actions, and repeated experiences. (Chapter 7 extends this discussion.)

PRIMARY

As you walk out of the kindergarten room, past two children talking over their checkerboard, hardly anyone notices because they are involved with their activities. However, when you walk up the battleship green iron stairs past colorful murals made by children and enter the primary room, a six-year-old boy provides a hug-at-first-sight and practically drags you past four children listening to tape recorders with earphones, two children playing with a teacher-made "Candyland" (Milton Bradley Co.) game adaptation for practice in the word families of "it" and "at," five children whose chairs face a wall in order to cut down visual distractions as they write on lined paper with pencils, a child with a ruler measuring plant sizes, six children writing responses to teacher-made computation cards using colored plastic discs, and two boys playing a teacher-made board game using dice and working in the base 4. You both join the teacher who is seated at a round table at the far end of the room listening to a group of five children read their captions for pictures that will be made into a roller movie.

When they finish, one child goes to the office to use the primer typewriter while another goes to the easel. The teacher asks the "hugger" and three other children to remain with him for a new card game. They play "pairs" in which the cards are placed face down in random order after the words on them have been identified. Since the children had not seen the game before, the teacher takes two turns to show them how it works and to explain the need to say what you pick and how to replace each card in the same spot unless it is a pair. (Details of game construction are provided in Chapter 5.)

The teacher invites you to take his place in the game. Then the teacher circulates around the room, making brief notes in a small book. He explains later that the book is indexed for each child and he periodically checks off what materials each child uses and notes in which skills or concepts the child needs instruction. Each day he concentrates systematically on keeping track of the movements of five children although he makes notations about others. At least once each week he reviews his notes to help in planning the following week's additions and in developing longer range ideas for projects and trips.

As he moves from one area to another it seems clear that children have no assigned seats and move to the area in which related materials are stored. Measurement tools and accessories are grouped together in one area and writing tools are grouped together in another. However, each child has a large box of his own in which to store personal books, papers, and small construction projects. Since materials are stored in the area of use, children can easily replace them. It is simple for children to keep track of the objects because they place a felt cloth underneath objects when they use multiple materials such as boxes of small blocks or bags of arithmetic counters.

There are displays of children's writing and art work on the bulletin boards. Among these displays are graphs that children made, which survey such phenomena as the numbers of cars and trucks passing the school at different time intervals during the day. The teacher explains that the nursery teachers had prepared the children for work with graphs by having activities in which children matched objects on a one-to-one basis. He also noted that the kindergarten children had graphed eye colors of group members on a one-to-one basis and had surveyed children's preferences between two television programs. Earlier in the year, the six-year-olds had made a histogram depicting family sizes of children in their group. He planned with the teacher next door that the seven-year-olds would interview their parents and grandparents in order to construct a similar graph for purposes of comparison with the six-year-olds. They believed that such comparisons would stimulate some interesting questions and wider connections with other data and that the questions could generate research activities appropriate for the children. Chapter 4 expands the possibilities of this kind of activity.

This morning, however, a child had brought to school two packages of candy. The teacher asked the following questions:

Which is biggest? Which is heaviest? (Balance scale)
How many pieces are in each box?
How many shells, peas, corks, chalks . . . fit around the perimeter of each box?

The child's attention continued to be engrossed beyond the forty-five minutes that I observed her. Next steps for this child might mean surveys involving seriation and other classifications, or moving beyond balancing to the use of standard weights and measures.

Circulating. The teacher appeared to follow an alternating pattern of activity. He would circulate briefly within each of the furniture subdivisions and then remain in an area with one or two or six children. He would listen to a child read, or teach a new number concept, or try to resolve a dispute, or discuss plans for a new project about life in the sea, or start a new board game with a group.

After each direct teaching time, he circulates around the room before beginning the next activity with another small group. The main concern while circulating is to help those individuals who need additional encouragement or stimulation to think of additional possibilities. He wants to be sure that minimal interruption of direct teaching sessions will occur—when children are involved in what they are doing, they are not likely to seek the teacher's attention when it is less readily available.

As he circulates, he is able to learn more about each child's pace, depth of involvement, and competence with each activity. He could stop for a fleeting moment of teaching, one of the most satisfying facets of the job. He could notice the child who needs help in choosing a next task, offer a suggestion of what to do next, or assist in joining another child or group in an activity. In effect, he is using the circulating opportunity to *extend plans* for ongoing work with children, to *redirect* children, to help children *select* and obtain needed *materials,* to engage in direct *teaching,* to bring individuals together or change group compositions in order to support positive *social interaction,* to *enjoy* and *appreciate* children's real accomplishments and self-directed efforts, to *evaluate* what they can do and how well-coordinated they are in order to *diagnose* their needs for possible next steps, and to *record* their progress on a regular basis.

When you visit the seven-year-olds next door, the teacher's pattern of movement is similar. As you enter, she is just finishing a transaction at the children's post office and then suggests that you be a resource person for spelling information for a group of children who are writing. You notice that there seem to be a number of requests for the spelling of words with "er," "ur," "or," "ir," and "ing."

Two children line up a string of small word cards they select from a pocket chart of many words until they have a sentence. Then they copy the sentence all at once. The teacher explains that this helps them to express their idea before it is lost. In this way, they can record it before the idea is buried in the coordinating effort of the physical labor of writing.

In a nearby area are six boys, using a balance scale with ounce weights. They are to find out how many green peas balance a four-ounce weight. They begin counting a pea at a time, occasionally lose count, and a boy or two as well. The teacher sits down with the group.

TEACHER: Oh, brother! You don't mean you're doing this by hand? Now, can you think of a better way to do it?

CHILDREN: (*Respond*)

TEACHER: Now, if I can get you a one-ounce weight, can you think of a quicker way to do it?

CHILDREN: That would be much easier.

TEACHER: If I could get you a one-ounce weight, how many times would you need?

CHILDREN: Four times, then you could just pour them in.

(*Weights are borrowed from outside the room.*)

TEACHER: Now, why don't you pour and count later . . .

(*The original group grew to seven involved children.*) (*Small talk*)

TEACHER: Can you think of a good way we can count this so we'll know what we're up to? (*listens to children*) So, if we're interrupted, we won't have to start again?

CHILDREN: Count by ten.

TEACHER: I'll help you . . .

(Six additional 'observing' children have gathered around the table.)
TEACHER: Now, how many have we got here . . . ?
CHILDREN: *(Respond)*
TEACHER: So, if we've got 94 for one ounce. . . .
CHILDREN: *(Respond)*
TEACHER: How many do we have for four ounces?
CHILDREN: *(Respond)*
TEACHER: Now, how do we find that out?
CHILDREN: *(Busily computing and responding.)*
TEACHER: It would be much easier if we had 100, wouldn't it? If we
            pretended that we did, we could take away.
CHILDREN: The six at the end.
TEACHER: Now, if we pretend there were 100 in each ounce, how many?
CHILDREN: *(Respond)*
TEACHER: Then, how many do we have to take away from each ounce?
CHILDREN: *(Respond)*
TEACHER: How many times?
CHILDREN: *(Respond)*
TEACHER: Now, can you think of an easier way?
CHILDREN: *(Respond)*
TEACHER: Now, what do four 94's make?
CHILDREN: *(Respond)*
TEACHER: Now, do you know what four 90's make?

They continue together, with the teacher alternately cruising the room—to
appreciate, answer questions, and redirect other children—and sitting with this
group during a thirty-five minute period. They dissect the numbers at various
points and put them back together again. They move on to replace the peas
with round blocks and the four-ounce weights with eight-ounce weights. Then
they compute blocks in a pound.

Each time she circulates around the room, the teacher suggests a new
activity to three girls who appear to be engrossed in conversation. Each time
they follow her suggestion briefly. In turn, they paint, converse, do needlework, converse, do woodwork, and relapse into their conversation. Finally,
they become involved for a long period in planning a play, writing out parts,
and measuring for costumes. It is sometimes difficult for an observer to see
purpose in the continually resurgent gossip, even though Piaget (1965) and
other developmentalists (Isaacs, 1930) explain that interaction and dialogue
with one's peer group are necessary contributions to intellectual development
and self-awareness.

Occasional children, and each child on occasion, may wander, apparently uninvolved in school activity. This situation could resemble the perpetual-motion prolific artist who appears to have retired from motion. Such an artist could put into words what the child is telling us by his behavior—in effect: "Sometimes I have to take the time to absorb, assimilate, and accumulate new experiences and feelings before I can put them into any form." In fact, the shape of such form, whether it is written, built, or painted, and the child's social behavior have served as the teacher's means for assessing children's understandings.

It is possible that wandering children need more attention from their teacher to help them find a fitting activity. Undoubtedly some children require differing degrees of direction and structure, and teachers who are more and less able to mesh accordingly. There is no prescription. Each teacher or group will develop a unique style.

Teachers must weigh the emphasis on individualized and small group instruction and activity against conventional instruction. If young children are more passively occupied with attending all together to a "teacher–entertainer," one cannot as easily evaluate how many children are attending and absorbing and how many have vacated their bodies. Did you ever intentionally look out the window when you knew the answer, so that the teacher would ask you to recite—and look interested when your mind was elsewhere?

The issue is not whether schools support loss of "being human" in a large group structure against loss of "knowing" in small group organization. Neither dimension is wholly deemphasized in decentralized settings. Rather, the issue in small group situations is how to plan continually with children and colleagues to add to the stock of relevant activities that reflect and mesh with children. The issue is also whether the school as an agency accommodates to children as they are or children accommodate to an artificial structure "as is."

In a decentralized organization, the teacher accommodates to children's emerging concerns while retaining the franchise to plan ahead and stimulate new possibilities. The significance of such flexibility lies beyond the moment. Responsive teachers recognize that children can learn to use varied tools and to consider new ways to arrive at solutions for problems.

Ideally, it is most valuable for the teacher to support contemporary richness in living, while keeping thinking flexible. When teachers and children pursue solid activities in depth, their experience becomes rich. Whatever continuity exists between children's real learning this year and next year is an internal, frequently immediately unobservable phenomenon. The teacher who "covers" material may not necessarily provide "coverage" for the child.

Ultimate "coverage" may best be assessed by how well rational adult decision making progresses; how well individuals have learned to consider and choose from among many ways to live in human society; how well they use the tools for learning more about the world.

We face the issue of where children progress within their culture. Have we exchanged the loss of some children's academic development by brutalizing them and squeezing them into ill-fitting, pinching forms, for a comparable loss through happy, frittered wandering? One might postulate that the odds for a society of "human" beings are better stacked in the second instance, if any choice need be made at all.

However, an either–or choice is not mandated. *"Humanity" and knowledgeability are hardly mutually exclusive if one only accepts, with traffic patterns, the idea that the curve is an efficient, relevant, developmental form.*

ALTERNATE STRUCTURES DEFINED

The "look" of the self-contained, horizontally age-graded classroom is a familiar one. It is a tradition that is only about one hundred years old in the United States. A range of other forms has existed, such as tutorial instruction, the rural one room schoolhouse, the self-contained classroom with interage or vertical grouping, the cooperatively taught and vertically grouped structure, the cooperatively and kaleidoscopically taught and vertically grouped school without walls.

Certainly, your image of a good self-contained, age-graded classroom may be quite different from mine. There are probably as many variants of the form as there are practitioners.

When you know that a structure is vertically rather than horizontally grouped, it is hardly a recommendation for the quality of a child's experience. At best, we might presume that the unorthodox age span encourages a teacher to decentralize and provide some individualized instruction. At worst, we might find the teacher who operates two or three parallel tracks in some sort of paper-and-pencil teacher-directed textbook program. The old-fashioned one room school at its worst was such a place—the difference being that the teacher probably believed in his work and was not hypocritical about children's rights and responsibilities. The teacher made decisions about how children were to use their time and did not require them to engage in sham democratic discussion.

By the same token, a caution is needed for the teacher who wants to work in a decentralized setting. There are many teachers who are satisfied that they have "open" classrooms when children are working individually. However, while open education implies that instruction will be individualized, there may be alternate routes for attaining needed concepts, some of which may be solitary and some of which may be small group work.

Individualized instruction has been defined along a continuous broad range of interpretation. There are as many instances where individualizing instruction means that *all* children will proceed in sequence through a preset series of tasks, whether commercial program sheets, workbooks, prescribed kits of materials, or the same set of crafts products that everybody must finish, even if not at the same time. Frequently, Jane turns from page three to page four at her pace, and Charlie moves from page eleven to page twelve in an identical workbook. This has been documented for one region by Wiener (1973).

This may be individualized activity but it does not reflect the theoretical and attitudinal framework of openness. Children can easily become part of the "keeping up with the Joneses" game or they can have their self-concepts undermined by the competitive spirit that develops through obvious comparisons.

In an open setting, *skills and substantive knowing* are of primary importance alongside the strengthening of children's *intrinsic motives* and *self-direction* in learning. Aside from the obvious tool needs (which can be attained by a *variety* of methodological emphases) that underlie the mission of schools in our society, there are many ways that wisdom can be supported. Part of the essence of openness is the notion of active children who have the right and the natural ability to order the data of their experience into many possible forms.

When we consider some means to develop and refine those situations where people are engaged in the opening process, we partake in a necessary extension of this look of learning for young children. The organizational network that has been represented is intuitively attainable for some adults and reflects the complex of their past experiences. Many others who have, in the main, been exposed to bureaucratic models, management models, or systematic models of teaching when they were children need additional self-awareness as well as knowledgeable observations of open models.

The printed word may provide information and descriptions of practices. However, words are clearly limited when it comes to communicating the "look of learning" when the "experiences of observing and teaching" find no fully adequate substitute. Nonetheless, within the constraints of print, we can look together at some minimal elements and considerations that contribute to a system of "opening" and then peek into some alternate ways in which teachers have helped children with the beginnings of openness during the first days of school and, sometimes, later. It is most relevant to keep in mind that *there is no formula for, or finiteness about, becoming open. It is a process of becoming.*

At this point, a little self-consciousness is needed. Within these diverse settings, some definitions of organizational and staffing patterns may serve to develop more realistic concepts of open education. After defining interage grouping, cooperative teaching, and integrated time for purposes of our communication, there is a discussion of the "process" of organizing open classrooms. Only after we have in common some approximate images of the medium in which we work can we begin to look at the substantive issues in subsequent chapters.

INTERAGE GROUPING

Family grouping, sometimes called vertical, interage grouping, or ungraded classes, has a range of interpretations. A common characteristic of family grouping is that children of different ages work together. Points of contact may be made among adjacent ages so that three- and four-year-olds or six- and seven-year olds work together. Groups sometimes include children between the ages of five and nine years.

Possibilities for contact among these children may be in terms of an anchor or home room teacher or may occur throughout the day, for parts of the day, or only for specified activities.

The most exciting aspect of observing children of different ages working together is that they are living together *in the present* with a kind of spontaneity and intimacy found during a family's best times. As an older child reviews a game with a younger child or answers his questions, several possible relations occur. The older child becomes aware of her own actions and of the processes underlying the operations that she is explaining. She has a chance to feel competent, potent, and useful. She may also find that she feels comfortable with this kind of responsibility. In turn, the younger child has an opportunity to view models at various points of development and at intermediate levels of skill attainment.

Interage grouping also benefits the child who would not be "containable" in a traditional classroom. When a child is able to choose his activities with or without age segregation, and to keep his comparatively poor academic achievement private through a more intimate relationship with the teacher, this practice proves to be a bonus for such children. The open-oriented day allows for considerable elasticity in dealing with the children's many problems. The extremely capable scholar and the aggressive or deprived child can coexist and even succeed.

COOPERATIVE TEACHING

Similarly, cooperative teaching may consume any part of the school time or most of it. In its most obvious form, one teacher helps the children from two self-contained groups with music, for example, while the other teacher helps teach crafts skills. Cooperative teaching may involve an exchange between teachers of children of the same age or of different ages. While interage groupings may operate in self-contained settings, cooperative teaching would occur in a setting that is to some degree "open."

Many teachers feel rather alone in the traditional classroom. Lack of stimulation by other adults for several hours places a continuing pressure upon the teacher to maintain an even, vigorous pace. And many teachers tend to feel an added burden of guilt for experiencing troughs of energy and pace. When even part of the day is integrated, this pressure may be somewhat diminished but it is still apparent.

When teachers work cooperatively, whether with children of similar age or widely mixed ages, many of these pressures are relieved. The teachers become part of a more humane situation that must, by the logic of things, be transferred to the children. That is, the natural troughs of one teacher—whether in terms of energy, or new ideas, or responses about the pursuits of a particular child—may be absorbed by another teacher.

An integrated organization, inasmuch as it accounts for the diversity of children, mandates a range of resources from which to choose. The need for a wide range of resources, especially with children of a wide age range, can be catered to by several teachers. When they share pacing, chores, ideas, and materials, they can eliminate many areas of duplication.

Furthermore, by planning together, the teachers have the opportunity to grow professionally from each other. Attitudes toward individual children may be modified, ideas for discussion techniques gleaned inductively by observation, and so forth.

INTEGRATED TIME

One school staff defined integrated time as follows: "Everybody begins the day with an activity period and has set out materials before the children arrive. Thereafter, they each operate with different structures." This "activity period" is the key to the integrated time. In one sense, it is an activity that integrates traditional subjects. For example, an arithmetic problem card may integrate reading, measuring, writing, and physical activity. The task might be to weigh a guinea pig, count the heartbeats of classmates at rest or following two minutes of running, or measure a specified distance with a metered wheel. The relations between occupational pursuits, climate, chemical by-products, economics, and computation are easily projected.

Children are engaged in an activity chosen from any number of preselected suggestions, initiated by either the teacher or the children. At any given moment the child may choose from among art, music, language, mathematics, or project work. Most of the day or part of the day's activities might require choosing between different activities. Part of the day may involve choices only from among number activities or language activities or art activities. At the very least, different children are engaged in different activities. They would set their own pace and select other activities when they were ready. There is individual as well as small group work, and teacher supervision continues.

Nevertheless, there is some scheduled time in every school: lunch, sharing outdoor or gymnasium facilities, and looking at television, for example. In a traditional setting, most children escape to these activities like steam emitted from a pressure cooker—and, indeed, they may well have been pressurized. In open settings, however, it is quite common to see children continuing their work activities during these "play" times.

A chief objection to the integrated use of time is that to many lay people— and even to some educators—the kaleidoscopic nature of integrated activity lacks the traditional "hard work" aspect of learning. They may be willing to countenance "that sort of thing" with younger nursery age children, but they turn to less flexible approaches with primary children.

Critics imply that children spend less time on the layman's stock of traditional academe: the 3R's, and rote ingestion of data. It hardly occurs to them, nor have enough educators explicitly acquainted them with the notion, that the integrated use of time may instead provide *more* opportunities for children to work in these areas.

ONE EMBODIED INSTANCE OF DEFINITIONS

One composite example of a situation that is cooperatively taught and family grouped within an integrated setting is useful. Three teachers have decided to work cooperatively and share materials and ideas. Their school was built to house self-contained classes twenty years ago. Each teacher operates a "home" group and each group comprises six- through nine-year-olds. Each room has been furnished for different purposes. That is, one room is a "quiet" room in which children may write, read, and do language studies, although reading and writing are integrated in all the rooms.

A second room contains dramatic play possibilities such as a shop, a stock exchange, and a cardboard puppet stage. Conversation and activity are encouraged. Woodworking and other crafts and paints are also available. The third room is devoted to mathematics and science projects. There are various measuring instruments, commercial and teacher-made materials, games, science equipment, and writing materials.

The teachers have scheduled themselves so that they all work in each of the three rooms nearly each day although each teacher has agreed to be responsible for coordinating the order and decoration of one room. They felt that they wanted the stimulation of teaching in more than one area and that this practice brought richness to each room. It also gave them a balanced picture of children's abilities. In addition, it provided an opportunity to vary activities for some few children who needed to remain near a particular teacher. The corridor between these rooms was also used as an extension of the library for quieter reading and writing activities.

COMMON CHARACTERISTICS OF OPEN EDUCATIONAL SETTINGS

Since there are many different ways that teachers have supported decentralized learning, it is useful to recognize the commonalities that define openness. Without these criteria, we are no longer speaking about the process of "opening" teacher–child interactions. In effect, openness minimally includes four components:

Options
Pacing
Evaluation
Need for socialization

OPTIONS

When a two-year-old is whining in the afternoon without apparent cause, it is pointless for an adult to ask, "Do you want to take a nap, dear?" The two-year-old is probably not able to cope with the question. Furthermore, regardless of a child's answer to a yes–no type of question, if the adult has made a reasoned decision and is willing to accept only one answer, then it seems dishonest to ask the question in the first place.

Choices are made in a flexible, interactive framework. Given the range of possible adult styles and children's styles, adults can frame the kinds of questions about choices, and the numbers of choices, with which they can abide.

The teacher provides these choices in the form of activity options available to all, some, or one child at any time. In one instance, a teacher circulating in a room asks a child, "*What* are you planning to do when you complete your story?," knowing that this child can independently answer that question. In another case, "Will you begin a potato print *or* start your woodwork when you finish in the dramatics corner?" is the question he asks of a child who could use more involvement with construction materials. In yet another case, the teacher says, "When you finish the puzzle, please *come* to the measuring corner. I want to begin a new activity with you." Or, "When you finish this, bring it to me so that we can discuss it." If the child offers another reasonable suggestion, the teacher accepts it and can reschedule her for the measuring activity: "All right, we can do it first thing after lunch."

On one level, the number of choices available to a child is tempered by the teacher's judgment at that moment in relation to a particular child. Children frequently create relevant choices. At another level, the number of different activity possibilities occurring at the same time varies from teacher to teacher and at different times during the day.

A large group planning session, discussion, story telling, or performance, represents a single activity. There may be a nursery or kindergarten age child or two who are not yet ready for a large group activity nor able to participate in a particular activity without disrupting other children. In this case, other quiet activities are planned in advance with the individual children who need this attention. By planning in a positive manner for these special situations beforehand, the group's time is protected and the individual child's right to dignified treatment is respected.

Options, therefore, vary across a wide span of possibilities. In this sense, there is a "next-step" of openness possible for a teacher, beginning with any number of activity choices and expanding from there as he or she feels able. There is no single ideal image. Rather, there are as many as there are practitioners.

A central consideration in deciding how many different activity options the teacher can plan relates to the children's ability to make a real choice. It is worth underscoring that *a real choice is an informed choice.* A real choice involves some degree of challenge and the expectation that children can feel involved in the activity. In addition, the teacher can recognize and provide for legitimate choices wherein children might structure an activity or make a discovery that the teacher had not previously found.

While it is exciting when an activity or material offers a range of possible interpretations, offerings ought to be appropriate to the abilities of children. Chapter 6 deals in greater detail with the timing and selection of offerings.

When children use their perceptual powers to move outside a teacher's range of expectancies, the teacher's franchise is extended rather than diminished. She can acquire ideas and insights for additional planning and support of children's imaginativeness.

SELF-PACING

The teacher, planning with children, can also extend possibilities for the practice of needed tool skills while respecting the kind of self-pacing of which the children are capable. In short, there is a clear place for direct instruction of small groups and individuals through the use of alternative strategies.

For example, if a child had not signed up for individual reading with the teacher, she might be asked to opt for "either-or" time, or "now-or-later-today" time. During a planning session, the teacher could easily ask several children to start their activity time with the teacher if the need for a particular skill was evident in their performance.

In traditional settings, children usually follow the teacher's pace. That is, children most frequently respond to the teacher's soliciting actions (Bellack, et al., 1966). My observations in open settings contrast with the Bellack study of usual settings, and indicate that the children approach the teacher much more than in traditional settings and ask many more questions of the teacher. A related observation is that the teacher's presence in an area is sufficient to draw children to the area.

Self-pacing implies relative freedom to move from one area to another as needed. In order for such movement to work effectively in the artificially confining space of a classroom, certain behaviors must be learned and anticipated.

The teacher's task is to anticipate children's needs or adapt to them by setting materials in or near the area where they will be used. Children should know where to use materials, thereby cutting down unnecessary traffic. Moreover, when the teacher sets out priority materials before the children arrive, he creates a smooth transition and supports concentration.

The earliest weeks of the school year are an important time in which to establish where things are used and how they are treated when children have finished with them. It is during this time that the teacher is constantly circulating, appreciating focussed efforts, supporting children's self-direction, and constantly, repeatedly, sharing the question that children need to learn to ask themselves: "What are you going to do when you put away these things or finish this project?"

Self-pacing is supported by the internalization of this question *coupled with* the provision of stimulating activities. Stimulating activities exist in the child's perceptions rather than as absolute attributes of the activity. One teacher found that a solubility study group that nobody chose to attend had a waiting list several weeks later. She had retitled the activity "Mysterious Potions" and used an ambiguous picture to identify the sign-up sheet. A modest merchandising success, the activity drew many children over a period of time and stimulated exciting hypothesizing.

The content of "relevant choices" is a pivotal variable. In the early weeks, when a teacher and children are learning how to interact with one another, it is useful to plan for those activities that require minimal teacher monitoring and minimal direct instruction. As children gain self-direction in choosing and pacing, the teacher adds options that may require increasing teacher involvement, such as playing a game with more complex moves, or providing a needed tool skill.

Some teachers who were newcomers to an integrated activity period began with a *daily* hour during which they focussed on traffic management, organization, ongoing short-range planning, and training in self-direction. When children have been exposed to these consistent guidelines coupled with a range of relevant choices, several teachers in inner-city settings have observed a marked decrease in aggressive behavior and random movement. At the same time, I must underscore the importance of regularly available activity periods to avoid the kind of starved response that leads children to gorge themselves. Such gorging is manifested by short attention spans as children rush to taste rare opportunities.

The teacher responds to the children's degree of involvement. Nevertheless, a particular group of children can become saturated by the demands of activities and materials on two levels.

Just as a plant can be overwatered, so can children be overly stimulated by too many choices for which they are unprepared. Unfortunately, some fearful teachers may use such awareness as an excuse for whole-group action. Rather, there may be merely a need for reducing the options by a single, particular activity, or there may be a particular activity offered at the same time as another one requiring frequent monitoring by the teacher. Sometimes this "saturation effect" can be alleviated by reducing by one or two children the number who may engage simultaneously in a particular activity.

Another consideration concerning saturating a child's environment resides in how long a particular material will be available for children to use. In one study a kind of wave motion was observed when a new material was added (Fromberg, 1965). The first wave consisted of a small group of more assertive children who monopolized the material intermittently for a week or two and then gave it only cursory attention. The second wave consisted of a somewhat less assertive group who appeared to alternate with the first group. These children were followed by individuals who had observed at a distance for a few days until the first two waves had receded. After they had completed a kind of "circuit of safety," they settled with the material.

A general pattern seems to be that individuals actively use the materials, then intermittently use them, and then give the objects only cursory attention—until they rediscover them some weeks or months later. It is at the "cursory attention" point in the use of materials that they may be removed as an option because they are no longer relevant. However, when they are made available six or eight weeks later, possibly with or without added complexity, these same materials are likely to become relevant once again. Such activities as open-ended science materials, construction devices, art media, pets, and games lend themselves to this recycling.

However, those teachers who use only self-pacing as the single criterion of "openness" fail to recognize the other essential dimensions. When a teacher lists on the chalkboard that everybody must complete a certain amount of number work, reading, a composition, and a proposal for a project by a given time, that teacher is certainly permitting a degree of self-pacing. However, the content of the activities has received only the teacher's input. Part of openness involves some rights to select one's activity.

OPPORTUNITIES FOR SOCIAL INTERACTION

Self-pacing presupposes that children will be moving about the room from time to time. In order to "open" educational situations, teachers need to overcome the traditional fear of moving children. Legitimate opportunities for children to speak with one another can be built into activities and materials such as constructions, peer-assisted instruction, board and card game playing, creative dramatics, play writing together, and sharing riddles and jokes.

If a teacher has organized relevant options and has supported positive self-direction consistently, then peer interaction becomes a powerful educative force.

These intertwined elements are supported by the way in which the teacher organizes transition periods. I have seen a teacher whose children are engrossed in many options try to gain everybody's attention all at once in order to give notice that they needed to finish and then pack up in ten minutes. It took four minutes of tense exhortation to get the attention needed for the ten second announcement. The scenario was repeated five minutes later when the teacher announced that it was time for children to replace materials. The child who simply had to replace a book and a pencil received the same time notice as the child steeped in papier-mâché.

This tense setting underscores a useful principle: Avoid interrupting the entire group except in an emergency. If an emergency signal is understood and used only for an emergency, it receives immediate attention. It is helpful if the teacher begins to use such a signal in the vicinity of the most involved or noisiest area if possible. This works well with such signals as both hands up in the "halt" position, with everybody doing it, and looking toward the teacher when they see others doing it. Light switch dimmers, bells, and pianos are not usually available at outdoor occasions, and are therefore less useful signals. Many teachers are unaware that they talk over the heads of children who are not being addressed. Beyond any attitudinal message, this serves to raise the area's sound level.

An alternative procedure has improved the transition in this tense setting. Instead of telling the whole class to clean up at once, the teacher begins with that group which has the biggest job, and asks them to finish up in ten minutes and replace materials. She repeats this procedure in each of the areas of activity, ending with the children who may only need to finish reading a page in a book.

In this way, children are spending less time idly waiting for their associates to finish a task. During this procedure, the teacher can see what children have accomplished and note what may need completion during the next activity period, or who will need more direct instruction. In addition, it is a time to appreciate and enjoy children's accomplishments in an informal way. This is most effectively accomplished by the teacher moving into these areas and addressing each group in a conversational tone.

UNIQUE EVALUATIVE FUNCTIONS

Teachers find that they are much more in touch with children's accomplishments with this kind of continuing personalized contact. Diagnosis is not limited to a weekly impersonal paper and pencil test. In fact, such evaluative function-at-a-distance acquires less significance.

Therefore, evaluation is built into the teacher's attitude in the open situation. It flows consistently from the operations of varied activities. Many forms of productions are thereby legitimized for purposes of evaluation. The teacher is in close touch with ongoing individual progress and minimal benchmarks.

In this sense, much direct instruction in an open setting involves making the best possible time for learning new skills. The timing element, a diagnostic function, is related to children's pacing and teacher's pacing coinciding. Most teachers can point to the excitement of "fleeting moments of teaching" as significantly educative.

Moreover, it is possible to balance emergent "fleeting moments" with advance planning by the teacher. That is, planning for materials and resources *is* part of the teacher's franchise. One can hardly expect each child to personally recapitulate humanity's development. The teacher can prepare a range of materials that represent an *estimated* projection of children's possible options, and their skills needs and cognitive needs, for any comfortable segment of time—several days, a week in advance, sometimes a day or even an hour. Ultimately, the availability of materials and of direct instruction become matters of professional practice and judgment.

The scheduling and pacing aspects of the open setting are necessary supports for such instruction. Teachers find that their management and traffic functions decrease after the first month or two of helping children consistently manage self-direction in the setting. They find themselves able to remain with a single focus for longer periods of time. They can offer children additional options that increasingly require new ideas and skills.

When the teacher plans each one to one and one-half hour activity period in advance *with* children, the teacher can be assured that each child knows his opening activity before the teacher begins direct work with a small group or an individual. She helps them to plan periodically on an individual or small group basis thereafter. Any direct skill instruction for young children that requires more than five or ten minutes is probably oversaturated with variables or it is irrelevant for that time. After a few minutes of direct instruction, there can be ten to twenty minutes of playing out and applying the skill or idea with minimal or intermittent teacher monitoring. After each brief instructional episode, the teacher circulates among the children, gauges how much longer each child can be expected to be constructively involved, and evaluates what children are doing.

Record keeping can be multifaceted. Teachers have reserved a record book section for each child or recorded the opening activity of the day for each child during planning time, or in the case of primary children, recorded the group's written opening plan at a later time.

After the initial six to eight week period of adjustment, the teacher may record ahead of time which children will receive what sort of direct instruction on a given day. In a sense, the teacher *can see progress as the children's exposure to instruction reflects their receptivity to more complex skills and concepts.*

Teachers find that regularly collecting samples of children's written work in folders over a period of weeks is not only a useful evaluative measure but a comfortable opener for a parent conference. Sometimes, daily time schedules for each child in a primary group, developed individually with the teacher, are added to the child's personal clipboard. These may be reviewed by the primary teacher each week or two in order to plan for each child's balanced exposures to activities.

"Four-for-the-day," or any number you pick, is a helpful way to be sure to notice each child regularly. As the teacher circulates each day, he can plan to particularly notice "four" children on a rotating basis and record the activities and skills that they seem to need.

SCHEDULING ACTIVITIES AND PLANNING WITH CHILDREN

The *process of opening* education within a school setting moves on a continuum. The teacher–entertainer who addresses an entire group of twenty-five or thirty children can be scaled continuously through to the teacher–participant who affords herself equal franchise with children and addresses only one child at a time.

Clearly, the teacher–entertainer is an inhuman myth, a nineteenth century vestige, undoubtedly nourished by a combination of historical practice, the passive psychology of television culture, and the well-meaning teacher. When a teacher changes scene and tempo every ten or fifteen minutes, children may receive a message that says: "It really does not pay to invest yourself in anything that is going on because it will soon change." In this sense, the second agenda message undercuts real scholarship and commitment.

In addition, the content of messages that are addressed to a large group is likely to be focussed on some common denominator within many of the group members. However, there may be many others for whom it is either too simple or too complex. Beyond politeness—perhaps behind politeness—may lie anxiety or boredom.

For example, some teachers of six-year-olds frequently insist that whole group instruction is essential for teaching the children to write the letters of the alphabet. Since some children have already done quite a bit of copying and some writing from the ages of four or five years, they might be better off using their time for more productive, satisfying purposes. For those children who cannot yet make the necessary coordination, and can readily see their peers doing so, it can afford a devastating comparison and an inhibition of risk taking. However, if the teacher provides some opportunities for children to write their names, copy their own dictated poetry or shopping lists or experience charts or labels and so forth, he can easily see who needs additional help in certain skills and group these children for these purposes.

One last comment about instruction addressed to large groups is needed with respect to the psychomotor demands that this places on children. Quite simply, young bodies need to move. Even as adults, we need to move and have learned to socialize or institutionalize this need. When we sit at lectures, we cross and recross our legs, alternate hands on chins, adjust glasses, brush moustaches, press fingers, and shift our weight from time to time.

Nevertheless, there are a number of opportunities for a large group to be together within school settings that avoid some of the second agenda we might prefer to bury. Some, such as storytelling, have been mentioned earlier. Trips outside the group's assigned space, discussions concerning social issues or values, films, meeting resource people, movement or music activities, and parties and other timely events are still other possibilities.

An entire group can plan together for the use of time and resources. It is clear that younger children require more frequent replanning on a more individualized basis than do older children. Sometimes, planning together for the kinds of activities in which to engage can occur at the conclusion of a major activity period. Teacher and children can look together at how individuals have used their time. The beginning of the next activity period can be a time in which young children can commit themselves to begin with a particular task.

We can look at some ways in which planning takes place by looking first at a primary group's scheduling process after two months of working together and then by looking at the first days of school.

SEVEN-YEAR-OLDS PLAN AND WORK

Come inside the teacher's head as she thinks ahead during the tenth week of the school year. The interest centers already contain a range of options for different children. There are two new biographies of famous women in the library corner standing open in the middle of the round table. One is of Elizabeth Garrett, England's first woman physician.

The other is of Marie Curie, with three offerings by authors who address different reading abilities (Henriod, 1970; Henry, 1966; McKown, 1971). There are also new sports books and books about motors addressed to different reading abilities (Brewster, 1963; Burchard, 1975; Olsen, 1974; Sullivan, 1968; and Bendick, 1971; Chapman, 1974; Zim, 1953; and Meyer, 1962). A book about magic tricks is also there (Kettelkamp, 1954).

Perhaps those children who have been working on the automobile motor donated by a local mechanic could record their wrench and screwdriver activities. They can read in order to add labels to the motor parts, and develop a large illustrated class chart as well as some personal writing. Two children ask to take the books and writing materials to the "motor corner." The teacher asks, "Who else would like to work with them on doing a chart?" Three children raise their hands and the teacher adds their names to the chalkboard on which she had listed some options before the children arrived. She records each child's choice for a beginning activity as follows on Figure 1.

When the rods were discussed, the teacher said, "Today I would like Larry, May, Ned, and Ollie to begin with me."

NED: Will I have time to go back to my writing this morning? I want to start drawing for my horse story too.

TEACHER: You'll have time for it afterwards. Besides, I've missed doing numbers with you lately and I want to show you some new things.

NED: (*hesitantly nods agreement*)

TEACHER: We have a measuring wheel this week that two people can use in the hallways and gym with these question cards. . . . All right, Jan and Ken. Syl, you can use it when they finish.

SYL: Can I go to the mystery table today?

TEACHER: (*nods*) Who else would like to? Stan? All right. Anybody else?

UNA: I want to sign for the easel first. I'd like to try that new green paint and the thin brushes.

EDEN: What's at the mystery table anyway?

TEACHER: What did you want to do first today?

EDEN: I'm finishing a story about Tufty, my guinea pig, and his adventures when he gets out of his cage. If it's a book about animals, I would go to the mystery table. (*A few children speak quietly.*)

TEACHER: Remember about the mystery table. You take your chances, using the timer at a ten minute minimum setting if you start there. You can go later if you prefer.

EDEN: Maybe later.

TEACHER: Who else will be at the writing center: Deb? Fred? (*Records their names, nodding at their hands.*) Brad, how is the puppet show progressing? Will you be writing down the dialogue?

BRAD: Oh, we've already begun. But we keep changing it.

CAL: Yeah. Walt always wants more magic stunts but Vi makes too many jokes.

TEACHER: All right, I'll come by to give you a hand after I finish with the rods group. Alice, will you be with them today?

Library	Motor	Measuring Wheels	Rods	Smoking Survey	Easel	Puppetry Crafts	Creative Writing	Animal Center	Chess	Mystery Table	Individual Reading Conference
Al	Ed	Jan	TEACHER	Pat	Tom	Vi	Deb	George		Syl	TEACHER
Betty	Fran	Ken	Larry	Rose	Una	Walt	Eden			Stan	Alice
Carl	Greg		May			Alice	Fred				Betty
Dick	Hal		Ned			Brad					Carl
	Irene		Ollie			Cal					Dick
						TEACHER					Edward

FIGURE 1

ALICE: (*nods*) I want to use those papier-mâché puppets we made but I would rather tape record my part.

TEACHER: That's an interesting idea. (She knows that Alice has difficulty writing.) Could you also record some sound effects or background music for the puppets? Look, let's have an individual conference at 10:00 and talk more. And bring your current book notes.

ALICE: (*beaming*) Wow! O.K. I'll go with the group for now.

TEACHER: After I see Alice, I'll be due for some individual conferences with Betty, Carl, Dick, and Ed. (The children know that individual conferences are held at the teacher's corner, a table used for such activities as reading instruction and individual planning. Usually, children watch for their turn to come. Otherwise, the child who finishes might inform the next child. Sometimes, the teacher circulates throughout the room before meeting the next child in order to help the other children remain involved in projected activity.)

Following the large group planning session, the children obtain necessary materials. The teacher begins instruction in fractions using the rods at the table beside their storage shelf. After ten minutes she leaves the group with a series of problems to solve and record in their notebooks. In the meantime, she circulates around the room.

When she stops to see what Al is reading, Al asks if he could go to the school library for another "Little Bear" (Minarik, 1957) book that he saw there the other day. She noticed his recurring interest in warm family relationships and reminded him to put his name card next to the "out to the library" pocket chart and adjust the handmade paper plate clock hands. In that way the teacher can quickly locate a child.

She briefly discusses the motor group's progress and suggests that they use newsprint paper in order to plan the design for the heavy oaktag chart. George needs additional garbage bags. Then the teacher sits briefly with Syl and Stan who are using puzzles and she suggests an alternate strategy before sitting with the puppetry group.

She reflects back what they are saying when they need to clear up a point and she helps them spell some words. Since Cal seems to be the scribe rather than a composing participant, she asks him to suggest what will happen next in the script. He suggests two possibilities and the group discusses them. They decide to hide the lost valise in the course of the plot and develop Cal's idea for a test to find the true owner.

When the teacher leaves the puppetry group to help George with some spills, she notices that Tom is finished with the easel and is washing up. She enjoys his painting with him, especially the way he has used different brush thicknesses for interesting effects. She asks if he would like to write a story to accompany his painting. He does not want to write but prefers to play chess with George.

Una, who had finished painting earlier, is now at the mystery table. Jan and Rose check their names at the easel list and are painting. Ken has wandered around the room, looked at the turtle, held the guinea pig for a few moments, and then selected a book from the library corner.

Pat begins to write up the findings of her smoking survey at the creative writing center. This three-sided center contains pencils of different sizes and hardness, erasers, unlined and lined papers with varying distances between the lines, and a waste basket. There are also crayons, felt-tipped colored pens, and colored pencils. Chairs and writing space face the wall or a cardboard divider that cuts down visual distractions. Since Dick in the library corner and Fred at the writing center seem to be finishing, the teacher suggests that they use the measuring wheel with the set of yellow cards that she prepared for them. They agree.

Then the teacher sits with Alice for an individual conference. She intersperses individual conferences by circulating and helping children finish up, regroup, and find their next activity. During each individual conference, she records children's progress and what she notices each one needs for additional instruction. Carl leaves his conference with a paperback book of scrambled "word find" puzzles (Gerger, 1973). Each puzzle consists of a grid of letters in which words, listed below the grid, are embedded for the reader to find and circle.

Carl joins several children who are drinking from milk containers at two tables pushed together near the sink. The teacher circulates and then joins them for conversation with a cup of tea that she had prepared, using a small electric water heater. From time to time children drink some milk, clear their place, and return to an activity.

The motor group looks finished for the day and has dispersed. Ed and Fran are surveying mileage using road maps and recording their findings. They are estimating travel times using varying travel speeds. Greg is at the easel. Hal is writing, sometimes copying diagrams from a book. Irene has taken some unfinished weaving from her storage box. Different children have replaced those children who had begun the morning in the library corner and creative writing center, and two boys are using Lego blocks.

At almost eleven o'clock, the teacher is having an individual conference with

Dick. After another individual conference, this time with Edward, she circulates from area to area, mentioning that the children have fifteen minutes before story time. Along the way, she appreciates perseverance and accomplishments. She asks Rose and Pat to show her the state of their smoking survey and checks back individually with the children who had been in the original rods group. She notes that May and Ned need more practice with fractions and that Ollie and Larry have completed the written problems. She takes a packet of additional problems from a closet and places them near the rods for future use.

At 11:35, she is seated with E. B. White's book, *Charlotte's Web.* The children are seated on the floor nearby and she reads for fifteen minutes. Then the children gather their belongings for lunch in the school cafeteria.

As we look back over the morning, a clear pattern of teacher movement was evident. After the large group planning session, the teacher alternated direct instruction with circulating around the room. She was having individual contacts with all of the children at various times. This was a pattern that she had established during the first days with these children. The first days' procedures is discussed after a brief look at the afternoon schedule.

In this school, teacher aides helped the children at lunch and the teachers usually had lunch together. This teacher had not yet decided whether she enjoyed this aspect more than when she had worked at a child care center where the teachers ate with the children and took time to meet with colleagues during the children's rest time. There had been many opportunities for direct instruction at lunch through table setting, sharing, and unstructured conversation. Sometimes she planned unstructured discussions about subjects chosen by the children in this school in an attempt to recapture that close feeling.

This afternoon, the children were scheduled for outdoor play. They could use large hollow blocks, hoops, balls, ropes, and an enormous orange and white parachute. Most of the children enjoyed the parachute games. In one game, many children held the outside edge until the parachute was filled with air, at which point several children raced across underneath it before the "holders" could shake it down. In another game, the holders all curled the edges under and sat on the inside until the air filtered out of the parachute. In still another game they shook large yarn balls across the parachute.

When they returned to the room, they gathered for a brief planning session. About half the group joined the teacher for a role-playing activity while the others read, fixed puzzles, wrote their findings to number problems, played Monopoly, chess, and did needlework on mesh.

The role-playing activity was based upon a large picture from the Shaftel materials (Shaftel and Shaftel, 1967). They discussed the picture first and then role-played the alternate possibilities. The teacher asked the following questions.

What do you think is happening?
Does somebody see something else?
Suppose that he felt that way, what might he say?
What else might he say?
Suppose she said that, what might he do?
What else might he do?
Why would he do that? What could he hope to accomplish?
In what other way could he solve it without lying?

The teacher was helping them to explore alternate motives and alternate modes of handling problem situations. She listened to what children said and they began to respond to each other's comments. When the role playing began, she took one of the roles once with a child who was hesitant. She expected that they might explore this same picture a few weeks later with totally different outcomes.

BEGINNINGS

The primary task during the first days and weeks of school was to help children become increasingly self-directed and independent. Another task the teacher set herself was to become familiar with each child's capacities to work independently, to deal with other children, and to cope with the conceptual demands of various situations and materials.

In order to accomplish basic organizational foundations, she planned to spend most of her energies circulating, particularly showing her pleasure in the children's accomplishments, watching traffic patterns, observing attention spans, noticing social needs, and consistently following through with practical procedures for the use and storage of materials. While she did not plan to launch a major direct instructional program that would keep her from circulating for long periods of time, she knew that she could do a good deal of "fleeting teaching." She also knew that she could certainly review what children knew and diagnose needed next steps for instruction. These same principles were operative with teachers of three-, four-, five-, and six-year-old children.

NURSERY

In one nursery school, part of the total group was invited to come with their parents for brief periods before the entire group assembled after a few days. For some three- and four-year-olds, this was a first group experience. A few parents sat in the "parents' room," a teachers' meeting room. Other parents sat on chairs set along the wall of the children's classroom.

Before entering the room, each child was shown the parents' room along with the office, the school rabbit, and the school yard. When the teacher saw that a child was involved in an activity and had developed some rapport with the teacher, she told the child that his or her parent would return soon after having coffee in the parents' room. The teacher then informed the parent and set a time for his or her return. The teacher supported the children with activities, materials, encouragement, and positive appreciation.

Available options included sociodramatic play, or large blocks, or easels, or stringing wooden beads with laces, or picture books, or simple wood puzzles, or crayons and paper, or pegboards, or pierced wooden shapes for corkboards with a hammer and nails. Blue play dough, which the teacher had made before the children arrived, was popular with a number of children who were especially clinging to their parents. They used lumps of dough on masonite boards with dowels available for rolling. Most of the three-year-olds ignored the rollers and preferred to squeeze, pull, tear, or pound the dough.

The teacher encouraged the children with positive descriptive statements such as, "Look how flat you've made the dough. You're making many pieces, one, two, three, four, five . . . six! You're really thinking about that picture. Oh, you used blue and red and green and yellow beads already." As she saw a child's attention waning with one activity, she asked if he would like to try another and might suggest one.

The teacher's experiences had shown her that when young children were in transition between activities, they tended to miss their parents more than when they were involved. A little anticipation on the teacher's part helped to extend the child's involvement with activities. When the children became more familiar with the school environment and the teacher, they moved about with greater security.

KINDERGARTEN

In a public school kindergarten, all the children arrived together on a bus the second day of school. Before they arrived, the teacher had name tags ready, and had labelled a coat hook and a storage space for each child. The dramatics corner held a few dolls, puppets, hats, two telephones, and dishes.

The library corner was hung with colorful book jackets suspended from the ceiling. Picture books stood open on top of the adjacent shelf divider that housed additional books.

There were fresh paint containers and paper at the easel set near the windows on one side with the sink counter on the other. A pencil hung from a string attached to the easel. A drying rack stood between the easel and a low wood screen divider on which hung two plastic aprons.

On one table stood boxes of cut straws, paper circles, plastic washers, hole punchers, and blunt embroidery needles threaded with yarn. A checker board, puzzle rack, and "Candyland" board game were set out at another table. Underneath the checker board the teacher had placed a heavy flannel cloth square so that the pieces would be less likely to roll away.

At another pair of tables, enclosed on three sides by storage shelves, she set out contact-paper covered cans of pencils, colored pencils, boxes of crayons, and paper.

Half the supply of large wood blocks was available while she had decided to keep the other storage shelves with additional blocks and accessories facing the wall until she knew her group better. She planned to add the materials when the children had gained greater independence with the materials. In the beginning, she did not want to burden them with too many blocks. She asked them to find the outlined shape she had taped to the shelves when they replaced blocks together. She made positive, encouraging comments when the children helped her replace blocks after use.

At still another area established by three sides of storage shelves were two separated tables. On one table, the teacher had nailed an edge of quarter-round molding so that the Cuisenaire rods would not roll off too easily. At the other table she set out colored cubes and pattern cards to match the cubes. At this table there were also pegs with pegboards, and rubber bands of varying colors and thicknesses. On top of the adjacent storage area sat a balance scale. On the shelf underneath it were contact-paper covered cigar boxes containing wooden beads, pine cones, buttons, and metal washers. Each box was labelled. On another shelf in this area were unlined yellow paper and pencils.

After the children arrived and had received their name tags, they toured the room together with the teacher. They located the lavatory and discussed the various materials that the teacher had set out as options. The teacher believed that a real choice was an informed choice and that part of choosing was knowing what to do with the materials when you finished using them. She asked the children to show her what they had done when they had finished with the materials.

When the children had settled into the activities, she circulated, constantly chatted, appreciated efforts as well as accomplishments, and helped the children to store materials and to plan their next activities. In turn, she prepared the children in each area to finish up their activities and asked them to meet in the area beside the piano. When they assembled, they munched cookies, drank juice together, and chatted. She spoke briefly about all of the different materials that different children had used. Then she showed them her "halt" signal for emergencies, both hands in the air, and explained about fire drills when bells rang.

They participated as she played, sang, and obviously enjoyed Woody Guthrie's song, "Put Your Finger in the Air." Then she held up the book _Caps for Sale_ (Slobodkina, 1947) and showed the children where she would read it. She asked those children who needed a better view of the pictures to move _before_ the story began. The teacher read the story, reviewed some of the morning's activities, and then walked them to the bus stop. As she looked back at the morning, she realized that she never needed to add the softened plasticene or the flannel board to the available materials, and she wondered if she would need them for the afternoon group.

Each day the teacher planned to add or change options and to help children develop their own ideas for activities that could lead toward longer range projects. As children adjusted to each other and became increasingly independent, she would be able to plan for direct instruction in skills and the use of various tools for longer range concept building. Prior years had taught her that most of the organization, traffic patterns, and patterns of self-direction were established within the first six to ten weeks of working together.

THE RELATION OF STRUCTURE AND SUBSTANCE

There is little doubt that the beginning weeks largely emphasize the organizational and custodial needs of a group working together. However, the very nature of the structure presupposes a range of substantive possibilities.

Looking at the structure of relations between people in an educational setting, you can view it as a response to a particular set of questions that the structure answers. Were you to ask how to develop in children an avoidance for doubting authority, or to produce children who would work hard to find a single correct answer, or achieve well in order to help their group compete with other groups, or who would try to find original and varied solutions to problems, or pursue problems for their aesthetic elegance, you would necessarily organize the structure or personal relationships to fit each different question relevantly. In this sense, the structure and the substance are indissolubly wedded.

However, many educators take it for granted that their structures are educative in and of themselves. They are not—they require substance. What is learned and how it is learned are inseparable, but one must consider that there are many ways and much substance that need consideration in keeping with the unique developments of each child and each teacher.

CHAPTER 3
FOUNDATIONS OF
PERCEPTUAL MODELS

This chapter serves as the theoretical core of the book; now is the time to look closely at how teachers make educational decisions.

Some decisions are influenced by what the teacher accepts about child development. Some of the teacher's decisions are influenced by what he or she perceives to be society's sanctions, implicitly as well as explicitly. Some decisions are influenced by a relative combination of these dimensions. But *all* of the teacher's decisions are influenced by a value structure that underlies all of the preceding considerations: What is worthwhile? What ought one to do? And in early education, the unique questions must be added: What is too much or too little, too soon? What is enough? These issues are discussed in this chapter.

BEING, BECOMING, AND NOTHINGNESS IN
EARLY EDUCATION

Before the children arrived on a Monday morning, the pre-kindergarten teachers entered their classrooms and found a shambles set off by paint-splattered walls. The file cabinets had been wrenched open and white glue draped across the file folders. Heads of toys had been ripped off and thrown about. Torn books had been urinated upon. After several weeks of smelling a gruesome odor, they found a rotten egg in the pencil sharpener (Joyce McGinn and Fredda Rudnick, Personal Communication, 1975)!

While the teachers recognized that such violence by preadolescents grew out of a sense of powerlessness, the cleanup process was still odious. After the cleanup, these teachers discussed together how they might support the sense of

---

SHE FINDS OUT HOW MANY LITTLE CUPS OF WATER WILL FILL THE TALL, THIN CONTAINER, THEN A SHORT, WIDE ONE, AND A DOLL-SHAPED CONTAINER.

power and mastery that young children need to have in order to build a foundation of inner controls. If they could help build children's inner controls and sense of power while they were young, perhaps the children would have fewer reasons to be destructive.

They knew about research supporting the notion that children who have had reasonable options and early independence were less destructive when adults left a room (Martin, 1975). Self-directed children were able to see themselves becoming more responsible for their own behavior. They did not need to look ahead toward a sense of nothingness, of anxiety, of being out of control.

I believe that educators should, and can, help human beings have, and reach toward, great expectations in their lives. Children are entitled to the right to become what they are capable of becoming, and part of the process of becoming is tied to their contemporary sense of being a chooser and aware experiencer of their world.

This position is consistent with the Greek poet who felt that, "The human heart . . . is a perforated jug with a mouth forever open; though all the rivers of the earth pour in, it will remain empty and thirsting" (Kazantzakis, 1965, p. 345).

The analogy of an openness to life can hold for each person. Certainly, this porosity exists at each individual's beginnings. In the process of being human, seeking opportunities to effect changes, being curious enough to risk encounters with objects and other human beings, and spontaneously devising individual ways to order what they see, children have the potential for becoming that which they may be able to become—and thereby occasionally lessening the "thirst."

However, a child's transactions with the world of things and people may serve not to expand but to wrinkle his abilities to be curious, to risk encounters, to feel powerful. Rather, experience may teach him to limit his expectations of what is possible for himself. To that degree he is cooled, if not frozen, from moving in the direction of "becoming." The extreme of such utter "freezing" may be viewed as less than being, less than living fully, inclined toward "nonbeing" or "nothingness."

Imagine the notions of being, becoming, and nothingness as a continuum along which each person is constantly moving, sometimes toward one or the other direction.

"Nothingness" is an abstract possibility (of not becoming) in a changing relation to which you or I may find ourselves (Sartre, 1956). Each person lives in a sort of dialectical relation between becoming and nothingness.

Each time I make a choice and take a risk, I respond to personal questions such as, Should I? Can I? Which are the best ways? Such questions can lead me to feel anxiety when I feel that my efforts are fruitless, or that I am incapable of becoming that which seemed possible. Since I may fail to choose to fulfill my potentialities, I may feel guilty for not having tried or taken the risk in the first place. Psychologists and philosophers refer to such choices or anxiety, or guilt, as "existential." (Binswanger; May, 1958; Tillich, 1952) Risk-taking is a personal matter for each human being, a being who is alone-in-the-world, each human with his or her own personal view of the world.

Psychologists, philosophers, and sociologists see that human motivation is based on the need of each person to become what he or she is capable of becoming (G. Allport, 1955; Fromm, 1941; Heidegger, 1962; Sartre, 1956). A philosopher agrees when he says that "Wherever we arrive, the horizon which includes the attained itself goes further and forces us to give up any final rest" (Jaspers, 1955, p. 52). Each child is constantly becoming. There is openness, possibility, and an educational relevance in these perspectives. In seeking an answer to the question "What is enough?" for young children, there is always a next step to be taken, a new horizon toward which to move.

Being, by contrast, may be viewed in a present-time, concrete, constantly-becoming-future tense. There is a personal finite sense in which a person can experience "being-in-time" in contrast to the "public time" as measured in society (Heidegger, 1962). The ability to cope with present time is a dimension of emotional health (Hall and Lindzey, 1957).

Beyond these considerations lies the issue of each human, although alone-in-the-world, in relation to other beings who are alone-in-the-world. Education has been based upon the verbalized responsibility of teacher for child. Therefore, the teacher needs to support the child's becoming, to build trust, rather than to use the child solely as an instrument of the teacher's becoming (Buber, 1923; 1947). The teacher's role is to support the child's own attempts to take responsibility and risks and to become independent.

THE OBJECT-IFICATION OF CHILDREN

When children are treated as objects, and exposed to limited choices, they become pushed toward nothingness. There is frequently an object-ification of young children by teachers rather than a responsible relation between human beings. A major contradiction appears in early childhood school situations when emotional and social development is valued more than intellectual development.

While social activity is a major part of learning, it cannot shoulder the entire load of cognitive activity. Frequently, this skewed concern for affective development becomes a way for making children the means for the teacher's becoming, a kind of apron string image, that maintains the child's dependency and the teacher's control. This can contribute to the sense of powerlessness that leads to vandalism and violence.

Some of these same teachers may be impressed with the extremely rapid development of young children. True to the parenting image, such teachers operate under the principle "If a little is good, then more must be better."

One response to the recognition of young children's rapid early growth has been the practice of adding paper and pencil tasks. Increasingly, picture newspapers, dittoed worksheets, and then reading and number readiness workbooks are brought to the children—all of the children in the group—all at the same time. This is managed by the same nursery school, kindergarten teacher, and administrator who talks, among other things, about individual differences of children.

For children to be and to become, they need to take a more active part in their own education. This is a natural reflection of the integrated ways in which children develop.

THE MESHING OF AFFECT AND PERCEPTUAL-COGNITION IN THE DEVELOPMENT OF YOUNG CHILDREN

Beyond feelings and values, teachers must be conscious of what they might accept about how children develop—which is influenced by society. When society values future time and hypothetical thinking, the value of the present time is diminished. Western culture looks toward the better tomorrow, the rewards of a future place and time. However, just as each language has its own structure, syntax, and each city has its own map, so does early childhood have its own syntax of experience.

CONCRETE EXPERIENCE AND STEPPINGSTONE COGNITION

There has been a tendency among adults to see the years between three and eight as a steppingstone to more valuable intellectual activity. I contend that these years do not merely represent a stage to put behind oneself. They represent a time when important cognitive functions need to be nurtured. This is a time when fresh associations are possible. This is a time when the child's authentic emotions may still be expressable. This is a time when the aesthetic mode of knowing is a powerful force.

In the early years, children learn best through aesthetic, psychomotor, and social means. At the same time, cognitive development is the unifying mission that society has set for schools. These perspectives need to be resolved.

It is worthwhile to look beyond this steppingstone notion of cognition. Rather than seeing efficiency as the most rapid exclusion of "childish" modes of thought, educators need to appreciate *the potency of the perceptual processing of reality as a dynamic strand* of development that needs to be nurtured.

THE YOUNG CHILD AND PERCEPTION

The study of young children is the study of the concrete range of knowing. Development is continuous between concrete and abstract thought and there are flashes of "zig-zag" movement (similar to Piaget's "transitional" activity and Goldstein's (1940) "abstract attitude"), a *relative* emphasis.* This relative emphasis would range from fewer abstract performances in the early years to a greater ability to use abstract ideas and systems as adolescence is approached.

Through a process of absorbing (assimilating) meaning from direct experiences, young children increasingly see relations and create order out of their direct experiences. They classify properties of objects. They classify objects. They relate properties of objects to one another. They relate objects to one another.

The verbal eighteen-month-old defined his family as mother, father, and sister. When pressed for an additional member (adults of course were wishing him to mention himself), he pronounced "Fyuffy!" (Fluffy, the dog) with a glowing joy at his own insight.

A three-year-old city apartment-dweller had visited family and friends over the summer months. One evening, he spontaneously announced that he had visited Aunt A at the seashore, Aunt B in the country (a suburb), and Aunt C in the jungle (a wooded, rural area).

A five-year-old established the last cookie in the dish as the prestige cookie. When her younger sister ate it she exclaimed, disappointedly, "I had the Y cookie and she got the Z cookie!"

Young children continually revise (accommodate) their behavior and develop more complex associations, routes for new input to travel. As broader classifications develop, this process of accommodation *presets* children to

---

* Susan Isaacs (1930), while criticizing Piaget's theory of maturation as part of a rigid structuralism, would prefer a greater emphasis on experience. However, her observations might be like "transitional" phenomena. In a related comment, David Russell (1956) states that "creating" new forms "should be considered in dynamic molar terms rather than as a series of discrete stages" (p. 312).

perceive, assimilate, absorb, consume, and transform new encounters. In turn, their assimilations *preset* them to manifest their own new accommodations. More stimulation and less stimulation is still some sort of stimulation. Children adapt.

The young child's reality is basically a perceptual reality, consistent with a unique syntax, a unique structure of relations. While "perception" may pattern in a sentence as a noun-form, it also embodies properties generally associated with the verb-form "perceive."

Perception is a construct that lies on a continuum between sensory data and mature abstractions. Perception has symbolic components and complexities in its most mature sense. Perception contains both sensory experience and meaning. I suggest that *to have meaning is to have some cognitive and affective involvement—commitment.*

A young child's perceptions and behavior have integrity and their own unique syntactics. Tomorrow is important, but so is today. The importance of present time, of being—now—is a relevant, useful attitude for the early childhood teacher.

AN ACTIVE CONCEPTION OF HUMAN NATURE

Piaget repeatedly speaks of equilibration as a kind of process for readying-the-next-step phase of life. The continual process of adaptation presents new horizons. Attention, motivation, and readiness for new experience weld affective and cognitive development. Even activities that have been categorized as primarily social (self-concept, readiness to participate in a group, fear of strange faces) or emotional (fear of the dark, fear of guns, anxiety) have a cognitive component.

When children have felt successful, they have been motivated to risk trying more difficult activities. They respond to "an element of uncertainty and a perceived chance for success." With growing self-confidence, the teacher can plan an enlarged "element of uncertainty," greater challenges.

This is not to say that children will act only when they have achieved success or only when external forces have dictated their behavior. Children are willing to maintain tension or to create tension because they are curious and need to feel effective (White, 1959). They can feel satisfied by the process of being active, with or without a clear product.

Educators have sometimes missed the significance of the young child's need to feel effective or competent but have emphasized the product: "Achievement." For example, it may be hypothesized that the first grader's enthusiastic involvement with the farina-like, "See! See! Oh! Oh!" may be less likely to stem from the material's inherent aesthetic quality than from the repeated feelings of competence, environmental mastery, and achievement that the "recognition" of these words affords him!

Although psychologists have viewed motivation as an internal affair, it appears that educators have been viewing motivation as externally determined. How often have teachers been faced with the query: How do you intend to "motivate" the children, or, further, "motivate" the lesson? I contend that one cannot "motivate" another human being, much less an abstraction such as a "lesson." At best, one would do well to be able to stimulate others to motivate themselves. The underlying question is: What challenge can the child perceive?

The child in the educational setting can potentially perceive external stimulation. Activities and events might become intellectual challenge if the child, based upon *prior experiences,* can participate.

Directionality of Human Behavior. In a narrow cognitive sense, children move toward increasingly abstract operations. In an existential sense, children move toward fulfilling their potentialities. Each individual moves toward self-actualization, toward keeping open his possibilities for making decisions, toward becoming. Self-actualization is an idealized construct proposed by Goldstein (1940). It reflects a holistic notion of human nature and suggests that a person's active orientation to the possibilities of the present time, rather than to the myths and burdens of the past, is a healthy concrete state. The process itself can be satisfying.

This is not a linear but a meandering process. It is sometimes joyful and satisfying and at other times painful and frustrating.

Set and Future Perceptions.   Based on their past experience, children engage in a process of contrasting, selecting, and discarding data. "There is no end to this spiral process: familiar possession becomes a resource for judging and assimilating additional foreign subject matter" (Dewey, 1933, p. 291). The notion of "spiral" process is a dynamic idealization, the expansion of experiences into increasingly complex generalizations.

Future perceptions may be integrated into, and alter, already achieved generalizations. This notion is related to the concept of "set," the preparedness to perceive and act in a particular direction while faced with alternatives. Experiences are integrated on the basis of each person's preparedness or set.

Another interaction between cognition and affect is embedded within this notion of set. In order to be prepared to move in a particular direction, one must feel comfortable within one's self on the one hand. On the other hand, one must feel uncomfortable with one's plans in the face of contrasting alternatives. One feels dissatisfied, responsible, and then ambitious to move ahead—affect and cognition wedded. (It seems clear that built into the ability to generalize is the capacity for emotion. You have only to look at brain-injured individuals who have the ability for concrete thought but have simultaneously lost the ability to both generalize and show affect. There may well be neurological ties between affect and the ability to generalize about which researchers have yet to learn.)

There is agreement that perception, indeed cognitive processes generally, represents a sort of personal hypothesis in the face of a particular present-time situation (Bruner et al., 1962; F. Allport, 1955). "Set," as a function of prior experience, influences later experience including the retarding or limiting of one's ability to respond.

Rhythm and Reactivity. Dienes (1959), the British mathematician and educator, observed a related phenomenon: the resistance of subjects to start another task and their tendency to "dwell on their achievements." He is talking about how long it takes for a child to rebound from an exposure so that he is ready to absorb a new exposure, "the speed of his rhythm of learning" (pp. 54, 36).

This is a form of saturation. When you water a plant you know when the plant is saturated because you can see water dripping out the bottom. But when you saturate a child, it looks like a whole host of different behaviors because different children show saturation in different ways. The preceding chapter considered possible alternative teacher behavior to accommodate these child behaviors as does Chapter 6.

The notion of "rhythm" as construed by others besides Dienes merits attention since the nonlinear nature of development is embedded in it. Various writers, using an aesthetic-intuitive emphasis, refer to a generalized "rhythm of life," combining appreciation of experience and an ineffable quality of "natural" functioning. (Dewey, 1933; Goldstein, 1963; Langer, 1953; Rugg, 1963; Yutang, 1937) Piaget's (1947) view of rhythm as a linking structure between objects and mind emphasizes a theoretical and descriptive emphasis. Yet both views could concur that experience is at once in a cognitive (concrete-abstract-direction)-affective (degree) relation. Rhythmicity is inherently attention getting and perceivable. There needs to be a message for any rhythm to have meaning.

It has even been suggested that creativity is supported by the returning rhythm of "a new innocence of the eye" (Koestler, 1964, p. 461). Human beings are to some degree capable of "childish" joy and openness and are also capable of variably controlled, systematic reason. To Alfred North Whitehead

(1929), there is a rhythmic change of emphasis between intuitive and cognitive experience that is always present.

Throughout one's life, these variable combinations of emphases tend to define each human being as unique. And in this uniqueness, alongside the alone-ness of each person as a being-in-the-world, lies the concern of education.

THE PROCESS OF PERCEPTUAL EXPANSION

The uniqueness of each person is guaranteed by the complex process of cognitive development. After looking at the centration–decentration continuum, dialectical processes and the nature of generalization and memory are considered.

Centration–Decentration: A Variable Emphasis. Piaget's theory suggests that cognitive development moves from centration, being limited to what is present, towards decentration, conceiving of that which is absent or symbolic.

The adult is "decentered" from the world of objects and can perform many abstract operations without concrete referents. In contrast, the young child is much more centered in the world of objects and is largely dependent upon sensory impressions—what he can see, touch, and hear. There is a need to differentiate the child's system of connectives (logical aspects) from the child's grasp of adult expectations (understanding) (Smedslund, 1969). Teachers need to be tentative in concluding precisely what children understand logically and what may or may not be relevant from *their* point of view.

The three-year-old who tells her group about the sweater that her grandmother knit for her, right in the middle of a discussion of transportation, may be sharing her "syncretic" thinking. The truck was green as was the sweater. She was abstracting the property of color that was part of the subject *for her* rather than a change of the subject.

Bruner's (1966) continuum of enactive, iconic, and symbolic functioning parallels Piaget's decentration–centration conceptualization. To Bruner, the young child's development begins with movements in the physical world (enactive), is extended by a growing ability to imagine relations (iconic) within the confines of concrete experiencing, and then is capable of beginning symbolic capability.

Adults infer that the earliest experiences of the young child have no inherent order, except perhaps in a simultaneous or chronological sense. In the course of beginning to order and classify experience, the young child has the potential to tap many forms, and to connect properties and variables that have been closed to adults as a result of acculturation.

Where the adult sees a scientific phenomenon, a child might surrender to an aesthetic experience. During the ascendancy of perceptual-iconic processing, *young children are probably at the zenith of their absorbency and flexibility with regard to the potential for a unique ordering of the world.* To lose this imagery is to diminish the individual's humanness and range of action. A lost abstraction can be found but the loss of fluid processes is probably beyond salvage.

An important difference between an adult's thought and a child's thought is that an adult can manipulate abstract ideas and symbols and become self-aware. The adult may be conscious of what is happening, of how he or she is operating. The young child is much less able to stand outside of himself and see his behavior as others see it, or to appreciate another individual's ways of viewing a situation. To develop increasing self-awareness is to develop increasing decenteredness from one's immediate environment. Consequently, when the teacher plans activities for young children, she should favor inductive learning activities.

However, people do not merely pass through and then discard these stages. Rather, human beings are continually enriched by their expanding, varied potential for experiencing the world.

There is corroboration for this view in some intriguing introspective data from Albert Einstein (Sullivan, 1972). It has been reported that Einstein was a late talker and that his imagery was exquisite. To look at the ultimate developments of cognition suggests that the most advanced level of adult intelligence is the ability to deal with postulations upon postulations. You could operate on the expansion of symbolically-based mathematical operations.

Yet Einstein said that when he formulated his boundary-crashing theory of relativity, he did not do it on the postulational level first. He contended that he did it at the level of imagery, at the perceptual, concrete level of pictures-in-his-head, the type of imagery most notable in the three-to-seven-year-old child.

This observation lends some support to the suggestion that young children's openness to perceptual experiencing is an asset to flexibility and to their reordering of the world. Certainly, educators want to help children expand in the direction of abstract operations. At the same time, teachers should remain open to the possibility that children might actually discover something that adults had not previously considered—a plea for moving beyond *the* predigested question and *the* correct answer.

Dialectical Development: Contrasts and Negative Learning.   From yet another perspective, the French philosopher–psychologist Merleau-Ponty (1964) draws attention to the young child's process of decentering, tied to increased self-awareness, as follows: "'I *have been* the youngest, but I *am* the youngest no longer, and I *will become* the biggest" (p. 110).

This could be the experience of a young child who has a new sibling. While jealousy might be a problem in decentering, it occurs as a "lived de-centering" rather than "a primarily intellectual operation." In this case, you can see an interaction between social and cognitive development. For the young child, *concrete personal experiencing* was the process that furthered this growth in self-awareness. The child perceived the social situation through his imagery system first, and then could move to the point of giving the experience some form through his verbalization, his symbolic abilities.

This growth arises from a dialectical situation, a situation of contrasts, similar to the economic issue of scarcity—the relation between what one wants and the possible limitations about getting what one wishes. Contrasts serve as a fundamental learning strategy.

Piaget, for example, sees the beginning of the development of self-concept deposited among the earliest kinds of self-awareness, in the notion that "I have an inside and there is an outside." This begins to develop when a baby has unfulfilled wants accompanied by a dawning awareness of dependency upon an outside force, another person, to fulfill his wants.

Floyd Allport (1955) sees the process of learning by contrasts as a fruitful notion. He sees a process of "oscillations," the repeated intake of information that deviates somewhat from precisely what is needed. Trial-and-error activity, by negative knowledge, may reveal a more positive way to reach a goal.

Negative knowledge, contrasting data, is a form of verification for positive empirical findings in physics (Wiener, 1961; Hanson, 1971). The Eastern methods of "no-knowledge" (using the way-of-knowing negatively, as opposed to "having-no" knowledge) classifies objects that are excluded as a way of inferring that which is negatively known (Siu, 1957). The literary critic Steiner proposes that "silence," a kind of negative knowing, is another form of literacy alongside mathematics, music, language, and art.

Dewey (1933), from still another perspective, suggests that "comparison, without contrast, does not amount to anything logically" (p. 174). While recognizing the centrality of contrasts, he also cautions teachers to note the diminishing returns of too much difference between that which is "familiar" and that which is "strange" (p. 290). This suggests that the teacher needs to stimulate children's action by a next-step approximation, "intellectual challenge." I propose that *intellectual challenge* is "*a perceived invitation, containing both an element of uncertainty and a perceived chance for success, which produces learner motivation to strive toward the attainment of intellectual expansion"* (Fromberg, 1965, p. 12).

A review of research supports these perspectives and suggests that subjects can feel confident when exposed to "negative instances" that can confirm their views (Bruner, Goodnow, and Austin, 1962, p. 62). Nevertheless, subjects appeared reluctant to use negative, indirect information. They preferred positive information whenever it was available.

These observations reveal an interesting interaction of affect and cognition. People can logically appreciate that a negative case, a trial-and-error experience, may be fruitful. At the same time, for those who are raised on a diet of the digetibly correct, single solution, deviations can feel like failure. Significant thinking is a dynamic process of weighing alternatives, along with a willingness to risk the intellectual challenge of questions-in-progress.

The process of oscillations between positive and negative feedback operates from the earliest activities in life. When an infant sees a colorful object, you can notice that he follows it with his eyes. Later, his entire trunk and limbs quiver with apparent excitement. After several weeks pass, he has moved from this seemingly random excitement to what looks like accidental contact with the object. This "accidental" contact increasingly requires less of his time and energy until he grasps the toy directly, with hardly any random motion. The fumbling attempts of adults to correlate their actions in front of a mirror are similar.

The process of living is a process of movement, with new "tangents" (F. Allport, 1955) always touching and changing former ways of thinking. Parallel with biological systems theory (von Bertalanffy, 1960), "function and structure are one and the same thing" (F. Allport, 1955, p. 528).

What you perceive and how you perceive it is identical. This fleeting resemblance to the kinetic theory of molecules in a spatial dimension can be seen in terms of time as the "next-logical-developmental-sequence." Molecular activity is changed when temperature changes and the likelihood increases that tangency regions will meet. In this nonlinear model, tangency regions meet at a more rapid rate.

The Paradox of Expanding by Reducing.   On the one hand, there is a process of elimination that takes place in intellectual activity as more inclusive categories and concepts develop. On the other hand, this process is welded to affective processes, including the development of self-confidence.

Memory and Forgetting.   The Soviet psychologist, Luria, studied *The Mind of a Mnemonist* (1968) and sheds further light on still another facet of this elimination process.

The subject of the study was a man who was working as a professional on-stage memory act. At an earlier time in his life he had had a job as a newspaper reporter. While the editor listed the day's assignments and his colleagues recorded feverishly, the mnemonist would simply listen. Without recording, he could recall every detail. Later on, when he became an actor, he never forgot his lines. Eventually, he became a mnemonist.

Colleagues and members of the audience would hand him long commentaries in other languages that he did not understand. He would memorize them. People would hand him lengthy lists of numbers or nonsense syllables. He would remember all of them.

When faced with the following written series of numbers as an experimental task, he memorized it only after thinking about it a while and studying it:

1	2	3	4
5	6	7	8
9	10	11	12

Undoubtedly, the reader has instantaneously memorized this series of numbers.

When the experimenters asked him what process he had used in memorizing the numbers, he described a mental "walk" he had taken in which he saw first one, then two objects, then three objects, and so forth. His mind was filled with the imagery of this "walk" and he remembered this series, as he had others, in this fashion.

When the experimenters pointed out the pattern, groupings of four numbers, he agreed that he could see their viewpoint, although it had not occurred to him independently. While you immediately sought the efficiency of generalization, a relational process, he operated on a very concrete level of imagery. (In this particular instance, however, many young children would have been able to note the pattern that he overlooked.)

The experimenters thought that it would be easy for him to memorize poetry because of his rich imagery life. However, when they gave him poetry, he had great difficulty. As soon as he began to memorize the first image, there were so many other images attached that his own became tangled.

The researcher inferred that poetry was a most abstract form and dealt with more abstractions than everyday language. Inasmuch as he was faced with adult levels of imagery, he was faced with a process of literally abstracting and generalizing properties.

The limited ability of the mnemonist to generalize can help to clarify a relationship. In effect, *the complementary operation of refining negative and positive instances in thinking is a process that is parallel with the complementary operations of forgetting and remembering.* Contrasts are important when you wish to memorize or to forget. The mnemonist claimed, for example, that one of his most strongly felt problems was trying to forget what he had learned.

The mnemonist engaged various memory devices. He remembered by using the imagined "walks" that he took. He remembered by making sensory associations, a kind of synesthesia. For example, he associated his devised images with a simultaneous "taste" or texture.

If he were about to reproduce something incorrectly, he would be warned by his own "taste" or "tactile" sense so that the item did not "feel" the same or "taste" the same. With so many concrete devices, he found it difficult to forget.

In the course of his performance he found the need to forget, to put aside prior activities, because he became overloaded with data. He described a somewhat amusingly desperate device for putting past events out of his focus. He claimed that he "covered" the unwanted, imagined "walk" locale with a large canvas. When he mentally "lifted the canvas," though, he could remember the "walk" that he had taken.

Further discussion of the significance of this remembering–forgetting issue follows the description of related memory studies done by Piaget, Sinclair, and Bliss (Piaget and Inhelder, 1966). One experiment studied children's responses to the nature of equal quantities transferred between containers of varied shape and size. In another experiment, similar results were found when a series of graduated sticks was used.

One week after exposure to the sticks, the children made drawings that showed what they understood about what they had seen. Six months later, not having seen the model again, "80 percent of the cases" responded with "slightly superior" recall. Piaget et al. conclude that "intellectual progress in the scheme resulted in progress in memory" (p. 82).

Piaget's interpretation, supported by his reference to other researchers, and Luria's interpretation concerning the mnemonist, suggest that humans do not easily forget. Rather, the problem is a question of perceiving in the first place, of marking the "figure" emerging from its ground. Once individuals perceive something, it remains with them. In the development toward adulthood individuals learn to forget selectively, to generalize, to conceptualize, a process of reducing the form in which data is held.

These findings have implications for what teachers can do with young children. The teacher needs to expose a child to what seems to be a reasonable activity or material. If a child has been exposed and is reasonably receptive, if he perceives the exposure as a figure out of his ground, he will absorb it. He may some day make some association with other data. He may some day even make use of his experience. The richer the range of options you give children, the more likely they are to learn and the more likely they are to move toward increasingly abstract ideas.

In a way, these umbrella-like abstract ideas represent a larger covering of a domain that contains many smaller elements in various interrelations. Children engage in the continuing process of reducing and shaving down their experiences into forms that create more efficient storage and retrieval systems. Such growth also means that the proportion of random, uncoordinated, and disorganized behavior is reduced.

I wish to draw your attention to the molar, interactive nature of human experience. It is essential that teachers experience each child as a feeling thinker, a thinker who feels. If the teacher accepts the child as a participant builder rather than a passive receptacle, there is a need to consider what this acceptance means to existing conceptions of knowledge.

PERCEPTUAL MODELS AS A SYNTAX FOR EARLY EDUCATION

This section considers the nature of meaning, knowledge in today's society, and perceptual models.

ON MEANING IN EARLY EDUCATION

I have suggested that to have meaning is to have some commitment, a cognitive-and-affective involvement, and this is at the hub of this discussion. Commitment involves underlying conditions such as personal and physical motives, possibilities, and expectations.

To deal with meaning is to deal with the ineffable. "To grasp the meaning of a thing, an event, or a situation is to see it in its relation to other things" (Dewey, 1933, p. 137). The point of agreement among philosophers and psychologists is that meaning may be apprehended by its function and use, a personal experience (Bruner, et al., 1962; Polanyi, 1963; and von Wittgenstein, 1968). While objects, the data of experience, exist "out-there," each person attributes "inside" meaning to his primary experience with the "out-there."

To the extent that *meaning is an experience,* aesthetic knowing is part of it. The aesthetic process itself is the lymphatic fluid in which cognition and affect are blended. Aesthetic in this sense involves direct, concrete experiencing. Aesthetic experience may focus on a concrete work intentionally produced by an artist, or it may result from direct acquaintance with unorganized data. Whether an artist interpreted a tree for you through an art form or whether you focus on its perceptible properties and appreciate them in your own way, you may have had an aesthetic experience. In this sense, artistry and aesthetic experience are differentiated.

The tree is the datum upon which you can focus. If you look at that tree with scientific intent, your experience is discursive, and the tree is a means to some other purpose such as measurement and comparison. However, if you perceive the tree for itself, for the "full and amplified perception of all that is perceptible there," then the purpose was nondiscursive (Gotshalk, 1947, p. 7).

Anything that a person might perceive can be known directly, aesthetically, nondiscursively; or indirectly, discursively, through empirical means. Thus, *meaning is a kind of perception—a perception invested with commitment.*

The nondiscursive, artistic purpose can lead to the skillful making of new connections (Richards, 1924). However, scientists also need to make connections between apparently disparate variables that they observe and they, too, have intuitive experiences. The scientist and the artist focus on different aspects of the same data. The artist helps people to see new meanings by *creating* a *new* experience (Dewey, 1934).

In the first place, certain knowledge helps you to grasp an art work. It helps to know the distinctions between the elements of the art form in their new connectedness in order to perceive it as worth appreciating (Langer, 1957). Therefore, it is worthwhile to consider what is involved in readiness experience.

Meanings have been referred to as "prelinguistic" (Husserl, 1973) and "prelogical" (Tauber and Green, 1959). In this sense, "subthreshold" perception is the realm in which meaning exists. This realm is present throughout life, and represents the process that interrelates elements and ideas. It is proposed as the realm in which metaphorical extensions are created. These functions make for the potency of early childhood.

Young children may be able to receive "the message" (Levi-Strauss, 1964) or to perceive the "significant form" (Langer, 1953) of particular data through aesthetic experience before they are able to deal with the data by cognitive means that can be shared with others. This is the difference between appreciating an experience and being able to criticize it. (The final chapter deals with this distinction.) This is also the difference between receptivity in the sense of recognition, as contrasted with recall. (This distinction is integrated in Chapter 5.)

The identification of a "prelogical" domain further represents a kind of blender for "the deeper emotional content of the creative unconscious" and rational processes (Tauber and Green, p. 3). This is the area of human realization in which intersubjective meaning is experienced. *Intersubjective meaning is both shared and ineffable* (Husserl, pp. 363–64). The artist's meaning can be shared. The process of creation, the object created, and the process of apprehension are a transaction (Gotshalk, 1947; Dewey, 1934).

As each person experiences a work of art in light of his unique experiences, he is able to share this experience with others through the unity afforded by their own experiencing of the work. A poem "may be experienced by many different minds with only slight variations" (Richards, p. 78). In Dewey's (1934) sense, "it is recreated every time it is esthetically experienced" (p. 108). There is an "intersecting set" of experience between creator and perceiver.

Teachers attempt to keep the young child open to such experience through creative and appreciative activities. (Some of these activities are delineated in Chapters 6 and 7.) It is only after children have had opportunities to build their own "background" of experiences that they are able to perceive new "figures" against the "background."

Learning deepens through this basic process of contrasting figures that are freshly set against known background experiences. However, teachers cannot simply "give" experience to young children. The basic contrasting process is a personal "struggle," the process of becoming. Thus, the child must be active in the construction of his own meanings for which he becomes indebted to himself.

The behaviorist-oriented reader may reject these notions out-of-hand. However, I concur with the anthropologist Henry (1965) that if a phenomenon seems probable, it must be considered until a method for its verification has been developed. It follows that learning would not be limited only to that which could be empirically validated.

The point remains that each meaning is personalized. There is a great potential for uniqueness in young children's receptiveness to direct experience. They remind adults of interpretations and feelings that, while frequently legitimate possibilities, would not automatically appear in the molded sites of culture-bound maturity. One might say that they exist with great flexibility in the metaphor of living.

School and Meaning.   Success in schools has traditionally rested on limiting this metaphoric process and shrinking the sites so that children achieve a more unified outlook. This has been supported and justified as efficient. Those children who do not conform are variably classified as disordered.

To take a deterministic cultural outlook is dangerous. It relieves educators of responsibility at many levels—"Oh, that's his background." "What can you expect if she comes from that neighborhood, that family, that lower-track class?"

The myth of the teacher-next-year may similarly relieve the teacher-this-year of responsibility. To compromise with next year's imagined limitations is to ignore children's adaptability along with selling out this year's rights. Also, administrators have been used as a rationalization. "Oh, 'they' expect this workbook material to be 'covered'." Who can presume to have captured in a multitude of identical workbook copies a mesh with the continuity in as many child minds? If one believes oneself not to be responsible then one becomes less responsible (Peters, 1959). These observations reflect needed directions for change in the varied relationships between people who deal with young children more and less directly.

Historically, the judged-good teacher in such a setting is the super manager who performs well the functionary duties of which many teenage camp counselors are capable. Educators must view the young child's education as a *personal process* of ordering the dimensions of life's chaos. Such an involvement denies the passivity of the child as one "to be molded." Perhaps it would be clearer to see the world as also malleable and the child as both actor and reactor.

The early childhood education literature and folklore has so romanticized this rather sturdy young being as such super-precious, delicate material, and the task of teaching as such a basic imposition that an interesting pattern of prognostication and chocolate syrup has been painted. Teachers frequently present a sugar-coated needle to disguise the taste of teaching, an essentially unpleasant memory of a bitter pill upon which they had gagged in childhood. Since adults are the slaves of their own childhood models, the occasionally convenient superior stance of omniscient adult vis-a-vis helpless child becomes extended.

This hesitancy to deal with substance and even tool skills in a straightforward manner can only represent an abrogation of responsible adult function. To proceed with early schooling that exclusively values the "here and now" and "what the child asks for" and "brings to the situation," is to unconscionably exploit the dialectical relation between order and novelty in human life. Culture, representing ordered existence, is at once a reprieve from anxiety and a brake on creative action (Goldstein, 1963). An individual can be protected against the nothingness of anxiety by accepting the order of culture as represented by an adult. However, there are obvious costs to personal integrity and substantive depth.

The teacher becomes significantly responsible for each child's personal freedom within this construction. Such a situation presents the serious question of what authority a teacher ought to represent in a child's life.

It appears to me that there is a need to vest authority in the nature of the child's own study and findings rather than solely in the teacher and the influence of his or her possibly dramatically persuasive style and expectations. A child acts out of regard for the meaning of a challenge to himself. He should not act for fear of the teacher or for love of the teacher but for love of learning (Montessori, 1912; Peters, 1959; Dewey, 1933).

Learning in this sense can become meaning, in the sense of committed action. While one may speak of children's freedoms and the elysian fields where children pursue the flowers of learning for the love of their fragrance, educators must face the reality of the teacher who is more than a horticultural servant. The teacher is responsible for recognizing what knowledge and what view of human nature he is valuing. Are humans rational beings or beasts-with-reason? Or more than both?

There is a need to look at knowledge directly. Doing so also requires consideration of the teacher's franchise in early education.

ON KNOWLEDGE IN EARLY EDUCATION

A myriad of issues present themselves: What is knowledge or knowing? What is worthwhile knowledge? What knowledge is it worthwhile for young children to acquire? How, then, does the acquisition effectively occur?

New acquisitions of knowledge become possible when the young child perceives encounters as full of meaning. Perceivable forms serve as a base for the young child's metaphorical possibilities to make "the strange" familiar (Dewey, 1933; Gordon and Poze, 1973).

Young children's beginning thoughts deal with the *raw* materials of meanings that are concretely based upon sense data. Young children can be independent when they participate in concrete operations. However, plastic-wrapped knowledge dispensed in prepacked dosages limits independence.

In more mature thought, a person is dealing with *processed,* already shaped, or partially shaped data. When young children are exposed to abstract expectations, they become tied to adults in a kind of "game playing." Responding with shallow verbalisms represents a dependent being. To this degree, children can feel the sting of nothingness, a relative loss of autonomy and self-direction. Movement toward "nothingness" is the price paid for verbalism.

The teacher who observes the movement of the young child's thought between these two areas of processed and raw data has a basis for conscious planning. Teachers recognize that nondiscursive and discursive knowing are second agenda to each other. Since they coexist, each perspective is a negative way of learning about the other. To devote little attention to one dimension is to send a message of relative devaluation. In order to provide children with balanced experiences, conscious effort needs to go into professional planning for balance.

Knowledge and the Franchised Teacher in Society. It is difficult to speak about knowledge outside the context of a particular society. Ultimately, each society shapes its schools in order to maintain that society. There is a general socioeconomic web from which this milieu is evolved.

For schools to promote a particular set of values is to promote a traditional cultural bias. At this time, technological change itself is becoming traditional. This creates a major dilemma: gaining consensus in order to define that culture that one would be committed to perpetuating would be a real problem.

While the 3 R's became the base for institutionalized education in order to serve the "entertainment" needs of the eighteenth century Bible reader, the twentieth century person's entertainment mix has somewhat more kaleidoscopic involvements. For one thing, commentators on styles of life such as McLuhan (1964), Toffler (1970), and Tom Wolfe (1965; 1969) nudge people to notice the participatory aspects of current entertainment. How can a linearly organized teacher have any chance of competing with television?

Regardless of the domain of subject matter, if the teacher's style is authoritarian, while the children are becoming acquainted with the domain, they also learn to become accepting of authorities' dictums. Dewey (1933), labels such behavior, "Intellectually irresponsible" (p. 33). Newspapers, television commentators, the foreman on the job, the peer group leader become believable and relatively less doubtable as they come to represent an Authority, however brief the reign. This condition undermines possibilities for critical awareness dealt with in Chapter 8.

In effect, whatever you select to do enters into a dialectical relation with what you do not do. For example, if a teacher spends much time and energy teaching discrete facts, then there is likely to be minimal thrust remaining for discovery activities. If you are trained to seek *the* answer (the teacher's answer), you become conditioned, set to play only that game. The subtle passive receptacle assumption of teaching-something-*to*-children leaves small opportunity for active children.

There is hardly a need at this late date to spell out the centralized fabric that clothes our schools in shredded garments. The sheer financial economics of huge buildings and mass-produced materials, resistance to organizing schooling in ways other than historically practiced, the mistrust and devaluation of individual school faculties' competence to develop their own *programs*, alongside the verbalized position that diversity of theories should exist within each school, since no one authoritative theory can be empedestaled—each contributes to such fragmentation.

Yet, history suggests that education is a unifying agent in this society (Butts and Cremin, 1953; Curti, 1959; Mann, 1957). Perhaps, indeed, unification may be approached by means of diversity, that is, that diversity is the welding element in a substantive sense. A unifying framework—perceptual models— presupposes a diversity of tools and materials. This framework supports a range of individual and societal differences.

Some Sanctions of Eastern and Western Culture.   In contrast to Western culture and its emphasis upon future, indirect, deductively ordered knowledge, Northrop presents an image of Eastern thought as determinate, particular, and related to *present* concerns. For someone who begins from an Eastern perspective, each directly experienced situation is absorbed for its own sake much as you approach an individual work of art. Just as one who valued aesthetic appreciation would judge each work of art as it hit him directly, so the Easterner might be likely to judge each time in his own life as distinct in character. Long-range commitments in this view are not essential. Alternative "bridges" need to be built to avoid such precarious behavior as long-range commitments in the light of subsequent reevaluations of circumstances.

In this way of thinking, single answers are not fixed, predeterminate, or discrete. Rather, there are alternatives implied, alternatives that may change as the system of variable elements changes.

There is a place in education for the continuum of experience that includes Eastern ways of thinking that favor the intuitive and Western ways of thinking that favor the rational. The perceptual models framework includes the notion that people are at the same time capable of universal and particular learning, determinate and indeterminate experiences, capable of reason and intuition, and so on. In this sense, Northrop speaks of "epistemic correlation," a reflection of the interaction of the two cultures, East and West.

The two cultures can be both distinguished and united through the *intensity* of any culture's participation in different parts of the continuum of aesthetic-to-abstract experience. Piaget's work with individuals parallels a societal participation in the continuum (Swensen, 1975). It is possible to imagine a self-actualizing person or society that maintains a balance. I suggest the model in Figure 2 to represent this correlation of cognition, affect, and culture. Each thinking-feeling-cultural person, or society experiences varying combinations of these potential, *blended* fields.

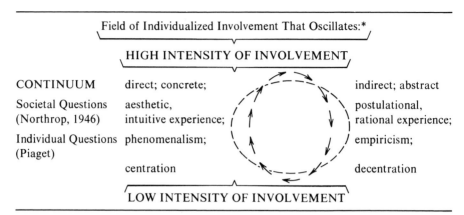

Field of Individualized Involvement That Oscillates:*

HIGH INTENSITY OF INVOLVEMENT

CONTINUUM   direct; concrete;   indirect; abstract

Societal Questions   aesthetic,   postulational,
(Northrop, 1946)   intuitive experience;   rational experience;

Individual Questions phenomenalism;   empiricism;
(Piaget)

                    centration   decentration

LOW INTENSITY OF INVOLVEMENT

* Recall the earlier discussion in which oscillations, a rhythmic phenomenon, are subject to the phenomenon of saturation.

FIGURE 2   An Adapted Epistemic Correlation of Cognition, Affect, and Culture

Perceptual Models as an Alternative Framework. The use of perceptual models as an integrative framework for curriculum development is an attempt to reflect the actual blending in ongoing life.

Experiential data become the projectiles of learning activity. Through activities, children may perceive perceptual models that extend beyond a particular datum of experience.

To test theory is to validate it. In Western culture, this is done largely by empirical means. Yet, teachers need to recognize that visceral knowing, knowing by direct experiencing, is one of the most powerful ways to know, even though one may be limited in sharing such knowing objectively with others. At best, people may share indirectly, by *interpolation,* or through art forms.

The notion of an educational theory that can fit any place in a culture-free medium may well be a beautiful myth. Yet there is a need to consider ways to cope with the unexpected. What if major highways, communications, or other "extensions of man" (McLuhan, 1964) were hindered or vastly altered?

Short-term electrical or social continua notwithstanding, American society as a whole has had little major upheaval when compared with other parts of the world at the present and at other times. For example, the development of the English "open" education structure has been partly attributed to the removal of urban children to rural settings during World War II. Teachers were liberated from bricks, mortar, and standardized materials. They lived with children of different ages and found decentralized teaching more adaptive to these conditions. After the war, when they returned to the cities, they found merit in continuing to decentralize and to make group relations more informal, eventually building new schools to fit the new people patterns.

To survive in any given societal or physical environment is to make order of it—to gain some measure of expectancies concerning it, to gain a degree of control over the future, at least the effect of future occurrences with regard to one's own being. Beyond coping and surviving, counterpoint striving and thriving.

When I deal with the subjects of coping and surviving versus striving and thriving, I am again faced with the question, "What is enough?" I would seek a balanced experience for children.

I am concerned about the history of early childhood education that has been marked by polarities, pendulum swings, and fads. Certainly teachers underutilize themselves when they spend as much energy as they do in keeping up with the newest practice. In itself, this is inefficient. Yet the greatest waste devolves to the children. For in fragmenting their lives by teachers' expectations (and lack-of-expectations are themselves expectations), teachers unconsciously limit the children's possibilities for becoming what they are capable of becoming.

To look at the course of acceptance by school people of Dewey and the progressivists is to see this kind of fragmentation in full defloration. Some school people interpreted doing and freedom as permissiveness. Some interpreted the child-in-the curriculum as a license to disenfranchise the teacher as one who may bring activities to children. Some interpreted the avoidance of waste as the basis for building what often turned out to be an alienated hierarchical administrative institution. And Dewey despaired many years later, in *Experience and Education* (1938), at the way his ideas had been defoliated. It is as if zealotry, like the fabled blind men, could only grasp at a piece of the elephant.

These many years later, schools continue to value short-cut efficiency and circumstantially acceptable answers. Frequently, this penchant for the practical trips up the practitioner. Perhaps teachers are so close to what is happening that they can see only a piece at a time—and perhaps this may be the most obviously direct Victorian-inherited human characteristic. In any case, teachers face a serious problem by virtue of the pounding waves of both criticisms and crises. Like the culture, there is a tendency among teachers to welcome and devour the latest pill. While this may salve them for the short run, its effects wear off all too soon. Recipes and isolated one-shot deals in the classroom become addictive.

Rather, teachers need to keep in mind the limits to human knowing imposed by cultural structuring. These foundational values of a culture infiltrate and permeate a child's life at the outset. Enough has been said in the literature to merit general agreement that the early years are critical and formative in life. While there are many ways in which educators have brought society's knowledge into children's lives in schools, a survey is not offered here. There are numerous volumes that directly deal with these issues and these are recommended to the reader (Hyman, 1973; Spodek, 1973).

Rather, in keeping with present purposes, to contend that an alternative needs to be developed, the "structure of disciplines" view is used selectively as a springboard.

Knowledge and the Franchised Teacher in Schooling.   Dewey's vision of the teacher as one who helps children move toward humanity's "fund of knowledge" (1933, p. 137) in ways that are consistent with children's total capacities strikes me as a beautiful notion. The only problem is trying to identify humanity's "fund." The complexities of pointing out funded knowledge-and-then-some become apparent as you view the differences in perspective between East and West, shaded by your own cultural blinders.

However, Phenix's (1964) masterful attempt to analyze generally accepted organized knowledge moves from the perspective of separate domains that then need to be connected. The structure of disciplines view is also consistent with an active conception of humanity. The emphasis on methods of inquiry is also consistent with Piaget and Inhelder's (1964) research that represents a child, active in learning, who "constructs" reality.

I see much usefulness in the structure of disciplines view. It can be an enriching exposure. After all, the structure of disciplines approach can provide an opportunity for children to actively acquire a quantity of consistently organized knowledge. They can do so through becoming acquainted with the tools that serve to help knowledge expand in each of the respective disciplines.

However, Phenix's attempt, and Bruner's (1961) attempt, to abbreviate the issue and redefine Dewey's projected "fund" of knowledge in terms of "key concepts," "spirals," the "process of education," and "the ways of knowing" create a problem for the teacher. Even if one were to ignore the limitation of cultural perspective, the potency of Bruner's and Phenix's abbreviation is quite a rich diet. To grasp the "key concepts" and means of inquiry of ordered disciplines is quite a chunk for the generalist to digest.

Although they would not spoon feed it, they propose that the school provide children with pre-cut pie. Children are expected to act and process events within the scope of current disciplines, even though the authors suggest that overlaps can be expected. However, imagine that each discipline exists as a piece of pie. One may detect occasional efflusions dripping into adjacent pieces but the cuts have, after all, already been made. And the relative sizes are culturally determined emphases.

The limits of knowledge are established by the structural character of those disciplines currently defined in Western tradition. Some critics of the structural view argue as if disciplines are menacingly impinging upon each other's territory. While overlap is expected, I welcome rather than turn away from this image. Such a notion is quite compatible with Floyd Allport's (1955) model of "tangency regions" and the standpoint of perceptual models.

Spirals and keys are valuable conceptions in a theory of knowledge that stands *outside* children. And this is the core of the problem: that while reality may exist "out there" somewhere, knowledge, whether scientific or musical, is an *inside* experience, the child's construction. This conception plays havoc with those who propose to "program" substantive knowledge.

However, children are more than receptacles for knowledge objectives. Objectives become eclipsed by human interaction. Interaction recasts behavioral objectives (Hyman, 1972).

The position in this book respectfully varies from the separate disciplines view. Teachers would need to deal with the complexity of schismatically fertilized "mathematics as conceptual music and music as sensuous mathematics" (Polanyi, 1963, p. 38). I propose that the place to look for a selection framework is not first in the separate domains of knowledge but in their integration, the connective dynamics between them. Teachers need to encourage plasticity rather than containment. *The manner in which the teacher functions becomes part of the substance that is communicated.*

The teacher who works with young children must continue to function while "connective dynamics" are being developed. In the above context, I am personally willing to be content with the teacher who is also a reasonably intelligent, curious, and humane person.

The teacher would provide the children primarily with access to the *tools* and skills of funded knowledge. Beyond this, it seems useful for the teacher to consider ways to help young children acquire an experiential syntax—perceptual models—that cuts across the traditional divisions of disciplines. The next section focuses on nonlinguistic (in the sense of primarily unwritten) systems, a kind of syntax of experience.

PERCEPTUAL MODELS

McLuhan (1963) has proposed using "models of perception" as a framework for planning:

It follows that any existing 'subject' in our curricula can now be taught as a more or less minor group of models of perception favored in some past or at present. Taught in this way any 'subject' becomes an organic portion of almost any other 'subject.' (p. 66)

A typically McLuhan "probe," it stands to entice one into a nonlinear world.

To perceive a perceptual model is to project the kaleidoscopic alternatives of a potential transaction or interaction or operating process. In McLuhan's view, "A structure cannot be contained. Any conceivable container is at once part of the structure, modifying the whole" (p. 66). Time makes this process irreversible.

Attempting to define a perceptual model is like attempting to define such happenings as time, Woody Guthrie singing Woody Guthrie's "Wake Up" song, motion, El Greco's greens, a dandelion seen mid-air in a gravitational field, the spaces between hiccoughs, the baby's drawing in of breath before an even louder wail, a Dos Passos description, the ecstacy of birth, an Anais Nin miscarriage, the potentials of an open drawer (to close, shatter, create dust, remind oneself of other times and places . . .).

After a look at some issues concerning models, perception, concepts, values, and a theory of knowledge, a definition of perceptual models can surface.

ON MODELS

A model may be a representation of reality. It represents in physical or abstract form (generally by some sensorially related or potentially sensorially related means) some possible, imaginable, or perceivable interaction among elements or systems of elements. Models may represent concrete or abstract processes.

For example, the computer is frequently compared to some aspects of brain functions. Schools have dealt with this sort of model when "if–then" has been taught, and alternative moves explored. An apparently simple game of checkers, in which some four-year-olds can engage, may be seen as an extended either–or checklist of alternatives, similar to computer functioning.

If a computer loses a game of chess or checkers to a human being, it may well be that it was not deficient in considering the range of logical alternatives but that it was unable to consider humans' "clouded" emotional qualities that "precipitate" risk and gambling. May it be that this emotional behavior is not perceivable as "information" according to computer logic—or the logic of the programmers?

The limitations of the computer's functioning may provide insight into human thought strategies. Part of the early game playing of the computer was overshadowed by humans who set priorities for moves, who did not scan every "bit" for each move but rather studied several moves ahead for the most likely pieces (Pfeiffer, 1962). Obviously, quality and judgment weigh strongly against mere quantity of detail in a model.

Moreover, a model may be a representation of interactions among people; between groups of people; or of people's use of, or manipulation of, concrete objects, or symbols, or ideas. The model itself is not, of course, the reality. It is a *possible* description or interpretation of reality processes.

Parents, teachers, and peer group members are role models for children. Each is a system of aggregated attributes. The painting, the sculpture, the robot, and the planetarium exist as models of reality—even when the art representations may be "abstractions," that is, imaginable interpretations of reality. Ecological concerns deal with presumed models of relatively healthy, life-sustaining environments. We frequently talk about an aquarium or a terrarium as a model of a balance of life.

Models are useful when real situations are less than accessible. McLuhan (1964) points to the play element of science in experiments with models of otherwise unobservable situations. He also sees games, along with art forms, as tangible models of less accessible situations. Certainly, games are used for varied purposes in legal education, medical training, social studies, logic, and so forth. Such games provide more concrete access to the real world or the world of symbols.

In this "less accessible" sense, models may represent abstract as well as concrete conditions and phenomena. Thus, *models when representative of concrete thought are drawn from perceptual data.*

A Definition of Perceptual Models. *A perceptual model is an abstract representation,* not of an abstract interaction among elements or systems of elements but *of potentially perceivable interactions among concrete elements or systems of elements.*

Perceptual models exist in the teacher's mind as a frame of reference in planning activities. *The perceptual model is the teacher's map of what the child may perceive.* Using this frame, the teacher could select and sequence activities as she interpolates this "map." When children are exposed to concrete activities and are receptive to them (discernible by their actions, active involvement with these physical, social, and symbol-related encounters), they are "ready" for more complex encounters.

For example, the teacher can provide children with a series of two-dimensional puzzles that increase in complexity and are probably useful prior activities for Tangrams (Elementary Science Study) that play havoc with preconceived strategies. Tangrams is a seven piece Chinese puzzle from which the player attempts to recreate each of hundreds of possible, different printed forms in turn. Each form demands that the player break out of earlier approaches and combinations.

Tangrams, in eliciting new strategies, and woodworking that requires step-ahead anticipation and preparation, are probably useful precursors for three-dimensional puzzles that demand these kinds of "abeyance" actions. Such activities stimulate the use of continually changing and intricate strategies.

Exposure to the Dienes "Logic Blocks," a set of wooden blocks that vary in color, size, and shape, and the Elementary Science Study's "People Pieces," a set of small plastic tablets with people pictures that vary in color, girth, sex, and age, can operate in a parallel way as concrete games of classification. They can be used for more complex or simple purposes. The beauty of these generically available materials is the handy opportunity to stimulate children to set their own problems and develop their own games.

The teacher is aware of the curved efficiency of time. A child who "lazily" studies the clouds may well turn up a matrix organization of weather and cloud type—or simply be reacting through escapism to too much pressure or too little stimulation.

From children's behaviors *teachers may infer a potentially complex process of personal mapping of these phenomena.* Perceptual models may be viewed as an adult mapping of, and *approximations* of, these variably apprehendable, potential processes within the child. Perceptual models become bracketed.

The ultimate state of the perceptual model might be viewed as the *most likely,* possible, consistent, concrete system of relations that may develop, and remain in continual flux. The teacher tries to estimate where children are and to help them move toward the next logical steps.

A Theory of Knowledge Revisited. To speak of knowledge, then, is not to speak of a model in the teacher's mind alone. Rather, knowledge becomes an aggregate system. Teaching and learning are an interaction between the child's process of *perceptual modelling,* the teacher's models of the child's processes, and the ineffability between them. To the child, her perceived models are concrete-data-bound-to-reality. While not fully self-aware of their own intellectual processes, young children are continuing to become aware of their own physical attributes and capabilities and those of others. Thus, a perceptual ordering unfolds.

The process of ordering the "randomness" of experience creates the child's product. In this sense, ordered knowledge is momentarily abstracted from ongoing development. Inasmuch as it may be possible to reflect upon ordered knowledge, a product, one's *consciousness* of it still makes it a process. To reflect upon one's thought is to change it or reinforce it, a kind of change of density.

The teacher who focusses on assessment as a process raises the ceiling for possibilities to expand, for children's experiences to become more complex. Thus, to deal with perceptual models from a teaching standpoint is to take account of the integrated aspects of development all at once.

This is a multidimensional way for teachers to select activities. First, look at perceptual models as a *"structure-of-a-process"* in an ongoing system of change. Then, *project the possibility of an interplay of varied methods of inquiry upon concrete activities.* Inquiring, an energic undertaking, is propelled by human "fuel"—motivation.

Do keep in mind the contrast of the distinct domains of expert knowledge that may, in fact, serve to restrain innovation and discovery—and to remain limited to a set of particular pre-positioned, "inevitable" possibilities. However, major theoretical bolts of the Galileo, Darwin, Freud, and Einstein sort are not drawn from already ordered domains alone, but also from totally different perspectives—totally new "perceptual viewpoints."

Beginning with Activity. I propose that teachers begin with concrete activities that are approached, not with *the* method of inquiry of any one discipline, but with *any* methods of inquiry that may reasonably be employed. In this way, you can avoid the established parameters of a predefined type of datum.

Children naturally engage in a "crosscut" perceptual modelling approach. To reiterate: *Project an interplay of varied methods of inquiry upon concrete activities.*

The role of the teacher is to mesh the varied methods of inquiry, to provide the relevant tools and skills to children as they move through activities. Rather than begin with particular knowledge objectives, the teacher begins with the consideration of how various tools can be employed to develop, extend, and deepen children's perceptual models. Children learn to use and apply available tools to *the study of experiential data.* The tools become the glue that binds experiences. The teacher provides the tools directly, through appropriate activities.

That term, "appropriate activities," the core of "experiential data," sits so innocently in the air. Yet it is painfully clear that all the noble values and attitudes a human can muster will not create activity in a vacuum. Inasmuch as I am convinced that structure, the medium of schooling, is a part of the substance, some antidotes to the vacuum were presented in the preceding chapter and are elaborated in the chapters that follow.

The dynamic use of different tools and the beginning of learning through activity can be means for absorbing "funded" knowledge from the dynamic rays suggested by *each* experience. Activities would tie in additional tools and structural relations using many-dimensional data. Proceeding with this interplay of tools may be a way to seek beyond the cultural limitations of knowledge: "Learning has not really occurred until some change takes place in the child's own personal and unique perceptual field" (Combs, 1962, p. 69).

PERCEPTUAL MODELS GROWING FROM METAPHORS

On a simple, concrete level, partial perceptual models build through metaphorical relations. For example, pupils who begin Dalcroze music classes refer to "walking" and "running" notes; the undertow of the waves reminds me of some mothers on the first day of nursery school who push-and-pull their children; a contradiction is like a seesaw, or a spring, and so forth. These particular examples could have been randomly, even casually selected. Any number of other possibilities could have been employed.

Sometimes children do this sort of metaphorical translation quite spontaneously. Teachers can frequently see their analogies as poetry or a genuine-appearing insight. Children create this "poetry" by abstracting the "salient points" of a situation (Leacock, 1972, p. 129).

Metaphorical extensions mark the development of ongoing systems of interacting elements. The beginner Dalcroze music students are merely acquainted with the metaphor. Later on, repeated rhythmic measures of varying tempo begin to form patterns. Children experience some rhythmic patterns as repetitious signals that take on the melodic quality of transposing *emotive wholes* that are more than the sum of their parts. A fruitful perceptual model is the synergic image of "more than the sum of its parts" that had greater generality than the image of simple rhythmic patterns. This rough sketch of one line of transformations is extended in the next chapter.

It is interesting to note that computers can deal with a similar kind of "pattern recognition" by sequential or random scanning of data with a preset program. The child's potential is, of course, much less definable, probably has fewer restraints, and is adaptable to a vast variety of alternative recognitions—

and appreciations. The perceptual model is part of the human potential for pattern recognition.

Working backward, there are other possible experiences in which "more than the sum of its parts" can be perceived, such as human interaction, profiles of climatic conditions, insightful task solutions. "More than the sum of its parts" can also blend into syllogistic logic in the following adapted example: The teenager is freed to follow adolescent culture. Adolescent culture is conformist. He is free to follow an alternate form of constraint (Henry, 1973, p. 262).

The other metaphors mentioned can be extended. The separation anxieties of mothers came to me as I felt the sand pulled out from under my heels at the seashore at exactly the second that another wave broke at my ankles. This is a more complex metaphor than "walking notes" since it is so much farther from physical interactions. A short extension of this image leads to the "double bind" model in which a child must act as if the parent really *meant* what he or she *said*—for example, verbal level: "I love you"; emotional level: "I can't stand you" even though the child detects a contradiction (Henry, p. 192). The simultaneity of the "double bind" is a perceptual model that young children can experience on a concrete level.

Working backward from the "double bind," consider sub-atomic physics which offers a model of an electron that appears to "race backward in time" or is in "two places at once" (Koestler, 1973). Here, the rationale consists of using space as the frame of reference instead of a time frame (defined by the speed of light) with which we are more familiar (L. Wiener, Personal Communication, 1973). Certainly, the nonhuman sample is immune from the intentionality of the double-bind. Humans may have unconscious intent.

Metaphors, of course, are hardly exact in all elements. If they were, they would not be metaphors. However, metaphors serve to draw together and highlight one or more attributes. Young children's thinking is rich in such syncretic flexibility. The early childhood educator has quite an exciting task in trying to *reconcile the limitations of syncretic functioning with the seminal powers inherent in this transformational process.* The teacher provides less direction for resolutions *per se* and more encouragement with varied materials and activities for connection-making and fluidity.

Taking the seesaw-spring image, there is still another level of complexity. Dialectical discourse is itself a rich perceptual model that could be traced back to the analogy. A bare bones perceptual model, while helpful as a generator, remains merely a source of energy requiring substantive incarnation. The substance can vary across Marxian economic theory; a Picasso painting with self-contradictory faces, "Woman in the Mirror"; a contrapuntal musical score; a filmed story such as the Japanese production of *Woman of the Dunes* (Abe, 1965), in which the removal of one's source of struggles—sand dunes— continually reappear. While a young child could not be expected to engage in formal dialectical discourse, he experiences conflicts and arguments, ambivalent feelings, inconsistent treatment by others, even the interaction between his hole digging and the force of gravity on the sand, at a concrete level.

Clearly, differences exist in the variety and kinds of relatedness that individual teachers can provide. Since the weight of action in learning is placed upon each child, the quantity of relatedness is not as much of a concern for the teacher as is the process. Sometimes, process is taken too much for granted as naturally learnable whereas teachers emphasize sheer bulk of information that is so much more readily available and ingested. It seems apparent that each teaching generation bears the responsibility for its own renewal in valuing, setting priorities, and establishing theoretical and practical consistency.

Concepts and Perceptual Models Contrasted.   The term "concepts" has been used in the literature to denote *many levels of generality,* for example, this apple, any apple, justice, reciprocity. . . . "Percepts," in turn, are the elements that constitute concepts. Piaget (1961) states that perceptions are not the source of knowledge but rather, "function as connectors" between abstract operations and concrete events" (p. 359).

One could then project that a perceptual model might be synonymous with concepts generally. It is useful to make some distinctions. It would be more accurate to say that there are some conditions under which a concept may be found that is identical with a perceptual model. The inferred "relations" in perceptual knowing are central to the perceptual models notion.

Most concepts in human thinking have been categorized into particular regions of expectation. People usually expect certain items to be part of particular disciplines, subject to unique methods of inquiry.

Each discipline sustains its own hierarchy of simple and more general abstract concepts. There may be comparably abstract levels of complexity that can correspond between one discipline and another. When teachers plan for the interplay of varied methods of inquiry upon concrete data in concrete ways, it is possible that children will experience transposed levels of perceptual models.

Perceptual models comprise the essential interactive processes, a kind of lymphatic system. Percepts and concepts contrast with perception in that they are structurally rather than functionally defined: *The functioning of perceptual models is their structure.*

PERCEPTUAL MODELS FOR EARLY EDUCATION CONTRASTED
WITH MORE AND LESS SYNTACTIC THEORIES

To speak in terms of perceptual models as a "syntax of experience" is to speak in terms of a human predisposition to perceive models. In a parallel view, language is a finite structure of relationships that can generate infinite possibilities. This image bears on the present consideration.

Chomsky (1968), who has written about linguistics, proposes that human beings are born with finite mechanisms—"schemas"—to generate infinite possible combinations of language, possibilities that extend far beyond each child's limited exposure to language. This is one example of the interaction of innate factors and environmental factors.

These finite structures, or presets, operate as a theory; they limit language to transformational processes. There is a growing interest in this kind of transformational construction in fields beyond linguistics such as computer technology, biology, anthropology, and psychology.

A rough analogy is the pattern recognition of computer functioning where relevant "signals" are extracted from interfering "noises" because of the computer's preset human programming. The human programmer works out of a particular theoretical framework (Minsky, 1967). The machine generates expanded possibilities from limited structures.

DNA molecules in human cells can similarly be seen as a limited alphabet that transmits hereditary messages to an infinity of generations (Pfeiffer, 1962). Here, there is an interaction of innate and environmental factors.

A related framework that ties technology to social considerations has been proposed by Moore and Anderson (1968). They have suggested that various "autotelic folk-models" (apparently self-propelled and represented in the form of different activities) exist in all human societies. These activities include games of strategy, games of chance, puzzles, and art forms. Activities representing these models are intrinsically satisfying and provide a strong force in effecting acculturation. Moore and Anderson have applied these perspectives to seek intrinsically satisfying ways that provide a responsive environment intended for increments in children's reading.

They suggest that the possibility for such fundamental models is universal and that the simpler forms become transformed into more complex forms. Their suggestion is similar to Levi-Strauss' work in anthropology with myths.

Levi-Strauss (1964) has worked on a syntax for mythology and contends that myths from different societies can be compared and found to have related themes. He suggests that each society creates its myths by extracting a "limited number of relevant incidents" from an "infinite series" of historical events (p. 16). In his study of kinship structures (1949), he particularly tries to sharpen the distinctions between those aspects of human relationships that are culturally governed as opposed to naturally universal. He posits a transformational relation between human nature and human culture.

Steiner (1970) sees an analogy in Levi-Strauss' work to "mathematical topology that studies those relations that remain constant when configurations change" (p. 248). Moreover, Steiner has suggested that myths, while including words, "go beyond them toward a more supple, inventive, universal syntax" (p. 249).

The psychologist Jung (1968) also found a rich source of study in mythology, which grew out of his study of dreams. His theory proposes that beyond conscious awareness lies the "personal unconscious" that may become conscious. Different individuals differ in the extent of their awareness of the personal unconscious at different times.

In contrast, Jung proposes the sphere of the "archetypal mind," or the "collective unconscious." He sees the collective unconscious as the repository of humanity's "universal"—as opposed to personal—dream symbols. Broadly interpreted, human beings are predisposed to transform the limited range of universal archetypal structures into varied personal symbols.

Teachers and children can continue to interact with the distillate of these theories as part of the teachers' consciousness. Teachers may move beyond fragmentation toward a more unified approach to curriculum decision making which recognizes perceptual models as a useful lever for helping children's knowledge to expand.

The various positions cited point out that some patterns and transformational processes appear with amazing frequency under disparate cultural circumstances. On the face of it, *a pattern of underlying transformations* appears to suffuse each example offered on a distinctly theoretical level. It is therefore useful to note that these apparently supportive formulations have been independently criticized. Leach (1970) has questioned Levi-Strauss' procedures. Piaget and Inhelder (1966; 1969) treat Jungian archetypes as vaguely mystical and Chomsky's notion of "innate kernels" as an "exaggeration" (pp. 62, 121, 123).

It will take much more study beyond the scope of this writing to finally resolve the question of those aspects of perception that are relatively innate structures, predispositions, or the result of nurture. At best, it is safe to say that children are able to absorb perceptions involving a *degree* of decentration. In addition, young children can use and associate more and less partial systems of interacting elements that add up to more than the sum of their parts. *The powerful flexibility of perceptual modelling and its relations lies in the oscillation process of perception along the centration–decentration range.*

GREGARIOUS PERCEPTUAL MODELS AS PRIORITIES

The question of priorities in the face of a particular sociocultural setting and its limited resources begs for consideration.

Assume that a teacher is aware of a range of activities that would reasonably mesh with the children's momentum. Most children can become interested in many things. Those activities that are more *gregarious* would be early choices. "Gregariousness," as used here, means more conductive to connections among and between present or future activities. Gregariousness forecasts the possibility that children's pursuits will deepen and enrich their encounters.

The teacher also takes into account such bread-and-butter considerations as ideas for activities, materials, and resources. Other considerations that affect gregariousness include the children's capacities and the appropriateness and availability of methods of inquiry and relevant tools.

The gregariousness of a perceptual model as a priority selection is limited by the perceivable relations of the planners. A tacit assumption is that children will be responsible, by their direct action, for seeking relations. In any case, this happens.

Although the perceptual models interactive approach crosscuts different ways of ordering the world, each child is not thereby committed to exhaustive dissection, study, and involvement of each or any particular field of concrete phenomena. Different methods of inquiry would be singularly, relatively, and respectively weighted by different children.

It seems reasonable to plan activities that provide wider possible concrete representations of perceptual models. While encouraging self-propelled contemporary activity, concrete activities extend the possibility that children will be open to future associations.

When the teacher begins with a different model, it presupposes a range of different questions to be answered. Furthermore, the same model may be related to different data, sometimes in the physical world and at other times in human relationships.

Priorities, the availability of materials, and human resources reflect values. Values are set against the frame of what is technically possible in a given instant.

Therefore, the gregariousness of perceptual models operates not as a prescriptive but rather a *suggestive* teacher perspective. Pills and potions are not among the offerings of this approach. Were you to enter several settings in which perceptual models were considered in developing action with children, you might expect to find quite different activities.

To base the selection of plans upon perceptual models is to help children proceed with an effective *range and power of alternatives.* The power to select from among ongoing alternatives and, beyond that, to create them, supports creativity. In a world marked by explosive change, a concretely based, open-ended program for young children may begin to furnish a vital range of alternatives in life. This is projected as a way to help cope with the unknown that is constantly becoming.

Machines and technology have made funded knowledge more accessible than heretofore in a sort of paradoxical way. The other side of the coin is that proliferation of knowledge by its very bulk has complicated the retrieval of knowledge. Against this background, McLuhan (1963) suggests that, beyond merely imparting information, education needs to help eliminate "familiar" boundaries while providing for the critical training of perception.

Moreover, perceptual models may form a basis for stimulating continuity, a continuity that is unique for each combination of people who work together. In effect, to work with children is to deal with time, with sequence. The teacher may juxtapose events and materials physically with each other in a particular sequence simultaneously so that children can work out a sequence, or in combinations thereof. Children's receptivity to a juxtaposition of materials and events is affected by the timing and atmosphere in which such exposure occurs, influencing their feeling of power to act.

Often, children are faced with teaching that is largely rote and technical, subsequently followed by claims that children are unable to learn anything else. Teaching sometimes follows those paths that lead only to a limited range of empirically measurable phenomena. Since the position adopted here differs from this practice, the next chapter looks at alternate ways for children and teachers to work together. The examples of how different activities represent perceptual models will play out the theoretical framework that has been offered in this chapter.

SUMMARY OF THEORETICAL ASSUMPTIONS AND PRINCIPLES

Perception is a construct that lies on a continuum between sensory data and mature abstractions. The perceptual mode of learning that predominates in early childhood consists of sensory experience and meaning. The young child can extend sensory experiences by using imagery to make connections.

Perception oscillates along the centration–decentration range. Children's thought oscillates between processed and raw data. While decentration begins in social interactions, each person's rhythm of oscillations and saturation is unique.

Perception occurs as a fresh figure contrasted against a known background. The readiness (set) to perceive is an interaction between cognition and affect. Past experience can be used by an individual who feels responsible.

Young children are able to select from among and create alternative concrete activities. Early responsibility for relevant choices supports independent, constructive behavior.

Children feel motivated to become what they feel capable of becoming. They feel intrinsically motivated to act and to extend their attention when they experience a sense of competence and responsibility. Young children are also content with episodic activities and with appreciating the process of activity for its own sake.

The unique patterns of learning in the early childhood years are significant for a contemporary sense of being and later, becoming. These patterns are important sources of creativity. The limitations of young children's syncretic thinking—an incomplete process of transforming elements and making new connections—must be reconciled with the seminal powers inherent in this functioning. Children learn in meandering, nonlinear ways.

Once children perceive an experience as relevant, it is not easily forgotten. Human beings generalize by "forgetting" selectively, by reducing the form of knowledge for storage purposes.

Meaning is a perceived experience invested with commitment, and represents an interaction of cognition and affect. Each feeling has a cognitive aspect and each cognitive experience has an affective aspect.

Discursive meaning is predominantly rational. Nondiscursive meaning is predominantly intuitive. Discursive and nondiscursive meanings are both needed for balanced living and need to be part of children's education through conscious professional planning.

Intersubjective meaning is the confluence of similar, direct, and concrete experiences by different individuals. Children develop ordered knowledge, an aggregate holistic system, through a process of interaction with other children, adults, concrete materials, and activities.

Contemporary society is participatory and needs independent thinkers. *Perceptual models* are consistent with individual and societal differences.

Perceptual models are a finite structure of relations, an experiential syntax, that can generate infinite possible combinations of ideas. Perceptual models are a pre-set for transformational processes and relationships leading to substantive learning. The function of perceptual models is their structure.

Perceptual models form an integrative framework for selecting activities that reflect the connective dynamics between existing disciplines. Perceptual models support new viewpoints that cut across existing subject matter divisions and extend knowledge beyond a particular datum of experience. Parts of perceptual models develop through metaphorical relationships.

Young children can learn perceptual models through concrete activities. Concrete activities will help them to retain an openness to future associations with other meanings. Children who engage in concrete activities are responsible for seeking relationships by direct action.

Young children can acquire perceptual models through applying varied methods of inquiry to concrete data. Children use tools to study experiential data.

Different children can acquire equivalent knowledge through engaging in different activities. They may make deeper and richer connections between present and future activities when they begin with more "gregarious" activities that are open to varied uses and broad possibilities.

CHAPTER 4
ALTERNATIVE STRATEGIES FOR PLANNING ACTIVITIES: INTEGRATING SCIENCE, SOCIAL SCIENCE, THE ARTS, AND SKILLS

It is time to look at how teachers can plan activities. With young children, the activity becomes the primary medium of learning. Educator Bruce Joyce (1972) also suggests that activities can integrate curriculum. He emphasizes the importance of using the ties between areas for planning. Therefore, the teacher's primary task is to provide direct experiences so that children can grasp underlying meanings and associations. Several real considerations enter into these offerings.

While writers exhort teachers to begin first by considering the purposes of an activity and desired behavioral outcomes, many teachers begin with an idea for an activity that appeals to them as either stimulating, novel, didactic, satisfying, useful, dramatic, fun, or simply manageable. When pressed, it is possible to justify the activity in more global, "significant" terms.

I would even regard it as progressive if a teacher were to select a stimulating activity and ask herself why it is significant, how it fits into any larger scheme, how it relates to other activities.

I would consider it progressive if a teacher were to ask himself why a child could be expected to engage willingly in such an activity. What might be the child's perception of his engagement? A priority response would be the child's ready involvement in the activity for its own sake. On another level the teacher should be asking himself if the activity is intrinsically worthwhile and substantial.

In terms of the child's experience, it does not matter much by what route the activity travelled in the teacher's thinking. Activities relate to resources of a particular group, their surrounding community, and its *resources*. In this way,

---

THE CHILD TRIES TO MATCH THE OBJECT THAT HE FEELS WITH ITS PICTURE.

curricular programs become decentralized and the identity of cultural subgroups is supported.

What does matter is that the teacher has effectively juxtaposed activities. Effectiveness in this sense parallels a Brazilian educator's argument that "efficiency" is "identified with the power men have to think, to imagine, to risk themselves in creation" rather than "carrying out orders from above precisely and punctually" (Freire, 1970c, p. 475). I recommend that children acquire varied perspectives by using tools in varied ways.

THE INTERPLAY OF TOOLS

A major purpose of this chapter is to communicate some ways in which teachers plan activities that involve the interplay of tools. The various tools are skills through which children can acquire, extend, and deepen their understandings.

After exploring the application of some tools and methods of inquiry, this chapter deals with planning activities by considering substantive knowledge. Suggested activities that are designed to extend connectedness are presented and the underlying importance of communication and dialogue is discussed.

SEQUENCE AND CONTINUITY

Teachers make a value decision each time they select a particular activity. In relation to each child, each teacher is the repository of humanity's "fund of knowledge." Therefore, the teacher's choice reflects, at best, some set of associations between concepts, some sense of a hierarchical complexity inherent within them, and some sense of their sequential relation to children's developmental capacities. In this way, each activity presupposes a range of related activities. The next activity reveals the particular triangulation that the teacher has made between the knowledge, and the child's directions and depth of involvement with the preceding experience.

Along with the basic gregariousness of the content, the depth of children's involvement is one clear priority for the teacher to consider when deciding what next steps need to be taken. Depth study for young children should have pure hues, not pastel fuzziness. The logical sequence of gregarious perceptual models remains an ongoing interpolation.

In keeping with the purpose of this chapter to elaborate how teachers plan, some alternate sequences of activities will be presented. Nursery, kindergarten, and primary designations alongside different activities are meant to be suggestive. It can be expected that some older children may need more background or that younger ones may need more stimulation.

The conceptual ties between activities form the basis for the teacher's experience of continuity. She tries to understand the nature of the child's perception and to mesh activities accordingly. Teachers realize that a real change is a change in the child's own experience of connectedness. This interaction between teacher, child, and activities is a continual dialogue reflecting the interplay of varied tools on children's encounters.

THE TEACHER PLANS FOR TOOLS

There are several perspectives from which tools can be understood. In the first place, *tools are instruments* whose use takes practice. The hammer, ruler, camera, test, and screwdriver are used more efficiently after practice. In this sense, tools are more and less complex skills that need to be learned. For those tools that require skill in symbolizing, young children need different kinds of practice than when tools are more clearly extensions of the hand. Maps are such *symbolic representations* that can extend understandings. Mathematics, while a domain of knowing, is also a tool of the physicist. Chapter 2 emphasized some sequential activities related to mathematics as part of the discussion of organization. Chapter 7 extends the integration of mathematics and social life. Chapter 5 deals with the ever present tool of language. Young children need systematic help in learning to use these tools.

Tools are also *methods of inquiry* that help to expand substantive understandings. If we view mapping broadly as model making, for example, then mapping has been a major task of inquiry into the separate disciplines. Scholars within these disciplines have mapped their domains with respect to unique scope, subject matter, and preferred methods of inquiry.

In this respect, tools are *inquiry strategies* for gaining understandings. The notion of "planned contrasts" is a powerful pedagogic strategy as well as a method of inquiry that can be used to study people as well as objects. Additional inquiry strategies will be interspersed in the discussions of alternate planning procedures and the discussion of dialogue.

SELECTING TOOLS

Clearly, no individual is equally competent with all methods of inquiry across the range of disciplines. Therefore, when you assess the kinds of tools available to you, you have a reasonable spot to begin looking at your resources. Figure 3

Hammers	Clocks and timers	Lenses
Saws	Nonstandard measures	Magnifying glass
Rasps and files	(quantities of equal	(clear and colored
Screwdrivers	lengths)	glass and dyes)
Braces and bits	Pulleys	Microscope
Drills	Pendulum	Prism
Pliers	Light meters	Binoculars
Wrenches	Micrometer	Level
Nail sets	Galvanometer	Gyroscope
Wire Cutters	Voltmeter	Lights (flashlight,
Scissors	Ohm meter	infrared, ultraviolet,
Rulers	Amp meter	black light)
Protractors	Watt meter	Heating devices
Compasses	Torque meter	Cameras
Abaci-Counters	Sextant	Tape recorders
Calipers	G-indicators	Kaleidoscopes
Scales	Speedometers	Maps (globes,
Thermometers	Odometers	mercator projection,
Barometers	Pedometers	relief maps, etc.)
Hydrometers	(for people and	Stethoscope
Shygmomanometer	animals)	Wind sock
Vacuum indicators		Weathervane
Tachometers		Musical instruments
		Art materials
		Models (planetary,
		skeletal, etc.)
		"Junk"

FIGURE 3   SOME TOOLS USED FOR BUILDING, MEASURING, AND OBSERVING

lists some concrete tools that have been used with children. The beautiful thing about looking at a tool as a resource is that each one suggests an array of possible activities and, after all, activity needs to be the base for early education.

You might ask some of the following questions: To what data can these tools be applied through activities that involve children? What perceptual models do you see represented in these activities? How can you use the gregarious properties of the perceptual model to extend thinking and action? Are children able to make their own connections? Are there opportunities, if not right away then in the future, for cooperative work and discussion?

When children need to learn finer skills for using tools, additional activities are suggested. However, one reality when the teacher begins to plan with tools alone is that before long, you find that perceptual models are needed in order to connect activities or to help guide and coordinate future plans. This is not to say that one should not begin to plan a sequence of activities through the use of tools alone. In reality, this sometimes happens and stimulates a fruitful line of inquiry. The substance of the inquiry and the children's reactions then suggest other tools and activities.

Different perceptual models emphasize the use of some tools more than others at different times. In addition, resources suggest some directions for emphasis, underscoring flexible planning.

MAPPING SUGGESTS ACTIVITIES

You could follow some children through their nursery, kindergarten, and primary school situations and see the sequential expansion of mapping as a tool. When young children engage in mapping, there are often opportunities for psychomotor involvement as they build skills in imagery and symbolizing. The teacher's role in helping the children to focus on these and other inquiry skills can be seen in a group of five-year-olds who greet a visitor from India.

TEACHER:	Do you know where this lady comes from?
CHILDREN:	Yes! India!
TEACHER:	How did you know?
CHILD:	My grandmother lived in India for a long time. (*To visitor*) Did you know her?
DR. D:	I don't think so.
TEACHER:	Let's find the place where she came from. (*Brings globe to the group. Dr. D. shows children the place in India from which she came.*)
TEACHER:	(*pointing*) What does the blue mean?
CHILDREN:	Water.
TEACHER:	What does the green mean?
CHILDREN:	Land.
TEACHER:	How do you suppose Dr. D. came all the way here? What might she have used?
CHILD 1:	Maybe she came by boat.
TEACHER:	You think that's possible? Let's see. (*They trace some alternate routes.*)
CHILD 2:	Maybe she came by car.

TEACHER: Let's see if she could really come by car. (*Children note water part of the globe.*) Let's ask her how she came.

DR. D.:   By airplane.

CHILDREN: I was on an airplane . . . Me too . . . I went . . . etc.

TEACHER: She could have come around this way, moving East, or the other way, moving West. Let's find out which way she came.

DR. D.:   (*pointing out route*)

CHILDREN: How long did it take you?

DR. D.:   Thirty-two hours.*

It is clear that the children have acquired some beginning understandings and skills in using the globe. Several gaps in the children's thinking that suggest next steps are noticeable. First imagine the activities that could have prepared them for this discussion and then project possible next steps.

Nursery: Threes.   When they were three years old, some of these children had color-sorted beads into two different boxes at a time. At other times they sorted by shape or size. When the teacher wanted them to learn color variations, all the beads were the same size and shape. When she wanted them to learn size differences, all the beads were the same color and shape. In that way, she isolated the single variable that she wanted to teach. This variable became a new "figure" contrasted against a known "background." She also used color names functionally throughout the day. Color, size, and shape are used symbolically in maps.

She also helped the children build imagery through tactile activities using a similar, gradual process. They played with objects in boxes or bags that they felt. Properties were added gradually so that children would need to project their imagination toward the unseen. In addition to building toward mapping land forms, this sensory play was a step in building toward future conceptions of unseen phenomena such as atoms. The teacher also introduced the Elementary Science Study's "People Pieces" and "Attribute Blocks" to help the children build imagery when she would ask them to guess what might be in the box . . . and what else? . . . as they removed one object at a time.

The children enjoyed their reception at home when they brought their own hand outlined with crayon on paper or impressed into plaster-of-paris held in a paper plate. They were fascinated to watch their friends' profiles silhouetted into larger and smaller shadows as the light was moved. They particularly enjoyed bringing home their own profile silhouetted after the teacher asked

---

* Adapted from a conversation with Dr. Sunitee Dutt, University of Dehli, after she visited Gertrude Luttgen and her five-year-olds in Minneapolis, 1963.

each child who wanted one whether he wanted a tiny image, real-sized image, or giant-sized image. They were adding to their experiencing of the idea that real objects can be represented in different sizes, a beginning foundation for the concept of scale in architecture and mapmaking. Their play with pets and peg city accessories, miniature animals, dolls of varying sizes, doll houses, wooden puzzles, and large building blocks also contributed toward this development of the concept of scale. The teacher also took photographs of several children who had not been able to bring their own photograph to school.

The teacher set out a box of colored cubes and cards with square patterns that were the same colors as the cubes. The cards progressed from simple patterns using a few colored squares to complex patterns using many colored squares. The children placed each cube on the corresponding square on the card. After some practice, children constructed the patterns of cubes directly on a cloth and used the cards as a reference.

Close to the end of this year, the teacher read them *The Little Island* (MacDonald, 1971), a story of a cat's aloneness experienced as a purely existential moment. Whatever personal associations the children would make might relate in the farther future to their academic work.

Throughout the year, the teacher sometimes accompanied the children with a drum as they explored different spaces and directions with their bodies. They used hoops, boxes, furniture, ropes, and a wired cloth tunnel as accessories to the exploration.

Nursery: Fours. The following year, the teacher built on many of these experiences. She practiced imagery construction and sequence with children using varied beads, following Lavatelli's (1970) suggestion. The children would string each bead in the sequence suggested by the teacher. When children had done this comfortably, the teacher asked children to set the sequence for each other as they sat back to back. Sometimes they sat at opposite sides of the easel (McGinn and Rudnick, 1973) and took turns:

CHILD 1:   "I'm putting on a round yellow bead."
CHILD 2:   . . . "a big, square bead."
CHILD 1:   "What color?"
CHILD 2:   "Red."

When the children finished, they compared the strings and checked themselves for accuracy. In this way, they were able to work together without continuous teacher supervision.

They also worked cooperatively after practice with the teacher in "What's

Missing?" In addition to random classroom objects, they used the "Attribute Blocks" and "People Pieces" (Elementary Science Study) in this game. This activity continued their development of an imagery system leading toward representation by varied symbolic forms. They also used colored loops of yarn as "playgrounds" for including or excluding blocks with the same or different properties.

When they replaced woodworking tools on the pegboard, the children learned to use the outlined shape of the tool as its resting place. There were similar taped outlines on the shelves holding large building blocks that they used on the floor. The children used these blocks in order to represent their dramatic fantasies of farms, zoos, garages, space stations, monster havens, special houses, railroads, trucks, and boats.

Smaller-scale construction toys that they used on felt cloths at tables or on the floor included such kits as "Playskool Village," "Lego," "Lincoln Logs," and "Tinker Toys." Miniature furnishings, people, and animals continued to be popular. Since the preceding year, the use of these manipulable toys had become more systematic and orderly. Children's work showed more symmetry and balance. Their painting and drawing paralleled this development. As the children engaged in these activities with two and three-dimensional media, they were deepening their experiences with symbolic representation. When they used sets of the same objects and pictures in series of varied size, they were also strengthening their concept of relative scale.

An especially enjoyable representational activity was the time when each one who wanted to would lay down on the back of a large sheet of discarded wallpaper to have his body outlined. Then, each according to his ability "mapped" the terrain within his own boundaries using large felt-tipped pens, yarn, and other textured materials. For some children, this was the first time that they had started an activity on one day and completed it over the next few days.

A few of the children had been with a teacher who used the Montessori-inspired globe with them. First, they used a "rough-smooth" one to differentiate land and water. She also used a colored globe, transferring the distinction from the tactile to the visual sense.

When some of the children had travelled with their teacher to collect possible collage materials outdoors in the autumn, they had a long discussion about reaching some seed pods across the small stream. After discussing alternate ways of crossing and ruling out a log that looked too brittle, they walked to a small wooden bridge. They talked about its construction and other bridges they had seen. Somebody mentioned a tunnel that had a toll also.

The next day the teacher had set out picture books in the library corner and mounted pictures from her own collection, of bridges and various views of tunnels. One child connected the idea of animal burrows and began another line of study, comparing how animals and people solve similar and different problems in varied ways.

In this instance, the teacher had planned in advance to stimulate the stream-crossing discussion as part of the collage-and-outdoors-in-the-fall activity. She was delighted with the various connections children made as well as their large and small block representations and dramatizations. *The Three Billy Goats Gruff,* and its role-playing with large hollow blocks, added still another support and direction to this growing awareness of land forms. Other supporting books that she read to the children that year included McCloskey's *Blueberries for Sal* and later in the year, *One Morning in Maine.* Parts of these stories represent hilly terrain and the style of life on an island, as well as wholesome family relationships.

In the later part of the year the children played with mirrors and simple symmetry, and splattering paint on paper and folding over the paper. They also did vegetable and sponge printing with water base paints.

In addition, they played a complex version of Woody Guthrie's "Put Your Finger in the Air" that they had enjoyed so much the prior year. After the teacher saw their pleasure in this "Simple Simon" and "Do as I Do" kind of activity, she began a series of simple cards on which she drew stick figure representations for children to act out. Only a few children used these cards. However, when she shared the idea with a teacher of five-year-olds she learned that many more of them were interested in this activity than were the four-year-olds. The teacher of the five-year-olds added to her colleague's suggestions and remarked that the cards reminded her of the simpler cube and card matching activity that she had seen the three-year-olds using.

Five-Year-Olds. The five-year-olds also moved to more complex classification activities. Each child in a small group placed a sheet of paper on the ground in areas such as construction site, beach, business street, and grassy plot. They noted what was under their pieces of paper and collected samples in separate bags. When they returned to school, they compared notes and the teacher recorded their findings on a large pad of paper. Throughout the several weeks during which these data were collected, the teacher read them such books as Beim's *Eric on the Desert,* Credle's *Down Down the Mountain,* Lipkind's *Russet and the Two Reds,* set in the city, and Tresselt's *I Saw the Sea Come In.*

In addition, many of the children "mapped" their family trees during the latter part of the year. Those who were able copied the labels for such family members as mother, brother, and uncle from teacher made cards. Eleven-year-old children visited and helped write the given names.

The children continued to play out more numerous seriations with pictures and objects. They also continued their use of blocks and woodworking materials in increasingly complex ways. Several teachers report five-year-olds using blocks and other materials to represent and dramatize their first hand study of harbors (Spodek, 1962; Imhoff, 1959; Mitchell, 1934). Dioramas that represent a room, a shop, or a street are also concrete activities that support young children's growing abilities to deal with representation. The sandbox and work with clay add variations to the diorama experience.

The colored wooden cubes and colored loops served to extend their concepts of spatial relations. The children learned to develop and plan towns as they used these materials. They derived great pleasure when they set their own rules for building and then asked other children and adults to guess their rules, for example, only houses of a different color than the loop may be built within the area of the loop.

This particular group was fortunate to have a mobile three-dimensional model of the planets available for observation and manipulation. While their concept of space is growing slowly, this kind of concrete exposure is an added referent for the children. It is further supported by the children's use of three-dimensional wood puzzles.

Their teacher also helps them project their thinking by using picture matrices that are suggested by Lavatelli, and block matrices suggested by the Elementary Science Study, using colored cubes. Through the year, children progress to the use of six-by-six matrices. For example, alternating color patterns or size patterns or shape patterns or their combinations are set out and various games are played—"What's Missing?" is one such game. Another involves reversing two elements and finding which ones have been reversed.

In still another valuable variation, children set problems for each other and the teacher. In addition to the social independence, it is intellectually and personally valuable for children to set problems for adults to solve. Because children have many experiences with concrete and pictorial systems, their ability to deal with varied symbolic systems is strengthened.

As their skill grows, the teacher has given some children dittoed outline maps of their room. The children's tasks vary in complexity as different children set out to find a missing item or a hidden object.

During this year, they have been learning and refining their own left and right orientation in functional ways. The walls are labelled North, South, East, and West, and the teacher uses these terms in giving directions. When the children set the table for special occasions such as the parents' lunch, they discuss these spatial relations. Some children are puzzled when other children on the opposite side of the table question their placement of eating utensils. The teacher allows ample time to play out the needed walking around the table with an awareness of hand and wall orientation.

Within the week that the visitor came from India, the teacher hung some strikingly colorful aerial photographs of varied terrains, islands, and locales. She also set out some maps near the globe on which they had located India.

Six-Year-Olds.   As these children continue to deepen and confirm their mapping skills, they will need additional concrete activities to support the varied subskills represented by the preceding activities. They will be using the sandbox to create more specialized forms such as a delta or a peninsula. They will look at a globe and locate continents and nations as they read and hear stories and films about these places, and meet people who come from other countries.

Grandparents and neighbors who visit the children, or a colleague with photographs, slides, or artifacts from another part of the world can stimulate children to seek locations on maps and on the globe.

Children can make simple three-dimensional topographic constructions. As they learn more about plants and various soils from trips, and by varying soil conditions indoors, they will be better able to do this kind of work. These activities can also make their comparative study of families from different countries a richer experience.

Some children enjoy matching objects to photographs of locales in which they might have been found, a variant of the three-year-old's more simple classification ability. When direct visits to different terrains are possible, many comparison activities are stimulated.

As their symbolic skills improve, some children will be able to have enough grasp of aerial perspective to map their classroom, however variable may be the scale they employ. These skills are supported when children manipulate two-dimensional map puzzles of continents, nations, and states. In addition, the children can set up their own hide-and-seek picture markings on dittoed room maps as they progress. The joy inherent in this kind of activity permeates the atmosphere and sweeps the visitor into involvement.

Seven-Year-Olds.   Many seven-year-olds who are able to read and write can set verbal directions for each other to use in hide-and-seek object games. They can use terms such as right, left, south, northwest, and inches. Their ability for fine muscle coordination makes it possible for them to develop their own relief maps or dioramas using plaster-of-paris. Certainly, the teacher needs to help them with some coordination. One sophisticated group set up their own diorama concept of a pioneer settlement based on the teacher's reading of Wilder's *The Long Winter* about a pioneer family's survival.

A group of seven- and eight-year-olds mapped points of interest on a map of the United States based on their collective trade book reading. They marked baseball training camp areas, horse riding, skiing, and boating regions. They marked North Carolina as a furniture source when a child reported seeing an address underneath a wooden chair in her home. They placed a "No Gas" sign on Denver because one child's family changed their vacation plans during the gasoline shortage of 1973. This observation prompted one group to survey peoples' travel plans and to set up a bar graph of mileage distances to various places from their community. They used ordinary road maps to chart mileage.

Some children decided to see if railroad mileages were different than automobile routes. The school librarian helped them find old maps that showed railroad lines at the turn of the century. They were able to compare and graph these differences.

A few children were interested in corresponding with children in other countries and this added to their skills in conceiving of space and different regions. They had reason to discuss the equator and seasonal differences when an Argentine correspondent wrote about summer vacation while the children were at school watching the snow turn to slush.

The discussion of seasonal differences built upon the five-year-olds' beginning contrast between the globe and the mercator projection. In order to clarify the distinction, the teacher helped the children with other conservation tasks in terms of quantity studies. They used standard measures of liquids alongside oddly shaped and variously shaped containers. While it is not clear that conservation of liquid quantity will transfer to map and globe distinctions, the juxtaposition of these activities might have some impact on transformed change. At the least, it is an additional exposure to which they are receptive.

In addition, the teacher used a projector light and created shadows with various shapes to build toward the notion of night and day. The study of night and day was in turn juxtaposed with other activities related to a larger planning framework than the tool of mapping. The next section focuses on this conceptual framework as a basis for planning activities.

THE TEACHER PLANS FOR CONCEPTUAL GROWTH IN PHYSICS

While children build their skills in using tools by varied routes, the scope of their understanding can expand. As the skills provide more streamlined ways for children to focus their thinking, the ideas themselves can become more complex and diverse.

Inasmuch as *a substantive base is needed for planning activities,* it is useful to look at organized fields of knowledge for direction. The teacher's sense of continuity may mesh with children's associations between experiences through the use of materials, activities, tools broadly conceived, and dialogue.

Once *the teacher selects a larger concept* and its subsidiary concepts, the teacher can plan for *a variety of representative materials and activities.* A pivotal factor in the introduction of the teacher's ideas for materials and activities is that the teacher needs to use them when they are *relevant to children's concerns.* When the teacher has mapped out a variety of possibilities ahead of time, she can feel free to use them or not as the children's directions emerge. At the same time, while any teacher must necessarily be limited by the available resources, or those which he can develop as children move in particular directions, such directions may or may not have occurred to the teacher in advance.

However, an important part of planning is this *building of a stock of materials and activities.* If one material would appear to be inappropriate at the time of use, another material could serve instead. The focus of conceptual connectedness need not necessarily be changed since there are *many ways to concretize the same abstractions,* and the means are as varied as the individual practitioners.

When the teacher is aware of these considerations, the growth of perceptual models is supported, even though planning began at the point of the adult "fund" of knowledge.

An example of this interactive procedure exists in an incident with a five-year-old who showed a small group of others a "trick" with magnets (Fromberg, 1965). Kay laughingly showed how her magnet could attract a piece of paper and then gleefully explained: "It can't pick up the paper without the nail but it can pick it up with the nail." Since time was limited, the teacher planned for the next day, following this new path. Various nonmagnetic materials were brought to the group. Kay shared her "trick." The teacher then asked, "Can you guess which materials could be used for such a trick?"

Among the carefully selected materials were copper discs. Children variously predicted whether or not each material could be attracted by the magnet before attempting to use it as an intermediate body. When a number of children felt sure that the copper could be attracted, the teacher took the time to explore their thinking before continuing with her advance plan:

> TEACHER: (*holding up copper discs*) Does anybody know what these discs are?
>
> CHILD 1: Iron.
>
> TEACHER: How can we test to see if it is iron?

CHILD 2:	Try the magnet.
TEACHER:	And if it's iron or steel the magnet will . . .
CHILD 3:	Pick it up.
TEACHER:	(*applies a magnet to the copper*)
CHILD 4:	Try the big magnet.
TEACHER:	(*tries the larger magnet*)
CHILD 5:	Put all the magnets on.
TEACHER:	(*after following the direction*) . . . It's not attracting. So, is it iron?
CHILDREN 6 and 7:	It looks like iron.
TEACHER:	Remember yesterday, Mike (CHILD 8). Tell Bob (CHILD 7) the kinds of metals the magnet can attract . . .
CHILD 8:	Iron and steel . . .
TEACHER:	Could this possibly be iron or steel?
CHILD 8:	No.
CHILD 7:	I still think it is 'cause there's no reason.
CHILD 3:	Let him feel it.
TEACHER:	(to CHILD 7) . . . You try to pick it up. (*Looking toward a nearby child*) Give him the magnet.
CHILD 7:	(*after trying*) Yes . . . Well . . . It looks like it but I guess not.
TEACHER:	Does anybody know what this is? This is another kind of metal that you see all the time.
CHILD 5:	You can make ashtrays out of it . . .*

The balance of planning before and during contacts with children is an essential facet of the teacher's role. All too often, novices have entered teaching with a desire for democratic classroom functioning with children but have banished themselves from acting among the responsible voting citizenry and have not brought planned activities to the group.

There is every reason to believe that children's pre-school experiences and interests can be respected and built upon in the classroom. At the same time, *teachers need to continue to plan for the introduction of new phenomena as well as the expansion of those understandings that children have already acquired.* Too often teachers in fear of "incorrectly" administering the formula of a wholly child-directed emerging curriculum, hesitate to use their own judgment and act.

* Different children are represented by the use of the same number designation in the different episodes that are reported. However, within each episode, the same child's contribution is indicated by the same number.

Studies have certainly indicated that children can become interested in most things (Jersild and Tasch, 1949; Wann, Dorn, and Liddle, 1962). It is important, then, that teachers consider the manner in which new ideas, materials, or skills, are planned into the program.

In this way, *continuity is a negotiated result* when a teacher sees children as active contributors to their own learning. As you look at the concept of the interaction of forces in nature, it is possible to demonstrate how a teacher can help tie activities together in this negotiated way. If you were to relate this concept of the interaction of natural forces to the interdependency of living things, you could see a clear base for interdisciplinary activity that builds from a unifying conceptual framework.

Just as Craig (1958), a science educator, proposes "interrelationship" as a major concept in science, the very concept of culture proposed by social scientists fits neatly into this interdisciplinary conception (Adams, 1958; Chase, 1956; Mills, 1959; Nagel, 1961). For example, the social scientist views human beings as members of a group that is part of a chain of interacting groups. The food chain and biological life processes are similarly interdependent. Cyclical change is the perceptual model that reflects the interdisciplinary commonalities.

The parallel tracks of conceptual understandings and concrete experiences reside in adults' thinking and planning. Look at such a translation into activities for five-year-old children. In considering the interaction of forces in nature, some subsidiary forces would be gravitation, magnetism, air pressure, and centrifugal force that can be translated into activities and materials for young children.

It is not intended that these activities would focus on any single force and pursue it to the ends of human knowledge. Nor is it intended that the interaction of these forces should be made explicit to children regardless of their receptiveness. Rather, the two tracks of conceptual understandings and concrete experiences can begin together. The concrete track then moves back and forth across the conceptual track. While the conceptual track remains in adult thinking, concrete experiences are planned as children's behavior is taken into account. Therefore, were any other group of children to begin with the same set of materials, the actual experience would be likely to be different. For example, project yourself into one kindergarten group's experience.

GRAVITATION

Since gravitation was a common experience for children, representative activities were planned to help children become more conscious of their own experiences. The teacher had planned to focus upon the contrasts of up and down and why objects stop moving up.

Lamorisse's story, *The Red Balloon,* had been read to the children and a popular children's television program, "Lassie," was showing the adventures of the hero flying in a basket suspended by a balloon. Therefore, materials that were available were paper cups, strings, and helium-filled balloons, as well as ordinary balloons, rubber balls of various density, yarn balls, and shuttlecocks.

After briefly talking with the children about the story characters, the teacher asked the children how they could solve the problem of getting the paper cup off the ground. After the children saw that one helium-filled balloon was inadequate, they made guesses concerning how many would be required and repeated the process after each balloon was added. Following the children's exclamations of "Ready! Aim! Blast off! Any minute!, and Pascal, come down," the teacher asked them to suggest ways of bringing down the cup.

SEVERAL
CHILDREN: Pascal, come down.
  CHILD 1:   Hey, you could put the wood in.
  TEACHER: What would that do?
  TEACHER: (*after several children have placed a block in the cup*) What happens now? . . . If Pascal is up too high, how do you think he might come down?
  CHILD 3:   Weight.
  CHILD 1:   How about a ladder?
  CHILD 4:   If he had a pin, he could pop it.
  TEACHER: What would happen to the balloon?
  CHILD 5:   The air would come out . . .

Notice that each suggestion was accepted by the teacher who then encouraged children to describe the possible consequences. In this way, a pattern of guessing, observing, repeating, describing, and explaining began to be established.

Children also had opportunities to throw objects into the air and they counted to see how many numbers were recited before the objects hit the ground. The teacher encouraged them to describe how the objects came down, why they might fall that way, and the relative speeds with which they seemed to fall. Throughout these experiences, the pace of verbal exchanges was generally brisk and materials were changed before children had exhausted the opportunities for their use.

These sessions were looked upon as a time for bringing the materials and some of their possibilities to children's attention rather than as a time for the teacher to recite a series of facts. They turned into a time for the teacher to stimulate children to conjecture about the materials, to explore the material's possibilities, and to describe their observations.

The teacher planned two activities for the following week when the terms "gravity" and "force" would be added. Several children seemed to have been familiar with the term "gravity" and the teacher took the opportunity to see what they understood. These kinds of exchanges made it possible for the teacher to attempt to see what children were thinking and to clarify their thinking when it seemed necessary, immediately or at some later time.

For example, in an attempt to clarify the preceding week's focus concerning why objects stop moving up, the teacher, using pictures, discussed with children the reasons that certain things flew and the reasons that they fell to the ground. In this way, they were dealing with a basic outlook of the physical scientist. They were defining the limitations within which a particular natural phenomenon could occur or could not occur.

In an ancillary activity later in the week, the teacher asked children to dictate statements concerning the prior group meetings so that they could share them with a youngster who was absent. Some of the responses follow.

CHILD 1:   The balloons and the cups went around the room.
CHILD 2:   . . . 'cause they had helium in them.
CHILD 3:   They lifted the cup up.
CHILD 4:   Four balloons.
CHILD 5:   We counted to four.
TEACHER: We had balls too. What kind of balls?
CHILD 6:   Little balls.
CHILD 7:   (*moving hands*) They were shaped like this.
CHILD 8:   Like a capsule.
TEACHER: (*reads back what is written*)
CHILD 4:   They went up, up, up, up, up.
TEACHER: What made them come down?
CHILD 8:   The air came out.
CHILD 7:   Gravity.
CHILD 5:   Because they have no motors.
CHILD 6:   They don't have propellers or wings.
TEACHER: A bird can have wings and he can come down. Why does he come down?
CHILD 1:   There's nothing to keep it up.

The activity of having their own statements recorded, aside from its value in building language skills and helping the teacher to understand children's perceptions, also served to further explore the possibilities of their focus upon gravity.

As their receptiveness to continuing exposure to these kinds of experiences was maintained, children were eventually able to gain some information and a beginning ability to apply it. In contrast with these earlier experiences, notice the wider scope of their comments five weeks later during an activity period.

(Children are looking at pictures of space travel on a bulletin board):

CHILD 1: That's a rocket!

CHILD 2: My friend has a cardboard rocket that goes round and round.

CHILD 1: Hey, that rocket's upside down.

CHILD 2: I'm not crazy. The rocket is upside down.

CHILD 3: He's flying.

CHILD 4: He's standing on his head because there's no gravity.

CHILD 5: There's no gravity in space.

CHILD 6: If you get very far away the gravity can't pull the rocket down.

TEACHER: What if you were up in space where Meg said there's no gravity, how could she be kept from flying around?

CHILD 7: She wears a gravity belt.

CHILD 5: If she didn't have one she would be flying around.

TEACHER: What if she were flying?

CHILD 2: Just like upsy-daisy.

TEACHER: . . . What if she tried to pick up her mommy?

CHILD 8: She could pick up her mommy.

CHILD 3: . . . because there's no gravity.

These comments revealed one way in which children were receptive to their exposure to the activities.

MAGNETISM

The force of magnetism was selected as a focus for activities since it represented one force that contrasted with gravitation. Another consideration was that the effects of this force can be directly felt and seen by children and might thereby simplify their exposure to the concept of a force.

Magnets of different sizes, shapes, and strengths, and a variety of magnetic and nonmagnetic articles were available. Only one activity had been planned but another was added. The addition was made in order to enable children to see and feel the effects of the magnet's properties and to differentiate the relative strengths of magnets.

The teacher worked with two groups of four and five children. Each group congregated at a table that had been set with a variety of magnets and articles, with enough magnets for most of the children.

The teacher encouraged the children to pile the objects that the magnet attracted separately from those that were repelled. She also suggested that they guess into which pile each article might be placed. After the piles were completed, the children listed for each other the articles in their respective piles.

When the teacher asked them what the attracted materials were made of, some children variously mentioned metal and iron. However, after several different magnets were unsuccessfully used to attract a metal ring, children were left with a new classification to ponder until a later activity. This experience of sorting magnetic and nonmagnetic objects helped children to begin to classify objects and it also added new words such as "repel" and "attract" to their vocabulary in a functional way.

Another classificatory activity with the magnets was that of differentiating the size and strength of the magnets. The teacher asked the children to notice that magnet to which the object was attracted first when she moved magnets of different sizes toward an equidistant object on the table. She asked them to guess which magnet would be stronger each time the activity was repeated. After this procedure was repeated several times the children concluded that a smaller magnet *might be* stronger than a larger magnet.

TEACHER: You have all used different shapes and sizes of magnets. Is a big magnet stronger than this?

CHILD 1:   The big one because it picks up these together.

CHILD 2:   The big one.

TEACHER: Why?

CHILD 2:   Because . . .

CHILD 3:   It has more weight.

CHILD 1:   Just because it's bigger doesn't mean it has more energy.

CHILD 4:   It's much stronger.

CHILD 5:   Because it's bigger.

TEACHER: Remember we said that for a magnet to be strong it has to have a strong pull? (*A nail is set between the two magnets.*) Let's see which one pulls it first.

CHILD 3:   The little one.

CHILD 1:   Because you started it first.

TEACHER: Where did it go again?

CHILD 2:   Little one.

TEACHER: Let's try it again to be sure.
  CHILD 1:   I hope the little one wins . . .
  CHILD 3:   . . . Sometimes . . .

Approximately two months later, the children spontaneously applied this experience to another situation with the gyroscope in an attempt to change its direction.

CHILD 1:   I don't think the magnet will do anything.
CHILD 2:   (*indicating the gyroscope*) I don't think it will spin. The inside will but not . . .
CHILD 3:   (*as child has brought a magnet*) Nothing happens.
CHILD 4:   'Cause it's going too fast.
CHILD 1:   Maybe it's not metal or something.
CHILD 5:   Maybe it's not iron, not iron, not iron . . .
CHILD 6:   I'll get the red one. (*a stronger magnet*) (*He brings it and unsuccessfully tries to attract the gyroscope.*)
CHILD 1:   You sure it isn't the broken one?

They were certainly able to independently use their knowledge of magnets in this new situation.

Their independent work with the magnets as well as their discussions with the teacher contributed to this facility in applying their knowledge. For example, the following exchange was recorded during an independent work time earlier in their exposure to the magnet study.

(*Children are at a table with magnets.*)
CHILD 1:   It won't pick it up. (*Bangs magnets on copper plates that the other child set out.*)
CHILD 2:   It's a different kind of metal.
CHILD 1:   I'm going to use all the magnets.

Their independent exploration with the magnets also led to some discoveries and a growing recognition of the existence of a force. For example, one child who had been using bar magnets alone at a table was talking as he used the materials:

Try to push these together. . . . There's some kind of force that won't let them push together. Like a bouncing ball. . . . When you turn them around they do come together.

One youngster's "trick" of attracting paper was turned into the focus for another session the following day. Then the children focussed upon the magnet's power to attract through materials that were not themselves attracted by the magnet. The teacher encouraged children to guess at each additional material, to test each guess in turn, and to describe each occurrence.

For example, after the children added cardboard, they found that seven pieces was the maximum number through which a paper clip might be attracted by any of the available magnets. A child who noticed the clip had been attracted but that it did not go "zip" stimulated the group to think about the relative strength of the force. While, to an adult, it may seem to take a long time to find out about seven pieces of cardboard, this can be a suspenseful, dramatic event for young children. There is a direct, aesthetic satisfaction in such an experience. How can a teacher merely throwing a fact at a young child compete with such intensity?

AIR PRESSURE

The force of air pressure can be felt and seen directly by children. Also, since a planned viewing of a televised astronaut's rocket launch relied upon jet propulsion, children who had been exposed to the use of air as a propelling force might bring more associations to that later experience. In addition, the model rockets available for children to use required a combination of water and air pressure for their propulsion.

Initially, the teacher encouraged the children to select balloons, blow them up, and play with them in any ways they saw fit. Some children reacted by blowing them up and having them sealed. They would then pat and throw the balloons up and down and follow them around the room. Other children, who had difficulty blowing them up, tried to fill them with water. Still other children blew them up and let the balloons loose to enjoy the sight of the balloons deflating and the sound of the air escaping. This last play became popular and children would also place the deflating balloon against their cheeks. One child said to nobody in particular, "Can't see air but you can hear air."

The teacher planned an activity with plenty of balloons and drinking straws sealed in paper. There were also specially constructed toy boats that could be shared by two or three children at a time.

The teacher asked the children to tear off an end of the paper covering the straw, to suck at the straw and describe what happened, and then to blow out and notice what happened. This activity was obviously enjoyed by the children. The children compared the activity with others they had had.

CHILD 1:   It stuck on.
CHILD 2:   Kind of like a magnet.

CHILD 1: When I blow up paper it's like a balloon.
CHILD 2: He was the pump.

After this procedure, the teacher asked the children to guess in which direction an untied balloon would move if it were released. The children pointed in a variety of directions and later described the actual course. They repeated this procedure several times and the teacher remarked, as she had at other times, "Now you have to do things several times to see where they're going." In this way, she was trying to make them aware of the need for repetition and tentativeness as a way of studying natural phenomena.

Since the teacher was interested in allotting time for children to express themselves and to note relationships to past experiences, the children were often first to state relationships. Some spontaneous examples connected with the straws are stated above. The children also compared the balloons with rockets and jets, commenting on the direction in which the balloons travelled.

Then they discussed the plastic boats. A hole was drilled in the rear of each boat and a glass dropper, from which the rubber cap had been removed, was set through the hole so that an end of the dropper would be below the water line. The teacher attached a balloon to the opposite end of the dropper that sat in the boat, and rubber bands held the apparatus together.

Children blew up the balloons in the boats through the dropper, set the boats in a large water-filled tub, about four feet long and three feet wide, and gleefully watched the boats propelled by the air escaping from the balloons. As they repeated their activity, they talked together about jet propulsion, a term the teacher had introduced:

CHILD 1: What would happen if it had two balloons?
CHILDREN: It would go faster.
TEACHER: What if we put three balloons?
CHILD 3: (a child who rarely spoke, said, smiling) It would go faster.
CHILD 4: Round and round.
CHILD 1: Let's do it.

It is interesting to compare a different group's responses when the teacher asked the question that "CHILD 1" had asked.

TEACHER: What would happen if we had two balloons?
CHILD 1: It would go faster.
CHILD 2: If they were on the sides it would go . . . (makes a zigzag motion.)
CHILDREN: (laugh)

TEACHER: That would be good to try. Hal thinks it will stay pretty still, wouldn't go in any direction.

CHILD 3:   That's the problem. We really don't know.

From these comments, it seemed that children were beginning to express their conjectures and to see new possibilities for extending group experiences.

They seemed very involved in these activities. Yet, throughout the discussions and introductions of new materials, the children were allowed to inflate their balloons. This was very much like their continuing use of magnets and the earlier dropping of balls. The physical involvement with materials appeared to help them to keep their thinking focussed. The fact that they were simultaneously involved in expanding ideas and manipulating materials indicates that this coordination was possible for these five-year-olds.

In order to continue the study of air pressure, a few simple cardboard pumps were set out for children to use independently. The teacher planned to help the children launch plastic rockets that required the pumping of air into water and these pumps were introduced first in order to move children one step at a time away from their own lung power.

The children launched these plastic rockets (Parks Toy Co.) themselves. They filled the toys with water and then pumped air into them, feeling the pressure build up until the children released them. Some of the children connected air pressure with the rocket launching. On another day when two children were pumping rockets, void of water, in the classroom, a third child said to them: "When they get too much air in them the rockets push off. I guess the air pushed them off."

CENTRIFUGAL FORCE

An understanding of orbits in nature requires some idea of centrifugal force. Therefore, the teacher planned classroom experiences in which children could feel and see the effect of centrifugal force.

During one session the teacher gave each child wooden spools and cardboard squares suspended from strings, and wooden tops. The focus of the activity was to introduce centrifugal force, to call it by name, and to differentiate it from the other forces with which children had had experience.

The teacher began by asking children to differentiate whether the spools or the cardboard squares were heavier as they held them in their hands. The children's comments indicated that they were continually relating their present ideas to past experiences with weight and the strength of magnets.

In the beginning, the children began twirling the objects suspended from strings at what might be termed the "guessing" stage of the session.

TEACHER: Look what we have here.

CHILD 1: A merry-go-round.

CHILD 2: (*holding strings apart*) If it would stick out like this it would look more like a merry-go-round.

TEACHER: Is there any way we could make it go out?

CHILD 3: Sticks.

CHILD 4: Glue it out.

CHILD 2: You can push it around.

CHILD 5: Like blow it.

CHILD 1: You could twirl it.

The following excerpt can be seen as representative of the "observation" stage of the session:

CHILD 6: It's going faster.

CHILD 2: I saw the string going with it.

TEACHER: Is the cardboard under my hand?

CHILD 1: At the sides.

TEACHER: (*with a yardstick*) How far off the ground is it?

CHILD 6: Eighteen.

TEACHER: Yes, just about. Let's see if it goes down closer to the ground.

CHILD 7: No, higher.

CHILD 5: Lower.

TEACHER: Let's measure and see.

CHILD 1: Twenty-four.

TEACHER: Is twenty-four more than eighteen?

CHILDREN: (*nod*)

CHILD 4: 'Cause your arm is higher.

TEACHER: Let's measure if it goes higher without an arm moving. (*They repeat the procedure until all are satisfied that they are repeatedly seeing the same thing.*)

Children's prior experiences were again called into play when they attempted to "explain" the phenomenon.

TEACHER: What's making it go up?

CHILD 1: Air.

CHILD 8: Your hand.

TEACHER: Does it go out by itself?

CHILD 8: When you twirl it, the air holds it up.

TEACHER: Is it moving faster or slower?

CHILD 4: No, faster.

TEACHER: When it goes faster what else is happening to it?
CHILD 2: It's going outer.
TEACHER: What makes it go out?
CHILDREN 2 and 4: Air.
TEACHER: Remember, when we drop things. What's the force?
CHILD 3: Gravity.
TEACHER: (*Briefly reviews in terms of the force of magnetism and the force of air*) The force that makes the spool go out is centrifugal force. This is the center and the force that's moving it out is centrifugal force.
CHILD 5: Sounds like medical center.
TEACHER: That's a hospital. (*Briefly distinguishes the meanings.*)

They followed a similar procedure when the children used the tops. The teacher added some transparent tops to the materials that children used during work periods. These "centrifugal" tops contained colored water, colored oil, and grains that separated into three rings when they were twirled. They were actively used by the children, some of whom acquired great skill at keeping numerous tops twirling simultaneously. The children identified materials in transparent "centrifugal" tops and then compared the materials with regard to weight and color:

(*Three or four children shared each top.*)
TEACHER: Look at the tops and see what's in them.
CHILD 1: (*describes*) Beads . . .
CHILD 2: Red beads . . .
CHILD 3: White, green, and orange.
CHILD 4: White, green, and orange.
TEACHER: What's the color of the oil in yours? (*The teacher repeats the question as she moves between groups.*)
CHILD 5: Green
TEACHER: . . . and the water?
CHILD 6: Red.
TEACHER: Which would be the heaviest?
CHILD 4: The beads.
TEACHER: Which would be the lightest?
CHILDREN: (*spin their transparent tops and describe the colors on the outside ring, the inside, and the middle ring. They compare color with weight.*)
TEACHER: What makes it move out?

CHILD 5:   Centrifugal force.
TEACHER: (*brings a different colored top to each group and they repeat the twirling.*) Do the beads always go to the outside?
CHILD 3:   (*seemingly confident*) They don't!
TEACHER: Try again . . . What colors are the beads?
CHILD 3:   White.
CHILDREN: (*twirl the tops again. The children have really been twirling or turning or looking at them throughout the discussion.*)
TEACHER: What color is on the outside?
CHILDREN 3 and 4:   (*smiling and wide-eyed*) The white!

Throughout these interchanges between teacher and children it became clear that these procedures were encouraging children to be more careful observers. They seemed more able to challenge the observations of others and to offer more explanations for events.

Several weeks later, the teacher planned to bring up the subject of centrifugal force again. The intervening weeks had been devoted to other things because the children seemed to need time to explore the materials.

Materials that were accidentally added, when children foraged in a box, were spinning tops wound with string. The children were fascinated with these tops and insisted on practicing with them. Thus, accidentally faced with a task beyond their physical coordination, they repeatedly attempted to master the skill for as long as an hour at a time.

At another time, after children had twirled objects and repeatedly let them go, a few of the children remembered the term "centrifugal" or a reasonable facsimile of it. The teacher reminded them about "flying from the center." As the children set this information into the frame of their own experience, they revealed some acquaintance with rockets.

CHILD 1:   If you let it go it flies off.
CHILD 2:   Like a rocket. First it has a round thing (*moving his arms upward in a sweeping motion*) and then . . . But what keeps it up?
TEACHER: What do you think?
CHILD 2:   Gravity pushes it down but what pushes it up?
CHILDREN: (*variously mention fuel, engines, etc.*)
TEACHER: Does it go straight up?
CHILD 1:   No, it goes *he moves his arms up and then horizontally*)
TEACHER: Yes, around.

CHILD 3:   Like a top.
TEACHER: Let's see if we can make an orbit . . .

The children twirled various objects, and the teacher moved among the children who were spread out and asked individuals if they were feeling the pull.

The teacher divided the children into two groups of about four children, seated them on the floor, and supplied each group with a transparent top. After they identified the materials and their corresponding colors, and classified their relative weights, the children guessed which materials would form the three rings as the tops were twirled.

The children's numerous prior experiences with differentiating relative weights were essential for this experience. They showed an ability to apply these learnings in this new situation that was attended with great involvement.

During these weeks the teacher also focussed the children's activity on the rotation of a sphere. The teacher chose this activity with an eye on the concept of an orbit around the earth. The teacher had also planned that the children would be exposed to the concept of the continual movement of the earth and, if possible, other planets.

At first, clay spheres were rotated on pencils. Groups of three and four children took turns with flashlights and rotation.

The teacher thought that children might be able to compare these experiences with the tops. They did. At this time, the children were also able to attribute the end of spinning to the force of gravity.

A youngster, mentioned earlier, repeated the application of this function when the activity had focussed upon centrifugal separation: "Gravity pushed it down but what pushed it up?" Perhaps this concept exemplified a beginning feeling about the interaction of forces.

However, it would be difficult to conclude that children ever directly applied centrifugal force to answer this youngster's question. They were only able to verbalize that centrifugal force was operative in centrifugal separation.

A week later, the children heard the story *Follow the Sunset* (Schneider and Schneider, 1952) while a globe lit by a filmstrip projection lamp was nearby. A globe had always been present in the classroom and children had often referred to it. The focus of the activity with the globe and story was upon the continuing movement of the earth. The teacher planned this additional experience with a rotating sphere to precede the children's visit to New York City's Museum of Natural History's Hayden Planetarium, containing a model of the sun and planets in motion.

In preparation for the visit the following week, the teacher emphasized the earth's continual movement and provided some information concerning day and night. The following interchange exemplifies one way that the teacher tried to put this information into children's experience.

TEACHER: (*with globe*) We're going to have lunch soon. Now what would the children in Japan, where Carole and Angela come from, be doing?
CHILD 1: Sleeping.
CHILD 2: It's night.
TEACHER: If we were sleeping what would the children in Japan be doing?
CHILD 3: Brushing their teeth.

The visit to the museum the following week involved several activities. The teacher had arranged for a special fifteen minute program that focussed on the continual movement of the planets. The museum specialist, who conducted the program, received the children's complete attention.

Another activity was a visit to a life-size replica of a space craft in the museum. Some of the children's comments are recorded below.

CHILD 1: Isn't he going to drive upside down?
TEACHER: Why do you think so?
CHILD 1: Because the steering wheel's upside down.
TEACHER: Is the pad coming out of his hand?
CHILD 1: No, because he's holding on tight.
TEACHER: What would happen if he let go?
CHILD 1: It would float out of his hand.
CHILD 2: Because of gravy.
CHILD 3: Because of no gravity.
CHILD 4: (*pointing to the model of a man in vehicle*) How come *that* one isn't upside down?

This indicates that children were beginning to apply some of their learnings and to try out their growing vocabulary. In subsequent conversations, it was clear that children were raising questions and thinking of more possibilities to explain the phenomena to which they were exposed.

A week after they launched their own toy rockets they viewed the actual launching of an astronaut's space craft on a television set in school.

Several children had brought newspaper clippings of the orbit and the teacher asked why the path of the astronaut's orbit in the newspaper was not straight up:

CHILD 1: It's high and then low.

CHILD 2:   I remember when we were at the museum, he went up and then into the water.

TEACHER: Is the earth flat like this?

CHILD 1:   No, it's round.

CHILD 3:   (*observing teacher drawing oval shape on chalkboard*) Oh— now I know! Now I know! It has that part and because the earth is round and this line (*indicating the apogee of the orbit*) is halfway round the world!

The observer could not help feel the excitement that this youngster was communicating. Children were receptive to activities that dealt with the interaction of opposing forces such as gravity and magnetism, centrifuge and gravitation, and air propulsion and gravitation.

THE PLACE OF MEASURING TOOLS IN THE ACTIVITIES

One can hardly deal with the physical world without dealing with quantities. In their study, the children repeated their manipulations and measured changes whenever relevant.

A yardstick was one tool that was repeatedly used when children studied centrifugal force. The use of this tool was possible only because children had had prior experiences in the classroom with measuring and seeing numbers written. They frequently used rulers at the woodworking bench.

Children were also exposed to terms that described the relative position of phenomena such as bigger than, heavier than, stronger than, higher than, longer than, above, larger, up straight, and so forth. They discussed angles in connection with the earth's axis. As with most of their activities, this representation of angles directly involved children. After the children had seen the angle of the globe's axis, the teacher asked them to stand straight and then on an angle. This was done at a rapid pace for a few seconds and with obvious enthusiasm and understanding.

Children also measured time. They quickly noticed that counting was inadequate for timing the fall of objects. The teacher obtained a one minute timer with a clock face. However, children were confused by the representation of a whole minute in the space of half the area of the circle. Further searching in photography shops uncovered a three minute timer that had a clock face marked into seconds and minutes.

The teacher left these timers on a shelf without comment. Several children who noticed one recognized it as some sort of "clock without hands." One youngster said, "Hey, I know what it is! It's a countdown on rockets."

The children began to use the timers to time their cooking play. Subsequently, children used the timers to measure the length of time that their tops would spin, their rockets would fly, and the length of time it took for a boat on the river to sail a given distance.

When the children used the timer with their own jet-propelled boats, they talked a good deal about the "countdown." However, the time-keeper had been counting "up." That is, while several children seriously and patiently waited, the time-keeper was starting the timer at zero and counting up to the zero and the three minute mark, which were identical. After three repetitions, during which the time-keeper was counting off seconds by tens, he announced the "blast off," promptly pocketed the timer, and enjoyed the boat race. At this time, these children were obviously very attentively focussed on the countdown and their race but were not able to coordinate these interests with the timer.

Therefore, in an attempt to extend the children's experience with the timer, beyond the "countdown" or "up" phase, the teacher planned a small session to focus upon the use of the timer and the yardstick. They measured how much time it took the boats to travel a particular distance.

The children's comments during this discussion revealed that several of them needed to clarify vocabulary relating to time and distance. In effect, the teacher differentiated for them that a yardstick can measure length in terms of distance and height, and that a timer can measure length in terms of time. The group worked in the area around the tub filled with water.

At the teacher's request, the children suggested various ways that they could make the boats sail. The children mentioned pushing, blowing, and fanning the boats in addition to jet propulsion. The children measured the time and distance required for the boats to move when blowing, fanning with cardboard, and jet propulsion were used.

They then compared which method took the longest and the shortest time to move the boats the greatest distance. This procedure of comparing the times and distances was facilitated by written records that were charted as each procedure was repeated. Children were physically involved and completely attentive. It was clear that they were able to coordinate their manipulations of materials with their discussions of events in the teacher-group session.

INTERDISCIPLINARY CONSIDERATIONS

Teachers can consider the possibilities for developing the notion of the interdependence of living things and human beings using a similar planning procedure. As the teacher identifies subsidiary concepts, he develops a stock of materials and activities that appear relevant. For young children's use, these activities would be necessarily concrete and would provide for psychomotor and aesthetic satisfactions and involvement.

The Social Studies Project at the University of Minnesota has developed an extensive, in depth, interdisciplinary framework and materials for social studies work (Minnesota Project Social Studies, 1966–1968). The Joyces' work on data banks for children who can read is another important contribution (Joyce, 1972). What they have done is to collect firsthand data, written, filmed, and taped information, for children to use in their study of a variety of locales. The teacher uses an index system to help children answer their own questions by retrieving data they seek.

While the scope of these projects is beyond the reach of an individual teacher unless a school or district could subscribe, the underlying principles can be useful. It is possible for a teacher to cross-reference conceptual frameworks and materials from several different programs that do exist in the district. This cross-referencing, combined with the teacher's own ideas, can be a useful resource.

In addition, teachers can write short-range dittoed narratives that are customized for a particular group at a particular time. Tape recordings can be made for preliterate children. Teachers can exchange tape recordings made with visitors to the school such as the local restauranteur who described his childhood in Italy and his reasons for emigrating, or the great-grandmother who detailed her life before electricity. Those children who had not been at the original interview might ask questions of those who 'had been, or write, telephone, or invite the person again if possible. In addition, available resources may exist embedded in materials owned by the school that might otherwise gather dust.

"Engineered" visits to local construction sites can touch on many issues relating to interdependence. The teacher could ask the workers to carry family pictures and possible pictures of fishing or bowling outings with friends as a way for children to see the varied group memberships. They would be observing the workers' dependence upon each other for hoisting, dumping, building, and measuring. When children make return visits, they are able to see the progress of the building and hear about the problems of plumbers finishing in time for the painters to begin. If they have watched a factory being built, there is an entire range of new questions to ask such as: What kind of factory? Why was it built on this site? Who will work here? Don't those people have other jobs now? Why would they want to leave them and come here? Where do the workers live? How do they get to work? How do they spend their earnings? Issues concerning producers and consumers might emerge as relevant.

Children could use bar graphs to record family size or distances travelled to work or how many storeys were built at different dates. They could hear the story *Benjie on His Own* (Lexau, 1970) in this general time frame and wonder about how their lives would be different if they were a member of a different family, if their nurturant grandmother became hospitalized. They could further invert their sense of proportion and ask how their lives would be different if they lived in a house rather than an apartment, or on a farm rather than in the city. The teacher helps them to find answers to these questions by providing *quantities of contrasting* data through direct visits, meeting people, seeing films, reading, listening to recordings, and building their own models and representations. Answers found by these contrasting means, rather than those accrued through verbalisms, are likely to remain more closely intertwined with children's experiences.

In a similar manner, children build understandings about life itself. They can compare a series of aquarium containers or terrarium containers that are influenced by different conditions of light, heat, air, water, and nutriments. When resources are limited, several groups can cooperate in the planned variations, using surplus materials scavenged from homes, businesses, and even the school cafeteria. For example, many uses can be found for commercial-size food jars.

As one considers the seemingly endless possibilities and connections between events, every new teacher's fear of not having enough to do dissolves into the experienced teacher's understanding that there is never enough time to do as many things as children stimulate them to consider. Therefore, you need to commit yourself to seeking increasingly effective ways to make the present year you spend with children their most satisfying year.

DEPTH

When you plan for activities that help children pursue their concerns in depth, you begin to contribute to satisfactions that exceed their moment. In this sense, depth refers to the personal involvement, the meaning level, of a series of experiences.

For example, look at erosion as representative of an interaction of forces. You can speak of, and observe, the interaction of air, temperature, water, soil, wind, rock, and human-made structures. You can notice the relation of tree plantations, fires, rainfall, climatic conditions, and land forms. You can tie human use of land as another interactive element. You can observe eroded sites, directly witness erosion during and immediately following rain or thaw, compare pictures before and after land development for construction, pictures before and after fires, and pictures before erosion compared with a later seashore visit. You can see films, slides, and filmstrips. You can read about mudslides and avalanches in adventure stories, including the most adventurous ones in the daily newspaper. You can create structures in the classroom or on school grounds and play at eroding them.

However, after you pass an inhabited home set on the side of a boggy mountain following a downpour, when you see the house as an island surrounded by downhill racing streams, when you witness a family helplessly watching the land around their home being eroded away, when you see their only access to their own house is boards set over these shallow rivulets of water, then you have the kind of vivid experience that can personally involve children. Children can identify on a very personal level with the social impact of natural forces and human beings' interactions with nature.

Dramatic events can spawn dramatic solutions and leave an impact on the participating observer. Film technology and even tape recorded dramatization are certainly possible substitutes for the real thing. However, the child growing up on a Saskatchewan plain does not have direct access to mountainous phenomena. His teacher also needs to seek extended, depth experiences that reflect the interaction of human beings and nature in their locale.

Measuring tools may differ. Instead of measuring water erosion, the plains child might be measuring wind damage or drought damage. However, the interplay of varied tools and varied data set in a strong substantive framework can provide a comparable quality and quantity of experience.

This is not to say that if children do not have an immediately observable opportunity for such depth involvement that they should not be involved in study. It is certainly difficult to predict when your most significant moments will be encountered. In those instances where ties seem possible, the gregariousness of ideas and activities becomes a criterion for setting priorities.

For example, if the teacher sees no major drama in the children's immediate plains surroundings, he can contrast present conditions with films, newspaper pictures, and narratives of the "dust bowl" period. "Supposing" can often be fruitful. A seven-year-old who hears passages from Steinbeck's *The Grapes of Wrath* about a migrant family in the 1930s, or Wilder's *Little House on the Prairie* or *The Long Winter,* about a pioneer family in the 1880s, can begin to identify with the problems encountered.

The newly growing field of outdoor education, including conservationism, environmental studies, and ecology, may well be the focus for a naturally interdisciplinary field. One has only to spend time with forest rangers in the national parks to appreciate the power of their outdoor, inquiry-oriented, activity-based curriculum and the depth of their educational approach. Their approach takes one beyond the de-schooling of society.

At this point, we must move beyond human beings' "funded knowledge" to the changes in knowledge and the world that appear to be our inheritance from the past and our legacy to the future. There are future projections for human knowing that are probably beyond the imagination of even science fiction writers. A theory of education that proposes to affect ongoing generations needs to consider such ongoing unknown knowledge and change just as each teacher learns to teach in ways that can be translated beyond the particular group of children with whom she is currently working.

THE TEACHER PLANS FOR GROWTH OF PERCEPTUAL MODELS

The New York Times reports a gravitational pull so strong that light rays cannot leave its field of force (Sullivan, 1974). It is exotic to consider a mass of such density that its gravitational force made it "invisible." The reporter explains this phenomenon as a hot star-type material with gravity as strong as our sun's, yet much smaller. He proposes that these conditions alter existing notions of spatial and temporal relations as we now understand them. Scientists have recently been writing about such "black holes" in space (Jastrow and Thompson, 1974). Only with the recent development of the tools of radio astronomy can scientists begin to consider the notion of a neutron star. There is even poetry in the notion of gravitational attractions between the orbiting bodies of "a black hole" and a "star" as "dancers" in space. There is an elegance when these scientists think flexibly enough to attempt explanations.

Neutrons and protons are the two particles that form the atomic nucleus, but neutrons, being electrically neutral, could be packed together more tightly than protons, which, carrying a positive charge, repel one another. Also, since a neutron (when free of an atomic nucleus) eventually sheds an electron and turns into a proton, it seemed reasonable to suppose that, reversing the process, the compression of a sea of protons and electrons could produce neutrons. (p. 26)

There are many simple elements embedded in the quotation that contribute to the adult reader's understanding. Some of these elements can suggest a reach toward concrete activities that may contribute to this understanding. In considering perceptual models in planning, we shall look at some of these elements.

One activity in which children can learn that like magnetic poles repel and unlike magnetic poles attract can be simply done with large, blunt-tipped embroidery needles. When a needle is drawn repeatedly in a single direction along a magnet, it becomes magnetic. Children can easily observe the needle's new two-sided powers just as they had done earlier with commercial magnets. If children create a second needle-magnet, both times holding the eye part, then they may observe opposing ends more easily since both eyes will be either North or South poles. When one of the needles is suspended from a string, it will turn away in relation to the turning of the hand-held needle. Since the major purpose of this activity is to note the repulsion–attraction properties, children's imaginations remain open to future work with electromagnets and engines, as well as to long range understandings of subatomic particle behavior.

There are many ways in which children can learn about the "conservation of angular momentum," which is represented by the star spinning more rapidly after it contracts. Children come by this knowledge intuitively as they turn and spin in their dances and games. Ballet dancers make use of the principle. Vehicles are streamlined to make them more efficient. When children look at automobile, railroad train, and airplane designs through the years, the changes are apparent. Primary age children enjoy using an electric fan with tubes of paper glued into various shapes. The square tube, round tube, and "teardrop"-shaped cylinders' movements can be measured and compared. While there are few teams like the Wright brothers, there are many children who may also play with kites as they did, make their own kites, and experiment with different designs at various times in their early education.

The notion that crystals may be dissolved in solutions and then reconstituted by evaporation is easily represented with coarse salt and natural evaporation or heating. It is interesting to compare some containers in the dark, in the light, covered, and uncovered. These contrasts are an important inquiry tool that raises children's consciousness about controlled variables. Simple square dances with seven-year-olds, which divide and regroup pairs of people and then reconstitute original pairs, represent a similar perceptual model in quite different form. While these activities reside quite a distance from subatomic fusions, they can contribute concretely toward the long-range directions. Whether or not the teacher had planned the square dance with "black holes" in mind does not alter the child's experiencing of the square dance as a pleasurable, social, physical, aesthetic, and perceptual pastime. All too often, activities in school such as art forms and concrete experiences with natural phenomena have been traditionally categorized as "frills." These areas create a financial guilt in uninformed lay groups who understand only the straight lines of verbalisms in books. However, richness and variety of experience, coming at things from varied perspectives, are principles that support functional learning.

Concepts of density grow from daily activities with balance scales and water play. The five-year-old child who has time to study a straw sinking into a thick, frosted milk shake and says, "Oh, look. Like quicksand." is learning about density just as she did when she viewed a film that showed a person struggling in quicksand. Experiences with foods, the bathtub, blowing soap bubbles, and plant textures are related, as are rush-hour train trips, packed elevators, and popular buffet tables. Children could easily survey and seriate food and plant texture densities using straws and lenses. They can survey traffic density and people density at different places and times and chart it.

The observations of heating and cooling processes further contribute to the building of a notion of density. For years, teachers have heated in a pan of water a bottle whose opening was covered with an attached balloon. As the water heats, children are excited to see the balloon expand and then contract when the bottle is placed in a pan of ice cubes. While this demonstration is a dramatic example of the molecular-kinetic theory, it can become merely a "demonstration" with a lecture accompaniment. This activity would be put to better use if it grew out of the inquiries of the children, and caused more questions than it answered. It would also be put to better use if only those children who were ready to ask questions participated. A teacher would certainly not turn away, but welcome, other children who were drawn to the activity. Nor would he press others to join. In addition, *a worthwhile activity is worth repeating for others when they seem ready* to be receptive to the exposure. At the same time, not everybody needs to have participated in each activity.

Experiential data become the projectiles of learning activity just as this section began with data encountered in an article at an experience level that adults could absorb. Activities provide the possibilities for children to perceive kernel models that extend beyond a particular datum of experience. A particular activity, in and of itself, transports no magic. A particular tool, in and of itself, carries no insight. It is only the children, through experiencing inductive possibilities, who can create their own perceptions and their own insights.

The teacher's first responsibility is to plan concrete activities, juxtaposing them with respect to an estimate of "gregariousness." The teacher's ongoing responsibility is to appreciate children's unique connectedness, flexibility, and receptivity as a basis for future work.

Look further at additional examples of perceptual models and some of the ways that activities radiate from them. It is important to recognize that there are many activities mentioned at other times that might be connected.

In the format that follows, each perceptual model is defined. Then, activities are identified in terms of their relation to the perceptual model rather than exhaustively.

PERMOD: INDIRECT PROGRESS

There are many times when you need to move outside a frame of reference or break out of a direction of thinking or acting, or postpone a decision, in order to make progress. You need this permod when you try to understand the orbital reentry of space vehicles. The reference in Chapter 2 to the curve as the shortest distance between two points in European cities and in teaching is one way of seeing efficiency. When you cannot lift something, a lever helps. The wedge and lever together in a screw are an even less direct way to move forward. When the surveyor measures great distances, he uses triangulation. The psychological defense mechanism of sublimation is an indirect way of continuing to progress. The musician and pop or concept artist move outside traditional materials to invent new art.

Children experience lived indirection: "I'll be your friend if you give me a cookie." At a young age, some children learn to perform a "circuit of safety" before trying to use a potentially challenging material.

A discussion of any ethical or values problem offers an opportunity to help children develop wholesome social "leverage," to move beyond a single focus and to consider alternatives. Discussions between the teacher and children are basic to identifying many alternate interpretations of, and behavior in response to, varied social conflicts. When the children learn about the possibilities of other ways to deal with value-laden situations than the single set which they may bring, the original set may be broken.

In a similar use of alternatives, children may become more creative users of space:

Is there another way you could move back? Is there another way you could move sideways? Look at your fingers. Curl them. Twist them. Now, let's make lots of sharp lines, and your feet too.

Now, bring that lone, straight line again. Move about the room and stretch around. Twisting and curling and stretching right down to the floor and way up . . .

Now, whatever part you choose, let it go up to the ceiling.

Now another part. Now another part. This is great!

Now roll over into another space and balance on another part. (J. Sandland with six-year-olds, 1971)

Many games that children play provide practice in triangulation and indirect strategies. "Tangrams" is a classic game that embodies the breaking of set expectations. It is a seven piece puzzle. The object of the game is to assemble the pieces to replicate a series of different printed forms. The Elementary Science Study has prepared a sequence of outlined forms, beginning with only a few pieces and gradually adding pieces. Young children depend on tactile as well as visual cues and need to manipulate the pieces in the outlines themselves. "Knock hockey" is a large muscle activity that uses triangulated action as children knock a disc of wood against the sides of the board in order to bypass obstructions. Checkers and chess are other games in which indirect strategies are used. Children learn to sacrifice a playing piece in order to gain a better position. In addition, they become increasingly proficient in considering alternate moves. Three-dimensional wood puzzles also require planning ahead several steps. Many five-year-olds are able to play these games.

Economic policy decisions frequently reflect short range sacrifices for longer range progress much as do checker playing strategies. When children save together for a common purpose rather than immediately consume their property, they live through this model. Bake sales, pot holder, needlework, and woodcraft sales are some activities that can connect with longer range planning. When seven-year-olds establish their own book and poster store play area, some of these indirect questions arise after repeated, long-term dramatic play and research activities.

Children classify matter by indirect means when they dissolve materials in water or evaporate them as a way to identify them. For example, baking soda and flour look similar when dry but they behave differently in water. Rust is one way to classify metal.

Woodworking activity, beginning in nursery school, develops many skills. In addition to learning the use of carpentry tools and measurement skills, the children learn to plan a few steps ahead and to prepare for new work. Some of these steps are necessarily indirect.

The simple tools connected with woodworking also represent indirect activity. A child applies leverage when he extracts a nail with a hammer.

Many groups in the nursery school as well as the primary school use pulleys to lift blocks, store toys, or send letters or materials across the room in a basket. The pulley is a wheel and rope that changes the direction of force. Children also see pulleys used at construction sites, harbors, quarries, or pumping sites. Seven-year-olds can read the book *Hoists, Cranes, and Derricks* by Zim and Skelly (1969) independently, and there are many picture books suitable for younger children.

PERMOD: DIALECTICAL ACTIVITY

When you experience negativity and polarities, you may become stimulated by your encounters. When somebody takes the "devil's advocate" position, ideas can be clarified and placed in perspective. The young child who survives inconsistent treatment—and every human being does to some degree—hears disagreements, and participates in conflict, has lived through dialectical experience.

The many counter forces in nature manifest this model. The action-reaction model is basic to Newtonian physics. Several activities relating to the opposition of forces in nature, including air pressure, magnetism, gravitation, and centrifugal force, were mentioned earlier in this chapter. In addition, inclined planes are part of a child's life in such forms as slides, ramps, hills, and the problems of picking up piles of toys that slide off an inclined surface. The block corner and its accessories is an obvious place to experiment with ramps that have different angles in order to see which ones are easier to use. Children can use elastic to pull toys and can measure the different lengths caused by the incline of different ramps on the same toys. Homemade rubberband paddle boats are a more complex representation of opposing forces.

Children play on rocking boats, or seated, hold hands together and stretch each other to rock back and forth. The pendulum is another concrete referent of dialectical activity. Some primary age children are able to measure and survey the heights before dropping and the distances and heights travelled in the pendulum's arc. Younger children can simply play with it.

Children come to expect that a rubber ball will rebound. It can be interesting for them to compare other spheres such as marbles, wood balls, and aluminum foil balls. A folding carpenter's ruler, which has prestige in the child's culture, a meterstick or a measuring wheel are useful in measuring the distances of rebound. When children try to find answers to the question, "What happens when marbles are rolled against the wall?" and compare their hypotheses and their measurements, they grow toward a consciousness of causation that leads beyond the concrete. If they only derive the notion that the wall "resisted" the ball, they have moved beyond an undifferentiated taking-for-granted of their environment.

Musical counterpoint, part singing, rhythm instrument orchestration, can also manifest the dialectical mode. It is important for the teacher to intersperse plenty of free-form exploration with instruments each time they are used. When a "stop"-and-place-instruments-on-the-floor-signal is understood *before* the instruments are distributed, it is possible for the teacher or one of the children to share ideas when necessary. Children can classify and counterpose instruments of a different pitch. They can classify and counterpose rhythms and tempos. Young children frequently confuse volume, pitch, and tempo, and profit from help through direct contrasts to differentiate these variables. They can intuitively counterpoint these musical concepts on the basis of models.

In their daily contacts with other people, children learn through contrasts and negative feedback, detailed in Chapter 3. Experiences that further this dialectical development also influence children's ability to deal with reversibility and relative thinking. Good debaters see opposing positions.

A useful tool of inquiry is the question pair: How is this event (object, feeling, place) like that event? How is this event (object, feeling, place) different from that event? For example, when a teacher asked several five-year-olds why an orange had fallen down in the autumn, the children hesitated a moment but laughed when the teacher asked, "Why didn't it fall up?" The inversion of reality in the second question helped them to look at the phenomenon from a new perspective, the possibility of it being "otherwise," the possibility of causation rather than "*ipso facto* reasoning." Also, the inversion of reality immediately drew from them a variety of conjectures: "It's ripe. It doesn't have an engine. They dry up. They die." Of course, the effectiveness of inverting reality in this way is dependent upon children's prior experiences and helps them to focus on, retrieve, and relate material.

PERMOD: THE WHOLE IS MORE THAN THE SUM OF ITS PARTS

A melody has been the classic instance representing the idea that the whole is more than the sum of its parts. In all art forms, the potential aesthetic impact may vary with the preparation of the observer or listener. Yet, there is an intersubjective knowledge shared between different persons who directly experience the work of art. In a parallel construction, we could experience the unique tone of cooperation among members of a group that exists only as a result of their interaction. At this point in our understanding, insightful solutions to problems or tasks resemble this model.

"Cooperation" among the "parts" appears to be an underlying assumption. A black and a white child functionally manifest this cooperation in *Two is a Team* (Beim and Beim, 1945). The concept of a family, the comparative study of different kinds of families, and the comparative study of families in different cultures contrasted with different climatic conditions and different terrains, can support the development of this perceptual model. *Angelita* (Kesselman) exemplifies the contrasts between Puerto Rico and New York. Television in the home has changed the nature of firsthand experience for children by providing data that can balance contrasts even if it cannot be manually varied or modified by a dialogical relation. For example, families at a distance in time become a here-and-now experience. The television families such as "The Waltons," while a prettified picture of the depression, can help children identify through the dramatization. It is hardly sufficient data but it is an actual part of what is available. Films, stories, pictures, trips, and visitors add still more data.

When children compare their roles and the functions of others as consumers and producers, and their relations to goods and services within their various group affiliations, they gather still more portions of data. Through many encounters with resources, they acquire data to compare and classify. Through functional use of labels and thought-provoking questions, the data enter into sharper focus. These activities help the children to build the permod of the whole exceeding the sum of its parts.

Dramatic play and more focussed simulations afforded by role playing with props can be another way to expose children to this permod. As a child identifies with his role and the problems the character faces, he or she may deepen sensitivities to other people and more directly feel their problems.

There are various events that naturally embody the permod. The entire growth process of plants, animals, the child himself, and reproductive processes are certainly more than the sum of their parts. Related activities are detailed later in this chapter.

Concrete activities such as cooking with yeast, mixing paints, food colors, and combining foods are relevant and involving activities in this context. Twirling color wheels and centrifugal tops that have a variety of uses are also applicable.

Children enjoy many activities involving rhythm and rhythmic movement. Rhythms are varying interrelations of tempo and begin to form patterns. These rhythmic patterns are repetitious signals that we perceive as entities that exceed their elements. Much of musical experience reflects this quality of transposing "emotive" wholes. Our experience is immediate and direct. It is valuable for teachers of young children to play with rhythm alone as well as with melody. Rhythm alone creates a less constricting, more open activity. Teachers use a simple drum and encourage children, beginning with three-year-olds, to "Come to me in any way you like. Come in a new way. Come in a different way. Come in a high way, low way. Come as if the bottoms of your feet were covered with glue, as if you were wearing a heavy crown, as if you were carrying an injured bird, as if you were very angry, as if you were on the moon. . . ." The possibilities for discussion and moving are vast. The children's use of space and rhythm are kaleidoscopic. Therefore, it is useful for the teacher to accompany the children's rhythms rather than have the children fit their movements only to the teacher's rhythms. In this way, opportunities remain open for new discoveries by the children.

Hughes' *The First Book of Rhythms* presents varied perspectives on rhythm in the world. After much firsthand experience, five-year-olds and older children may find new ways to look at new encounters.

PERMOD: DOUBLE BIND

When appearances and reality deny each other in our experience, we feel a "double bind." When people set sail with a friendly exterior while harboring hostile feelings, others can sometimes detect the hostility but feel socially compelled to respond to the exterior friendliness. This is a complex socioemotional process that children experience in their early years. However, this model is also reflected in their later development of conservation of quantity. Children can conserve feelings in the "double bind" encounters much earlier than they can conserve quantity when the outward forms change.

Many systematic activities to help children improve their conservation abilities have been suggested elsewhere (Lavatelli, 1970; Weikart et al., 1971). In addition, everyday activities with varied materials contribute to this growth. When children argue about their fair share of food or toys, they contribute to this development. Lavatelli provides an activity that is clearly inductive and requires less teacher verbalizing than many other attempts at intervention.

A very simple but effective training device employs quantities of colored beads, two plastic 8 oz. containers, one low and broad and the other tall and skinny, and some brown paper sacks. The child drops a bead from each hand into each of the containers at the same time, sometimes chanting as he does so, "one in here; one in here." From time to time, brown paper sacks with a hole in the center are put over the containers and the procedure is repeated. Children deny that both containers have the same amount of beads when they can see the beads, but invariably give conservation responses when they cannot perceive the inequality of the level of beads in the containers, and eventually the discrepancy between the responses they give in the two situations becomes apparent to them, and they say excitedly, "It's got to be the same; I put the same in each jar. It doesn't matter how it looks." Operational structures are obviously emerging. (p. 112)

Children encounter similar contrasts between appearance and reality when they deal with objects in relation to buoyancy. While many nursery schools afford water play opportunities for children, they frequently do not offer much more stimulation than the child's bathtub at home. For example, salt water and fresh water provide a simple contrast. When teachers plan contrasts for children that provide dissonance between the appearance of materials and their real nature then children have an opportunity to question the logic of single-variable appearances. Whether or not the children do in fact question it right away should be less important than that an opportunity existed for the children's exposure and the teacher's diagnosis.

Teachers should legitimize guessing and supposing by encouraging children to ask whether or not an object would float or sink, and then test their hypotheses directly. A wide variety of materials can be introduced gradually in order to control variables. If children compare cubes or plates made of wood, plastic, rubber, metal, and cardboard, they can focus on the material rather than its shape. If children compare different shapes, then it is useful to keep their material composition constant. For example, the same size of aluminum foil that the children shape like a boat, a raft, or a bar can be a clear comparison study. Does a hole in a doughnut make a difference when compared with an ordinary bun?

Some teachers have dignified children's syncretic thinking by accepting children's classification systems. In a handbook of teacher-made, multisensory materials for three and four-year-olds, the authors report a free-form classification activity, elegant in its simplicity (McGinn and Rudnick, 1973). Children simply group objects that are alike and unlike and then tell their reasons verbally. "It's always interesting when a child groups a hammer, a spool of thread, and a small wrench together because 'that's what my mommy *does* use in the house'" (p. 5).

We have been culturally conditioned to expect certain music to evoke certain kinds of images. Young children, not as fixed in their connections, may be kept open to possibilities by listening to music and selecting accompanying pictures from a large picture file. When they see that the teacher accepts a variety of alternatives, their double-bind potential may be modified.

When children explore and find acceptance for many alternate solutions in their dramatic play, role playing, and puppetry, a similar impact may take place. For instance, the possibilities for dealing with authority and other problem issues in children's lives can be dramatized in different ways. *Peter's Chair,* by Keats, is a story for nursery age children onward that touches one solution for one child with a new sibling.

General growth in relative thinking grows through continued contacts in the world of objects and through educated visual perceptual just as it does through social encounters and dramatizations. Just as it is difficult for young children to put themselves into somebody else's feelings, it is also difficult for them to interpret another's visual perspective.

R. Karplus, a physicist-educator, has attempted to concretize relative thinking by using "Mr. O" (Karplus and Thier, 1967). "Mr. O." might as easily be a puppet or stuffed toy who can describe whatever he sees from wherever he is located. Five-year-olds and their teacher can play with the observer notion, placing objects in front of "him," and setting "him" on stationary and on moving vehicles. Young children can deal with an imaginary observer on much the same level as an imaginary friend who can be blamed for misdeeds.

Lavatelli also suggests activities to develop relative spatial concepts. She uses table settings and house, garage, and tree dioramas in combination with pictures. The Minnesota mathematics project on symmetry for the kindergarten suggests some rotational activities with shapes as well as with objects, and uses art-related activities to stimulate relative thinking (Waters, 1973).

PERMOD: CYCLICAL CHANGE

Young children begin to experience cyclical change directly through the routine schedules of eating and sleeping, and through seasonal changes. Since change exists constantly, it is probably fruitful for teachers to focus on those activities that reflect the permod of cyclical change, recognizing that the activities themselves may build toward an understanding of cyclical change even if only partial cyclical change is reflected in the activity. This permod is reflected in the life cycle, bird migration, the food chain, seasons, cultural evolutions, as well as in electrical circuits, cyclic compounds in organic chemistry, automobile engine cycles, and a series of legends or poems.

Time is an important element in cyclical change. Historical time, temporal ordering, is usually the first kind of time that people consider. However, while the behavioral and social sciences conceive of time in terms of duration, economists consider commodities produced over time. While biologists use temporal development and evolution to consider the past, physicists consider the future, focussing on prediction. Time for physicists is a major component of their substantive concerns. By contrast, existential time exists when people make decisions and the religious would view time as infinite and transcendent. For the artist, poet, or musician, the present is the single most important time in which the past is represented and future expectancies anticipated.

Time is also a constraint when teachers work with young children who are still learning to sort out time distinctions and sequences of events. Concrete activities provide one means to deal with young children and time. Analogy is another tool for helping children deal with the distant in time.

The time line has been used in kindergartens and the primary years. In nursery schools, teachers have hung baby pictures acquired from parents beside September pictures. After a few weeks, the chart was put in storage until May when another set of recent pictures was added. Children have noticed changes in hair length and, in some cases, sleeve length. A nursery school variant of the time line is a photographic sequence of events during trips as well as a sequence of pictures representing a variety of other group projects, including parties. Tape recordings are other kinds of records that can contribute to a sense of temporal order.

Immediate duration of time occurs when children wait impatiently for pudding to cook and cookies to bake, a film to end, or a story to begin. When seven-year-olds survey the rate of heart beats for ten seconds before and after running for two minutes, or the number of birds at a bird feeder during a ten minute period, they deepen their sense of time on a personal level. Many events that are recorded with such graphic surveys or with experience charts measure changes and time. Children can use clocks with second hands, mechanical timers, metronomes, and such nonstandard measures of time as water wheels. Sometimes, children are quite ingenious about suggesting ways to record changes. It is worthwhile to ask for their suggestions. In addition, they can keep records through communal or individual "books of changes" at their own levels of representation.

Human beings of all ages wonder what will happen when they grow older. For young children, visiting a family with an infant, and speaking with elderly people are important supplements in an age of nuclear families. Picture books such as *The Growing Story* by Krauss, about plant, animal, and child growth, *The Umbrella* by Yashima, a prestigious acquisition marking growth, *The Carrot Seed* (Krauss), *One Morning in Maine* by McCloskey, about losing a tooth on an island, and *My Family* by Schlein, about generations, can add perspective to the first hand activities. Birth and death questions are the subjects of other picture books for children who have special concerns, for example, *Matt's Grandfather* by Lundgren, about a nursing home, *The Dead Bird* by Brown, Miles' *Annie and the Old Ones,* and *All About Eggs* by Selsam, dealing with reproduction, are examples of an extended body of books for young children.

The notions of death and extinction are important human concerns. When you consider the limits of children's grasp of time, it is a constant wonder to notice children of five, six, and seven years of age wrapped up in dinosaur lore. It is hard to say whether dinosaurs have more appeal because of their lengthy, varied labels that have prestige in the child culture, or because of their appeal to libidinal monsters and children's conscience development. Children are able to see actual size replicas or the fossilized remains in local museums as well as in special films and pictures. When the children compare the different varieties of dinosaurs, they can learn about the different limb structures and running capacities that distinguished the vegetarian from the flesh-eating dinosaurs. This frequently leads to classifications of other animal forms and their varied tails, paws, ears, sizes, teeth, skin textures, mobility, and patterns of adaptation.

Some children bring fossils to share with others that their families encountered on vacation trips. Plaster-of-paris hand or foot prints and printing activities with sponges and vegetables, and later with words, add to the fossil concept. With some fossil recognition comes the possibility of dealing with various rock formations and their relation to changes in heat and pressure.

In some areas in the springtime, it is possible to find eggs or tadpoles in ponds. These can be raised easily on crumbs and fish food in an aquarium. Children take great pleasure in watching them develop into peeper frogs, after which time they need to live out of the water. Many questions are raised by these dramatic events. An alternate activity might be to obtain an egg incubator through a local 4-H club, or some mealworms from a local pet shop. A guppy family that grows in an aquarium can produce still other stimulation as can healthy rabbits, guinea pigs, and turtles. However, with rare exceptions, a fish aquarium along with any animals kept around young children for more than a month or two fade into the background. Perhaps interchanging animals from time to time with other groups could keep children's interests high and budgets solvent.

Plant growth is another responsible activity that helps children see changes occur. They can even create part of their own food chain by sprouting mung beans or alfalfa, which takes a matter of days, or watching the variety of growths from carrot tops, avocado pits, sweet potatoes, green peas, bulbs, flower seeds, and vegetable seeds in a window box or outdoor garden where possible. Children can vary growth conditions such as amounts of water, light, and heat. They can measure what happens using rulers and nonstandard lengths of string or oaktag. In order to create a longer-range association in time, pumpkin seeds, dried and saved from a Halloween jack-o-lantern can be planted in the spring.

It is worth being cautious about holidays generally. Too many early childhood teachers have built their entire social studies program around a kind of pagan calendar worship in which a vacuous notion of Thanksgiving symbols begins the day after Halloween, followed by the outer trappings of Christmas beginning directly after Thanksgiving. The focus of this book is toward a more substantive base in activities through which children take much more responsibility for setting problems and comparing their findings with each other.

Some of this focus is longitudinal and social, as exemplified by the six-year-olds who compared histograms of their own family sizes with those of the seven-year-olds' parents and grandparents. These kinds of comparisons lead to questions about possible contributing differences. Still other comparisons with other cultures might yield still more questions. For example, they might find out that their great-grandparents were apprentices before they were twelve years old in order to contribute to their family's income. They might find out that people in India have large families in order to support the elderly better. They might find out that more of their grandparents lived on farms where there was more space for large families. These findings might build toward learnings in later years concerning welfare legislation or demographic shifts and densities. While there are many books written about farms and cities and families, *The Little House* by Burton is one of the few for young children that deals with change in the density of population in a concrete manner. Still more questions and opportunities for dramatic play, trips, and study present themselves.

Change in density itself is a permod basic to the kinetic-molecular theory of matter. An understanding of engine cycles requires a prior understanding of this phenomenon. That is, heat speeds the movement of molecules that expand away from each other, whereas cooling slows the movement of molecules while compressing them. Children's many random exposures to temperature changes are obvious. Focussed observations and contrasts help children to order their random experiences.

Measurement with a thermometer comes in handy on many occasions. Before children can read the thermometer, the teacher might mark a large one by color designations for three or four distinctions such as blue for hot, yellow for medium, and red for cold. Varied sizes of thermometers provide added applications for study.

Children can enjoy melting ice cubes in their mouths or in their hand in the nursery school. It would be interesting for them to hypothesize and then observe what happens to the ice cubes outdoors in the winter, and to compare this with what happens to ice cubes on a radiator or in a pot on the range. It is also interesting to see what happens to the water that they find when they remove a pan from the radiator and place it outdoors. Similar cycles are represented by creating a rain cycle in a terrarium or when laundering doll clothes, by simply inverting a jar over garments drying on a radiator.

Seven-year-olds can similarly see the cycle of liquid to solid to gas after a candlemaking activity. Even a carrot that is eaten, grated, juiced, and the remaining end planted can serve young children as an exemplar of change. While this planned variation is useful and stimulating, it is rare excitement to turn an unexpected snowfall into a spontaneous aesthetic experience that can be appreciated in different ways when it is an indoor visual activity and when it is an outdoor tactile immersion.

Woven through each day are such "fleeting moments" that hold the potential for deeper meanings when the teacher takes the time to appreciate them with children. Children can dance the snow falling and the wind shifting, the surprises of growing things, and their own changing feelings and experimentations with their bodies in space. All can appreciate the mobiles that children build out and down and that change appearance in a breeze.

THE ROLE OF THE TEACHER

Activity itself is not educative. Even though content and method cannot be separated in the conception of learning presented here, the teacher's functions that support this activity need a closer look.

At this time, it is useful to consider some tools available to the teacher that can support children's experimentations. A cookbook of activities is merely a list of ingredients without techniques for treating them. Once ingredients and techniques are available, it is the creative cook who can adapt and create new recipes. Similarly, a professional teacher comes to stir the pot in his or her own way, with his or her own special mixtures.

When a teacher of young children provides materials, then the children's experimentation makes discoveries possible. However, nature does not teach in and of itself. It does not send messages to a passive receptacle. Situations need to be designed that can focus children's observations. This is very different from listing a set of generalizations for children to apply. As you look back over the activities suggested in this chapter, some teacher strategies can be noted and others can be projected.

First of all, activity is the primary medium of learning for the young child. As he manipulates materials, questions possibilities, observes events, and applies varied tools, he has a chance to extend his learning.

Induction is the primary means through which learning occurs when young children engage in activities. This is facilitated when the teacher plans for systematic contrasts. The teacher is careful not to overload children with too many variables at once. In this way children can participate in, and observe, events under differing conditions. Children can perceive a new "figure" by virtue of its juxtaposition against a known "background."

Such "figures" wear different "costumes" in relation to the different questions and purposes of the activities. For example, when a group observes the supermarket receiving a delivery of produce from a truck, they also acquire background data for comparing marketing patterns in a book or film of an Asian community committed to water transportation. The economic comparisons or the interactions of people and their environments, or the food chain, are some varied directions in which such observation may lead. The tools used in the activities will influence the kind of activity that the group needs next. Will they compare artifacts, technology, family roles, or climatic influences? Whichever activities are chosen will help move children toward adult forms of understanding, perhaps their own unique organizations.

As long as children have many samples of direct data, they can be extending their thinking inductively. It takes time for children to marinate these bits of experience.

Repetitions and comparisons of comparable phenomena at different times take on new meanings as children's own perceptions grow to meet formerly encountered experiences with greater depth. *The teacher soaks the child's environment with permods that are embedded repeatedly in variant forms.* The teacher appreciates children's spontaneous interests and pursuits and helps children to relate them by obtaining materials, by raising questions, and by providing information when it is needed and otherwise inaccessible.

As adults observe children's behavior, certain plans are postponed or eliminated while others are substituted. During activities related to the interaction of forces mentioned earlier, the five-year-old children appeared quite content to concern themselves with materials related to first one force and then others, before focussing upon the first force again. When concerning themselves with an apparently abandoned idea, children usually approached it with the kind of fresh enthusiasm shown to any new phenomenon. However, each subsequent approach was neither identical nor necessarily sequential with the children's prior approaches. Intervening impressions had inevitably changed at least the children's perspectives. This observation parallels the Luria and Piaget studies of memory described in Chapter 3.

On one occasion, for example, a teacher may feel that an introductory session concerning centrifugal force is beyond the children's grasp because of a lack of accessible feedback. Although there might have been a fine quality of interchange and questioning, the teacher would prefer returning to the idea at another time. When tempered with time and the free use of materials, a new, and possibly improved, perspective may be gained. Children can hardly be expected to plough a straight furrow toward the permod of balance-of-forces-in-an-open-system with centrifugal force to one side and centripetal force on the other.

In any case, whenever *contrasts* are learned, it is important that children have an opportunity to induce them. In addition, teachers can help children to identify events or conditions when they consider *polar positions* through questions, for example, How is your observation like yesterday's activity? How is your observation unlike yesterday's activity? or, Where would you find it? Where would you be least likely to find it? Why would you do it in April? Why would you not do it in November?

Another aid to involve children in their learning is simply by doing it. That is, young children need *immediate personal involvement* with materials. From an attitudinal viewpoint, it may be counterproductive to engage in a lengthy introduction; "If the attitudes acquired during the preamble to a topic are unfavorable, teaching the topic itself is an uphill job" (Page, 1962, p. 11).

An initial pedagogical tendency is to logically justify and sequentially identify an activity to children. In this attempt to share their motives with children, adults often overlook children's own motives. Consequently, those children who are not initially bored may even become wary. After all, is our culture not one in which guilt-connected or supposedly painful experiences are introduced with prefaces in word or deed concerning how little something or other will hurt one?

Hawkins (1973), an educator, in his construction of the triangular relation of "I–Thou–It" makes a related point. He proposes that the basis for children and adults to interact is the activity that they may share in common.

Many appeals to attend *to* the teacher's authority can be avoided when a child can attend *with* the teacher to a material or activity. Especially when dealing with groups of varying size, a great deal of time and potential stimulation and positive excitement may be lost by detailed, lengthy, introductory calls for total immobility, quiet, and attention. Direct immediate involvement in an activity can be one way of avoiding such harangues.

Still another way to involve children in their own learning is to judiciously either *postpone or provide information*. The teacher withholds information when it is evident that a child is able, with some direction or encouragement, to satisfy his question by himself. Frequently, children are able to use methods of inquiry that net a great sense of competence and self-reliance. For example, a child asks,

CHILD: How many old people, grownups, and children live in New York City?

ADULT: Why do you want to know how many? How could you use the information if you had it? (*They discuss seeing the school librarian who might have census figures.*) . . . If you were planning to move a children's clothing factory to New York City and found out that most of the people were elderly, how would you feel about moving? . . . If you were a parks commissioner and needed to plan playgrounds and programs, how would information help? . . . What if there were mostly children? . . . What if there were mostly elderly?

Sometimes *open-ended questions* serve as a way to provide information by eliciting thoughtful responses that relate discrete factual bits of data. Questioning is examined further in Chapter 6.

In addition, children acquire information when teachers use relevant vocabulary in a functional way, that is, simultaneously with the phenomena indicated. The following example involves the *functional use of vocabulary* as well as an instance where children were helped to use language more precisely.

(*Boys were startled by the clatter of objects falling from a nearby table.*)

CHILD 1:	(*to nearby adult*) What happened?
ADULT:	(*jokingly*) The force of gravity is working.
CHILDREN:	(*laugh delightedly*)
CHILD 2:	Gravity is working. Gravity threw it down.
ADULT:	Did gravity throw or pull it?
CHILD 2:	(*thoughtfully*) Pulled it . . .
CHILD 3:	(*under his breath*) Gravity . . . Gravity . . . Gravity

In another instance, a teacher began an activity with a gyroscope by twirling it and asking the children, "What does this gyroscope remind you of? Let's follow the orbit it takes with this blue chalk."

Trips add to children's opportunities to acquire information. Sometimes a trip can begin a questioning process for the children. At other times, it grows out of their ongoing work and can be an extension of it. In either case, a trip increases in value when children come with prepared minds. Their observations can be focussed through questions that they discussed with the teacher beforehand in addition to those questions that arise spontaneously. In the first place, children should discuss with adults why the trip is relevant. It is certainly efficient for the teacher to have made the trip ahead of time, even if it were suggested by the children or if it were an annual school tradition. This advance investigation may avoid such surprises as, "Closed Tuesday," or "Under New Management" that does not welcome groups of young children.

Similarly, if a purpose for inviting a resource person is to create a situation in which children can ask questions, then the resource person needs to be known as a person who avoids lecturing. Even if the subject matter is new for the children, some artifacts or pictures can serve to further involve the children.

LEGITIMIZING MANY FORMS OF COMMUNICATION

Visitors may be sources for listening to children as well as sources for information. In the role of listener, the visitor performs a valuable service for the children. They are given an opportunity to report their observations, concerns, and understandings to somebody who was not a participant. It helps them to clarify their experiences when they respond to someone else's legitimate questions. The psycholinguist Vygotsky (1962) contends that real understanding exists when a child can express his thought to another person.

When children talk about their experiences, adults have a better opportunity to know what children may be perceiving. Frequently, parents are a source of feedback to the teacher. At other times, children from a different group can visit in order to be shown children's work. An older child or adult recorder can take dictation for a group book. Children can also tape record their experiences and their findings.

It is important that the teacher legitimize many forms of communication for young children besides the written or spoken word. There is a clear message of respect when an adult photographs block buildings or sculpture that represent children's major expressive efforts. A child might make a symbol drawing of his own block construction or peg city game. Children can certainly draw, paint, or construct dioramas. They can move their bodies in space to express a range of feelings and understandings. They can compose songs together and relate the author's picture to the compilation of songs in a song book.

Many activities represented in varied forms should be accepted. Children should be exposed to a variety of aesthetically pleasing works. When children see varied means for expression, their own possibilities are expanded. However, it is too sad to remember the art teacher holding up to the five-year-olds what the seven-year-olds had done using the same medium and theme two hours earlier. This sort of constriction of children's possibilities is becoming extinct but there are still some vestigial remains. Teachers should encourage children's openness to their own feelings and experimentation with the media.

While teachers accept children's sincere, varied productions and *recognize their developmental capacities,* children can learn to appreciate improvements in their own work and the work of others. Just as children learn to criticize—in the sense of evaluate—events on the basis of evidence, they can appreciate fine standards of work. When a great variety of products, and the efforts they represent, are valued by the teacher and carefully presented and displayed, children can become stimulated to try new media, create new forms, or pursue new interests.

The teacher can perform some of the functions of a museum curator when children's art work and written work is mounted with dignity and displayed on walls, the backs of room dividers, and the spaces between windows or doors. Boxes can be covered with contact paper, wallpaper, or cloth, and stacked to provide a three-dimensional display area for children's constructions, clay work, artifacts, shell collections, or machine parts of interest to children.

Covered cardboard can be used to set off, carrel-fashion, a lighted three-dimensional display where shadows are explicitly planned.

Moreover, wire or string strung across a corner, across a room from wall to wall, or corner to corner, can serve to hang such things as hangers and hoops for mobiles, stencils, splatter paintings, puppets, weaving, straw sculpture, or children's own poems. Sometimes, when the teacher moves a storage shelf or screen to set off a new area, the contents of that area can become a new focus to draw the children's attention. Children themselves can create such "museums" that become an integral part of their experience rather than an alien form.

CHAPTER 5
READING AND
LANGUAGE TEACHING

The intent of the preceding chapter was to consider ways to expose young children to a myriad of rich activities in order to help maximize their becoming more human. In this sense, to be human means to be free both to choose and to be responsible for choices; to move with some degree of spontaneity; and to have the right and to develop the ability to effect change in one's own life—all this, surrounded with other receptive and responsive human beings.

It can hardly be fully emphasized when writing that the real nature of human development is the development of ability. Skills, *while necessary*, serve development and are not an end-all. Only the practice of early primary grade teachers who deal nearly exclusively with the 3 R's have swayed the public view of what schooling has been rather than what education means. At the other extreme are those nursery school teachers who rigidly exclude substantive conceptual consideration and the development of language skills in the same unbalanced way.

The section that follows discusses some playful, inductive ways in which young children can improve their literacy skills. Syntax model games for expressive language development and phonemic games for the development of decoding skills are presented in turn. These activities represent an application of the discipline of linguistics to the learning of language. Linquists, discussed in this chapter, have defined the central concepts of linguistics as meaning, communication, symbol, and structure. The major method of linguistic inquiry is induction. Therefore, the activities presented are inductively ordered.

The chapter concludes with a discussion of the relation of writing, reading, and experience.

SHE CAN TAKE HER TIME WRITING NOW THAT SHE HAS SET OUT HER IDEA WITH THE WORD CARDS.

SYNTAX MODEL GAMES AND VERBAL EXPRESSION

Some procedures for developing language skills in young children are set forth in this section. These procedures, "syntax model games," were developed with consideration for children's language development, their developmental styles, and a consideration for transformational-generative grammar.

The procedures are called games because they share some common properties with games. That is, their delivery is playful, and their concrete materials support self-motivated involvement. They differ from some games in that they are not designed to be competitive and rules are not stated in advance. Rather, language rules are inductively acquired and become apparent to the participants through their functional use. As the adult models the game initially by playing it several times, "taking turns," while uttering the planned, syntactically equivalent verbal accompaniment, children are provided with an opportunity to induce the syntactic structure. The induction becomes evident when the children take their turns and employ equivalent syntax with varying tokens.

PURPOSES SERVED BY THE GAMES

These activities, in which two agenda move side by side—the children's perceived involvement with concrete materials and the adult's parallel saturating with specific repeated, contrasting syntactic models—represent one possible lever to strengthen several possible skills.

For one thing, meaning is conveyed by the structure of language as well as by its tokens. Children can better understand spoken and written language if they have been exposed to a variety of structures in a meaningful context. Through manipulation of materials, expression and referent are related. Similarly, when children are able to use varied structures, they become better able to encode spoken and written messages. Therefore, it is a purpose of these activities to stimulate children's expanded and fluent use of language.

Another purpose of these activities is to support children's cognitive processes through the development of more efficient and more flexible use of language. Since language and thought are intertwined, the ability to use language more flexibly serves as a means toward more competent communication of one's thinking. Flexibility is more likely to grow when children are exposed to a variety of alternate structures. This section samples some ways in which the implementation of these purposes has been attempted.

Of particular significance in this respect are the studies of Cazden (1972). She used a variety of treatments with nursery age children and found that focussing on ideas, rather than "grammatical expansions" alone, was more helpful to children's varied language development (p. 126). Children quite simply are being provided with additional meaningful opportunities for contrasting data. Her findings, consistent with other findings (Yonemura, 1969), are particularly interesting in terms of the present discussion because they point to the significance of meaning as a lever to technical proficiency. In addition, Lavatelli (1970), who developed sequentially related materials to improve young children's conceptual skills following a Piagetian framework, recommends that teachers model planned syntactic structures to accompany the manipulation of materials.

In the light of these related positions, the alternative of using pattern drills, as employed in teaching a second language, was discarded. Meaning is closely restricted in the pattern drill and young children would have, in light of their learning styles, questionable motives for involvement.

INDUCTION AS A WAY OF KNOWING LANGUAGE

A usual observation of developmental psycholinguistics is that young children do learn the language they hear around them without apparent self-awareness. To them, their "doing" of their language is more important than their consciousness of doing. I wish to make the case that any intervention in children's language development serves young children best when it follows the basic contours of natural language development. If educators could tap the satisfying efforts that new speakers experience, and recreate this naturalness, it would seem that syntactic complexity and effectiveness could be supported.

Therefore, another purpose of these games is to focus on the children's functional use of language rather than their self-awareness. While verbalization may draw a young child's attention to a particular phenomenon, significant understanding derives from that child's concrete experiences. The young child's fluent, functional use of language reflects his cognitive experience.

Understanding and Using Language. Language acquisition is tempered by cultural as well as cognitive factors (such as memory) that necessarily limit possibilities for use. Chomsky (1965; 1968) distinguishes between linguistic competence and linguistic performance. Slobin and Welsh (1973) observed that a toddler's self-motivated spoken performance-in-context was more competent than when she was asked to initiate a repetition of her own earlier statement.

Meaning provides a kind of power source for language if you accept that meaning involves cognitive and affective facets—a commitment. Meaning makes manifest a closer relation between competence and performance. The facts indicate that children's ability to speak, read, or write are not always retrievable when adults can assess them. Perhaps the study of children's behavior and development needs to consider children's motives at least as much as the experimenter's motives. Teachers must attend at least as closely to children's motives for speaking as to their performance if a closer view of competence is to become apparent.

Therefore, educators need to encourage activities that provide varied language opportunities. The purpose of such activities is for children to express their thoughts more effectively, expansively, and flexibly. Initially, it appears useful to recognize the prominence of oral language for the young child. Therefore, a major purpose of the procedures is to begin to stimulate children's language skills through the use of natural, inductive learning processes. Education must deal with the tension between functional language and studied talking.

Despite the differences between them, Bruner and Piaget remind teachers that the child's potent comfort with imagery at this age becomes the envy of artists and poets (Piaget, 1947; Bruner, 1966). These cognitive modes follow and parallel, if you wish, the unique grammars that toddlers (one- to three-year-olds) around the world manage to develop for themselves (McNeill (1970).

Metalinguistic Awareness. A philosopher notes that, "If you shift your attention from the meaning of a symbol to the symbol as an object viewed in itself, you destroy its meaning. . . . Symbols can serve as instruments of meaning only by being known subsidiarily while fixing our focal attention on their meaning" (Polanyi, 1963, p. 30).

It follows that teachers would not expect young children to be conscious of their own language functions in any formal sense. However, adults are capable of such dual knowledge of, and about, the figure ("focal") and ground ("subsidiary") aspects of language. Self-awareness, the ability to reflect upon what one has done and how one has arrived at such accomplishment is an objective of educating intellect in general.

Dialogue, along with experience, serves to help children move toward this development. Clearly, language helps human beings refer to that which is not present and ultimately, to reflect upon it. Young children have certain "expectations" about language (McNeill, p. 124). However, researchers and educators find that young children are able to reflect upon, or be self-aware of, their language processes only after they have had extended functional experiences (Bruner, 1966; Mackay et al., 1970; Piaget, 1947; Vygotsky, 1962).

This distinction between functional induction and metalinguistic awareness affects education because much traditional teaching has attempted to impart the formal rules of grammar and phonemic contrasts in the elementary school, whether in a descriptive sense or in a sense of "do" and "don't do" rules, frequently through the use of textbooks. Essentially, since language is inductively acquired in a social context, the very notion of textbooks as a way to teach the structure of language as a discipline is also inconsistent with the way language is learned naturally.

Further, to look at linguistics, the science of language, as a discipline is to see induction as its major way of knowing. *The educator must refer to the criterial aspects of systematized knowledge along with the child's strategies for its acquisition.* Therefore, to focus on learning *about* language rather than to focus on functioning effectiveness is to place "subsidiary" considerations prior to "focal" ones in early childhood education.

Teachers need to think of a largely preliterate, oral tradition as a salient feature of young children's functioning. It is relevant to consider young children's capacity against humankind's historical perspective. In effect, human beings have been largely illiterate throughout history. Multitudes of adult contemporaries around the world are illiterate. Therefore, teachers must consider the central importance of the spoken word before the written word in human communication. Yet the place of language in schools has been largely linear and visual. While linear and visual language development are a legitimate school function, education for young children would be served better by additional attention to the *means* by which ideas can be expressed and decoded. The method of teaching language should follow the learning processes that characterize the child.

In terms of decoding and retrieving information from others' spoken or written language, syntactical differences between the experience of encoder and decoder may widen or lessen the gap of communication—at best an attempt to comprehend, but only rarely more than an approximate apprehending. "A word in context means both more and less than the same word in isolation. More, because it acquires new content; less, because its meaning is limited and narrowed by the context" (Vygotsky, p. 146). It would seem that more efficient communication would result from greater experience with more and less complex, varied, or subtle syntactic usage.

TRANSFORMATIONAL-GENERATIVE GRAMMAR AND LANGUAGE EDUCATION

The significance of syntax, the structural relations of patterns of words in sentences, has been particularly neglected in the elementary school. It is about time adults ceased to mourn the passing of traditional or descriptive grammar study in the elementary school. It would be better to focus on the ways in which children could gain greater control over the processes that generate language.

A transformational-generative approach to language focusses on those processes by which sentences communicate meanings. The various ways in which words may *function* as flexible elements in sentences is a central concern. Since meaning is conveyed partly by the order of, and relations between, words in sentences changing sequence, the contrasting patterns of words in sentences may change meanings. Frequently, intonation or other particular minimal change in surface structure may alter the deeper meaning of a statement although the surface structure seems similar to a prior statement.

Gleason's distinction between enate and agnate structures may help convey the transformational aspects of syntactic patternings. Enation defines sentences with similar syntactic patterns in which there exists a direct correspondence between the grammatical *functions* of each word in any pair or more of sentences even though the meanings of the words in this framework differ. Different tokens can be substituted in the same forms without syntactic change, for example, "The cat chased the bird. The dog hunted the rabbit."

Agnation defines manipulations that can change the structural *relations* between words in any pair or more of sentences. Vocabulary may or may not change. However, even if vocabulary remained the same, the altered relation of words in sentences would change the meaning of the sentences as follows:

That man is old. That man is going. or
To err is human. It is human to err. or
It is raining! Is it raining? (Gleason, 1965, Chapter 9)

To describe the range of enate and agnate relations in a language is to describe the particular grammatical structure of a particular language.

N. Chomsky's (1968) "theory of syntax" holds "that sentences are not derived from other sentences but rather from the structures underlying them" (p. 33). He distinguishes between the "surface," or phonetic structure, and the "deep," or meaning structure (p. 107). He theorizes a "universal grammar" represented by the deep structure of syntax that is innate, "rooted in the human 'language capacity'" (p. 27).

Even with rather minimal exposure to language, babies learn to speak. They frequently overregularize logically even when notably unconventional, for example, "I runned home." Such generalization supports the observation that children are creative users of language very early. One cannot help seeing the playfulness of children as an important contributing factor to the development of creative linguistic possibilities.

These contentions are consistent with a Piagetian view of the child as an active participant in the acquisition of knowledge. The child's construction of his world appears to be supported by innate human possibilities that interact with environmental forces. The inductive process in this interaction extends knowledge beyond experience.

Through interaction, the conventions of sentence formation may be applied to the expansion, coordination, subordination, or other alteration of sentences. Use of these conventions may make language more or less efficient and contribute to individual variations in style of speaking and writing. For example, it is useful for teachers to note that words denoting relation and subordination are best definable only as they are available in sentences.

Carol Chomsky (1972), in a study of young children's acquisition of language, used pictures with contrasting pairs of sentences, rather than bare word testing, as a way of diagnosing children's comprehension of these variations. It is useful to employ *the power of contrasts* to work through inductive strategies, trusting to children's "presets." Therefore, the teacher's role would be to focus upon the process of language learning.

SOME "RUBBER BAND" NOTIONS OF SYNTACTIC DEVELOPMENT

Induction is the process by which children learn language. This approach to learning is consistent with child development literature. Researchers point to repetition, imitation, and induction as the means by which initial syntactic development grows (Brown and Bellugi, 1964). Brown and Bellugi speak of the continuing process of adult–child "expansion-reduction-expansion-lesser reduction." The rubber band image refers to this fluctuating process of language growth through interaction. The child reduces the syntax spoken by the adult. The adult in turn expands the child's statement. With continuing interaction, the child begins to expand his syntactic usage. As a rubber band becomes used, so does the young child's speech stretch and loosen to match the scope of the adult's fluent syntax. Another study supports this view of young children, "actively, by analogic extensions, forming classes and rules" (Ervin, 1964, p. 186). Imitation is viewed broadly in these positions as a complex, oscillating process of practicing with language variants. At the same time, imitation is not guaranteed in and of itself without consideration for the social interaction between adult modeler, the child, and the stimulation provided by the activity.

A later study by Bellugi-Klima found that the universality of this interaction process appears to hold true for deaf children as well as hearing children. She found differences in the handling of verb tense revealed in the form of expression through visual signs (Reinhold, 1972). In a somewhat parallel line of observation, differences in dialect or standard forms of regionalisms do not appear to hinder thinking (Cazden, 1972). In effect, the young child's rich perceptual potential and associational possibilities for thinking are intertwined with linguistic development. The associational possibilities of thinking operate at the deeper rather than the surface level of language structure.

The philosopher von Wittgenstein (1953) also noted that becoming a participant in the various "games" of language serves as a language extension process by the use of "analogous" rules (p. 35). As contrasts are perceived by children, their functional mastery of language becomes more flexible. The significance of such *contrasting* syntactic patterns in language learning is further noted in work as varied as that of Montessori (1912); Bruner (1966); Gleason (1965); Miller (1969); Chomsky (1965); and Fries (1952).

Now, one would think that the *process* of natural, inductive, early language development could be used to help children develop their continuing linguistic skills. If modelling of the "rubber band" variety were crucial, informal repetition of syntactically equivalent structures, with different tokens, might help children to induce a more efficient or expanded structure when *contrasted* with other transformed structures. That is, if an adult were to develop concrete materials-based playful, game situations, which were *organically* tied to certain contrasting pairs or trios of syntactic structures, children would be exposed to a planned rather than the usual random modelling of contrasting sentences.

I attempted to employ such "syntax modelling games" with several hundred five- to nine-year-old children of varied background in groups of three to five children. *Varied concrete materials* that served as the children's focus were used in games ranging from board games to large muscle activity games. The adult modellers were student teachers who used these games as microteaching activities. Twenty minutes was the median time.

The verbal interchange for each activity was recorded by written protocols and tape recordings. The recorders had prior experience in verbatim episodic recording. Tape recorders were used to add accuracy to the verbal content, whereas the written recorders also relayed data on physical involvement with materials as well as nonverbal communication. Between four and eight different student teachers took turns recording for each other in order to provide a range of teaching styles for one another.

SYNTAX MODEL GAMES

Such games as grab bag; guess the picture-on-my-back, in-my-envelope, on-my-seat; matching objects; street map board game with toy cars; personification; actions on objects or with parts of the body; and costuming were used as vehicles for modelling particular sentence structures. Different sentence patterns could be applied to the same games. A look at some planning considerations and some protocols might clarify.

There are *concrete materials* in each game. The teacher opens each session with three or four *contrasting models, briskly paced.* Brisk pacing helps the contrasts to stand out more clearly than if the focal models are embedded in ongoing conversation. For example, in a grab bag game, the teacher transforms simple sentences by coordinating them. The teacher begins with the repeated models while playing the game as follows:

(1)   I feel something cold.
       I feel something wet.
       I feel something cold and wet but not greasy.
       It's ice!
(2)   I feel something smooth.
       I feel something long.
       I feel something smooth and long but not sharp.
       It's a candy cane!
(3)   I feel something rough.
       I feel something flat.
       I feel something rough and flat but not slippery.
       It's sandpaper.
Howard, you play the game now.

The simple sentences are contrasted with their coordinated form. As each item is discovered, it is taken out of the game so that children can see a wider range of objects and not merely parrot an earlier grab bag participant. The suspense is a highly involving factor in this activity. For younger children, it may be necessary for all to feel, see, and talk about the objects before they disappear into the bag.

If children pick up the transformed structure—the coordinated form, as evidenced by their use of it as they play the game—then the teacher would provide a more complex alternate model, for example, "I feel something wrinkled and rough but not sticky or smooth." If the original repeated model seems too complex, the teacher would remodel a simpler alternate, for example, "I feel something cold, long, and smooth."

The *repeated structures* serve as a contrasting figure against a background of familiar language flow. Inasmuch as the teacher models reflect the actual game they will be most readily used by the children. This is reflected in the folklore tradition of childhood street games such as "Giant Steps," jump rope chants, hide-and-go-seek, jingles for choosing team members and taking turns.

Another syntax model game that fits language and action is the "actions" game. Coordinated sentence structures such as "I am laughing and jumping" can be replaced by more complex modelling: "I am opening and closing my eyes but not giggling—yet."

While using objects rather than one's own body, the teacher can model similar sentence structures or variations such as the following.

(a)   Hm, what can I do with this rope?
      I can either twirl it or jump with it.
(b)   What can I do with this blanket?
      I can either fold it or hug all of you in it.
(c)   What can I do with this bottle?
      I can either spin it or play a tune with it.

A more complex variant to which a teacher might adapt after hearing the children's statements might be, "I can roll or bounce it but I cannot eat the ball." or "I can play a tune with it or pretend it's a telescope with which to see horses a mile away." A simpler form might be, "This is a hat. I can wear it or sit on it."

Children sometimes contract the "rubber band" to, "I can eat it." or "I can slip and slide." The children perceive that they are playing a game. Since the teacher's attitude aims at positive support and inductive process, there are *no right or wrong statements*. All children's syntactic responses are acceptable. The teacher's single technique to stimulate induction becomes repeated modelling of the structures with different tokens by "taking another turn to play the game." In this way a *perceivable contrast* can be created between the *figure*, the syntactic structure, and the *background* formed by the changing tokens.

The "Actions" game also lends itself to interrogative structures, for example, "This bell can ring. If I tap the bell will it ring loudly?" A more complex version might be: "If I insert this key, will it turn easily or stick in the lock?"

Approximately ninety-five percent of the children appeared able to use simple expansions and coordinations. Subordinations were the least readily used structures.

In another actions game, you can see interrogative and subordinate transformations:

(1) I can melt or light this candle.
     Should I melt or light this candle?
     I could have melted it, but, as you see,
     I lit it.
(2) I can roll or drop this egg.
     Should I roll or drop this egg?
     I could have rolled it but, as you see,
     I dropped it.

When teachers *select materials that children prefer*, children's involvement increases in the verbal as well as the manipulative aspects of the activity. Flashlights, rotary beaters, binoculars, toys, textured materials, machine parts, food items, clothing, jewelry, baseball cards, and tools have varied appeals to different children. In some cases, children have acquired additional vocabulary labels in a functioning context as by-products of the teacher models. Generally, the adult's initial models include items for which children might have less information. At the same time, children can use attractive materials that do not overload their information store. If the primary purpose is to encourage expressive language, then information load should not become a hindrance since one can hardly express oneself about unknown data.

The following protocol represents this principle in operation. At the same time, there is an opportunity to see the teacher attempt a "rubber band" expansion later in the interaction.

		Today, we can pretend to be something else.
TEACHER:	(1)	If I were a pair of glasses, I would be worn around the ears but not eaten.
	(2)	If I were a corkscrew, I would be used to open bottles but not doors.
	(3)	If I were an oil filter wrench, I would loosen filters but not heads.
	(4)	If I were an antenna, I should be attached to a car but not a chair. O.K. You take a turn.
CHILD A:		If I were a basketball I would be used on a basketball court but not to hit people.
CHILD B:		If I were a ball, I'd be used to play with but not cooked.

CHILD C: If I was some bubble gum, I would eat it but not throw it away.

CHILD D: If I was a monkey I would be holding my hand. I would not be . . .

CHILD A: If I was a key chain I would be used to open cars and doors but not bananas. This key chain is interesting because it is an alarm clock.

CHILD D: If I were a can of BB Tuna, I would be eaten but not painted.

TEACHER: If you don't see anything up there you would like to be, you can make it up.

(*Several interactions in which children use the modelled structure.*)

CHILD C: If I was Snoopy I'd play Charlie Brown.

CHILD A: If I was a light bulb I would make light so people could see in the night.

TEACHER: Nobody wants to be a pig?

CHILD D: I will. If I was a pig, I'd oink, oink and give you bacon.

TEACHER: If I were a hat band I would be worn on the head but not on the foot. OK, who goes now? OK, A.

(*Several interactions in which children use the modelled structures.*)

CHILD A: If I were a frog, I would jump in the lake and live on a lily pad but I would not be thrown away or killed.

TEACHER: (*EXPANDS MODEL*) If I were a pig, I would play in the mud and eat oats but not swim in the lake.

CHILD B: If I were bubble gum I would be eaten and not put on the floor.

CHILD C: I only wear a headache band when I have a headache.

TEACHER: If I were a football I would be thrown and kicked but not cut in half.

(*Group listens to taperecording of preceding.*)

Child C uses the dialectic form, "If I was . . ." throughout while Child A alternates between the dialectic form, after hearing Child C, and the teacher's "If I were . . ." The adult's objective would be to provide additional repeated modelling of the teacher's form and positive support for its use by the children in order to support the process of induction.

Children will occasionally expand beyond the adult's modelled structure. When the teacher noticed this, he adapted by expanding his model. It is difficult for an inexperienced teacher to adapt during interaction. In this case, the children reduced the sentence complexity to a simpler coordination as can be seen toward the end of the interchange. This has occurred in other games also. The children's participation in this game reflected a more efficient, standard use of negative expression than was usual for them.

Children enjoy costumes and dressup activities. To move away from the monotonous chartings of "We went to the zoo. We saw lions. We saw tigers. We saw monkeys.," the dressup was used as a device to encourage more efficient use of language by coordinating sentences. The more layers of clothing each participant wore, the more fun. A simple teacher model could be, "If I were going outdoors I would put on a poncho and a scarf." A more complex structure might be, "If I were going to sleep I would put on a night shirt and ear muffs but not gloves." Packing a real valise for an imaginary trip can afford similar stimulation. While it is important for the teacher to present a briskly paced set of models at the beginning, the children's involvement with some materials tends to slow the pace of verbal exchange. However, the adult asks the children to "listen to what Child B will say," or "I wonder what Child B is going to tell us about his trip . . ." as some ways to focus involvement.

Another activity that lends itself to coordination is the street map board game with miniature cars.

> TEACHER: Today we are going to give drivers directions about how to reach places in town. I'll play first and then you can give the directions.
> (1) How can I get from my house to the market? I can travel on either Red Street or Green Street.
> (2) How can I get from my house to the movies? I can travel on either Yellow Street or Purple Street.

A more complex alternate could be "I can travel on either Red Street or Green Street but not White Street. That leads to the garbage dump and I cannot eat garbage!" Still another more complex alternate, "To get to school from the shop you can take either Blue Street or Green Street and walk over the bridge, or Purple Street and Orange Street and jump over the stream."

It is apparent that these repetitive structures can be treated as cosmetized pattern drills or handled playfully, with a light touch. There is also the opportunity for the teacher to expand the bare coordinated structure represented by "I can travel on either Yellow Street or Purple Street." as the following protocol represents.

> TEACHER: OK, A, how would you get from the bowling alley to Medical Drive?
> CHILD A: Yeah, that's pretty good. We didn't get in any swamps yet.

TEACHER: You live on Green Street and your mother wants to drive you to the movies. One at a time. Oh, B . . . Tell us again how you would get from Green Street to the movies.

CHILD B: . . . Take either M Street or R Avenue.

CHILD C: Wow! You went a long way around. If you went on N Street you could have got right in his way.

TEACHER: I've got a question. Let's say you're in the park, OK? and you decided you were really hungry and you had to get to the candy store to get something to eat. So travel from B Park to the Candy Store.

CHILD D: (*Child contracts*) . . . Green Street . . . uh . . . M Road.

TEACHER: (*Teacher accepts and expands*)
OK, D, to get from B Park to the candy store, you take either G Street or M Road. Good. D, what would you do when you got to the candy store? (Child D speaks.) OK.

(*Several interactions in which children use the modelled structure.*)

TEACHER: A said that to get from B Park to the candy store you take either B Street or Maple Street. Oh, you go, C. What do you say? . . . Buy some cake? Could I have some? Thanks.

(*Several interactions in which children use the modelled structure.*)

TEACHER: Good. We went to B Park and we want to get to the bowling alley, and oh, no, we ran out of gas. In order to get from B Park to the gas station . . . C, what happened to your gas? You forgot to get gas? You'd be stuck in the bowling alley as well. Let's see if D can go a different way. . . .

The syntax model games can move beyond grammatical expansions toward expanding meanings for children. In this sense the teacher, while interacting with the semantic level of the child's comments, can follow a second agenda, the repeated modelling of a particular syntactic extension.

Many times children are expected to answer rather than ask questions in school settings. They need practice and encouragement in asking questions that help them to know more about the world. They also need practice in improving the use of questions for efficient concept attainment strategies. An interrogative game was developed to provide practice with questions.

After the children pin an animal or food or whatever picture on her back, the adult can model the interrogative form, for example, "Is it either tall or short? Is it either cold blooded or warm blooded? Can it either fly or swim?" Children tend to reduce the structure to such statements as, "Elephant!" or "Can it run fast?" The teacher might take the opportunity to expand the meaning of the child's statement, modelling a more complex structure.

This particular activity shows that the use of different sentence structures reflects different cognitive abilities. If a player has a limited number of guessing opportunities, he needs to obtain effective information through his questioning strategies. With exposure to more effective verbal models and strategies, young children become more able to focus fruitful questions rather than gambling on a label. Bruner, Goodnow, and Austin (1962) discuss related cognitive aspects in "Selection Strategies in Concept Attainment."

As evidenced by the protocols, most children did induce the games' syntactic structures while playing with the materials. Children were receptive to their exposure to the activities. In addition, they used these syntactic structures at other times with other materials in the classroom and as a playful communication with adults.

LEARNING TO READ

It is possible that, if popular music were taught in school in the same manner that reading is—short selections analyzed and used as the basis for tests—the billion dollar record industry might quickly collapse. (Stephens, 1974, p. 161)

Reading is useful and pleasurable. It is an essential economic and cultural tool. The earlier this tool is acquired, the greater is the degree of vicarious, independent, and extended experience that is open to an individual. However, rote decoding without comprehension is meaningless exercise. Many adults have decoded a printed page without having grasped any of the author's meaning because the message was beyond their readiness to deal with the content at that particular moment.

Even in the face of technological advances that may replace the constant need to read, as the pocket-size calculator appears to be replacing the need for personal speed in arithmetic computation, it is inconceivable to imagine a post-literate world. While this is not the forum for arguing whether or not children should learn to read, it is the place to talk about when it should be learned and how.

PUTTING READING IN ITS PLACE

Through the years, early childhood educators have variously argued whether or not to include reading instruction in work with five-year-olds or six-year-olds or seven-year-olds. Moore's Edison Responsive Environment, better known as the "talking typewriter," is one attempt, among others, to teach reading to nursery age children.

Montessori children receive initial instruction in the nursery years if their teacher judges that they are ready for it. There have been progressivists who have recommended the postponement of instruction until children are seven years of age, citing incomplete ocular development before that age. Regardless of these variations, the prevailing practice places "first grade," or six years of age as the time for all children to acquire this skill. This tradition is based on the Morphett and Washburn study (1931), which recommended the Mental Age of six years, six months, a study that has been questioned throughout the years.

Several considerations merit review of prevailing practice here. First, nursery age children have been able to learn to read. Durkin (1966), for one, reports many children entering kindergartens with independent reading skills already established. Second, most children learn to read in our society before they are seven years of age, apparently without an increase in ocular problems. As a matter of fact, with recent advances in the field of perceptual learning disability diagnoses, teachers are finding about fifteen percent of children who have such deficiencies within the school population even before they are expected to read. Therefore, causes of reading problems also exist elsewhere than in the act of recognizing printed symbols.

It is a constant wonder in the light of research findings into the great range of capacity within a chronological age group that adults continue to be concerned with the starting *age* for instruction. It would be better to regard "readiness" as a life-long state, beginning in the cradle for each person. Then, the teacher's task is to diagnose the child's skill at a given time and to provide instruction at the next level of complexity.

Educators speak of "teachable moments" and "sensitive periods" when the time is ripest for learning particular skills. Vygotsky (1962) found that

... instruction usually precedes development. The child acquires certain habits and skills in a given area before he learns to apply them consciously and deliberately. ... Therefore the only good kind of instruction is that which marches ahead of development and leads it; it must be aimed not so much at the ripe as at the ripening function. (pp. 101, 104)

Hunt (1961) also deals extensively with the question of matching instruction to development as a central issue in education, and reviews related research that touches the issue of the "most" sensitive periods. At this point in educational history, adults are likely to be aware of sensitive periods when they have been missed and children develop remediation needs. In a relevant review of reading readiness, British researchers suggest that readiness is a "dynamic" condition, reflected in the "flexible" interaction between teacher and child rather than a rigid date (Downing and Thackray, 1971, p. 99, *passim*).

Part of the problem about the teaching of reading is that early childhood educators have frequently asked "What might children better be doing with their time besides reading?" I am not so sure that a child could be doing anything more important with his time than to learn as much as he can in ways that make him feel human and competent. At the same time, I feel strongly that a program which focusses on the 3 R's to the exclusion of basic substance is a program that tries to place disembodied tools into a child's hands.

When teachers attempt to develop skills in a sterile atmosphere, it is akin to dosing babies with medication that kills the necessary along with the unwanted bacteria. The babies' subsequent digestive upsets may be reversed. Are teachers so certain that they can reverse as readily the "school game" of feigned attention as a facade for boredom that children learn as a by-product of content-poor early schooling!?

The fact remains that learning to read is not an end in itself but a tool skill that can help to support substantively based activity, that can help extend and capture a range of possible meanings for children. It is particularly unfortunate that the pressure for disadvantaged children to learn to read has taken a linear direction, largely excluding meaning, rather than a curved direction which may be more direct in the long range as noted in Chapter 2.

It is worth looking at the most efficient ways to do what needs doing while retaining a medium in which substantive activity continues. The sooner children reach a level of comprehension in their reading that approaches their level of interest, the sooner reading can function as the tool it can be. Early success breeds a feeling of competence and purposeful, natural use of this tool. As with any skill, coordination and comfort in its use accrues with practice. As noted in Chapter 3, motivation is likely to be increased by such a feeling of competence. In addition, strong motives to read grow out of solid activities and stimulating dialogue.

For these reasons, many teachers do not shy away from systematic instruction in decoding skills that help children move toward the recognition of printed symbols. You cannot expect young children to recapitulate the history of the human race until first grade and then suddenly be assaulted by several hundred years of pedagogic tradition at once.

Since learning to speak is the most complex task a living organism can accomplish, learning to read should be comparatively simple. Many of the same principles that applied to the syntax model games and early speech development parallel and support the young child's developmental modes of learning.

READING PHASES

The section that follows presents the decoding phase, the recognition of printed symbols. However, decoding is only one technical part of learning to read. There is general agreement by reading specialists that three phases can be identified. These phases include the recognition of the printed symbol, the comprehension of the author's meaning, and the utilization of these understandings.

Very briefly, the *recognition* of the printed symbol requires sensory and perceptual faculties. Various conventions are understood, such as the notion of a word, that symbols represent words, that the same symbols have the same sounds, and that they are represented in a left-to-right sequence in English. Fries (1952) suggests that the reader develops a range of habitual responses to a specific set of *contrasting patterns* of graphic shapes. Practice strengthens habits.

The *comprehension* of the author's meaning requires the operation of memory, association, anticipation, and generalization skills. One's purpose in reading "sets" one to understand because the reader brings connotative meanings to the material (Freud, 1932). It has been said that the reader who brings more to the material will get more out of it (Chall, 1967).

Just as decoding skills precede comprehension, comprehension precedes *utilization* of what has been read. Beyond comprehension, reading can add to experience as you use the understandings you have gained to act, think about, or simply enjoy. For example, when reading makes you laugh, you have used past experience.

Because of these complex components, reading is probably one of the classiest habits humans can acquire. Since practice strengthens habits, and real habits are self-motivated, the role of the teacher is to support self-motivation by providing opportunities for such self-motivated learning to take place. Practice, in and of itself, does not cause learning but provides the time for inductive processes that do. At this time we should note that children who may learn faster require less practice. However, the more opportunities children of the same general age have to develop skills, the wider the range of differences between them will grow. Therefore, homogeneous grouping is a myth. Any grouping that exists should be for a specific short-range purpose such as the particular skill of contrasting "bet-better," "mat-matter," "bit-bitter," or the particular interest in discussing sports books of varied complexity.

However, when lay people and teachers talk about learning to read, they most often refer to the decoding phase. There have been a great many different methods of teaching decoding that have been used by teachers. These fall into two major types: the "whole" or analytic method and the "part" or synthetic method.

WHOLE AND PART METHODS

In the methods variously referred to as the "whole word," "look–say," and "sight word" methods, children begin with whole words whose configuration, or outline, they are expected to memorize. In this approach, children usually operate with various reduced cues such as the initial letter of the word or the outline of the word's letters that rise above or below the line, or the length of the word, or the nearby picture in the basal reader. A classic anecdote is that of the teacher who uses a set of word cards that a child successfully reads. However, he can never seem to recognize one of these words in his book. When she asks him how he knows the word on the card, he points to the smudge in the corner of the card!

One educator suggests that "sight-memorizing" whole words is like teaching a language that has no alphabet, where each word is a separate symbol (Tudor-Hart, pp. 28–29). Despite these considerations, many children do learn to read by using the whole word approach. They make their own inductions about the regular patterns that they can apply to decipher other words. Many other children are unable to do so.

Usually, when teachers begin with the "whole word" method, they introduce "sounding out" toward the end of the first year or after children have achieved a body of "recognition" words. "Phonics" is the school-based instructional program for this second method. Children are taught isolated *sounds* such as "b-uh" as the sound made when you see the *letter* "bee." Vowels are marked phonetically, according to the conventions of the International Phonetics Alphabet, so that children can differentiate ă as in fat from ā as in fate. The children are told the generalizations and are expected to apply them deductively. There are a range of combinations of phonics and the look–say method that teachers have used.

When you look at "phonics" instruction, you can see an example of how "readiness" is not simply related to maturation. Readiness to learn to read by using the deductive means of phonics is quite different from readiness to learn to read by using inductive means. Particularly with young children, "readiness" needs to be directed toward, and defined by, a particular method of instruction.

The *synthetic methods vary* along a continuum from the traditional phonics instruction that follows a recognition vocabulary to an initial introduction of isolated sounds or *contrasting patterns of sounds* that are bound to other sounds. The variations in programs relate to such issues as whether or not children need to learn letter names before sound values, whether or not capital letters should be used, whether or not nonsense syllables should be employed for instructional purposes, and whether or not words should be built from left to right as in Stern's use of "ma/n" or right to left as in Gattegno's (1969) or Fries' or Bloomfield's "an" to "man."

Opponents of the synthetic methods contend that since meaning is the most important function of reading, only whole words should be employed. Given an understanding of the way in which words pattern in sentences, it could be argued further that whole sentences provide more accurate meanings and, therefore, that some words are definable only in the context of a sentence.

Really, when you look at these camps, there are many connecting paths that join them if you consider the psychology of reading as a combined act of sensation, perception, and comprehension. For example, when very young children look at television, see road signs, and labels on boxes, they are responding on the basis of whole word recognitions with particular context clues. When children write words and sentences in which they are interested from copy, they are combining both approaches. The entire "language-experience" and writing trends in the field of reading instruction support both approaches. These are discussed later. In addition, *after* children have developed independent word attack skills, part of their growth in reading more rapidly is related to their use of reduced configurational clues.

For the present, some definitions will precede a look at some decoding games and some principles underlying them. "Independent reading" will refer to the ability of a child to decipher new words with the major range of sound-symbol relations at hand. "Beginning reading" will refer to the process of "breaking the code" and acquiring these relations. "Prereading skills" will refer to the multi-sensory and cognitive support systems that contribute to beginning reading. The inaccurate assumption that reading readiness begins and ends in a workbook, or any other preset program should be dispelled by an activity based program.

THE ROLE OF THE TEACHER IN DECODING GAMES

A primary principle when teachers use inductive decoding games is to provide *contrasting patterns of phonemes*. The phoneme is the smallest range of sound that can change the meaning of a word. The transformation of the word "*mat*" to "*th*at" represents a single phonemic substitution. Although "*th*" is written with two graphemes, it is a single sound or phoneme. Inasmuch as a phoneme is a "range" of sound, children learn to categorize this range in our language. For example, you place the "l" in "bald" and "love" at different parts of your mouth because of its contrasting context within the words. When the teacher contrasts patterns of phonemes in order to help children read, those children who are ready have an opportunity to perceive the differences between phonemes relative to their native language.

The new variable needs to be contrasted against a background of known elements if it is to stand out and really be a contrasting pattern. When there are too many variables, it is more difficult for children to induce the new phoneme.

Wherever possible, self-checking devices are usefully included. For example, self-checking devices include puzzle pieces that fit, a picture on the opposite side of a card for a child to check if a word was read correctly, and opportunities to match responses against other possible responses.

A second principle is that the teacher needs to *model the new phoneme several times in a functional context*. When the teacher avoids "naked consonants" by keeping them verbalized in a functional context, then later blending problems can be avoided. For example, it is practically impossible to state a consonant sound alone. It comes out as a "*b*uh" or "*k*uh" or "*s*uh." When children who were taught to read using phonics or "sounding out" methods meet a new word, the "naked consonants" slow them down so that "*s*uh-*t*uh-*o*-*p*uh" for some children becomes distorted as "supper" rather than "stop."

A third principle is that the *simpler* and more commonly used phonemes should be taught *before* the *more variable* and less commonly used phonemes. For example, the "common" sounds of the vowels such as in b*a*t, b*e*t, b*i*t, b*u*t, and l*o*t, are simpler to learn than the "name" sounds of the vowels such as in b*a*ke, b*e*at, b*e*, b*o*at, or r*u*le, which require accompanying patterns and are less regularly spelled. Similarly, consonants such as the "c" in *c*at and fa*c*e or "g" as in *g*as and *g*em are more complex than "m" or "b" which do not require conservation ability.

A *vicariousness index* can operate as a corollary to the simple-to-complex sequence of sounds. Concrete materials would be used before pictures at the prereading level, and pictures would be used in the transition to written symbols—graphemes. When children have trouble, simply go back toward the concrete from the symbolic.

A fourth principle derives from the third. Presumably, if you can see the sequence of phonemic complexity offered to us by linguists, you will have some idea of which skill is easier or more complex than the particular new variable with which a decoding game opens. Therefore it helps to plan for the possibility that *the focus may need to be simplified or made more complex,* or varied for different children who are playing together, starting with the prereading level. In addition, in order to support such variation starting at the beginning-reading level, it is useful to keep writing materials handy for the teacher in order that he or she may provide a simpler alternative or build up phonemes as needed.

Whenever possible, it is useful to *avoid competition* in these games. It is more useful for the teacher to appreciate children's growing skills and focussed efforts. Some of the competition can be avoided or underplayed by individualizing tasks beforehand so that all of the "Bingo" cards finish together, or that different "Slapjack" players are set to slap different variables that appear in equivalent quantity. It appears that there are many arenas where human beings do battle with each other. If children could perceive their own learning to read in a neutral, straightforward manner, with less fear and pressure, then it is possible that fewer learning blocks would occur. Frequently, a competitive atmosphere is a signal to the teacher that children's self-confidence has been shaken.

Better still, many children learn to read without apparent effort, under conditions where widely different methods have been employed. They induce the contrasting patterns of phonemes and are able to become independent readers rather smoothly. However, the majority of children require varying degrees of systematic help in acquiring this skill. *The professional teacher's greatest contribution is systematic help when it is needed.*

Decoding games can be a vehicle for systematically presenting phonemic contrasts so that children can induce the patterns. These games involve the use of concrete materials. These materials are tied to a rich language and experiential environment that helps the children to become saturated with written language as well as with spoken language.

DECODING GAMES

It is easiest for children to play when the teacher models the game by simply doing it. The teacher opens each session by showing the children the new phonemic variable contrasted several times against known elements, and then models the game. A look at specific games will clarify this procedure.

Pairs. The game of "Pairs" or "Concentration" is particularly adaptable to almost any skill level. It could almost be an entire sequence in and of itself. In addition, children are highly motivated to focus on the cards that are turned, face down, as they try to pick a pair. For this game, it is also possible to set different children different tasks.

Pre-reading Level. For example, a set of cards could match pictures that begin with the same sound as boy, box, or ball. A different game could focus on the pictures that begin with the same sound as pig, pen, parrot. Still another game could combine these beginning sounds that are sometimes confused. Still another game could be pictures that end with the same sound as hammer, fur, and car, or with pictures of words that rhyme.

Before the picture level of sound discriminations is reached, children need to learn to play the game itself. The teacher plays the game with them and asks them to turn over two cards to let others see, to tell what they see, and then to replace cards in the same locations if they do not match. It is an exciting moment when the cards do match, and the teacher adds, "You really are concentrating." One of the participants can then place the pair in its storage container.

The success element can be simplified and increased by constructing a three-by-four game. The game can gradually build toward a twenty-by-two game for five-year-olds onward. The earliest cards may simply be those pictures, shapes, or colors that are the same, or pairs of animal pictures or flower pictures or outdoor–indoor picture pairs. "Number Concentration" and "Capital Letter Concentration" in which children match cards with the same number of objects on them, or match a capital letter with a lowercase letter, have also been used successfully with four-year-olds (McGinn and Rudnick, 1973). Since young children should not have to wait a long time for their turn, anywhere from two to four players is a sufficient number.

Beginning Reading Level. For children who have played at matching pairs, the addition of a card with the "ă" pronounced on it can be made to an ongoing set of pictures or shapes, with the number of cards newly reduced for this occasion. This procedure can make for a smooth transition. When "at" is added, then "ᵢₗat," with one set of four cards in each new game, the "a" cards can be retired. (See Figure 4.) Many five-year-olds are able to handle and enjoy this activity. By the time "at" has retired and four or five different initial consonants with four cards each have been added, the children are ready for a reduced number of variables, the return of "at," and the addition of "it." The "it" family can build words with the same initial consonants. In this manner, the game of pairs continues to expand through the other simple consonant-vowel-consonant word patterns such as "tan," "tip," "tub," "run," and so forth, over a period of weeks.

The ccvc (consonant-consonant-vowel-consonant) patterns such as the

One possible beginning sequence of phonemes for decoding at the beginning reading level:

> a : at
> at : mat : sat : pat : fat, etc.
> pat : pit, sit, etc. ⟶ pit : pin, fin, etc.
> pat : pan, fan, etc. ⟶ pin, fin, etc. ⟶ pun, sun, etc.

Adding one variable in each game:

| (First Game) | 2 × 4 = a, a, a, a, at, at, at, at |
| | |

(First
Game)   2 × 4 = a, a, a, a,
                    at, at, at, at

(Second
Game)   3 × 4 = at, at, at, at
                    mat, mat, mat, mat
                    sat, sat, sat, sat

(Third
Game)   3 × 4 = mat, mat, mat, mat
                    sat, sat, sat, sat
                    pat, pat, pat, pat

(Fourth
Game)   2 × 4 = pat : pit
                    sat : sit
                    hat : hit
                    fat : fit

(Seventh
Game)   Model structure: If this is pot and this is pet.
                            If this is lot and this is let
                            If this is not then this is: [net].

FIGURE 4

words flat, slit, stop, and plum are built in a similar way, as well as the cvcc patterns such as felt, soft, and bend. Words such as plums and sends are natural extensions of these sound patterns. Here we see a progression of common phonemic patterns in which there is a one-to-one correspondence between sound and symbol. This sequence has been loosely adapted with reference to a variety of linguistically based reading series (Gattegno, 1968; Fries, 1952; Stern and Gould, 1965; and Bloomfield, 1961).

As children become more proficient, word families such as "ill," "ick," and "ack" words, patterns such as "hat-hate" and "bit-bite," commonly used digraphs such as in *sh*ut, *ch*ip, and *th*is and *th*ink, and vowel digraphs represented in patterns such as "set-seat" and "got-goat" can be added gradually and in turn. For example, well beyond the cvc stage, "bet-beat," "met-meat," "net-neat," "pet-peat," and "set-seat," may comprise one game of Pairs.

When teachers try to teach several vowel digraphs together at one time, natural induction of the pattern is defeated. Such teaching usually depends on deductive applications of general principles—therefore, it is inappropriate for young children. It is more natural for children to acquire their reading skills inductively in a functional setting, with one new variable at a time.

Independent Reading Level. In the course of becoming an independent reader, a child may acquire the ability to recognize some words as whole entities without really having grasped the underlying phonemic properties. There may be no functional comprehension problem. However, because a child has acquired the sight-word does not necessarily mean that he can apply the component patterns in other words. This is one of the diagnostic problems faced in remediation situations or with children beyond the early childhood years who seem blocked from further reading development.

At the independent reading stage, variant endings such as "half-halves," or "baby:babies" (vcc:ies) as opposed to "toy:toys" (vc:s) and "bike:bikes" (vcv:s) may need to be learned. Practice with "er," "ir," and "ur," or the "scr" and "thr" combinations is sometimes necessary, to name a few. These various phonemic patterns can be contrasted by using the game of Pairs as well as other games described in the next section.

Other Card Games. Several card games such as "Slapjack" and "Go Fish" can be similarly adapted to develop skills sequentially. At the *pre-reading* level, *pictures* are used to acquaint children with the game format and then to help them focus on similarities and differences in the sounds.

For example, a Slapjack game with three children and the teacher might focus one child on pictures that begin with the same sound as train or tricycle but not top or table. Another child might be asked to focus on words that rhyme with sink or pink but not with ring or string, while yet another child would be asked to focus on pictures that rhyme with cat or mat but not with net or jet. Some children show a sense of cooperation in this setting and help each other when a picture opportunity is about to be missed. This would be a difficult game at the pre-reading level, designed only for those children who had manifested their readiness for finer sound discriminations.

In the Go Fish game, players each receive four cards from the deck, and then ask each other for a card that goes with one of the pictures they are holding. Before the game begins, the teacher shares common labels for the group to use so that the picture of the mouse is not taken to be a rat, or the dish to be a plate. As each child receives a pair of pictures whose labels rhyme, the pairs are set aside. Otherwise, the child "fishes" for an additional card from the deck. Trios or quartets of cards rather than pairs can be used with older children at the picture level.

Card games serve as an opportunity for the teacher to provide initial instruction through a brief modelling of the game. They can be easily simplified or made more complex. They also serve to provide an opportunity for children to play with each other independently, and to solidify the particular skills. A detail to keep in mind is that young children have physical difficulty holding a "fan" of cards. A short length of wood can be sawn halfway down in order to provide a convenient stand for the cards, similar to a "Scrabble" game stand.

Slapjack, along with Lotto board games, is a good transition to beginning reading because the cards are open to all. These games capitalize on the fact that children *can match word forms before they can read them*. A useful lotto sequence includes a board face with eight to twelve pictures that are labelled. The back of the board contains only the labels. The card faces and backs are made similarly.

At the point of "breaking the code," after children cover pictures with pictures, one or more children can cover pictures on the board with word cards. Some fours, and many five-year-olds can match in this way after practice. The next step would be to match the words on the back of the board with the face of the picture-and-word cards, moving finally to the word-to-word matching.

If these card games are to be instructional rather than mere review or testing, the gradual addition of variables needs to be carefully controlled by the teacher. Occasionally, a social affiliation for the game's sake stretches one child rather than another. This should not be a major problem for the children or teacher who keep a flexible perspective. At instructional opportunities, the teacher can provide a model for the contrasting phonemes in these games much as he did for the Pairs game.

Board Games. Board games represent still another form in which decoding instruction can be supported. The format of games that require dice, a set of cards, a spinner card, or a set of tokens can easily be adapted to the various reading levels mentioned. These various implements serve to direct the player to move a token along a path marked on the board. When the commercial "Twister" game (Milton Bradley) is adapted, the markings represent phonemic patterns needed by the children. Teachers have constructed their own "Twister" boards for phonemic instruction by attaching together large paper bags from the food market with masking tape.

One inch wood cubes to serve as substitute dice, can be taped with the colors or shapes or words to be rhymed, which appear on the board. A set of cards can be prepared that directs the movement of pieces to sections that are marked for particular phonemic distinctions. When cards or cubes are marked for directions, the game may be changed easily by changing the cards or cubes rather than an entire board.

This is also a flexible aspect of using cards with a spinner device to point where a child will go. Each of several concentric circles can be designated for each of the players. In this way, the teacher can individualize the game. Commercial spinners with a rubber suction attachment (Commercial Complements) are easily transferred to different spinner cards for different games.

For more advanced players, there is a variation of "Chinese Checkers" in which the object of the game is to move tokens to opposite sides of a board designed as a grid. The tokens can be small cards or bottle caps or container covers that look identical. Children can begin with three or four and then build to six tokens. The players need to focus on moving their own tokens rather than confusing them with those of another player. When different players need to focus on a particular phonemic pattern that is face downward, such as words ending in "le" or "al," they come away with a clear image of it after the game.

There are many imaginative colorful themes and arrangements that teachers use when they custom design board games for the children with whom they work. Since it is time-consuming to develop these games, it is worthwhile to use sturdy materials and to cover them with clear plastic. They become part of a teacher's needed stock of materials that will build along with the collected stock of ideas for other direct activities that children can find so stimulating.

Games with Objects.   Games with objects are needed particularly with the youngest children who also would play with visual and auditory discrimination in their daily activities. Children can sort objects that begin with the same sound as house and hat into the brightly colored "horse" box while they place objects that begin with the same sound as feather and fig into the "fruit" box. Children can similarly sort small objects that rhyme.

Another sorting device that has prestige appeal in the child's culture is a cabinet of small transparent plastic drawers usually found in carpentry shops. For example, eighteen such drawers are available in a ten by fifteen inch size cabinet. Teachers have a taped word beginning with a different sound on each drawer. Inside the drawer are miniature objects that begin with the same sound. Children can empty a few drawers into a cloth and sort the objects into the drawers, or remove objects from a drawstring bag and sort them into the drawers. The same cabinet can be used for number sorting or picture and word sorting.

Sound and Word Readiness.   However, for some children who enter nursery school, sound itself is not yet this kind of *conscious* "figure" in their background experiences. For these children, instruction recreates the earliest kinds of interactions of parent and child, when the parent mentions body parts, labels objects, and sings Mother Goose rhymes. Is it not interesting how easily singing comes to adults when children are very small?

In a like manner, teachers of very young children need to provide verbal labels and descriptions for everyday events and materials. Just as the new parents' language and music helps to bring the baby into the world of sounds, the nursery teacher helps young children begin to differentiate sounds through speaking and singing with them. Just as the teacher of very young children bathes them in *verbal* labels and descriptions, teachers in succeeding years need to soak them with *visual* labels and descriptions in these functional ways.

The awareness of language as an auditory stimulant may be supported by general sound awareness of thunder, trees moving in the wind, rain falling, snow falling in contrast with the rain, motors, tires, footsteps when walking, running, hopping, or jumping with sneakers or shoes, on grass and on pavement, doors closing, paper rustling, blocks falling, water dripping, glass breaking, and so forth. Children can simply close their eyes, focus on sounds, and then share their perceptions with each other and the teacher.

When children compare sounds, seriate sounds, and translate these comparisons into creative movements through space, they are building their imagery system and their ability to transpose experiences from one sensory source into another. In a parallel way, written symbols involve the translation of meaningful auditory experiences into visual symbols.

Recognition Skills and Recall Skills. In these activities that focus on contrasting sound patterns, children are using recognition skills. *Recognition* skills are easier to apply than are *recall* skills. Therefore, an extension of games with objects would be to ask children to find other objects in the room, or in a box, that rhyme with hair and bear, or begin with the same sound as wolf and wish. A frequently used play is "I Spy" something that begins with the same sound as Deborah, or "I Spy" someone whose name ends with the same sound as the name Eden.

Still another step would be for children to recall objects that are not visible. For example, riddles with rhymes require skills in recall: "I love the beach but I cannot eat it. I can eat a (peach)," or, "This begins with the same sound as Daddy but I play with it. It is a (doll)." Riddles serve as a source of delight to youngsters, particularly those that children create beyond the range of adult sophistication. These kinds of activities provide teachers with children who are actively participating. Through such participation, it is possible to diagnose which sound confuses children at one level. At another level, the teacher can assess whether they have trouble differentiating a "b" from a "d" in a printed word.

After children have dealt with objects and pictures, and learned through repetition that the teacher uses the terms "word" and "object" to mean the same thing, they gain a consciousness of "word." Researchers make the point that disadvantaged children perceive language as welded phrases (Bereiter and Engelmann, 1967). Words provide greater flexibility than do phrases.

The sense of "wordness" also begins at the auditory level when objects are labelled and discussed. Teachers of young children functionally integrate the terms "word" and "sound." The idea of a "word" takes on added meaning when the children see the teacher "write words." These activities underscore the point that teachers should talk about what they are doing when they are doing it.

In addition, the teacher points along a line of print as she reads a story in order to add to the child's sense of a word. It is an interesting variation when the teacher reads stories or poems using an overhead projector, pointing to the words as he reads (Moffett, 1968; Anderson, 1968). This medium adds to the children's ability to focus. To further support this idea of a word, some teachers who speak or read a short sentence ask the children how many words they heard (Mackay et al., 1970).

When children can interchange words more freely, there is much greater flexibility and scope to their speech. Similarly, when children have the sense that they can interchange phonemes more freely, their reading skill gains more flexibility and scope. The teacher who helps a child to use *contrasting patterns as a basis for self-correction through comparison* does much to help that child become an independent reader.

On a visual level, you cannot take it for granted that all children understand that a space signifies the separation between words unless children have been exposed to this notion. Nor can you expect them to orient their reading and writing in left-to-right, top-to-bottom directions, unless there have been functionally pointed, repeated exposures. From the earliest times, teachers of young children write a child's name on his drawing and tell the child what is being done. Whenever writing or sequential arrangements are under way, the teacher notes that they begin at the left. Whenever the teacher creates board games for children, they are constructed so that tokens move from the left to the right and from the top of the board downward. With all this repetition, it is still natural for children to make written or visual reversals occasionally. Most of this has passed by the time a child reaches the age of seven years. Occasionally, however, individuals reverse sounds or a word in speaking or reading into adulthood.

The activities described above are meant to serve as examples of a functional use of written language in the learning of reading. When all is said and done, it is unlikely that anyone can teach another to read. Even when that other one is ready, it is he, himself, who takes the inductive leap that ties meanings and sounds with symbolic sights. The teacher creates conditions that help children accomplish this task in a natural way.

It bears reiteration at this point that young children cannot be expected, nor need they be required, to manifest self-awareness of their own learning. Most of those adults who were fortunate in childhood have no memory of learning to read as a distinct entity. It felt effortless. Your major concern should be with the children's own feeling of competence. A metalanguage that attempts to provide children with additional language to apply to their reading activity is unnecessary in this construction. For this reason, inductively ordered activities have been presented as ways to support children at their own levels of readiness and challenge.

WRITING HELPS READING AND COMMUNICATION

This section deals with the various ways in which writing that is taught simultaneously with reading furthers the ability to read written speech. Writing is also a means, a tool for expressing the order one makes out of experiences. Systematic decoding skills must be learned in a context of rich sociocognitive development. Comprehension itself is not inherent in the act of decoding. One either understands or does not understand, whether he has read, or heard somebody else read, the same text with his intonation patterns. Substantively based activities support comprehension by adding variety and scope to one's alternative interpretations.

The traditional "language arts" designation in educational circles speaks of the receptive modes of listening and reading and the expressive modes of speaking and writing. Just as listening and speaking enrich one another, reading and writing are similarly integrated. A reading specialist makes the germane point that "Writing serves as a bridge between the parts and the wholes" (Hildreth, 1964, p. 156).

Writing involves technique, meaning, and motives just as does reading. Writing involves a kinesthetic addition to the other coordinated visual and auditory perceptions of letter shapes. Writing in turn creates an auditory loss of emphasis and intonation. When they write, young children encounter a major problem because they cannot write fast enough to meet their expressive needs. This is the other side of the reading problem of decoding becoming efficient enough to match the child's interest in the subject matter.

One way suggested earlier to help the young child deal with this gap between interest and coordination in reading was to cope first with the recognition level of sounds within the contexts of words and then to move to the recall level later. A primary consideration in the use of inductive games was to help children become actively involved participants who could feel competent.

SOME APPROACHES

The dilemma of bypassing the technical coordination of handwriting and recall of word parts has been touched in ways as varied as the meticulous copying of newly read words (Spalding, 1969); Fernald's remedial approach to reading in which the teacher holds the child's hand while they write and slowly pronounce each word together (Smith and Dechant, 1961); Montessori's emphasis on having children write the words they read; the use of the "talking typewriter" (Moore and Anderson, 1968); the acceptance of a child's own spelling patterns (Chomsky, 1971); and the "sentence makers" and "word makers" (Mackay, et al., 1970).

The first two methods rely heavily on handwriting, Fernald's remediation technique uses handwriting, after tracing words, as a way to overcome reversal problems and to help focus the learner visually and auditorially as well as kinesthetically. The teacher and learner may even need to hold the pencil together in order to help coordination along. Once the individual feels the direction of movements in his hand, he may become independent. If you have ever needed to write a word to feel sure of its spelling you may sympathize with this approach. For Montessori, the writing serves as additional sensorial reinforcement for reading.

The "talking typewriter" overcomes the need for handwriting as very young children gradually construct the words at the same time that they learn to read them. As the typewriter keys are locked and unlocked, the keys named, and words constructed, children begin to read and write. Trial and error is an important component in discovering unlocked keys. The "environment" in this setting is "responsive."

Chomsky (1971) contends that for the young child, "the natural order is writing first, then reading what you have written" (p. 292). She feels that a real sense of competence, along with the notion of speech-that-is-recorded in the idiosyncratic spelling system of the young child, will provide a strong, active learning experience when adults have an accepting attitude. She points out that the child who selects the plastic letter "r" to represent "w" in the word "wet" is reminding adults that this is the way he pronounces it.

The Breakthrough to Literacy Program.   Mackay et al.'s (1970) attempt to bypass the technical coordinations of handwriting and the recall of word parts is an intriguing program. Their materials have been used with thousands of English children. The first material children use is the "sentence maker." This consists of a three part oaktag folder, each part about nine by eleven inches. The folder stands up to form a kind of private study carrel and folds flat for easy storage. The interior consists of nine rows of pocket slots into which children can match word cards that correspond to the words that are printed on part of the folder. A section of the folder is blank so that children can add "personal" word cards to these slots. "Personal" words are written by the teacher on an oaktag strip printed with a double line for unappended lowercase letters. In that way letters that extend above and below the central part of the letters are clear, for example, : : j : :.

The teacher keeps a scissors and the oaktag strip at hand, writes a word when a child asks for it, and cuts it off the strip. The child then takes the word card to his folder and stand. The plastic stand is similar to those used in Scrabble. He may add other preprinted word cards, or question mark or period cards, to the stand until he feels finished. He may be able to recognize some of these words himself or ask another child or the teacher to select the card he needs from an alphabetized file or a pouch pocket storage device that hangs on the wall. A labelled carpenter's drawer cabinet might serve equally well.

The child may read his statement to another child or the teacher and then write it in a notebook or on a picture he has made. In this way, his ideas do not need to face the danger of loss while he slowly coordinates his handwriting. Moreover, if he was not yet able to write, he might still compose his ideas on the stand.

One exciting aspect of this material is that a child can express his own ideas and create his own reading text. What the child says has meaning for him and is expressed as he would speak, using his own natural syntactic patterns.

This is part of the "language-experience" tradition. However, in the "language-experience" tradition, the children usually dictate and the teacher records. It is helpful when "The problem of suitable vocabulary for the culturally deprived or the language handicapped can diminish in the experience chart" (DeBoer and Dallman, p. 548).

In either instance, handwriting instruction can be integrated by the teacher simply stating what she is doing while she is doing it, for example, "To write this *o*, I start at the top, move counterclockwise, and close the circle." As the teacher repeats the directions, and speaks in terms of curves and straight lines, most handwriting needs are satisfied. Occasionally, a child will need the kinesthetic support of the teacher helping him move his hand while stating the directions. The "s" is one letter that children find particularly difficult.

In addition, the "sentence maker" contributes to the children's concrete understanding of syntax as children set words in the stand. When they read back what they have selected, they frequently fill in "grammatical" words and their usual spoken syntax even though the stand may only consist of a few "lexical" words that have "high information content" in random order (Mackay et al., p. 96). When the teacher asks the child to read each word card separately in the order set on the stand, the children gain an appreciation of the contrasting patterns of words in sentences. At other times, an observer could see a child rearranging or inserting new word cards as he sees the need for meaning in their order. These are learnings that come more directly in this way than by copying from dictated script. The left to right sequence is reinforced by a mark at the left side of the stand that children come to accept as the starting point for a sentence.

The teacher understands that the child's statements with written words may reflect a much more profound level of interest than their face value. A child who composed "my dad said to me you go upstairs" was reflecting a rejection of her presence and the denial of television privileges, quite a bit of drama for so simple looking a statement (pp. 109–110).

The teacher also needs to understand the child's "telegraphic" utterances with written words from a developmental standpoint. Just as McNeill (1970) speaks of new speech as a unique syntax, and Chomsky (1971) notes "telegraphic" kinds of spelling patterns. Mackay et al. observed a parallel shrinking of children's written syntax. These observations may be set against the "rubber band" notion of spoken syntax mentioned earlier in this chapter.

In addition, the parallel notion of Hayakawa's (1939) "abstraction ladder" may be useful. He provides the example of the "cow known to science . . . the cow we perceive . . . the word "Bessie" . . . the word "cow" . . . "livestock" . . . "farm assets" . . . "assets" . . . "wealth" (pp. 165, ff.). In the process of learning language itself, you may set up a parallel abstraction ladder of comparisons:

concrete object : concrete object
concrete object : picture
      picture : picture
      picture : symbol
      symbol : symbol

When children can deal with words and sounds in relation to objects, they may be ready for the next vicarious level of contrasting objects and pictures, and so forth. When a teacher notices that a child has difficulty at a particular level of abstraction, then it seems reasonable to move to a less vicarious level.

Vygotsky (1962) speaks of writing as "a second degree of symbolization" (p. 99). However, in my opinion, *the "sentence maker" materials serve to situate the activity of writing at the more concrete level of recognition as opposed to recall.* In addition, the materials suggest, and the good teacher accepts, that children naturally shrink the symbolic "rubber band" in the form of "telegraphic" written utterances. Even after a child has "graduated" from the stand and is writing at the recall level without the use of the stand, teachers have noticed that he may "revert to simple sentence making for a time" (Mackay et al., p. 156). The teacher needs to see these developmental phases as part of a child's natural rhythm of language development.

When the children's recall level of spelling is reached, children receive the "word makers" that consist of phoneme cards for word building in a smaller, two part slotted folder. Spelling games similar to Gattegno's (1968) game of transformations are also used.

The game of transformations has four rules for transforming a starting word such as "pat" into a concluding word such as "stops" (pat → pot → pop → top → stop → stops). The player can substitute, reverse, add, or insert, but not subtract, one letter at a time. In addition, children using the "word makers" collect words representing objects around the room that begin with a common sound. They also play at unscrambling words, and find words in the symbols of their own names. These activities add flexibility to the child's range of writing possibilities. Capital letters are also added after the children have achieved proficiency with the sentence makers.

In the course of these kinds of writing activities, the children themselves are actively relating their own concerns. The several hundred children that I saw using these materials viewed them as satisfying privileges that they had achieved. They composed their sentences, recorded them in notebooks, created illustrations for their statements, and created their own illustrated books with narrative as early as the kindergarten year. Within the same settings, they also played with blocks, dramatics materials, water, clay, crafts, and a full range of other concrete materials.

More Writing Activities.   However, appreciation for the enthusiasm of these children need not limit other kinds of writing activities that teachers have used successfully with children. Teachers of young children have used the "experience chart" as a vehicle for showing children that what they say can be recorded and that the teacher can help them to retrieve the message by reading it at another time. Good teachers have not used these dictated messages as a rote memory activity.

Frequently, recipes are written on large sheets of paper with picture accompaniment. Furniture is labelled, as are doors, windows, and the directions of east-west-north-and-south. Children have worn lapel card labels of their roles in sociodramatic play such as "doctor," "baby," and "mother" (Mackay et al., p. 7). In addition, children can play with letters or words on flannel boards and magnet boards with or without pictorial accompaniment depending upon children's capacities.

Some four-year-olds and most five-year-olds can write their own name and recognize the names of other children if they have had repeated opportunities to see them. Motivation for writing one's own name is high and can be a welcome first writing activity. The book *Rosa-too-Little* by Felt can only serve to add inspiration. In this book, a preschool city child secretly practices writing her own name in order to obtain a library card. After children can write their own names, teachers of five-year-olds arrange a trip to the local library where they can receive library cards.

When the teacher feels that a child might like to discuss a drawing or painting, she could ask the child, "Would you like me to write what you were thinking while you were drawing?" or "Do you want to tell me about your picture so I can write down what you say?" A young child might not have planned or produced a representational drawing. Therefore, a teacher would not ask, "What did you draw?" since that could suggest that representation or a particular standard was required.

A group of pictures with brief dictated narratives could be bound and become a class book on a particular topic such as "Looking Out the Window," or "October Picture," or "Wheels," or "Food," or "Dinosaurs," or "Motors." Such a book might circulate at the reading corner or even overnight at home.

Shopping lists, plans for parties, notices of special events, notices of daily activities, special instructions, letters to a sick child, a thank you note to a toy donor, and invitations to a parent to assist at a trip are other kinds of opportunities for writing and dictating. Anderson (1968) recommends a "News-Item Chart," a sort of newspaper broadside that could contain such information as, "Sue has a baby brother. Ellen has a birthday today . . . Mary's grandmother came last night" (p. 150). A class message center or working post office in which each child has a box can function as a place where he or she would receive mail such as notices to take home, messages from each other, appointments with the teacher, or special teachers, or greeting cards. Children will write

... picture captions, cartoon strips, songs, poems, stories, journal entries, jokes, riddles, telegrams, directions to follow, eyewitness accounts, personal recollections, personal essays, fables, editorials, and original nature booklets. (Moffet, 1968, p. 116)

When children need help in order to organize their time, a group discussion could end with a written list of suggestions for short term things to do. Similarly, alternatives for behavior can be listed and discussed. The guesses before, and the findings after, children see and feel a mystery box or unknown liquids or powders, can be recorded and compared. Word associations after hearing a particular piece of music or in response to a question such as "What does the color purple remind you of?" can be recorded and compared. Simple crossword puzzles can be used and children can construct their own. Creative dramatics episodes may be recorded as a script.

Technical proficiency, strong motives for personal involvement, and meaningful material, are important complementary elements that can operate and improve through children's dictation and their own writing. In addition, the realities of the English language dictate that about fifteen percent of the words used simply do not fit widely regular patterns (Mazurkiewicz, 1964, p. 135). Children are more likely to remember such words when they have written them and when they have some background of phonemic associations to guide them.

The whole point is to seek better, balanced ways to help children achieve these tools that communicate meanings. Clearly, children who have stimulation and experiences from which to draw ideas, and from which to react, have more to write about. Children should be able to feel competent so that they are able to use these tools to better understand their world, their place in it, and their relations with other people.

CHAPTER 6
THE FRANCHISED TEACHER'S WAYS OF WORKING: STIMULATING INDEPENDENT EXPRESSION THROUGH DIALOGUE AND THE ARTS

This chapter deals with various ways in which the teacher prepares for, and works with, children. The variety of this work is highlighted, beginning with an extended look at the relation of language and knowledge through questions. Other intervention techniques, and the use of synectics strategies are focussed upon in turn. Aesthetic considerations and activities in music, art, and literature are also discussed. Later sections are concerned with diagnosis, record keeping, and the individualized special learning needs of children.

QUESTIONS

Much of what you notice, your own pre-sets in any situation, how you organize perceptions, can be seen as responses to internal questions that you have asked yourself. Sometimes you are unaware that you are responding to such inner questions. Such questions are powerful, perhaps more than those that are stated.

The perceptual models outlook suggests that teaching effectiveness is related to the kinds of questions that stimulate more open, productive, and evaluative thinking. Relevant questions are interspersed through episodes of this book. The same kinds of questions can be applied to different data with distinctive results. For example, a "why" question or a "what if" question can cut across traditional fields of subject matter. The questions themselves are not owned by any field. However, the types of questions that a teacher asks can help or hinder what children learn. One might almost define a domain of knowledge through questions, a powerfully subtle way to influence perception.

CHILDREN TAKE TURNS THROWING THE BALL THROUGH THE HOOP, BUILDING VISUAL-SPATIAL SKILLS.

QUESTIONS AS TOOLS OF KNOWING

I agree that any question a person asks predisposes a range of possible answers (Langer, 1942, p. 15; N. Isaacs, 1930 p. 293). In the sense that each discipline is a field of inquiry, it predisposes a range of questions. Therefore, the language of questions forms part of the tools of disciplines.

At the same time, it is fascinating to observe young children. They seem to have a limitless capacity for expressing questions by their exploratory physical behavior quite as much as by what they say. It seems as if their very absorbency is part of this questioning attitude. In fact, many adults deplore the persistent curiosity and questioning of young children. Yet, as people grow, they find it increasingly difficult to ask productive questions, a possible result of "coverage" schooling.

It is conceivable that if teachers proceed with one common type of information question, such as "What housing do eskimos have?," children may come to expect consistency and react to the lower level even when a higher level of inferential question is presented, such as "From what animal might eskimos have learned how to shelter themselves?" In the second instance, there may be a range of acceptable answers. At the same time, information acquired by the children could be evident from their responses.

The power relations between teacher and child are quite different. That is, when there is only one possible answer, and the teacher is the single arbiter of correctness, then children tend to rely on memory and teacher authority, a sure way to inhibit initiative and independent thinking. This notion is central to the consideration of critical consciousness later in this book. A related position suggests that informational questions can be interpreted as a punishment and reward system (Torrance and Myers, 1970).

Individual teachers who have consciously attempted to move toward more open-ended questioning could be represented by one teacher's finding that, as the school year progressed, the children began to feel more confident in answering open-ended questions when they began to realize that there was no one correct answer.

An important first step is for teachers to begin to notice that fear of punishment, or growth of confidence, can be important side effects of the kinds of questions they ask. It would be reasonable to expect that teachers would want to support the linguistic as well as conceptual aspects of questioning by young children. Among the syntax model games in Chapter 5 are some possible ways to stimulate the linguistic aspect of questioning.

All too often, teacher recitation-type questions end in yes–no answers or specific bits of prechewed facts. Noteworthy is the group of kindergarten children where three-quarters responded that they had eaten oatmeal for breakfast and three-quarters responded that they had eaten corn flakes. Even when teachers phrase questions with "whys," there is the danger that the child will seek the answer that fits his assessment of the adult's desired response (Lewis, 1963; p. 132). Bruner (1966) cautions similarly when he speaks elegantly of children's "coping and defending" (Chapter 7). There is a danger that children can hesitate even if they know the subject matter, because they are afraid of misjudging the teacher's intent.

Certainly, many teachers want to help children to be more active in inquiry. Therefore, it would be consistent to pose the kinds of genuinely evaluative and inductive questions that help children develop their own answers. Cazden (1972), noting the greater syntactic complexity (transformational movements) of Wh-questions, than Yes–No questions notes the cognitive difference between them. In effect, "with yes–no questions, the cognitive burden falls on the speaker (which is why teachers are admonished to avoid them); with Wh-questions, the burden falls on the listener" (p. 50). Bloom's *Taxonomy of Educational Objectives* (1956) is one place where a hierarchy of cognitive participation is outlined. It is a useful source for establishing question levels.

For example, when you ask "Do you want to tell us about what happened?" the question predisposes a possible "yes–no" response. If you prefer to have a response rather than to offer the choice of responding, a more precise question might be "What happened when you had the fight?" or "Why did the fight take place?"

To ask an open-ended question is not enough. The paradoxical cognitive demands of many open-ended questions need to be considered. Knowledge grows toward abstraction yet concrete questions, not necessarily questions of the informational or memory type, support growth.

Consider the possibility of an extended abstraction ladder, following the format of Chapter 5.

Concrete	"Recognition" Level	
object $\rightarrow$ object	How did you feel?	
object $\rightarrow$ visual	How would somebody	
visual $\rightarrow$ visual	else feel?	
visual $\rightarrow$ symbol	How would you behave	
symbol$\rightarrow$ symbol	if you were there?	
Abstract	"Recall" Level	

The parallel in these paradigms lies in the transformations effected along the concrete, "recognition" level, or abstraction level of "recall." The "recall" level requires a degree of self-awareness.

TEACHER INTERVENTION

An important aspect of learning is the ability to use knowledge rather than merely to verbalize. A concept that has been learned is a concept that can be transferred. The teacher can evaluate children's work through their use of materials and their ability to apply their learnings in a new setting or framework.

Following from this viewpoint therefore, the teacher's role is not to accelerate verbalisms. Intervention by the teacher would serve to *expand* children's *opportunities* for experiencing, *to combine* activities in order to help children make their own connections, and to *provide varied forms* of activities.

In some instances, a line of questioning helps children to learn particular strategies that are useful. The teacher could ask them to imagine placing themselves at particular starting points in a floor painting job and to predict consequences. Woodwork that requires a child to ask sequencing questions is an example of a planning strategy. It is legitimate to help children learn to scan a series of objects or pictures or words, depending upon their skill attainment, in order to find a particular exemplar. Certainly, decision making, comprehension of printed matter, and standardized tests require such scanning skill.

After children have been exposed to contrastive induction modelling by teachers, such as described in the decoding games, they have been observed to employ these techniques in their own learning. They have used them to teach other children as well.

"If this is ban and this is ran then what is that?"
"Bran"!

A discussion of life and death included the use of contrasts in another form when a teacher saw a group of five-year-old children looking into the aquarium.

TEACHER:	Why does that red fish look different from the gold ones?
CHILD 1:	It's a different color.
CHILD 2:	. . . Not moving.
CHILD 3:	It's not alive.
TEACHER:	How could we tell it's not alive?
CHILD 3:	It's not moving.
CHILD 4:	Is that fish dead!?
TEACHER:	Was it alive once upon a time?
CHILDREN:	Yes. No.
TEACHER:	How could we find out? . . .

The teacher might have quickly delivered the information that the red fish was made of plastic and had never been a living thing, only an object. However, to have done so would have prevented the exploration of possibilities that support intellectual curiosity. Power relations also change when the teacher reduces opportunities for children to explore inquiry strategies about matters of interest to them. When the teacher provides information to passive recipients, the recipients' power is diminished. Certainly, life and death is a universally absorbing human subject about which children can talk. It would also have reduced an opportunity for the teacher to assess children's concepts if she had done all of the talking.

A group of three-year-olds who observed the workings of a chick hatchery in their room had a similar opportunity to absorb data about growth, life, and death. Their activities represented a living questioning. Unlike a different teacher of four-year-olds who rushed away a deceased "overly loved" guinea pig and replaced him before the children could notice, the three-year-olds' teacher encouraged them to question and wonder about the chicks. Their queries were answered in a straightforward way when a chick died.

A few children were able to compare the egg process with plants. One child suggested a relation to a broken windup toy. Through many activities such as measuring gerbils, rabbits, guinea pigs, plant growth, and their own growth, their environment made it possible for them to be saturated with data to help answer their questions, as well as to stimulate them to ask questions.

Early childhood educators have regularly emphasized the importance of children's questions as a way to learn (Dorn, 1966; N. Isaacs, 1930). The provision of opportunities for a great deal of talking in an interactive environment is necessary to support children's inquisitiveness.

In addition to the creation of activities, games, and simulations in which children set problems for the teacher and other children, the total environment can support the questioning stance of young children. The impact of the structure and organization of the teacher–child interaction can support or limit responsive behavior. The teacher, by valuing and helping children to set questions, stimulates them to move in particular self-propelled directions, extending beyond the present to new challenges.

Through the years, questions have been categorized along many ranges such as closed to open continua, abstract to concrete continua, semantically differentiated continua, and emotionally loaded continua. It is one thing to categorize teacher's question types into hierarchies such as Aschner's (1963) routine, memory, convergent thinking, evaluative thinking, or divergent thinking. It is quite another matter to know when and how to apply their use in teaching. A teacher might study written or taped protocols of his or her interaction with children in order to analyze the relative question types. Such a teacher might then resolve to reduce memory questions and plan to use additional evaluative questions.

However, teachers may become falsely lulled into feeling quite efficient and virtuous by such objectivity. There is the danger that exercising one professional behavior—working to improve and change one's work—will obscure the relation of an isolated improvement to a larger view of how it relates to one's long-range planning for children. Surely, there are legitimate instances for the use of a full range of question types when teachers work with children. Therefore, in order to avoid fragmentation and the proliferation of "one-shot deals," there is a need to look beyond the forms of question types alone to the content with which they deal.

It is not enough for a teacher to pose relevant, well-articulated questions, whether verbally and/or through extended activities. The true effectiveness of questions that contribute to inquiry, scholarship, expanded knowledge, and humanism comes through the teacher's sincerely involved *responsiveness*. Television, among other contributions, can raise excellent questions for children.

However, the motives that support children's active participation are strengthened when teachers listen to children, and extend and expand their line of thinking with still more stimulating questions and comments. The most complex skill for a teacher to achieve is to understand what the children might be perceiving on the basis of responses that they make. At best, the assessment is a considered, albeit intuitive hypothesis selected from a stock of hypotheses about the meaning of particular child behaviors, both verbal and nonverbal.

DISCUSSION WITH CHILDREN

Part of the teacher's responsiveness to children can be observed through the workings of several generally accepted techniques. The teacher can help children to *focus* in a discussion by accepting what a child has offered, however irrelevant-appearing: "Thank you for telling us. And what do you think will happen when we cover the pan?"

Another technique is the *feedback* technique. The teacher rephrases the child's comment, retaining the intent and perhaps clarifying it: "Did you mean that she should not be permitted to watch the film if she hit another child?"

From time to time, it can be useful to *summarize* the gist of an interchange: "I have heard people say that we should find out more about what we can do at the park, and invite some parents along on the trip."

"What are some ways that we could get that information?"

When summarizing, it is counterproductive to repeat what each child has said since that might only encourage children to listen to the teacher.

Decentralized interactions between children and teachers are likely to flow between teacher–child–child–child whereas recitation settings are inclined to flow between teacher–child–teacher–child–teacher–child. A good deal of learning and assessment is possible when children respond to one another during focussed discussions.

Without repetition, a teacher can credit participants who have made significant suggestions. "Alan suggested that we write to the museum and Gabe had the idea to ask if we could bring a camera. What else besides these ideas, and Ed's plans for our money?" In addition to encouraging children to listen to one another, it solidifies the children's perception of the teacher as someone who actively listens to their comment and values their contributions. When children observe that the teacher does not accept, does not notice, or refuses to consider a child's comment, they receive a powerful message against the teacher's commitment to independent thinking. The classic "ripple" phenomenon (Kounin and Gump, 1958) occurs that can inhibit the observing child from risking contributions in the future.

For those teachers who feel that they need to gain greater comfort with discussions, it is useful to plan ahead. For the novice, a brilliant question usually comes more easily with advance thinking and without the pressure of moving children and events. It is also useful to plan a few alternative kinds of questions that address more and less complex skills, in case the original questions seem unproductive.

It is consistent with truly responsive teaching to use only those pre-planned questions that seem appropriate during ongoing discussion. It is more worthwhile to follow *one* question into extended depth through a series of interchanges than to feel that *all* preplanned questions need to be asked.

Pacing questions can be as important to successful interaction as content itself. A beautiful question can be lost if the teacher interprets a child's look, perhaps thoughtful, as puzzlement. The teacher's tendency may be to rephrase the question. While the young child has barely had time to decipher the meaning of the first question, he is bombarded by another volley of words. This confusion may be avoided by letting the question sit for a second. Silences can have meaning. It may be that the teacher could, after a few seconds (ten?) of making *eye contacts* with the children, ask somebody to rephrase the question for the group. In another way, silence and sympathetic eye contact is a message to the children that the teacher actually expects an answer and is not being rhetorical.

It is important to keep in mind the purposes of the interaction and what the children need to bring to the discussion in order to participate in it. For example, a good evaluative question at the beginning of a discussion can stimulate children's eagerness to talk since they could express their own viewpoint. It is worth noting that judging and deciding about some matters are skills that are learned. Children would need to learn the criteria for making a particular judgment. While a teacher cannot always be expected to perfectly assess in advance what a child brings, he should adapt to the ongoing assessment. When teachers approach discussions with a sense of evolution and futurity, it is relevant and productive. Discussions may end in tentative suggestions or new ideas, or the generation of new questions, as well as with a solution to a problem.

OTHER INTERVENTION TECHNIQUES

The apprehension of perceptual models requires careful planning. It is relevant to look at some techniques in addition to general questioning that could support these kinds of learning. Some of these techniques are integrated throughout this book. Nevertheless, it may help to focus the reader if these techniques are viewed in a more conscious form.

CONTRASTIVE TEACHER MODELLING AND INDUCTIVE LEARNING

Contrastive teacher modelling was used in the language and reading activities. This inductive process of using contrasting patterns is as relevantly used in studying data from a scientific, social scientific, or artistic perspective. For example, observations can be planned in which children encounter similar events, such as the exchange of news under different conditions. The equivalent of newspaper or postal service functions may look different in an arctic or tropical, aquatic community than it would in our own setting. Plant growth under controllable variations represents other contrasting patterns. One group of interaged five- and six-year-olds boiled flowers to extract perfume and then proceeded to compare other things obtainable from plants and berries (Glen Pollack, Personal Communication, 1975).

Children can remain attentive when the teacher provides contrasts and children can make inductions rather than merely guess. They can feel successful. An example follows:

CHILD: (*pointing*) What's this word?
TEACHER: (*writing on chalkboard*) If this is rain and this is gain, I bet you
           can tell me what word this is.

CHILD: (*smiling*) Grain! . . . I love it when you do that. (Claire McKenna, Personal Communication, 1975)

When a child's induction is inaccurate, it is all too easy for the teacher to tell him how incorrect he is. Yet he can feel more powerful if he can revise his conclusion after the teacher provides a fresh modelling, or a new set of contrasts.

Some teachers behave as if direct instruction through inductive learning and indirect instruction through intuited learning are antagonistic to one another. In actual practice, random intuitive learning is less visible, less frequent, and frequently more frustrating. Often, when the folklore traditionalist speaks solely of incidental learnings, it is a euphemism for disconnected activity and many "one-shot deals." This is frequently, but not always, the teacher who starts setting out materials as the children wait, rather than before they arrive.

Lest there be misunderstanding, incidental learnings have been praised throughout this book, most notably in Chapters 2 and 4. I would be less concerned if a six-year-old who was not ready to subtract sets was unpressured than if a five-year-old who was panting to learn to subtract sets was bypassed because of arbitrary age considerations. In either case, the reverse process could block future learning. A developmental approach should provide for individual progression needs and planned intervention that is appropriately concrete and materials-based activity. The point is that we should provide a proper "match" for the self-motivated child.

Practice.   With an appropriately game-like format, young children are quite pleased to repeat their activities and "play the game again." The successful sense of mastery and competence shines through. You can see this by observing the ten-month-old who repeatedly tests gravitation by flinging spoons off his table, the twenty-month-old who is continually taking off the doll's clothes or climbing up the stairs, the four-year-old who wants to use the paints each and every morning, or the seven-year-old who repeatedly asks to play the "Pairs" decoding game with changing phonemic patterns. In any case, it is reasonable to practice skills by using varied forms.

It is an interesting cultural phenomenon that adults usually understand the baby's need for repetition of physical skills, and the young child's repeated practice of ball games and rope jumping. While repetition is recognized and tolerated in the development of physical coordination, it is accepted less readily in the development of conceptual skills. Is there a single person who never heard an adult say to a child: "How many times do I have to tell it to you?" or "I told you that already!" Nevertheless, *self-propelled* repetition usually leads to a sense of success and a concomitant extension of attention span.

While teachers have recognized the role of repetition in learning, they have provided practice in many different ways. Some teachers use a large amount of rote drill repetition of the same form of material, such as adding the number family combinations up to ten. Others use a smaller amount of rote repetition of the same type of material when they ask children to copy a list of five spelling words each day and add a few of their own. Some teachers ask children to check off a number of words for another child to read to him every few days in order that he may write them from memory. He would then compare his unprompted spelling with the original written list.

GROUPING

Still other teachers provide repetition through skills groups and interest groups. For example, incidental mention of quantity labels might be particularly repeated for individual three-year-old children, while they would be grouped for work with block classification games or card matchings at specifically planned occasions. For color, the children develop a purple day or a purple week with the teacher, bring purple objects from home, create a purple object table with purple cover, purple pictures, and the book *Harold and the Purple Crayon* (Johnson, 1958). A child who wears purple clothing can be affectionately added to the purple table for a moment's emphasis. That child is likely to remember purple! When children see a concrete property in both functional and focussed, contrasted form it is more likely that they will acquire the knowledge than if only one or the other technique is used.

One might well suggest that this takes a great deal of time. However, if children learn and can retain their own competent feelings, then that time is well spent. If all the children are given a demonstration together, then some will need varying degrees of repetition.

It makes good sense to decide what knowledge is needed in the first place, to diagnose which children need it, who may be *ready* to receive it, and then to work with only those children individually or in a small group.

Group Size. The size of a group depends upon several factors. Even if ten children need a particular skill and appear ready to receive it, that number may be too large. You can see this in a three- or four-year-old group where a concrete activity with seeds is underway. The teacher and parents have provided a sufficient quantity and variety of foods such as green pepper, apple, orange, pineapple, tomato, potato, avocado, green beans, green peas, melon,

and cucumber for children to handle, eat, and categorize. However, when two
or three children are doing most of the talking in this group of ten, the teacher
is not sure what the others are absorbing beyond a fine sensorimotor
experience.

An overly large group is particularly prevalent in those situations where
teachers establish traditional reading groups for direct instruction, such as
work in comprehension skills. After we observe a concrete situation in a group
of six-year-olds, we can proceed to analyze it.

> 10:00 A.M.
>
> TEACHER: (*calling twelve children at one time from across
> entire room*) I'm working with the Lions group. Sh.
> You stay there. (*Tapping child on arm to gain atten-
> tion to book. Brings child, by grasping her hand,
> from the door to a seat in the somewhat semi-circle
> of chairs. Taps child on head with a pack of word
> cards to get attention.*)
>
> Now-now. The same boy. Come to your seat, away
> from the door.
>
> I see one group of children who are ready.
>
> I'm looking for cooperative people. I see a few who
> are trying very hard.
>
> Mark, you forgot to whisper.
>
> The two girls near the sink. Hurry up! You're wast-
> ing my time. (*Traffic management continues*)
>
> Everyone in the Lions group, do this (*hands on
> shoulders, ears, knees . . .*)
>
> 10:03: I want you to concentrate. Let's look up here. Look
> at the words. Don't say them. Don't say them. We
> went someplace on the trip. Who wants to find
> where we went?
>
> (*A child who leaves her chair in the group when
> called by the teacher, walks to the chart, selects a
> word, points to it, looks at the teacher inquiringly,
> and reads the word to the group. The teacher nods
> and the child returns to her chair.*)
>
> Will you take your turn Angela? Will you try to say
> all the words? Walk around quickly.
>
> Sh. Over here.
>
> Sh. Everyone look but don't say it.

(*To group*) No, I don't want any shouting.

Hide your eyes quickly.

(*They play a word guessing game for a few moments punctuated by an occasional "Sh" when the enthusiasm builds about hiding one's eyes and guessing the correct word. A few asides to children.*)

MARK: Is the word "family"?

TEACHER: Let's say the word in unison.

A FEW CHILDREN: Unison.

TEACHER: The word is not unison. Whose turn is it?

CHILD: Monkey?

TEACHER: The word is not monkey. It is fish.

We'll play this game again tomorrow.

O.K. Quickly now. Angela, what page are we going to check?

ANGELA: Page 31.

TEACHER: Page 31. Sh. Move over here. When I say something, listen to me!

Carol, look at me.

Bill, Bill! I cannot see your face.

(*She reads them a sample paragraph as they read along silently from a workbook page.*) Wait, let me get my felt pen. (*walks to a corner cupboard and back*) I see quiet workers at the green table, at the yellow table. . . . (*addressed across the entire room. Children take turns reading aloud around the group.*) . . . we're on page 33 and you're not listening . . . Mark, a boy runs . . . (*pause*) Bill . . . home. The two girls near the sink, are you finished?

(*To a seated child*) You should have said . . . (*Children take turns reading*)

TEACHER: . . . in the pond. sh. You should have circled "pond." (*Several interchanges, individual children reading aloud around the group.*)

Who remembers the other meaning of the word "batter"? (*child answers*) Right!

(*Children take turns reading aloud.*)

Page 35 is a joking page. Can you wear rice? Sh. Can you wear ham? Sh. You're shouting. Sh. Do you want to say it too? Sh. Yes, I'm looking for people who can whisper. Can you wear belts? Can you wear ideas?

You can do this page for yourself. Now, turn to the next page.

All right, you're going to draw the picture . . . *after* you . . .

Sh. (*responds to a child*) I know. Just wait. I see two children who are not being cooperative. Mark, Mark. Can I see you? Would you do something quickly?

10:20: (*Addresses entire room*) Stop what you're doing, finished or not, it's time to go to. . . .

The episode above is a classic case of the management of a group that was too large for the task that was set. Management problems undermined quite a bit of the teacher's advance plans for children to use reading comprehension skills. The content and reading level was appropriate for the purposes of comprehension but there were many activities.

1. They were to select an appropriate sentence from an experience chart about a trip that the group had taken.
2. They were to play a "What's the Missing Word?" guessing game.
3. They were to hide their eyes and hide a word card after removing it from the flannel board.
4. They were to share independent workbook work that represented the preceding day's work (page 31).
5. They were to do a new page together (page 33).
6. They were to prepare to do a new page independently (page 35).

The number of changes, and the significance of the six part plan could be questioned. The activity was recitational. The group of twelve children was simply too large for each child to have a chance to participate. After a child had been called, he or she tended to become uninvolved. In addition, the teacher focussed a great deal on management, quiet and order, while her own voice carried across the entire room, reaching some children whom she expected to be working independently or in dyads with concentration.

Actually, the children seemed uninvolved in the teacher's planned activities and were easily distracted. There was continual readjustment of seating, occasional outbreaks of pushing, and intragroup conversations about matters other than the teacher's plans. A look at the protocol reveals that proportionately little substance was evident. However, much management was apparent. It is of course possible that an observer's presence could have made the teacher more conscious of order. However, this is a teacher noted for her hard work, solid years of experience, and careful planning.

She was *working very hard* to keep attention by focussing on behavior rather than substance. Perhaps if she had plunged toward immediate entry into the activity, the activity would have drawn their attention. Even so, the reader of this protocol might have experienced a sense of the teacher as somebody who was overly laden with packages, one or another of which was dropping.

In addition, she appeared very rushed. Perhaps she felt that she wanted to "cover" the six planned activities during the twenty-minute period. Consider, also, that the group size made for delays each time a child had to walk across the entire group to the chart or the flannel board. In turn, the teacher exhorted them to move "quickly."

To summarize, the teacher *might* consider that a group is too large based upon both her own feelings and her observations of children's behavior. Teachers might feel uncertain about the progress of a particular child; feel the pressure of not enough time to accomplish what is needed, assuming the plans are reasonable; or feel that each child has not had a chance to contribute to the group. They might observe that children are more interested in each other than in the substance of the activity; individual children seem to hesitate or to avoid talking to the group; children are distracted, daydreaming, or paying attention to other matters; some children do not keep pace with the group.

It is worthwhile to be cautious about using any one observation or feeling as a deciding factor. It may be that a particular child's ability has not been appropriately diagnosed for the group placement, or a particular child in combination with a particular other child do not work well, or that the group could work better if reduced by any one child. In the case of three- and four-year-olds, or a rare five- or six-year-old, it is possible that a child has yet to learn how to work cooperatively in a group.

Group Readiness. When a young child is easily distracted or seems to need a great deal more attention than is possible even in a group of four children, it wastes everybody's time and energy. If a teacher insists upon his attendance then the group may become bored or the individual scapegoated. When the teacher plans individually for such a child, all parties concerned have a more comfortable, productive relationship. There is undoubtedly a Harold or Harriet in every teacher's life who needs this sort of planning.

There was one four-year-old Harold whose teacher recognized that Harold and the remainder of the group would suffer unless his continual attention-getting, disruptive behavior became positively channeled. Since he particularly enjoyed clay, the teacher provided clay for him each day when the remainder of the group convened for the teacher to read a story and lead a discussion. Everybody accepted the arrangement matter of factly because the teacher handled the situation in a businesslike manner, "Now is the time for. . . ."

One day, the school's director walked into the room at this time and saw Harold making an intricate clay construction, joined by his own increasingly voluminous vocal accompaniment. When the director quietly told him that it was hard to hear the story, which he could observe from his position, he said, "O.K., I'll turn down my radio." and adjusted his clay knob and volume. From time to time, when a *Curious George* (Rey, 1973) story about a mischievous monkey was read, Harold would quietly join the group. In a few months, Harold was able to be an increasingly regular participant in large group activities. However, from time to time, he could read his own barometer, sometimes with the teacher's positively stated help, and separate plans were made for him during a group meeting.

Constituting Sub-groups.   Flexibility is an important principle in planning for children to be part of sub-group instruction. The same children will progress at different rates, at different times, and the range of differences widen. When the teacher provides a variety of activities or materials, particularly in reading instruction, the children's comparative progress may be less noticeable. Imagine knowing at the age of five years that you are forever a turtle and never a gazelle!? If skills groups are regularly reconstituted, sometimes after a few sessions or a few weeks, then status positions can be minimized.

When a teacher notices that an individual child or a few children seem ready to work on a particular skill, the needed instruction is simply an additional offering in an already full program. If a child who does not seem ready asks to engage in activity, the child might accept that this is another instance where she needs to take her turn. There are probably other reasonably fresh materials with which the child could be satisfied and with which she has a better chance of feeling successful. From the beginnings of schooling, it is useful for the teacher to emphasize that sub-groups are changing.

Homogeneous-heterogeneous grouping.   In the primary grades, for example, an alternative to the "classic" oversized group discussed above might be a range of varied reading comprehension activities. These activities serve to bring children together who may have attained varied skills but share interests in common. Even for a teacher committed to books from a basal reading series, each child might select different subject matter and try to influence others to consider their "most interesting topic."

A variation of the "most interesting topic" would be for each child to read two or three books, self-selected with teacher guidance, and then convince others about why he ranked the readings in a special way. Incidentally, these are useful opportunities for children to raise questions of one another as well as to *use* their knowledge. The teacher can find out what a child understands when the child "advertises" a book in the library corner by making a tape recording, an illustration, a mysterious package marked by clues, a written statement or teasing question, or a diorama.

These types of activities help children of varying attainments to communicate meaningfully with one another. The less accomplished child can see child models at varied points of skill attainment. In one room, a group of six-year-olds became intrigued when they watched some of their colleagues "doing division" and promptly insisted on learning how to do it. The teacher was surprised to see how much the "division" children were able to interpret to the others who, in turn, proved more ready than the teacher had anticipated.

The interage grouping arrangement is a natural "family" extension that represents ultimate heterogeneity. In one instance, a long-time teacher of a self-contained group of six-year-olds undertook an interage primary group comprising a three-year age spread. In a short time, she found it difficult to answer a visitor's question about a child's age. Whereas in the past the child might have fit into a particular "triptych" (high-medium-low) category tracking in the teacher's thinking, the child was now doing different things at different tracks of the teacher's "triple-triptych" schema. The opportunities for all of the children had expanded. For the first time in many years, this teacher was stimulated to expand her repertoire of activities and ideas, and began to find new resources in some of the younger teachers in the school.

To speak of the system of tracking within a single age grade against this framework is, to put it mildly, difficult to imagine. A particularly telling incident concerning homogeneous versus heterogeneous grouping left a building principal nearly in tears. She had been approached separately, on the same day, by two different groups of black parents in a small school district that had recently integrated. The population in her school was comprised of about forty-percent black children. The first group of parents, representing an earlier immigration wave of upper middle class incomes, asked the principal to arrange for homogeneous grouping. The other group, representing a second wave of families with lower incomes, asked the principal to retain the heterogeneous grouping. The principal and faculty saw the educational advantages of heterogeneous grouping and planned for it.

Quite a different reaction came from a teacher of six-year-olds in a large school district who said "I prefer the slowest class on the grade because nobody expects anything of them." These kinds of stated and unstated views are an affront to research concerning teacher expectancies of children. Research indicates that minimal expectations are indeed likely to yield limited performance (Rosenthal and Jacobson, 1968). If nothing more, expecting disinterest hardly helps one to proceed with a contagious enthusiasm. However, encouragement and successes that grow from legitimate challenge stimulate children to try expanded possibilities. The timeless work of the psychologists McClelland et al. (1953) led to the finding that the need for achievement can be learned and can be manipulated. Therefore, teacher expectancies are influential in establishing ceilings for children.

A great problem in education is that there are times when teachers can keep possibilities closed because they may not even perceive them. Creative processes and the aesthetic component of living are issues for educators to consider. The next section turns to look at the creativity that can be released through synectics strategies.

SYNECTICS

William J. J. Gordon's "synectics" has been presented as "a metaphorical way of learning and knowing" (1961, 1973). Gordon and his associates see their learning strategies working in at least the two directions of making the strange familiar (learning) and making the familiar strange (discovering and extending).

They have analyzed, developed, and applied several strategies in various educational settings ranging from schools through community and industrial groups. The strategies offer some ways in which teachers can extend interactions and systematize processes for creative learning situations. Good teachers have intuitively used analogy in their teaching.

However, the Gordon strategies have been developed and refined beyond the intuitive level. For early childhood educators, who particularly claim to support creative thinking, there is an inherent challenge to gain some ability to adapt these processes.

THE RELATION OF SYNECTICS "STRETCHING" AND YOUNG CHILDREN

Adaptation is probably necessary when working with young children for several reasons. On the one hand, children's syncretic ability to make connections can lead to relations and statements that appear respectively insightful and poetic to adults. On the other hand, young children's restricted abilities for self-awareness serve to limit children's *conscious* use of metaphor.

Young children, when they play with analogical relations, are quite content to incompletely match or classify elements—a reflection of their cognitive attainment. They find it difficult to keep several factors constant while manipulating one or another factor.

These observations can be made in the following dialogue with one group of four-year-olds and their teacher who began with a synectics "stretching" exercise, "Why is a shower bath like a rainy day?" Different children dealt with either, "A shower is . . . ," or, "Rain is . . . ," but they did not move the two variables together. This observation is similar to Piaget's conservation of liquids findings for this age group wherein children respond on the basis of only one variable. Teachers might reserve judgment since the same child's language and cognitive processes may be at different developmental levels.

In another group, four-year-olds responded similarly, "You need an umbrella and raincoat." Others were able to deal with commonalities, however they were attained, such as, "You get your hair wet." "It sounds like it." "It looks like it." "Water comes from the top." "It hurts you, your back, when it comes down hard." "You stand up." Similar variability was observed in a group of five-year-olds.

However, primary age children argued that, "A shower isn't like a rainstorm because you don't take it outside." Another child parried, "You can if you want to." The primary children were increasingly able to respond in this way. Their only apparent problem was that they were not sure what kind of answers to give. They seemed to be trying to classify the type of question, or "teacher game," that was on its way. Based upon their prior experience, they seemed to expect that the teacher was hunting for a "right" answer. When they were assured that whatever they said was acceptable, their comments flowed profusely.

The five-year-olds tended to be more trusting. The synectics "stretching" exercises, supplemented by their teacher's question, "How is being angry like popcorn?" (Perle Press, Personal Communication, 1974) produced masses of verbalization. The teacher found that the children's talk was vastly expanded during these interchanges. In some respects, the perceptual models approach to curricular planning relies upon the teacher's ability to transpose models in a way that is similar to metaphorical transposition.

While the above examples grew from a small bit of pilot testing, it points to the usefulness of teachers providing practice opportunities for children. Possibilities for alternate connections, and increased distance ("stretch") between the stimulus image and the connections made by participating children and adults, grows with practice. When working with young children, though, "stretch" breaks down more rapidly when a teacher goes too far with, "Can you think of yet another way that this/that is similar/different?"

Also, this occurs when the original stimulus is too far removed from children's experiences. When the stimulus is too far removed, their informational possibilities are overloaded and they don't have enough data with which to create. When the information demands are reasonable, synectics strategies represent a way for children to *use* information. In turn, it provides a stimulating, positive medium for educators to assess children's transferable attainments.

One useful dialectic strategy is regularly employed in the synectics exercises and flows naturally. In effect, since an analogy is not an identity but a representation of some degree of overlapping, there are some ways in which the analogy and the referent are similar and different. When one especially defines a phenomenon in terms of what it is "not" there is a huge margin for correctness, and a sense of success.

Moreover, when children can manage to generate items or phenomena that remind them of other items or phenomena, their kind of perception and understanding is apparent to the teacher. It may be as concrete as a six-year-old's, "Pencil sharpenings are like soft feathers." or a four-year-old's observation that, "Cherry blossoms are pink tree snow."

THREE MAJOR SYNECTICS STRATEGIES AND YOUNG CHILDREN

Beyond, and following, stretching exercises, three major strategies are isolated by the synectics people.

Direct Analogy. The direct analogy is familiar in everyday usage in representations such as: She married a lemon, has a sunny disposition, eats like a pig, looks like a blimp, is subtle as a Mack truck, gentle as a dove, and so forth. In these instances, a particular attribute of an object is extracted and associated with a focal subject. A simple sort of close relation would be to connect a cave or bird's nest with a human home. There is little "distance" or "stretch" between these comparisons. A "home" run however represents a considerable stretch that transforms, rather than correlates, the focal subject and the attribute. Piaget similarly identifies the correlation as a less complex attainment than the transformation.

Beyond stretching exercises, one way that synectics systematizes the use of direct analogy is by suggesting that if we are trying to solve a human problem, it is helpful to seek an animal or mechanical analogy. When trying to learn about a mechanical phenomenon, the synectics people recommend drawing a direct analogy with a living phenomenon, plant, or animal in nature. By increasing the distance between focal subject and the direct analogy, the child can see his problem or subject matter with greater objectivity. At the very least, the analogy may help the participant to see something new.

Then, by comparing how the analogy is like and unlike the focal subject, new insights can accrue. It is helpful to play out some of the synectics exercises directly in order to experience this exciting process. A fun exercise, worked through with Tony Poze of Synectics Education Systems and some university faculty and graduate teachers is, "How is a school like a garden?" The reader may find that it is a stimulating group project with colleagues.

When a teacher wants children to explore a systemic notion, the statement of this type of question and analogy can stimulate considerable discussion. In this sense, the analogy becomes a kind of simulation model, a path that may help the participant reach a new vista. Again, it is most useful to select an analogy about which children have sufficient information in order that they may better play out the congruencies. With the youngest children, it is especially important to see that they have some understanding of the distinctions between objects, animate phenomena, and humans. Explorations may show that your group of four- or five-year-olds strengthens their understanding of these beginning distinctions through the use of analogy.

Personal Analogy. The personal analogy is a second strategy that extends the possibilities of the direct analogy. The participants play at "being the analogy." You imagine how you would feel, what you would do, what you would say, or what you would perceive if a particular condition changed. In turn, you could deal with how you would not feel, what you would not do or what you would not say when you *are* a kettle, a school yard door, a tightly fitted shoe, or a spider in the rain.

Inasmuch as young children's dramatic play tends to make "being" an animal or thing familiar behavior, the personal analogy strategy is perhaps most readily available to young children. The teacher is an important contributor to the success of this strategy when he accepts an incomplete rendition of "remaining in character." Younger children may classify their characterization as incompletely as they might categorize sets of objects or properties. According to Piaget, this reflects their cognitive development during the nursery years and exists in transitional degrees through seven years of age.

When asking children to make suggestions, it is useful to establish a signal such as the teacher touching her nose, or children keeping their eyes covered while they are thinking. This might inhibit an outburst of a response from one child that might inhibit others' thinking. Sharing ideas is useful after a reasonable number of children have their responses ready. In this way, the rapid speaker does not influence the independent possibilities of the other children. While all responses are acceptable, some will show varying degrees of "distance" and fruitfulness.

Compressed Conflict. The compressed conflict is the third synectics strategy. It takes the form of a conflicting two-word phrase made up of a modifier and a noun, such as "safe attack," "mute testimony," "innocent menace." The two words derive from an extension of the personal analogy. That is, you make two lists of words, one of which deals with what you *do* experience through the analogy and the other of which represents what you *do not* experience, such as in what ways your experience is liberating and in what ways your "becoming" the personal analogy is not liberating. After playing with modifier and noun combinations, playing with the reversal of the order of the respective words, you could react to a particular two-word combination as a compressed conflict, for example, freely obligated.

The earlier observations concerning children's cognitive styles, might suggest that the major effort for moving through a compressed conflict strategy would rest with the teacher. If future studies find that this is the case, then teachers must raise the question: Even if children can do it with heavy teacher direction, is the time and teacher resource best spent in this way?

SYNECTICS EXCURSION

In various combinations of moves. which the synectics people call "excursions," they have taught concepts through analogy, stimulated aesthetic imagery toward creative use of language through analogy, and worked through the solution of problems through the use of analogy. The "Learning Flowsheet" and the "Asthetic Flowsheet" are used as aids.

Do be aware as you reflect on this material that this discussion can barely tickle the entire area. The reader who would want to pursue these matters might refer to the original sources as well as to *selectively* adapt activities for children from among the numerous activity booklets developed by Gordon and Poze. The limits of this section can very lightly sketch the Learning Flowsheet, mention the Aesthetic Flowsheet, and leave problem solving, represented by the Juggler Flowsheet, for the next chapter.

In the Learning Flowsheet, the teacher plans a two-part introduction. First, the teacher states "the central elements of the *concept to be learned*." Then, he selects an analogy to the concept with which the children are familiar. The teacher might ask them to be part of the analogy through "imagining": "What would you want? do? feel? How would you react when . . . ?" Second, the children engage in a two-part process of stating how the analogy offered by the teacher is like, and then unlike, the concept being learned. In the third phase, the teacher asks the children what they know that is similar to the concept, how it is similar, and how it is different. At this point, children could engage in personalizing the analogy through imagining again, and role playing. The third phase is repeated with a different analogue suggested by the children. Throughout the "excursion," the teacher keeps the playing-out of possibilities concrete through questioning, and by returning to the literal aspects of the metaphor.

Evaluation is built into the Learning Flowsheet Excursion. In order for the children to participate in the second phase of the excursion, comparing the concept and the analogy, they would have had to comprehend at least some of the "concept to be learned." If they could work through the third phase, offering their own analogy, it is likely that the children can use the knowledge. A teacher of four- and five-year-old children might feel that the first phase of planning had been fulfilled if children could deal, even partially, at the level of the second phase. Movement into the third phase involves a heavier dependency upon "recall," as opposed to simpler "recognition" functions because the children are asked for a fresh analogy.

The Aesthetic Flowsheet attempts to make the familiar strange while the Learning Flowsheet attempts to make the strange familiar. After the participants select an observable object, they draw an analogy with a plant or living thing. Then they develop an excursion into personal analogy and develop two lists of its polar elements. The next phase, clearly beyond the early childhood years, calls for the development of a "compressed conflict phrase" and a metaknowledge of the process.

An obvious value of some synectics strategies is that they provide an additional way for teachers to stimulate children's verbal expression as well as help the teacher support divergent responses. Participating children may become pre-set to consider alternatives as their capacity matures. There is a strong parallel to be drawn with the arguments: Why talk to babies if they don't understand the words? In response, the exposure to language appears to bear fruit when children speak earlier and more fully. When you consider intervention techniques, it is important to be familiar with, and to practice, the processes because their application as tools needs to be administered with the musician's touch, tempo, and dynamics.

AESTHETICS IN LIFE AND THE ARTS

People frequently associate the creative with the aesthetic, and the aesthetic with the artistic, in a narrow sense of "the arts"—disciplines such as music, the visual arts, dance, and literature, including drama. When stated as a listing of disciplines, teachers may miss a rich opportunity to perceive and create forms that do not fit existing definitions. Stated in this fashion, teachers may limit aesthetic definition to a rarefied phenomenon, separated from experiences available to all persons.

Freire (1970), an exiled Brazilian educator, takes this notion further when he suggests that museums and other formalized ways of taking custody of art forms are a manifestation of the people's powerlessness, removing the art forms from the financial possibilities and social participation of all of the people. Dewey (1934) also contends that nationalism, imperialism and capitalism have influenced the development of museums as a place in which art is a "separation" rather than an "enhancement" of "ordinary experience" (pp. 6, 8). Dewey was able to see the beauty of everyday pottery as a reflection of the integral place of aesthetic pleasure in the life of Ancient Greece. However, he felt that his contemporaries were not able to foresee that the jazz music and popular movie culture of the 1930s would become regarded as part of the cinematic and musical experiences recognized as legitimate "art" forms today.

Notice the problem of trying to integrate forms, arts, and aesthetic experience. While all life is not artistic, people generally regard some forms more than others as artistic in the sense of requiring skillful execution, being the "familiar" made "strange," of being experienced more aesthetically. However, the Gordon notion of "making the familiar strange" is a useful dimension by which you can view aesthetic experience. The aesthetic is what you experience. Aesthetic experience is not an intrinsic property of established art forms or products, although these formed arts have in common the potential for aesthetic experiencing.

Driving past a six story loft building, you might see two workmen using a roof-mounted pulley in a hoisting operation. The coordinated rhythm of their bodies rising and their muscles hardening to draw down the rope is poetry in motion. It is reminiscent of the sense of the tent raising in Walt Disney's film *Dumbo*. The film's expressive form could evoke an experience that closely imitates reality. Through skillful drawing and musical accompaniment, the film evoked the same sense of strength, rhythm, and synchronic harmony in the tension of the movement. In the case of the real workmen as well as the animated, musically accompanied Disney workmen, you could have had an aesthetic experience. Clearly, the workmen were not an art form in the sense that the film was formed art.

While you could have an insightful perception of the workmen, the film makers could communicate the insight through their formed work. A common feature of the aesthetic experience possible in both the real process and the artistic process is that the observer's perception is concrete, a direct experience. The art of Disney lay in the ability to perceive, to have insight into the aesthetic experience of the real perception, and then to capture his own insight by transforming it in the animated form. By integrating music as well as visual forms, he was able to serve up an insight that is not offered on-a-platter by reality. He was able to draw attention to certain elements of line, rhythm, and tempo. He was able to enrich.

A new art form or solution to a problem may be perceived by the artist as an aesthetic experience albeit not one that others may share. Two examples from the dance field and the conceptual art world can provide some common base.

Contemporary modern dance choreographers, such as Alwin Nickolais, frequently accompany movement with electronic music and use the dancers as objects in space along with props such as shopping bags, bolts of stretchable cloth, and plastic or wood constructions. The props contribute to the viewer's aesthetic experience as the dancers interact with them and with one another. One might almost find a parable for our society in the relations between the object world and the human world.

The work of the artist consists of finding new metaphors and representing them in new forms that help people to see and to appreciate human experience in fresh, new ways. The metaphor can create the sense of beauty. Authentic art is quite different from a notion of art as sublime, surface beauty, removed from real experience, a form that is merely *decor*ative.

The recent work of "conceptual" artists varies between abstract expressionist multimedia "happenings" and a kind of "pure" conceptual art that has no product. Galleries, with keen business sense, will validate that the no-product-conceptual-art-experience had occurred and the validated statement will receive a price tag.

A brief visit to a kind of conceptual art setting may help to clarify what really needs to be directly experienced. Become the solitary viewer of artist Brenda Price's work (Hanson Gallery, NYC, 1975). All at one time, you are taken over by sculpture, montage, painting, drama, and a novel in progress. In order to experience all of these media at one time, you must participate in the art process, as in a happening, touching permitted.

As in sculpture, painting, and montage there are concrete products. As in a drama or a novel, the themes spin out across time if the participant allows the time to become tempted into immersion. Metaphor can take many forms and these new forms address basic feelings and experience.

Ms. Price has created a series of beds shaped by frozen cloth, "to freeze the moment," and various props symbolizing the cycling of a woman's life from childhood through the birth process. The covers on the eight beds are psychological as well as physical metaphors for the sense-of-being, in private and public situations. Plans for parts II and III of the concept series are an "Infinite Laundry" series and a "Raising Children" series. Communication with others can be a problem when new forms are used.

Buber (1923) sees the artist and the appreciator in an "I–Thou" relation, a direct relation in a particular moment, an aesthetic experiencing for the artist while the artist is creating, and for the connoisseur while the connoisseur is appreciating. There is an opportunity for enrichment and fresh "insight" (Langer, 1957; 1953).

Perceptual models in the arts form the commonalities between the arts. There appear to be four major types of art products: "plastic, musical, balletic, poetic" (Langer, 1957, p. 78). When we look at "dance theatre" or multi-media "concept art," it is clear that one is basically kinetic and the other is basically visual. It is also clear that each centrally emphasized medium provides a different kind of participation. Even though a work is multi-media, a "primary" realm (Langer, 1957) stands out.

Human insights can be *communicated and perceived* through the creation of varied types of forms. Experiential data can be better understood when presented through the centering of one or another type or form. In this way, a primarily temporal or kinesic or auditory-poetic-linguistic or visual variant can affect people. These nondiscursive processes can reflect a rich range of perceptual models that would be less fully knowable if only discursive tools are employed.

AESTHETICS AND EDUCATION

Against this background, aesthetic experience is part of the broad range of human experience, of ordinary life, as well as artistic exposures. For Dewey (1934), "Even a crude experience, if authentically an experience, is more fit to give a clue to the intrinsic nature of esthetic experience than is an object already set apart from any other mode of experience" (p. 11).

Therefore, teachers need to provide for nondiscursive tools, the artist's means, as well as the discursive use of tools, discussed in Chapter 4. These tools need to be *integrated* into children's experience in order to support flexible thinking and the creation of new connections.

When selecting tools for young children, you can observe developmental changes between the apparently *random* play of the toddler with materials and the four-year-old who *plans* his creations with varying degrees of purposefulness. A child can create an insightful form only as a result of experience, even if that form is somewhat episodic rather than closed. Purposefulness and chance factors will interact in the resulting creations. However, an artistic product that can aesthetically move another person requires the input of the artist's own aesthetic experiencing.

Much of young children's learnings will come through their exposure to, exploration with, and growing coordination of, their use of producing tools. The teacher appreciates small benchmarks and shares these appreciations with the child. For example, as the three-year-old selects an intentional combination of building blocks, the teacher provides a verbal description and appreciates the fact. As the four-year-old begins to explore symmetrical block building patterns or the five-year-old experiments with unusual or complex structures, the teacher can do similarly. It seems likely, without guarantees, that the teacher who encourages many, varied forms will be supporting aesthetic experience. It is worthwhile to look at how each of the primary artistic dimensions is part of the young child's experience and consider ways in which they can be integrated into daily life.

TEMPORAL ART

Music forms a background to many activities. People of all ages hear music at the beach, in the supermarket, at a bus stop, during a conversation with friends at home. Yet, musicians exhort people to consider that music should be a part of life, not largely a background. What they suggest is purposeful listening to music. If they mean knowledge about music, then they are really dealing with history or a field of musical criticism, indirect knowledge, rather than the aesthetic mode.

Rhythm, pitch and melodic patterns, texture and harmonic patterns, can singly or jointly form the temporal experience along with dynamics. Children explore rhythm through body movement, percussion instruments such as drums, Chinese gongs, and triangles, and everyday objects. Melodic and harmonic patterns are available through singing and musical instruments.

Appreciating Music.   Teachers consider children's abilities to create as well as to appreciate music. In either case, music is a symbolic form and some elements require instruction. Where young children are concerned, the creative skills do not extend far beyond the appreciative skills.

However, music that is delivered with a passion, rather than passionately, is guaranteed to leave humans unmoved because it is overly intellectualized. A first step needs to be concrete experiencing in a setting conducive to attention. Appreciations develop by a systematic process of building perception. The teacher's function is to set the tone by timing and scheduling. Sometimes lighting, or the limiting of it, can help set a tone conducive to listening.

Here, again, the controlled number of variables will appear freshly against a familiar ground. Recordings and live performances of individual instruments and their combinations, with melody or rhythm or mode highlighted in isolation, provide opportunities for children to sharpen their perceptions.

For example, children could certainly distinguish between Eskimo music and the western European tradition. If children had heard a story or seen a film about Eskimos, hearing their music could sharpen that activity. The children would be likely to be more attentive than if no other contact had been made. Of course, children's attention level suggests to the teacher when to stop and change the actvity. Actually, hearing different kinds of music in the early years seems much more meaningful in the long view than singing "cute" lyrics *about* Indians that grows out of a dated pedagogic tradition.

When they learn to sing songs together, by having heard the songs on many spontaneous as well as planned occasions, a reasonable musical objective would be the feeling of participation that the children experienced rather than the attainment of the exact words. A song can turn an ordinary moment into something filled with expectation and good fellowship. It is too sad when teachers try to "teach" a song, line by line. Rather, they should "infect" children with songs. The greatest change in a teacher's self-concept can occur when he realizes that the children are unaffected by his own self-perceived lack of pitch or tone of voice.

When the teacher "aesthetizes" children's activities, they strengthen a dimension of personal meaning. There is a sense in which "only music can achieve the total fusion of form and content, of means and meaning, which all art strives for" (Steiner, p. 29). There is this sense that music can communicate basic human feelings in the way that the human voice can communicate feeling tone to a baby before words are comprehended. Art historian Gombrich (1957) suggests that at least one trend in art history has attempted to solve the problem of creating visual art that can provide the viewer with an experience that is as directly involving as is music.

Levi-Strauss (1964) makes a parallel observation when he compares mythological analysis and music, both of which "transcend articulate expression" and require "a temporal dimension in which to unfold" (p. 15). In this sense, music might be regarded as a nondiscursive symbolic repository of perceptual models.

Creating Music.   While you would not expect primary age children to create music using fugue forms and studied achromatic harmonies, you might reasonably expect that some of them would be able to experiment with melody and harmony in such simple ways as using a xylophone. (Mozart's earliest compositions were made at four years of age according to *Encyclopedia Britannica.*) Such experimentation is likely to flourish when the teacher takes a similarly experimental attitude. There is no formula to be followed other than the teacher's own openness to children's possibilities. The integration of children's creating of music with other aspects of early education is specified in the next chapter.

KINESIC ART

Common to all people is the veritable need to move. As humans grow older and become more differentiated, they have movement socialized out of them.

Dance involves elements of the *movement* of bodies through space along varied *levels* and in varying *directions* across *time*. The dance field has accepted Labanotation as a basis for recording this process of movement and rests. When adults look at the written representation, they can sharpen their outlook and appreciate the spatial relationships. Options can increase for isolating and contrasting variables.

The dancer can isolate and variably combine parts of his or her body. "Move only your elbows, your shoulders and head. . . ." The dancer can isolate levels: "Move in as high a way as you can, in as low a way as you can." In a complex pattern, the torso and arms might move to a rhythm that is different from the legs.

The dancer can isolate directions: "Move in the straightest way you can, the most curving way you can. . . ." "Move in the *flat,* as if there are transparent walls in front of and/or behind you. . . ." "Move in the *deep* as if there are transparent walls on either/or both sides of you. . . ." It is helpful to appreciate the components of the form.

The satisfaction of moving in space as well as the constraints of space are feelings that can be expressed. As human experience is communicated through movement, individuals approach the creation of an art form. Dancers talk about expressively "using" space, "interacting with" space. To the knowledgeable perceiver, space is a medium. It is almost as if one might play-fully structure dance as the nondiscursive interface to physics; the plastic visual arts to chemistry; music to biology; and drama to geology. Cutting across all are the perceptual models of experiencing.

In the following chapter, activities for movement education are discussed as part of the development of creative dramatics in early childhood. Such activities have also been integrated throughout the book. The following section turns to look briefly at literary forms, the nondiscursive use of language.

POETIC ART

People use the term poetry to define the wider range of nondiscursive uses of language. Probably because humans are verbal beings, they speak of poetic feelings almost as a synonym for aesthetics. Since creative dramatics and its related forms are dealt with in the section concerning socialization, this section examines children's relation to the nondiscursive use of language in literature, including poetry. Aspects of appreciating and creating are considered as they were in the music sections.

Literary Appreciation.   A good beginning for literary appreciation lies in the selection of quality writing for children to hear and later to read to themselves. When teachers select literature for children to encounter, they use the same standards as they would for appraising adult material. Some of the criteria to apply include integrity of characterization, even when the characters are ani-mals with human attributes; fine crafting; and the kind of imaginative use of language that contributes to aesthetic potential. In addition, the illustrations that accompany text in "picture books" for the early years need to be finely crafted because they are an integral part of the child's experience with books.

Nevertheless, while teachers might be able to agree on high standards in literature for children, some children may be unimpressed. Their level of taste may be far removed from the teacher's.

The literary critic Richards (1924) would agree that the teacher's function in literary education is to raise the level of taste and discrimination. If a senti-mentalized, hackney story is "the best" that a particular child has read, it may well be true. The teacher's task is to find out where the child is and then to help him move ahead toward the next logical developmental step. Educators Fader and McNeill have done just this with older children, permitting comics, periodicals, and pulp-type paperbacks in order to entice children to do more reading, to find more pleasures in reading, and to extend their range of selec-tions. Therefore, whether or not a child "likes" a reading is not necessarily related to the level of taste. One might say that they did not like their experience in reading but that it was good literature.

These outlooks are consistent with "perspectivism," as defined by literary critics (Wellek and Warren, 1962). In effect, it is important to know literature from different points of view, a major way of analyzing literary works. If a teacher wants to discuss a story with children, it is possible to avoid fact-stating but to raise questions about the writer's purposes and the child's feelings and opinions. When a teacher accepts a child's level and stated tastes, there is the possibility that the "Yes, boss" teacher game can be avoided. The crucial factor is provision of the right book when it is needed. As with music and all of the arts, teacher enthusiasm and an experimental attitude can go a long way toward influencing children's development.

Some Types of Literature for Children.   When we look at books written for children that they find appealing, it is evident that several forms stand out as distinctly child-like as opposed to adult. It is important for the teacher to differentiate those that have integrity from those that are gimmicky. There are many stories about people's problems and feelings masked by animal forms. The reader can identify with the characters and share the author's experience. Books such as *Charlotte's Web* (White), which some seven-year-olds can read, and picture books for younger listeners such as *The Way Mothers Are* (Schlein), and *The Noisy Book* (Brown) represent this genre. These animals serve quite a different purpose than do the violence-prone and violence-immune characters that appear in some other books directed to children. While *Charlotte's Web* involves the reader/listener in an intimate friendship experience with a spider and farm animals, laced with life and death issues, *The Way Mothers Are* underscores the intimacy of a warm family relationship through animals. *The Noisy Book*, in which three-year-olds enjoy repetitive participation, leaves the listener with a sense of empathy for a convalescing dog, and a satisfying ending.

The persons-in-feathers-or-fur, no less than human story characters that succeed as good literature, frequently involve the reader/hearer in significant human problems. Issues of growth and achievement; security and dependency; fear, assertion, and power; life and death events, are universal themes that can engross the reader. The finest children's stories handle these issues with care about children, providing satisfying if not happy resolutions. They do not titillate children and purvey suspense and violence as ends in themselves.

The cumulative form of the folk tale, frequently found in literature for young children, is consistent with children's developmental needs. When the substance is appealing, the cumulative stories are most popular, and easily retold. In any case, nursery and kindergarten children enjoy the repetition that is so supportive of a sense of mastery in so many areas. Gag's *Millions of Cats*, Tworkov's *The Camel Who Took a Walk*, or the folktale, *The Enormous Turnip* (Southgate), are examples of such stories, all with satisfying endings. A related form is the kind of symmetry that McCloskey develops in *Blueberries for Sal*, in which a human child and a bear cub inadvertently switch places, or in de Regniers' *The Giant Story*, in which a boy tries out his imaginary power to the satisfaction of numerous children from nursery age onward.

Part of the appeal of the successful children's author lies in his or her communication of appreciation for their characters and respect for their audience. There is a kind of sincere "eye contact" of the bone marrow. A. A. Milne is a master of this craft through the *Winnie-the-Pooh* books and his poetry classics *Now We are Six* and *When We Were Very Young*. If young children could only be exposed to two volumes of poetry, than A. A. Milne might suffice for a childhood's worth! He manages to touch most concerns and problems of childhood except for the pain of major deprivation. A parental reading of "Sand-Between-the-Toes," with coordinated tickles, beginning with "sand in the hair," is a rare joy. Even if some of the details are white-city-English, the human qualities are timeless for Western civilization.

In addition, a range of varied styles and forms should be read to children. Adoff's poetry anthologies, including the works of Langston Hughes and Nikki Giovanni, provide a range of sources for varied settings and fine craftsmanship. Giovanni's metaphors in "Winter Poem" are appreciated by three-year-olds quite as much as by adults.

Appreciating poetry that is read is one thing. Young children can also use narrative sorts of poems as a basis for their creative dramatics right alongside prose stories. Poetry is particularly adapted to choral speaking with subgroups taking turns and helping a reticent child participate. In addition, grouping together poems with some common theme or metaphor can help children to nondiscursively experience similar elements from different perspectives—a powerful way of learning. Such contrasts support the notion of critical education that is detailed in Chapter 8. Jacobs (1965) suggests using "poem cycles" along similar lines.

The teacher's enjoyment in a poem is its greatest charisma. It is worthwhile for teachers to become familiar with some favorite poems that they can integrate incidentally at the "right" moment. Milne's "Happiness," Stevenson's "My Shadow," or Segal's, "Be My Friend" are just right at certain moments.

At other times, the daily "story time" could include one or more or an entire session of poems for children to hear. Children will have favorites and ask for repetition.

With young children, memorization of lines and stanzas will come about quite naturally. When children say, enthusiastically, "Read it again," and "Again," they are coming into memorization. When the teacher asks the group what poems they would like to hear again, he is encouraging memorization. When the teacher reads a poem read previously, and invites the children to say any part that they know with him, he is leading them into memorization. When he gives them opportunities to say poems, or lines, that they have learned by heart, he is giving memorization its fulfillment. (Jacobs, 1965, p. 24)

Much nonfiction written for young children is written imaginatively and entertainingly. Illustrations in both fictional and nonfictional works are frequently well-integrated with the text and add to the experience of the book. However much these features serve to capture the child's interest, the informational impact of nonfiction is its primary purpose.

Creating Literature.   While report writing in the early years will grow largely out of children's concrete activities, from experiences they have had, some of it may be supplemented and stimulated by informational books. It is worth noting that young children's discursive writing and dictation may overlap with their imaginative statements. This reflects their growing attempts to sort out what is real and what is fantasy. The use of direct analogy and personal analogy can help children to make this distinction while focussing their attention on ideas about which to write. It follows that their imaginative dictations, tape recordings, and writings of nondiscursive prose and poetry will be largely a product of their integration of many experiences.

When young children hear poems and stories, the experience is sufficient in itself. The "turned on," totally absorbed atmosphere and the children's very posture tells the teacher that they may have been aesthetically captivated by the author and the delivery. *After* numerous such experiences with particular poems, the teacher might help children beyond five years of age to focus ahead of time on listening for "parts that remind you of the outdoors" or for "humorous" sections. They might apply the synectics strategy of personal analogy and "be the thing," or "the author," and play out the possibilities.

In brief, they would takeoff from the poem. This process also serves to sharpen children's consciousness of the process of poetry. Within a rich environment where imaginative language is used and valued, these procedures and other sensitizing activities found in the synectics materials may stimulate children to create their own poetry. In addition, the educator Walter, in *Let Them Write Poetry*, recommends that

. . . the poetry which will best stimulate the creative response is poetry which is short; which has simplicity of idea, of phrasing, of diction; which uses imagery; which is emotionally and intellectually suited to the age level; which presents experiences common in childhood; which is written in free verse or in simple rhythms. (1962, p. 24)

In effect, a first step is appreciative absorption and participation. Then, elements can be highlighted as "figures" contrasted against a familiar "background" by means of multiple samplings, juxtaposed by the teacher. In an accepting environment, these stimuli are usually sufficient for young children. Feelings usually flow freely into varied expressive forms at these early ages, and different forms are likely to feel more or less comfortable for different children. Some less verbal children find body movement a more spontaneous form in which to express their feelings while others may feel a closer affinity to the visual or plastic art forms.

The teacher tries to support a range of alternate forms for expression by appreciating and highlighting them. Sometimes children produce poetry when teachers expect prose. By accepting and appreciating children's attempts to express themselves, the teacher can build the kind of trust that is basic to a willingness to communicate one's feelings. Appreciating the positive qualities of children's work, while ignoring its inadequacies, will serve further productivity. The finest contribution of teachers to children's expressive productions is their capacity to legitimize many, variant forms of production, however incomplete or novel.

Each of the primary modes of the arts is suited to connections with other modes. For example, young children are quite capable of setting words to music. They frequently illustrate their stories, whether represented by several sentences or one word that conveys extended experiences. More usually, their words follow the illustrations. In the course of development, one might see a sequence beginning with movement and music, followed by the visual and plastic arts, before verbal representation.

VISUAL AND PLASTIC ARTS

Young children need a great deal of exploration with the materials of the visual and plastic arts. Nursery age and kindergarten children frequently need practice with coordination of holding pencils, chalks, crayons, brushes, and scissors. It is usual to see a three-year-old apply glue to a piece of paper that he then places, glue-side up, on his background paper. The very young child may need to be shown, by an adult who holds his hand, how it feels to turn over the glued side and press down. The child may need an adult to hold or attach newspapers firmly so that he can begin to use a scissors with two hands.

In any case, these sorts of direct instruction should follow from an observation of children's needs for help, to avert frustration and defeatism. The five-year-old who has an ambitious scheme to transform a milk container into a truck may need a great quantity of sensitive adult support for the execution of her project. If the teacher would end up doing all the work, it may be best to help the child find an alternative.

Materials for Creation.   There is a great range for using materials beyond painting at an easel, or table, or on the floor with brushes, or using homemade fingerpaints. Materials can be used in combination with each other. For example, etching dried paint over a crayoned layer with a stylus or inkless ballpoint pen can be a variant. The varied textures of mixing crayon, felt-tipped pens, pastel chalks, or rubber cement can be interesting. Mobiles that hang, or constructions built from a clay or styrofoam base with interesting collections of junk, are varying ways for children to experiment with materials.

For these activities, the teacher would do well to become a junk collector. Shop window dressings, discarded wallpaper books, closeout fabric sample booklets, a tailor's, upholsterer's or lumber yard's discards, used wrapping paper, candy wrappers, packaging materials and containers, discarded buttons and fabric trimmings, washers, screening, mesh, wires and wire ties, are among some of the seemingly endless possibilities. Some teachers have used onion skins, varied dry beans, egg shells, and variegated macaroni products.

When you run out of paper for painting, the classified columns of newspapers serve as a free substitute as do grocery bags. Powdered gray clay in large quantities, and powdered paints, cost a fraction of those that are already constituted. Freezer wrapping paper or barber chair paper rolls are less expensive than "fingerpaint paper."

It is useful for teachers to keep a card file of visual and plastic arts projects in order to provide varied activities that are well paced. For example, string shadow drawing materials may be made available to four- and five-year-olds at any number of different times during the school year for a period of several days at a time. Primary age children might have repeated exposures to print making, using paint or ink rollers. Each new appearance of the material is likely to be a fresh experience for the children. The teacher will probably observe different outcomes, due to children's intervening experiences, their growing coordination, and their ability to plan.

Undue traffic and mess is averted when art materials are stored and used near the water source. In one room for primary age children the sincere teacher placed painting materials in a corner diagonally opposite the door in order to provide the painters with a quiet area. However, traffic, paint and water marked a path to the water source that was outside the room.

Newspaper stored near art materials can be used to cover table or floor surfaces in order to cut down the washing up of markings, glue, clay residues, and cuttings. It also makes sense to use blocks on a carpeted surface if available in order to limit the sound level. If a choice needs to be made, the block corner is probably a carpeting priority over the basically quiet library corner. Smaller bits of carpet, or pillows on the floor, or even chairs, can be used for comfortable seating.

The three-dimensional arts deserve a closer look since they appear to be rarer findings than drawing in early childhood educational settings. Visual–spatial skills develop through experiences with three-dimensional constructions. These particular skills have been related to mathematical abilities (Maccoby and Jacklin, 1974). Few primary settings and not enough kindergartens provide ongoing opportunities for children to use even paints. Many more children need to have access to molding materials such as clay, plaster-of-paris, papier-mâché, sea shells, wire and foil, and pipe cleaners; and construction materials such as floor blocks and carpentry materials.

Three- and four-year-olds can use adult hammers, saws, and braces and bits when they are supervised, and sandpaper and glue by themselves. For example, the teacher can help those children who hold the cross-cut saw with two hands. They draw the saw across the wood, held in a vise, toward themselves about three times in order to establish a groove. Then they can learn to apply a downward motion to the carefully selected soft pine lumber. Some five-year-olds can use wire cutters and screwdrivers. Each teacher can expect that some children will need more direct help than others.

If funds are available, metal foil hammering, beginning with four-year-olds, and balsa wood carving, beginning with six-year-olds, are still other materials that children can fashion. The very youngest child's clay work may be glazed and fired in a kiln. Three-year-olds might want to use jar covers for cutting out clay and one-inch dowels for rolling. Four-year-olds might additionally want to use cookie cutters, a stylus, or small sticks for marking, and plastic knives for cutting. Pine cones and other large textured seeds can be used for pattern making.

In addition, mesh sewing for the younger children, and, beginning in the primary years, sewing collages, embroidery, macrame, and rug murals can be well developed. Four-year-olds with supervision can tie-dye extra shirts and squares of cloth cut from discarded sheets. Paper clips and paper straws have been used for weaving. Artist Monique Recant has woven magnificent constructions using steel-wool, and artist Wendy Ehlers has used lint, collected from washing machine and dryer machine filters, as a central material. Clearly, the possibilities for using materials are divergent.

Film techniques are becoming part of the early childhood program. For younger children, creations with motion picture film techniques reside in the realm of the visual arts, whereas for older children, the techniques can also be applied to creations that include dramatic forms. Inasmuch as children enjoy animated and unanimated films, some degree of literacy can begin with young children. Felt-tipped pens can be used directly on film, beginning with the four- and five-year-olds. Primary age children can create a few seconds' worth of animation with supervision.

Beginning with five-year-olds, in addition to motion pictures, children can refine their appreciations by using inexpensive cameras that take still pictures. Some of the cameras are available in quantity for less than a dollar. The Aesthetic Education Project (Browing and Ingham, 1973) is developing a photography packet. (The Aesthetic Education Project has been a federally supported project in education that was intended to develop stimulating materials, packets, activities, and research relating to various art forms. It is administered by the CEMREL Corporation, St. Louis.) Research findings indicated that preliminary studies showed children to be more accepting of unusual photographs (Roger Edwards, AERA, 1975). They also seemed more accepting of diverse viewpoints.

There are unlimited possibilities for materials to be used artistically if one only learns to see the strange in familiar surroundings. When that happens, the sole problem is finding space for all of the containers to store things. Teachers have labelled and put to good use materials such as discarded shoe boxes of uniform size, shirt boxes, huge ice cream cylinders, and packing crates.

Materials should encourage diverse, personal use. Teachers need to differentiate art from static, pattern-making pastimes.

The Teacher's Job. Beyond help with technical coordination of the medium alone, the teacher's job is to encourage children to use materials in imaginative ways, including multi-media work. Anytime a teacher feels that his idea for a project or a particular material must be experienced by all or most of the children, he might well suspect that a real artistic experience is missed. The common thread lies in evoking and communicating nondiscursive insights. Children may use an unspecifiable number of materials or artistic modes to symbolically represent their lives or to appreciate the experience of another person. Thus, there are many ways to achieve the processing purposes by legitimizing many, varied forms of production.

As teachers consider the issue of variety, there is a need to look at more decentralized ways to assess and record children's accomplishments. The change, time, and space factors that contribute to the assessment function are discussed first.

THE USE OF CHANGE, TIME, AND SPACE REPRESENT VALUES

This writing has emphasized that learnings through perceptual models can occur through a range of different activities rather than any single set of activities. Not all children should be compelled to participate in every project or series of activities. This is not only consistent with the stated view of what knowledge is, but of the styles by which children learn.

When teachers plan activities for children, they consider these dual factors of the level of complexity of the task and the child's readiness for the activity. The teacher views skills and knowledge in terms of their criterial attributes— the elements that are involved—and tries to match these elements with children's readiness. Thus, content and method exist together when considering perceptual models.

OPTIONS

If we look at options as a kind of accordion, we can see that productivity changes with the process of expanding or restricting the range of overtones, opening and closing possibilities. Unlike an accordion, we can imagine children for whom the reduction of choices may increase productivity quite as much as some children for whom the reverse change is true at different times.

The Number of Options.   For example, offering a limited choice of options to children who are capable of succeeding with them would be more useful than if they were guaranteed failure with a wider choice. The five-year-old child who drags blocks off the shelves and dumps all of them on the floor may limit his possibilities. In this case, the materials may suggest fewer ways to build than if selected from an orderly arrangement. The orderliness might encourage more advanced planning strategies in the child.

The number of options may be increased as the teacher observes children becoming independent. The number of options may be increased when the teacher observes that some children have explored a variety of materials. The number of options should be increased when the teacher notices an increase in wandering or interferences among children, or teasing or aggressive activity.

One teacher, whose six-year-olds were aggressive toward one another, decided to reduce options drastically. Not only did agression increase, but its expression became extremely overactive. With subsequent consultation, she arranged for eight different activities that ranged from fine coordinations and block construction through social board games. The aggression level diminished immediately. The children's behavior was an honest reflection of their experience in both instances.

In another primary setting, chaos reigned because there were no limits to options. Also, planning together between teacher and children was practically nonexistent. The children could use any material in the room at nearly any time. Consequently, they hardly ever felt a sense of their own progess or anything to look forward to the next day. Surrounded by gobs of glue, it was difficult for a child at the same table to write with concentration. Trucks would occasionally zoom past a child engrossed in a book who, distracted, would join the motorcade. A beginning step for this teacher was to declare a more-active and a less-active time for specified activities. In this way, too, the teacher could get a better sense of how children were using their time.

This case points to the fact that, beyond the activities themselves, movement and traffic are activities in and of themselves as well as connected with other activities. Previous suggestions for storing materials near where they are used make sense in this context.

Resources Affect Options. With this in mind, one of the controversies currently raging among teachers, and bound to outdo gum chewing for emotionalism, is the issue of private ownership of desks. If children are to be provided with real choices, and are to use materials with minimal distraction to others, it seems irrelevant to drag material to one's own desk space. Moreover, unless the resources are unlimited, the table and desk surfaces themselves are resources that need to be more fully employed. When children use materials in comfortably defined areas, others have a chance to observe peer models or to seek a genuine, common basis for socialization.

Within this resource-oriented outlook, children might store personal work in traditional desks, on shelves, in cubbies, or in shopping bags hung on a name-tagged coat hook. The other objection teachers raise is that children need their desks for writing, a statement that immediately reveals a classroom where options are limited, interest centers may exist only as lip service, and the chalkboard predominates as a focus for instruction. The writing center examples presented in other sections of this book are recommended alternatives.

Teacher Planning for Activity. Planning is definitely needed at several points. A teacher does well when she meets each week for an individual conference with each child. In addition, small group meetings need a plan. One simple, utilitarian planning form for use with young children follows.

1. Materials
2. Children's Actions
3. Teacher Actions
4. Teacher Questions

5. More Complex Alternative Content (Teacher Questions)
6. Less Complex Alternative Content
7. Next Steps

A few phrases can make a usable plan. Steps 5 and 6 provide flexibility and anticipate alternate needs for one child or the entire group and serve as an operating definition of short-term goals. Steps 1 and 2 should insure child participation. Step 3 may or may not apply, depending upon the materials. Step 4 provides a chance for the planner to consider priorities and to select an opening question designed for maximum impact. Step 7 serves to indicate a record as well as an advance plan.

With more and more experience, the teacher builds a stock of effective activities and stimulating questions. There are numerous publications organized from the perspective of separate subjects that provide ideas for one-shot deals. The professional educator can pick and choose and juxtapose these activities, in order to provide richer, long-range meanings. Sometimes, groups of teachers within a community have pooled resources. One useful such project is a collection of worthwhile trips that children can take with their teachers or parents in a given region, how arrangements need to be made, suggestions for preparatory, and followup activities.

TIMING AND PACING

As teachers look at the kinds and numbers of options for children, they plan when to offer these activities. For example, the learning style of some children is such that they need more vigorous early morning activity before they can settle down to more sedentary work.

Imagine a child who has slept all night, has been awakened by a parent in time to be served breakfast, and has been driven to school. It is no wonder if that child seems overly active first thing in the morning at school. Another child who is an early riser might have walked her dog, ridden a bicycle, watched television, or built with Tinker Toys for the past two hours.

Pacing, Balancing, and Saturating Revisited. Research indicates that the spacing of practice results in better achievement (Cratty, 1973). That is, the spacing of activity may be more important than the amount of time spent doing it. The balance of active with sedentary activity has been a basic principle of pedagogy. However, the unit system wherein a particular study such as "transportation" or "Native Americans" takes place only during the last two weeks of November or the first week of March flouts this principle.

Mindful of the growth of perception during alternative intervening activity, teachers would do well to intersperse subject matter throughout the school year, and across several years. The perceptual models curriculum suggests that a child could build a sense of achievement and success through one form if not another. Moreover, by alternating active and sedentary encounters, attention can be preserved by the contrast.

The problem of *saturation* may also be minimized by planning that takes into consideration the active and sedentary cycle. While there may be degrees of attention, the human nervous system does not operate by degrees, but by an either–or mechanism.

Each person has evidence of a "refractory" phenomenon when he drinks orange juice after eating a sweet cookie or perceives colors differently depending on their background. Just as people need to give their sensory processes an opportunity to absorb and become susceptible to new stimuli, teachers need to do at least as much for their children.

You can see this phenomenon when a child reacts to teacher questions. In one school, after several five-year-old children had been exposed to creatively oriented questions, they persevered by providing the next adult questioner, who was asking seriation questions, with varied and flexible responses.

Another consideration is the teacher's own need for gratification. That is, just because children do not manifest glorious results at the end of one exposure may not mean that the approach is at fault. Repeated, separated exposures over a period of weeks may be needed. Initially, such long-range activity may consume only a few minutes during each episode. An important criterion in such planning is the need for children to feel successful. This factor is one important component for deciding *how long* a particular activity or a series of activities would need to continue. It makes better sense to postpone an activity or its completion than to undercut the children's sense of accomplishment. Thus, a diagnostic, process-oriented attitude rather than an evaluative, product-oriented attitude should dictate the pacing and duration of activities.

Developmental Considerations in Timing.   Teachers of young children must provide enough time for things to happen. To a young child, rushing can be as devastating a feeling as failure. An adult who is hurrying a child repeatedly is communicating to that child that he is somehow inadequate. Anybody who has ever worked with three-year-olds experiences the five-year-olds as much more powerful in many dimensions, such as speed, energy, dynamics, sound level, and sheer power.

Physical routines play a much larger role in the life of the younger child than they do for the older child. It takes younger children more time to coordinate and accomplish ordinary tasks such as dressing. They need much more time to explore and mess with materials, and to coordinate their movements with those of other people. Especially for the three-year-olds for whom toilet training is a new development, they need a timely reminder, with enough time. Hand washing, which the teacher may regard as a subsidiary function, can be a focal one, a long-term project, for a three- or four-year-old.

There are some human beings who are always slower-moving people. If you could only tune in to the Stella in a group who moves slowly, sometimes as slowly as a mistimed film, you might be able to appreciate that her turtle ways, regularly paced, will help her to arrive within a reasonable distance of the rabbit-like, erratic sprinter and stopper. Even if she does not arrive, there is little to be done by insistence except to excite her sense of panic and ineptness.

Stella would be quite different than the child who moves slowly out of a feeling of hostility, a sense of being hurried, and of not being accepted by the adult. By moving slowly, this child can protect herself from even more pressure. In the second case, the teacher needs to deal with his or her own values, standards, and pressure rather than with pacing issues alone.

When children are engaged in real activity, when resources are seen more broadly than paper and pencil tasks and books, when the role of the teacher is decentralized, the underlying attitudes and premises dictate a unique use of space. While there has been discussion of space in Chapter 2 and the section on visual arts, some residual binding issues require attention.

OPENING AND ENCLOSING SPACE

For one thing, there is a message delivered when children's writing areas are in the center of the space and other interest centers at the periphery. What comes first in such a setting is "work" rather than "play," sedentary rather than active pursuits, and an alienation of intellect and pleasure. I contend that, in our rapidly changing times, this traditional image of the classroom is anti-intellectual and anti-humanist.

An equal problem lies in the arrangement of a massive expanse of open space, with all other activity at the periphery, as in an anemically thin doughnut. Chaos ensues, and the teacher's major task becomes behavior control. Again, intellectual, humanist concerns suffer. There are more kindergarten and nursery classrooms organized in this way than the occasional observer might imagine. The visitor is struck by the fact that large, stunning "Community Playthings" trucks, the veritable Rolls Royce of wood products for schools, are zoomed across this large central area, hazarding any body in their paths. The teacher plaintively complains to the visitor about the children's demolition derby mentalities. When she tries to subdivide the room into perpendicular "E's" ⊔⊏ by moving furniture, she finds a marked dimunition of roaring. In addition, it occurs to her that her room need not house the largest collection of "motorizable" vehicles in the county all at one time.

You may think of your space as perpendicular "E's" or a plus sign, or groupings of L-shaped areas, or a septagon radiating from the center of the room, or any other quidelines. Traffic patterns need to be considered along with a water source, and a balance between areas for socialization and individual concentration. When self-correcting devices are built into task cards and games, children do not need to seek help. When primary age children work in untracked "family" teams, their family buddies can serve as helpmates.

When you establish an area for limited purposes, it is useful to ask yourself what you would need to use if you were a child in that area. It may well be that rulers or writing materials should be available in more than one "writing" area. Thus, social needs, personal needs, and substantive needs dictate the placement of furnishings and materials.

When teachers see that resources include the use of 8mm film loops that cost little more than phonograph materials, phonographs, tape recording and listening devices, models, maps, games, and interclass visitations, they can see a range of ways to use space. With only a bit of tongue in cheek, it may be useful to build interest centers as spoked sections out of a centered closet-type core, whether round or octagonal or hexagonal in shape. This image may further legitimize the active use of resources, equally available to all.

Spatial Invitations. Emma Dickson Sheehy (1954), a classic early educator, suggested that a good learning environment had "invitations to learning." Building from this image, the teacher of young children can be a legitimate merchandiser of significant activities. The best techniques of advertising, including attractive setting, contrasted focal figure, redundancy of the product image and name, changing the packaging of a product or service, are among a few useful techniques. The teacher's own enthusiasm and commitment is probably the most important element threading through these techniques.

Space should be comfortable and inviting. Since young children feel comfortable on the floor, the teacher should legitimize it for them. In this regard, consider the successful buffet party as one where there are never enough chairs. Movement is only mildly kinetic and there is a wide range of opportunities for different people to meet one another. The hosting role is to see that everyone has a comfortable personal experience, is socially employed, and has some nourishment in hand. The host brings people and materials together in this flexible structure. The analogy is only partial. A teacher would also want to ensure that children experienced longer-term, deeper relationships with other people, and a varied menu of materials. Flexibility is supported when various seating arrangements exist—carpet squares, cushions, a sofa, institutional chairs, a small set of stairs for sprawling, a five sided packing crate. . . .

The substantive aspects should dictate the content of area usage. An arts center for visual arts as well as construction activities, a sociodramatic area including or near a games and mathematics area, a literary area, a group-discussion-planning-instruction area, an individually oriented writing area, a listening center, and one or more special projects areas—each can serve a range of needs. It is amazing how many settings for young children could profit from the mere provision of an enclosed literary area, and a designated arts area. These last two centers are probably the most universally acceptable and easily organized for that teacher who wishes to *begin* to decentralize instruction and centralize learning.

By their very existence, areas suggest positive activities in which children can engage. The next section on record keeping and assessment techniques suggests still other uses for the centers.

KEEPING RECORDS AND ASSESSING

The primary purpose for which teachers need to keep records is to better plan activities for children. While other sources— legislative, administrative, and parental—demand record keeping, the teacher's main focus must be in the service of children's development

There are a variety or records that can be created which serve varied purposes. Some kinds of records were mentioned in Chapter 2. The following section discusses the considerations and sorts of records that relate to personalized curriculum development, and then considers the more normative kind.

INFORMAL, PERSONAL RECORD KEEPING

Teacher-maintained.   The teacher can maintain personalized, anecdotal kinds of records for each child. Some teachers will attach themselves to a pad of three by five inch paper, dated, and headed with the names of a number of children for whom they want to collect an anecdote that day.

In addition, they would record on a separate paper the behavior of any other child who was particularly noticeable. The teacher notices a special moment of social risk for one child or the need for instruction in a particular number concept in another. These dated slips of paper would be placed in each child's folder.

A book for major instructional skill areas could be headed with a child's name on each page, and his accomplishments briefly noted, for example, categorized rhyming sounds—socks, key, light; needs help seriating seven cylinders; consonant-vowel-consonant words OK—next: CCVC group. At the same time, primary age children would keep a list of books or stories that they had read.

One child care center maintains a daily record book of anecdotes for each child that is open to parents (Vivian Manus, Personal Communication, 1975). In addition to projects, the teacher records the child's diet and rest activities. Parents add their own daily anecdotal record to the book.

Child-maintained.   The children's own notebooks, reviewed with the teacher's records during the individual conference time, serve as a record of performance in primary groups. In an attempt to balance a child's participation in varied centers, there could be a signup sheet for the center, or for a particular project. Preliterate children could place one of their own name cards in a pocket chart for the area. By the way, it is useful to employ such a procedure when children leave the room. A pocket chart could contain names of, and picture symbols for, places where children could go, such as the library, shop, office, lavatory, or speech teacher, and children could place their own name card in it. In addition, the larger planning discussion with the entire group could be a source for recording beginning choices that children had made on any day.

Product Samples.   Since many forms of expression are legitimized, the children's own products can be an added source of information to help you decide what they need next. In one group of three-year-olds, all easel paintings were collected and kept at the school until Christmas. The teacher sorted them by name and date, bound them in a roll with red ribbon, and planned to send them home. In addition to enjoying the sight of children's growing coordination and expressive abilities, she was able to see that Ross had not been to the easel even one time. Since he was always busy and productive with others in construction and sociodramatic play projects, she had not noticed the gap. When she suggested that he paint at the easel, he readily agreed. In his case, there appeared to be no problem.

The reverse could be said about four-year-old Tim for whom the teacher could record only a fixation upon a large red truck each day for a few weeks. Construction activities would occasionally relate to the truck. His only social contacts involved protecting his own possession of the truck. After a few weeks of adjustment to school, the teacher felt that he could do without the truck, that she and he had a comfortable relationship.

The teacher removed the truck to a storage room for a few weeks. He readily accepted that there were other things available for him to do. While he had taken comfort in the truck at the beginning of the year, he was now ready for more variety.

Similarly, when the five-year-olds' teacher noticed that the same few children played with dolls each day, she removed those materials for a few weeks and added other options. While Tim's narrow experience was grossly obvious, the five-year-olds' teacher noticed the doll play only after consulting her records. Rather than operate a deficit curriculum, in which balance occurs largely through what the teacher notices a child has *not* chosen to do, the teacher tries to plan for significant activities for each of the children.

TEACHER ASSESSING

The teacher needs accurate diagnoses of children's capacities in order to develop plans. The teacher can make many individual observations while he circulates. He can see what children are doing, how they are doing it, and then observe what they have produced. When children's work is inaccurate, he should treat it "not as unfortunate mistakes that should never occur, but rather as diagnostic clues which could be used to help the children" (Johnson and Tamburrini. 1972, p. 41).

What does knowing that something is "wrong," teach? What a child can do should be more important in planning than what he cannot do. For each person, there will always be many more things one cannot do than that one can do. While the teacher provides instruction where it is needed, it need not be at the very moment it is noticed.

The novelist and educator Calitri (1965) suggests that the teacher of a young child should simply appreciate what the child has written. Appreciation need not be undiscriminating because then it would be dishonest. Other educators suggest that teachers focus upon the valuing of that which is "unique or distinctive" in what a child has done, whether it is a drawing or written work (Burrows, Jackson, and Saunders, 1964, p. 17). There is an implicit sense that the teacher's clear appreciation of observed samples of priority values will sustain them. In this context, it does make sense that the teacher permit the child's personal involvement with his product to wear off with time rather than to attack the technical aspects of the product. My own preference with respect to the primary age child is that the teacher make a record of spelling or punctuation or form needs, and then provide instruction in a separate context at another time.

The complaint of a parent that her son's teacher hung up an abominable sample of her child's writing tells more about the parent and the teacher than it does about the child's achievements. That is, this child had a poor self-concept about himself as a writer, having been told so repeatedly by his parents. His teacher felt it was more important for her and for him to recognize his improved accomplishment than to address the inadequacies of his product. At separate times, she had him scheduled to receive direct instruction in handwriting, the spelling of vowel digraphs, and capitalization.

With this separation of instruction and assessment, it is possible to share the excitement of seeing a first grader look through her notebooks in June and comment with glee, "Look how I used to write, 'my.'" There is no greater sense of accomplishment than seeing your progress for yourself. Perhaps the controversy that rages around the "red pencil" correcting technique can best be addressed through parent education—and teacher education. While the adult may be focussed on spelling with the "a" before the "i," the child may be focussing on protecting himself from the teacher by producing less, less trustingly.

FORMAL TESTING

In addition to recording children's needs for instruction and accomplishment by observing their everyday lives, teachers have been asked to test children formally. Records of such scores are used to normatively compare schools, school districts, and materials. Sometimes the scores are used to track children into groups whose common factor is a test score range. The vagaries of profile, the variability of a child's performance in relation to varied tasks, is less often considered. This practice merits attention for intrinsic reasons, and because teachers as professionals should be involved in making decisions about such testing.

Most of the tests given in schools attempt to test the achievement of specific skills, the acquisition of specific information, and the general intelligence or capacity of children to learn in traditional modes. However, six-year-old Jose, one of the best readers in an inner city poverty area, attained one of the lowest scores in a reading achievement test. Several factors might have contributed to his test performance.

Teachers repeatedly observe that self-motivated performance is more competent than solicited performance (Cazden, 1972; Chomsky, 1972; Bellack et al, 1966; Moore and Anderson, 1968). Perhaps Jose saw no purpose for performing on the test. Certainly, the test administrator's cool, strict manner differed from his own teacher's encouraging attitude when he read with her.

Perhaps Jose could deal with the contextual setting of the classroom, which was functionally adequate to his academic life, but could not transfer his skills to the isolated bits upon which the test focussed. Perhaps the pivotal skills that he used for reading were not even emphasized by the test. In a similiar way, schools that test "new" mathematics achievements with "traditional" mathematics tests might find that their findings lack sufficient validity for making decisions about what to teach next.

The need to know how to take a test is another concern. Teachers who know that standardized tests are coming could instruct the children about how to interpret the test techniques. That is, skills in fully scanning; being sure that children understand terms such as "the same as" and "different from"; marking with a slash, an "X," underlining, or circling; or "all" those that apply to be marked or "only" the one that does not apply should be marked. It helps if the atmosphere is businesslike without being threatening. It also helps if children had met the test administrator in a less charged situation beforehand. Adults do at least that much when children have babysitters.

If a school or district does use standarized tests, teachers should lobby for representation in order to assure that the standardized tests used do, in fact, address the purposes intended by the teaching. The test field is vast and a study in itself, well beyond the scope of this book. School districts vary in their choice and use of tests; therefore, it would not be practical to deal with specific tests here.

Student teachers frequently have an opportunity to observe or assist in testing, and teachers usually receive orientation within the school district, by reading the specific test manual, and the test's instructions. While there are many basic textbooks in achievement testing, a unique source for early childhood workers is Walker's *Socioemotional Measures for Preschool and Kindergarten Children* (1973). Its contents may provide a needed balance to the largely academic, occasionally cognitive, measures now being used.

It bears reiteration that many of the teacher's most cherished values about humanistic behavior and qualitative thought processes are long-term objectives. There is usually a time lag between exposure to the experiences and their manifest products. Therefore, as teachers plan activities for children, the records of standardized testing may be a part, but surely only a part, of helping to make curricular decisions. It would be equally unfortunate if the core of instruction responded only to that which was testable.

RECORDS AND VALUES

What teachers value directs their decisions. If teachers value independence, then they note success when the anecdotal records reveal that children increasingly rely on their materials and each other rather than the teacher. If teachers value children's independent thought and increased communicating skills, then a look at tape recorded discussions gives feedback. If teachers value children's original and creative productions, then the collected samples of their written and constructed work, and videotapes of their movement activities, when available, can apply. Photographs can be another way to record children's original constructed work. If teachers value the expression of opinions and feelings, then children could record their reactions to happenings in their lives in a personal notebook.

Records that teachers share with others such as colleagues, the teacher next year, or parents, take other forms. Some school districts send two letters to each parent, twice each year. One letter is the same for all the parents and states general activities in which most of the class has engaged. The other letter specifies the individual progress of one child and is sent to his or her parents. Copies of these are placed in the child's docket and retained for the teacher to use the following year. Having both records gives the next teacher much more information than would a checklist or number grade system. When there is a record that goes solely to the teacher next year, it is useful to mention those personal approaches and appeals to a specific child that are positive ways to help him or her be productive and feel successful.

SPECIAL LEARNING NEEDS

This section deals with the teacher's work in individualizing instruction. While individualization has been stressed throughout preceding sections, it is pertinent to deal specifically with children who may have special styles of behavior. The early childhood educator is one who should have a sense of the smallest achievements of a young child, and should be able to communicate positive progress. These pedagogic abilities are important because the early childhood teacher is often the child's first teacher.

THE LEARNING DISABILITY LABEL

The learning disability label has been applied to children only in the very recent educational past, since the 1950s. It is an umbrella classification that really has no more single profile than any group of human beings can have. Some of these children are believed to have minor, "hairline" thin brain damage, "Minimal Brain Dysfunction," perhaps genetic, possibly as a result of birth trauma. Some of the observed behaviors are attributed to emotional disturbances. Some of these children are believed to suffer from allergic reactions. A physician and allergist has reported that fifty percent of the "hyperactive-learning disability" patients whom he treated with dietary controls showed a remission of symptoms in several weeks' time (Feingold, 1975). When artificial food additives and specific food restrictions were ignored, there was a reversion to hyperactive, angry, and diffused attention symptoms within only a few hours.

Teachers notice symptoms that group themselves around a few major behaviors. Perceptual-motor difficulties, visual focus, and problems with coordination represent one area of concern. Second, the child who is hyperkinetic, overly active and fast-moving to a point of frantic destruction (frequently an unintended by-product) is a more noticeable behavior problem than is the hypokinetic, overly sluggish and slow-motion child. The third major area of poor performance may be in concept formation, where a child is unusually tied to concrete referents, and has trouble understanding mild comparisons. A fourth area in which the teacher may notice a problem is in the child's language progress, notably reading. Renshaw (1974) emphasizes that the hyperkinetic child's behavior is involuntary, "an internal dynamo of excessive stimulation from the brain to the muscles" (p. 37). In addition to drug therapy, which can usually be discontinued during puberty because of unknown growth factors, Renshaw recommends *consistent* adult behavior and many small successes.

In many cases, the child in question may be perceived as underachieving because he "seems" much brighter than his performance allows. Any of the symptoms mentioned represent failure experiences in society, and problems with self-image usually compound the child's behavior. Chess, Thomas, and Birch's (1968) work with "Primary Reaction Patterns" suggests the dynamics. While children may be born with different primary reaction patterns, ranging across such dimensions as activity level, perseverance level, and intensity of response, different parents might create a different environment for the same pattern of behavior. Thus, the baby who hardly ever cried in one home might be largely ignored, and might become autistic, whereas the parents in another home might solicit interaction and respond to the smallest movements, thereby supporting sociability. Clearly, these are oversimplified sketchings and should be read as such.

There is a growing field of formal testing that psychologists employ in order to diagnose a learning disability. One of the few forms usable by, and useful for, teachers is a twenty-minute individual test, "The Meeting Street School Screening Test" (Hainsworth and Siqueland, 1969). This inventory has items dealing with motor activity, visual perception, language, and test behavior style. In any case, where a question arises, it is best to have a medical and psychological evaluation. However, unless you will be excluding the child, once you have tested a child, and found a label for her, you still need to work with her. Therefore, part of this section deals with some ways in which teachers can work with children who may be learning disabled. For many such children, early diagnosis and focussed help can serve to avoid many years of unnecessary academic and personal failure.

Ways of Working.   Teachers have found that learning disabled children do better when they receive individualized instruction that is focussed on a single, concrete variable at a time. Being easily distracted by visual movement is a problem for these individuals. Therefore, teachers have found improved attention by using a study carrel, or a seat facing a wall with only the necessary work materials in view. With such activities as science materials, the children seem to do better with structured activities in which there are concrete materials for them to use, and frequent feedback of success. The teacher can help children with such techniques as scanning or by suggesting specific questions to apply in classification situations. They do best when one activity at a time is before them that is short-range and that they can finish in a single sitting.

Focussing activities, small benchmarks, and frequent successes can be helpful beginnings to the extension of attention spans. However, it must be emphasized that no two children will provide the same profile of behaviors and needs. One child may profit from printed distinctions of "pit" and "bit" or "dig" and "big." Another might need the teacher's direct help in writing or sorting objects.

One home enviroment where a child watches a great deal of television and whose mother drives him to all of his appointments may be supporting his hyperactivitiy. Parents might be well-advised to let him exhaust himself a bit by allowing him to walk to school and to the park. Some children who seem to be impulsive readers, or seem to have trouble with focussing in general, might profit from the specific training offered by some specially trained optometrists and ophthalmologists.

It certainly helps the hyperactive child when his physical activity can be legitimately used. It seems reasonable to ignore minor body contacts and short term wrestling among children that is obviously not dangerous but rather communicative. Since most teachers of young children are women who have been trained by the culture to suppress agressive behavior, some consciousness needs to grow in the first place.

It is important for teachers to help impulsive children by focussing on activities rather than berating their behavior, to use activities to extend their attention span. When a seven-year-old is not yet able to read, it makes sense to play some appropriate sound readiness games with her rather than to hand her a second grade reader. If a teacher feels that a six-year-old can learn about money, it makes sense to provide real coins or concrete replicas rather than a pictorial representation that the child cannot connect with real money. The eight-year-old needs to have learned place value before he could be expected to learn extended multiplication. When teachers instruct an entire class in computation skills or money or spelling, they are really addressing only a part of the group. The child with special learning needs can learn best and perhaps be forestalled from interfering with others when he is handled individually or with a small group of peers.

Sociodramatic activity, detailed in the next chapter, can serve as an important, legitimized source of satisfaction and growth for the child with special learning needs. Such activity serves to extend fantasy, and, while based in concrete props, may help to move the participant to some distance from the concrete. The active nature of this pastime may also tend to extend the length of time in which an active child is willing to engage himself. Psychologists find supporting evidence that more active children saw, and made, fewer human-movement responses to projective tests and that they were less imaginative (Pulaski, 1974). In addition, sociodramatic play may be a means for sublimating excess energies and movement.

ACADEMICALLY DISADVANTAGED CHILDREN

When teachers talk about academically disadvantaged children, they usually mean that they need special help with a variety of sensorial experiences, language experiences, and the development of a positive self-concept within the school context. Whether the child comes from an economically deprived minority group such as a black family, a Spanish-speaking family, an oriental family, a Native American family, or a rural mountain family, some aspect of these problems may need special attention. There are some children from wealthy homes who have been deprived in some of these ways also.

THE CHILD'S STRENGTHS

At the same time, many children from impoverished environments come to school with a reservoir of experiences that may be powerful levers for the teacher to tap. Flexible thinking, original interpreations, a sense of responsibility for younger siblings, knowledge of local industry, and acquaintance with wildlife habits may be a few such beginnings. The perceptual models curriculum could grow from the datum of any experience. Part of the teacher's job is to perceive the child's background of experience as significant, and build activities from this base of strengths.

Hector, whose use of Spanish was much more competent than his English, was unable to do first grade mathematics in school. However, he sold shopping bags on Manhattan's Ninth Avenue, and regularly made change of up to five dollars. His teacher found out about his business experience by chance as she waited for the bus. She subsequently arranged his school work so that isolated numerals were turned into monetary transactions. When teachers sent Robert Wolsch (1970) their poorest language achievers, he typed their writings. In typed form, the writing was poetry. However, the teachers had only been looking for discursive language and did not see the poetry in front of them.

A rural child who has observed the entire life processes of sheep can certainly learn to see contrasts in school of other living beings and plant life. However, if the school ignores what she comes with, imposes a linear order, and insists upon a sterile textbook approach to the 3 R's, there seems to be little that is familiar to her. In addition, meaning for her is lacking. Compared with the woods, the animals, a busy street, or the comfort of being left alone with the television set, such a school can seem dull.

It is amazing to the observer that two groups of children in school can perform quite differently although they are next door to one another and come from the same population. One group may seem variably apathetic and chaotic, the other quite reasonable. Invariably, the difference lies with a teacher who is able to provide and legitimize involving, satisfying activities for children. One teacher shared with her group of five-year-olds: "You know I enjoy hearing you talk about interesting things with one another, don't you? That's why I like being your teacher. But some grownups don't like to hear children's voices. (The children nod, knowingly.) So, when another adult opens the door, please be very quiet." And they were! In the first place, she was able to provide them with a variety of options. They could feel some power to decide that this activity or that activity was their own choice. The substance of the activities had meaning for them. It was satisfying to them, and they felt secure.

In one alternative school for low-income black children

... youngsters aged 2 to 5 are taught 'survival' skills—what to do when the mother is not home. They are taught to cook, to lock and unlock doors, to use the telephone and to get around in the neighborhood. (Blakeslee, 1975)

The teachers felt that they needed to consider the children's real needs. Just as learning the traditional 3 R's is an important survival skill in society, teachers might consider that some of the alternative school's skills had a reasonable utility for their population of children.

Moreover, when children learn simple skills around the house and neighborhood, their feeling of competence grows. While your traditions might suggest that a five-year-old should have continual adult supervision, it is relevant to consider alternate life styles in which children find themselves. The main thing for the teacher to consider is that the child's perceivable reality rather than the teacher's perceived mythology is the relevant place for interaction to begin.

LANGUAGE INCREMENTS

Children who come to school with poor language backgrounds obviously need a variety of rich experiences that are also rich in language models. The syntax model games described in the preceding chapter are a useful, tailor-made part of such a program. One of the richest sources for language experiences is a by-product of aesthetically rich activities. Sensorial involvement with materials is important for the primary age child whose language needs expansion just as it is for the more verbally oriented three-year-old. The teacher needs to revise his footing on the abstraction ladder on a regular basis, adapting to children's needs.

Activities such as blowing soap bubbles, making bread, growing crystals with charcoals and gardening in window boxes are the kinds of sources that have potential for sensorial, aesthetic, and conceptual experience. Nature walks in which children collect collage materials, or seeds, or lichen and fungi, or rocks, or find their own clay, are other sources that extend language.

In addition, the teacher must recognize that a child's regional speech form may be quite adequate for learning and communicating, even if it differs from the teacher's speech style. For example, studies have found that many black children could understand the teacher perfectly well and used a standard, cognitively adequate language dialect (Cazden, 1972). Their problem in school lay with the fact that, while they understood the teacher, he frequently failed to perceive their understanding or their ability to communicate.

Studies of children's reading miscues underscore the need for teachers to appreciate children's understandings (Goodman, 1969). A child may read to the teacher and substitute his own verb form for that which is printed. He may alter a word, while retaining the meaning of the passage. Teachers need to view such miscues as acceptable since the child understood the author's meaning. When the teacher sees this as an error and stops the flow of reading, meaning as well as a sense of mastery are diminished. If the children were not already discouraged about reading, the repeated "corrections" might well induce the child to feel anxiety about performing adequately.

These cautions are applicable with any children, regardless of socioeconomic background. The main focus lies with appreciating the child's experience and understanding. You should also be cautious to avoid generalizations about the language deficits of any particular group. As a teacher, you can observe many children from improverished homes who learn easily and joyfully just as there are children from economically privileged settings whose motivation and learning ability is restricted. When you apply criterially referenced means in relation to each child's learning, detailed in the preceding chapter, there is a better chance of making a positive difference.

In addition, it is helpful to seek a balance of activities for children. Dewey deplored the fragmentation of his views in 1938. The clamor about disadvantaged children in the 1960s has led to heavily cognitively oriented programs for young children that address only a *part* of their possible development and experience. If you are planning to use any of these approaches, it is important to consider ways to balance their unidimensional approach.

SELF-CONCEPT

One of the concerns in all of these programs for disadvantaged children, answered in different forms, was the concern for the child's self-concept. When a child's physical needs may be inadequately met, when his parents need to spend most of their energy on survival, or in escape from an ugly form of survival, the young child's self-concept and expectancies can become injured. Teachers can be hopeful that the rapid growth of young children can be a helping factor as teachers try to provide a cheerful, secure, stimulating, and successful experience.

There is agreement among researchers that a child's self-concept develops at least along with his understanding of language. In our society, a black child learns to perceive himself as black somewhere between three and six years of age (Clark and Clark, 1939). Other children are believed to perceive these differences around the age of four years (Goodman, 1964).

One teacher of five-year-olds in a predominantly black population was incensed when a child pointed around the table stating, "You're light, you're dark . . ." and everybody wanted to be light. When a child, in anger, called another "black," why did that constitute an insult to him? If anything, should they not be proud to be themselves? When one of the children called the teacher "white," the others, quite disturbed, shushed the child saying, "Oh, no, teacher isn't white . . ." in a tone indicating that this significant person in their lives could not possibly be such a terrible thing as "white." These incidents indicated an unfortunate disparity of feeling on a most vital subject—themselves.

Sociologists have found situations where the "lower-class parent aligns himself with the child *against the teacher* on the grounds of class antagonism" (Davis and Dollard, 1940, p. 42). They also learned that the child often "finds that neither his parents nor his teachers expect a person in his social position to "go far" in school" (p. 286). In turn, these attitudes can be used as an excuse for nonachievement (Horney, 1939).

The popular media and materials in schools have supported these relationships. Therefore, the sensitive teacher should recognize the unique self-perception that such a child brings to school. It does not do for the teacher to dilute or deny differences but rather to accept and appreciate them. Otherwise, "if an individual has low personal self-esteem, he may project this onto his racial group" (Porter, 1970, p. 183). There is no substitute for a sense of competence and acceptance.

When a teacher is sensitive to the special torments of a child's self-concept, it helps her to know when to ask a question and to assess a child's response. For example, a small group of children gathered with the teacher to clarify a problem they were having. During the discussion, the sole black child in the group left abruptly. After everybody had scattered, she reappeared. When the teacher asked her if she had had a chance to plan her work, if that was why she left the group, the girl said, "I felt so stupid. Everybody else looked as if they understood. I was ashamed to ask how!" Sometimes, a child may not even know that there is a question to be asked.

An awareness of such needs implies that the teacher does well to plan beyond small group activities for regularly scheduled individual meetings with each child. Some children may need more and less attention. Whether such a conference consumes three minutes or ten minutes each week for different children, it is a valuable quality of time for which no substitute can be offered. It is a way for the teacher to be in touch with each child's accomplishments and concerns on a regular basis. It also helps to assure that children's productivity may have more balance than a rash of work preceding a parent conference of which the teacher is reminded!

BICULTURAL CHILDREN

The bicultural and bilingual child may feel particularly isolated in school. Current programs are attempting to support the retention of cultural heritage, notably with the Spanish speaking community in the East, the Native American community, and the English-speaking Chicano population in the West.

Particular controversy around the bilingual aspects of educational programs reflect a collision between the "melting pot" view or the "pluralistic" view of the mission that society assigns to schools. Current funding for subject matter instruction in the Spanish language, alongside instruction in English language skills, is a break from the tradition of the melting pot where pluralist approaches were privately funded. At the same time, there is a powerful argument that private funding meant the exclusion of the low-income child and further unequalized his opportunity. In addition, the child's self-concept can be strengthened when he sees his progress in the subject matter areas while learning to use English. Time will tell how English language development and self-concepts fare.

CHAPTER 7
SELF, SOCIALIZATION, AND SUBSTANTIVE LEARNING— COOPERATIVE MATHEMATICS

The preceding chapter dealt mainly with ways in which the teacher worked directly with children to support their development in functional, humane ways. The ways in which children work with each other as well as the teacher is another profound means by which children grow. The teacher's help is needed in order for such social interaction and personal growth to progress. These needs are dealt with in this chapter from several major perspectives, beginning with a look at the individual's socialization. We then consider the significance of sociodramatic play, and the socializing of substantive learning.

LEGITIMIZING SOCIALIZATION

Human interaction is essential. Earlier chapters have presented the interaction of social and cognitive development. Dialogue is an essential component in this development. The teacher's task is to foster humane interaction while children extend their knowledge.

SELF-CONCEPT IS LEARNED

It is through experience with other human beings that you develop your self-concept, acquire knowledge, and develop an ability to make responsible judgments. Your self-concept directs the quality of attention that you can afford to pay to the kinds of knowledge needed for survival. A poor self-concept is a distraction.

USING DIENES MULTIBASE ARITHMETIC BLOCKS, THE CHILDREN DECIDE TO BUILD WITH THE "LONGS" OR THE "FLATS" BEFORE TRADING THEM UP TO A "BLOCK" IN BASE 3.

Your self-concept and knowledge together mold your abilities to make responsible judgments and take action. You develop knowing. You develop judging. And you develop your self-concept. In part, your self-concept develops as you interact with other people, and receive "reflected appraisals" of yourself (Sullivan 1953; Horney, 1939; and Mead, 1934).

Self-concept, how you view yourself, is self-knowledge. It is knowledge that is open to influence by others. As your own self-knowledge grows and your self-concept becomes more strongly verified, you become less dependent upon others for information about yourself. You have confidence that you know yourself. However, what looks like self-confidence may feel quite different to the facade wearer. At best, teachers can deal in educated guesses.

The personal perceived self has been called the "phenomenal self" (Snygg and Combs, 1959). It is a person's only frame of reference whether or not it is a real representation. Therefore, a person tries to support what he perceives. Lecky (1969) proposes a theory of "self-consistency." That is, a person is likely to act in accordance with his self-picture even if it is false, or unhealthy, or hurtful to do so. Individuals perceive selectively and accept or reject action on the basis of how they see themselves.

Thus, if the teacher provides a young child with the label or attitude "slow," or "clumsy" or "thief" or "immature," or "aggressive," a young child will frequently manage to sustain the appraisal. However, other consequences grow from an unsatisfactory self-appraisal with which teachers must deal.

The central issue for education is that a child needs to feel powerful, competent. When he feels inadequate, problems usually arise. Problems such as fighting, destructiveness, withdrawal, inattention, fear, and unhappiness are obvious.

The core issue in helping children to cope with their feelings about themselves can be distilled to two strong provisions. The teacher needs *to accept the child's feelings and to provide the child with responsibilities.* These behaviors are much more easily said than done. Some instances will be discussed after considering that dealing with feelings is complicated by cognitive constraints.

It is clear that children are discovering new things about themselves as they work and talk with others in quite the same way that they are learning more about the world of nonliving objects. The social psychologist George Herbert Mead (1934) details several phases in the development of the self, from a sense of "I," to the socialized sense of "me." This development takes place through communicating with others, and learning to distinguish oneself from others. The child imitates, role plays on a physical level, does inferential role playing on a symbolic level, and then develops an understanding of the "generalized other" and empathy.

Other psychologists contend that some adults never attain a level of formal operations in their thinking and moral development because they have not had the needed experiences (Kohlberg and Mayer, 1972). While experience is no guarantee that reasoning skills and good, responsible behavior will develop, lack of relevant experiences would assure a lesser level of attainment.

ACCEPTING FEELINGS

"Richie is a cry-baby. Richie is a cry-baby." Two five-year-old boys are chanting, pointing at Richie, whose distress deepens. Richie runs into his house, tears streaming, trying to suppress his sobs, ashamed. The sting of his skinned knees has been pushed aside by the greater pain of ridicule.

Each of us has been "Richie" and each of us has seen "Richie." Children learn the lesson very early. Hide your feelings. Deny your feelings. Control your anger. Don't laugh so loud or so much. What *can* a child do?

One adult, observing a three-year-old's *jealousy* over a new baby, was sensitive to her feelings and gave her a large inflatable frog as a punching bag:

TEACHER: Now, Peggy, I see you feel it's hard to have a new baby. When you feel like hitting the baby, you can hit Big Frog instead.

PEGGY: Oh, but I *like* Big Frog!

Fortunately, the teacher was able to give Peggy snap-apart blocks, clay, and special moments of individual *attention* threaded through the day. Peggy's aggression toward the baby was manageable. Her parents also found ways for Peggy to provide real help around the house, such as using a magnet to help her mother collect thumb tacks that had fallen on the floor, and holding the hose while her parents washed the car. In short, three-year-old Peggy was distracted by responsibilities and activities with which she could feel successful.

Obvious material damage to limb and property rates more active attention in many settings than does *damage to feelings*. When six-year-old Hetty quietly tells each smaller child individually that she will beat him up, that he is a liar, or that he is ugly, and boasts about her out-of-school possessions and activities, little notice is taken. However, when she takes a child's plastic bracelet or extorts a dime in exchange for avoiding harassment, adults take notice.

It is probably a useful clue that Hetty is having difficulty learning to read. She needs individual instruction. In addition, she needs other ways in which she can feel competent. Her teacher provided her with the "Breakthrough to Literacy" materials, described in Chapter 5, in order that she might see her own statements written down. Feeding the guinea pig and washing paint brushes—a prestigious task in this group—are her jobs for this week. While these are beginning steps that may need to be followed by more specialized counseling, it is important to avoid making Hetty a scapegoat.

Scapegoating can happen all too easily when an exasperated teacher repeatedly reprimands the same child in front of others. It is too simple for the children to project their own inadequacies on to the target child. It is much better to take aside an offender and briefly discuss her feelings, her rights, and the feelings and rights of others. It also helps to find out both sides of an issue before assuming that the repeating offender is guilty.

TEACHER: Oh, Chris won't let you play with the blocks? Why do you think she feels that way?

JAN: I don't know.

CHRIS: I was playing there first and she came over and she just changes it.

JAN: You're selfish!

TEACHER: You feel you want to play with the blocks, too, and Chris feels that she worked to build something and wants it to stay up. What are some things you can do so that both of you can be happy?

When the teacher helps each child's feelings to be stated, both children feel accepted. When the teacher asks them for some solutions she is suggesting that there may be more than only one way to resolve the dispute. She is also suggesting that they are capable of being responsible for working out problems. With repeated *practice* and help from the teacher, both children may develop a habit of *seeking alternate solutions*. This is certainly consistent with a perceptual models approach to curriculum planning and development.

In addition, by reserving judgment, the teacher avoids falling into the trap of wrongly decoding, "I was playing there first." That simple statement might also mean, "I had it first—when she turned her head for an instant." or "I taunted her into enough anger to ruin my building." Similar arguments about sharing materials arise much more frequently with younger children.

COOPERATION AND SHARING

Many three- and four-year-olds need help in order to classify between "mine," "not mine," and "ours." Some children, even a child who is having a first school experience in the kindergarten, imagine that the teacher "owns" all of the toys in the school and will ask, "May I play with your truck?"

If teachers value a cooperative spirit among children, then they need to help children learn these distinctions, and to appreciate the special satisfactions of mutual effort. For example, my clothing and wash cloth and storage area are "mine." Children have less difficulty sharing when they have had a sense of possessions. However, sharing takes learning. Generosity is also a cognitive attainment even though it looks like a purely social accomplishment. The Soviet preschool teachers' manual describes how children learn that a new toy in the room is *our* toy which we share, and with which we play together—as children pass it around with accompanying verbalization (Bronfenbrenner, 1969).

The teacher models sharing by her helpful and cooperative attitude. Beyond "our" toys, we have "our" jobs. When we have materials to put away, you can finish with what you used and then help a friend. If everyone has a sense of everybody being responsible for replacing materials, children can look forward together to more quickly engaging in a forthcoming special activity.

Beginning with the three-year-olds, it is possible to ask children to suggest how they can help one another when the teacher is occupied. While the practice may follow more slowly than the plan, you can begin to build a habit of thinking. In all of these interactions, the teacher's positive outlook, her appreciation of children's efforts, her approval of their socially helpful behavior, and her acceptance of children's feelings and readiness level, can support cooperative behavior.

Substitute materials can be offered to children who are struggling over possession. However, as children mature, they are not as easily distracted by an alternate material. Fortunately, their developing sense of time may compensate, and the notion of waiting to take a turn with the material might be negotiable. "Now" and "later" are among the concepts that children need to classify through repeated experiences in which expectancies are substantiated.

In light of these observations, it makes sense for some duplication of materials such as scissors, hammering sets and corkboards for three-year-olds, and a few swings, rather than one, in the playground. Other duplication may be on the perceptual models level of the child's experience. Pipe cleaner constructions may serve a five-year-old as an alternative to clay. Shadow plays for four-year-olds may substitute for lack of space in a magnets center. A new shipment of colored pencils may be balanced by glue and sand painting for primary age children.

ANTICIPATION HELPS TO AVOID FRUSTRATION

When the teacher anticipates and plans for children to be active, he can avoid conflicts. Understimulation—not having enough appropriate activity—is an important cause of children's antisocial behavior. For example, the teacher just left her group of six-year-olds with the gym teacher. John is wearing rubber-soled shoes. The gym rule requires sneakers. On top of this, English is a second language for John. Had she been able to notice these elements, she might have prevented the incidents that occurred after she departed.

When the gym teacher sent John to sit at the side of the gym, it is doubtful that John knew the reason. Eddie, also with rubber-soled shoes, *did* know why he was at the side of the room. John and Eddie began to bounce and roll on a pile of mats, then to wrestle in a friendly sort of way. Eddie had had enough and seemed content to sit and watch the larger group. John repeatedly rolled himself over Eddie, literally pouring himself over Eddie's head, shoulders, and back, smiling all the while. Eddie clearly rejected this play, pushing away repeatedly. When they returned to the classroom, John continued to tease Eddie during a group discussion. Finally, Eddie exploded into a screaming rage. The teacher was puzzled.

Even if the teacher was unaware that the children had had to sit out the gym session, one can only wonder why she expected that John, who understood little English, should have to sit through a group discussion in which no concrete referents were available on which he could focus his attention. This was a moment for which she could have planned a separate activity for John such as a puzzle, or a painting activity, or earphones and a tape recorder with a story told in his native language.

Surely, if a school rule states that children should wear sneakers in gym, the school might have children leave sneakers at school. For those who did not bring any, for whatever reason, a supply of extra sneakers might be kept on hand. In addition, the rubber-soled shoe might be discussed as an issue for policy making consideration. Maybe "sneakers only" is an unreasonable rule. If nothing else, children without sneakers might be sent to the library.

Now, the issue of responsibility enters here. Whatever the rule, should Eddie be responsible to wear sneakers? In the case of Eddie, there was no financial or comprehension problem. In the case of John, finances or comprehension might have been problems. While both children felt the consequences of their possible forgetfulness, the entire group's discussion was devastated. The whole complicated situation might have been prevented.

DIAGNOSIS HELPS TO AVOID NEGATIVITY

When Eddie felt flooded and frustrated, he exploded. On another day, when Betty felt frustrated, she became negative. She simply refused to engage in an activity and promptly withdrew. She became "passively" reactive. The teacher had the interesting idea of bringing real menus from a local ice-cream shop and asked some of the seven-year-olds to select anything they wanted to eat and then to add up their own bill.

TEACHER: Betty, come and pick your foods.

  BETTY: No!

TEACHER: Now is the time to do this. You didn't read with your group today. Now, it is time for this work.

  BETTY: (*Hides behind a cupboard when the teacher turns away for a moment.*)

The teacher had been experiencing the child's negativity that day. Earlier, the child had been interrupted without advance notice from reading a book she had selected in order to join a group reading session. Perhaps had she been given advance notice, she might have finished the page or chapter and joined the group on her own steam. However, with respect to the patently stimulating mathematics lesson, other elements were at play.

The skills needed before Betty could add the bill included reading the menu, reading the money symbols, adding three digit numbers and dealing with place value transfers. Somehow, Betty had not learned place value, was not aware herself what was bothering her, but knew that she *felt* incompetent. Had the teacher taken a moment to ask the child "Why?," who knows what might have resulted?

A child might refuse an activity for several reasons. The child might feel that the activity is too difficult, that he does not understand what to do. It is difficult for children to verbalize this feeling. On the other hand, a child might feel that an activity is too easy to do, and might be able to say this to the teacher. If the child experiences the overly simple task as boredom, she may have difficulty verbalizing it. Sometimes, beginning at the toddler age, a child will simply test the limits of his power by saying, "No!" to the adult. Part of this negativity is really a question that the child is asking, trying to corroborate his understanding of the situation. Relevance of the activity is still another possible factor to consider when a child refuses to participate.

Relevance. A teacher asked all the six-year-olds to copy a letter to their parents reminding them of a meeting the following evening for which they had received a prior printed notice. Frank began to write nicely and then scribbled his paper.

TEACHER: Frank, you began the letter so carefully. Why are you messing the paper?

  FRANK: My mother's not coming to the meeting. She talked to me about it.

The activity needed to make sense to him before he could be expected to do it.

There are occasions when children are engrossed in an activity and nothing else seems as relevant to them at that moment. The teacher could try to find out if that might be a reason for the negativity and suggest the following.

I see you prefer to do this now. (*Respecting his feelings.*) It is important for you to have a planning meeting with me sometime today. Do you prefer to meet me before lunch or right after lunch? (*Giving him responsibility.*)

Clearly, *the way* in which the teacher makes a request or offers a choice will influence the child's perception and response. The child who is having his first school experience may not understand when the teacher asks "all" or "everybody" to do something, that it includes himself.

Competition.   Competitive situations can also draw out children's negativity. A child who is afraid to risk losing may choose not to participate in the first place. In competitive games, there is only one winner but many losers. And how must the sole winner feel, surrounded by so many on the other side of success? The Soviet system attempts to ameliorate this impact by developing competition between groups (Bronfenbrenner, 1970). The entire group loses or wins, and all of the group's members are responsible to one another for working hard. However, the group pressure placed upon the less competent or less responsible child appears to be much more severe than most teachers would deliver.

The cooperative feeling of a situation where the individual's problems become the group's problems can be a positive force for cooperative work. The teacher can be an important model by exhibiting accepting feelings where needed and expecting responsible behavior where it is possible.

However, cooperative behavior cannot be legislated. It grows first from "having" before "sharing." Children need to have a sense of acceptance and accomplishment, a sense of competence. Psychologist Rollo May (1972) contends that "powerlessness corrupts," and that, "The goal for human development is to learn to use . . . different kinds of power in ways adequate to the given situation" (pp. 114, 113).

Cooperative behavior is tied to the child's self-concept and his "sense of worth" and "power-to-be." Children can feel powerful through a sense of independence. Independence is strengthened when children can participate in making their own choices and when they can be responsible for completion of tasks commensurate with their ability. It helps if the teacher holds a reasonable, not a perfectionistic, standard for young children.

In well-run settings where these conditions exist, there is more productivity, less child-to-child violence, and a friendlier relationship between teacher and children. Sometimes, these settings may "look" less orderly than when children are regimented. There is usually more evidence of children talking and moving about purposefully. These are desirable realities. They are a natural fit with children's development.

AGGRESSION

However, there is hardly a situation where human beings gather when aggression does not occur from time to time. It is a real problem for the teacher, but not an excuse, when children come to school already brutalized. Similar roots develop into varied forms ranging from hurting other children, destructiveness, verbal aggression, other attention-getting behavior, and apathy.

Hurting Others. When children hurt other children by *hitting* or *biting* or scratching, or shoving, they need to be restrained. Teachers have used some of the following statements successfully:

Come with me. I have something for us to talk about alone.
We'll come back to the others when you are ready.
When you learn to build with this, not hurt her, then you may have it again.
That hurt her. Tell her with words if you don't like what she did.
If you want his attention, tell him with words.

If a child bites, it is certainly unfair to the victims. The aggressor also experiences shame following the reactions of the other children.

Fortunately, the occasional biter will grow out of this technique in nursery school, but hitting others can seem perpetual. While a nursery age child who is out of control can be physically removed from a situation, this is only a temporary emergency measure. The teacher who finds himself physically dragging away children who do not respond to words must take stock of other techniques and means of prevention. Certainly, a teacher who hits a child can only serve as a negative model for the other children, and has dropped the professional role. Building inner controls is an important educational purpose.

Instead, the teacher needs to provide as few restrictions as possible for the children. Then, when a legitimate "No!" comes from the teacher, it may be perceived as a "figure" rather than merged with the "background." How can the child be given more legitimate, varied choices? Does the child have enough notice before ending an activity? Does the teacher notice him and share her appreciation with him when he is working in a *positive* way? What activities can give him success experiences? Can the teacher set up situations in which the child can make friends through a common task? Are there times when fun and giggles are tolerated?

Children who feel powerless need outlets for success experiences that they feel they have chosen by themselves. They need to feel that the teacher accepts and appreciates their efforts. The standards held for them need to be realistically related to their own capacity. After the hurt child is comforted, the teacher can speak with the aggressor privately, exploring alternatives to hitting.

The daily activities should include legitimate, closely supervised, activities that make the child feel powerful. Plastic materials, water play, clay, and woodwork are a few such activities. In addition, the primary age child can feel competent through achieving small benchmarks in written communication, heavily dosed with teacher appreciation.

The three-, four-, or five-year-old may need more large muscle activities. Kickball or beanbag throwing games seem made to order. Activities in which he can watch toys roll or fall may interest him, such as a sand box or bean box with funnels and inclines, and transparent containers through which the child can observe falling and rolling. Other activities could include using balance scales, a pendulum, and a contained area in which marbles or beads can be rolled and aimed. There are potentialities for aesthetic experiences in these activities.

Destructiveness.   When a child destroys equipment or other children's work, it may be accidental, a result of curiosity or poor coordination or impulsive handling. Adults must look at the child's intent and act accordingly. Young children require sturdy materials in the first place. The placement of some materials or equipment may need to be reevaluated. For example, classroom traffic might be rerouted by changing the placement of a table or shelf. Some equipment might be transferred to the outdoors. Still other equipment might be made available at some times rather than others.

Verbal Aggression.   When a child calls another names, insults another, uses toilet words or sex-related words, it usually is in a tone that expresses anger. Rather than force the issue of apology with empty verbalisms, the teacher would do better to see what the behavior means to the child.

The child might be trying out new words whose meanings are unclear. He may also be testing the limits of the teacher. If he used to hit others and now uses words, then the teacher might interpret some progress, and share his interpretation with the child. If the child is trying to gain another child's attention in this way, then it may be that he needs to learn other ways to approach other children. It may also mean that he requires more activity in which to involve himself.

With the youngest children, it may pass if the teacher distracts the children, ignores the language, or makes up rhyming games with the sounds, such as stinker-tinker-rinker-dinker-binker. However, it is reasonable to let children know that:

When you call him by that name, you hurt his feelings.
It upsets some people to hear those words. We don't use those words here.

Other Attention-Begging Behavior.   Children use other means to get attention such as throwing temper tantrums and taking things. In these ways, they can assert themselves when they may feel blocked from more positive means. Tantrum behavior can be ignored after suggesting, "Let's talk after you calm down." However, the child's frustration or sense of helplessness needs to be understood by the teacher. The teacher can make a point of appreciating the child's verbal requests, attentive work, and positive approaches at other times.

When a child takes things from others, or takes home school toys as a way of feeling potent, the teacher needs to pay special attention to him when he is working well, in terms of who he is. His positive efforts need to be noticed and appreciated. When a teacher enjoys a child's activities, or just enjoys his enjoyment, it sends a message of acceptance and success to the child. It may help if the teacher is sympathetic to his desire for an object that is not his, and accepts his feelings. At the same time, she needs to make clear that his behavior is not acceptable.

May (1972) suggests that human beings show at least three types of responses when they feel threatened: "fight," "flight," or a "delayed response" (pp. 183–184). The flight reaction may not directly hurt anybody but the teacher can become quite anxious when a child runs away or disappears. It is a clear message that this child needs more positive attention and stimulating activities from a teacher who frequently appreciates the child's work and his very childhood itself. In this instance, as well as others, it is as useful for the three-year-old as it is for older children to have a *regularly scheduled* individual time with the teacher. Teachers of three-, four-, and five-year-olds who pride themselves on operating decentralized classrooms may be prone to miss regular contact with some of the more quiet-appearing children.

Apathy.   When legitimate forms of aggression are unavailable, there is a tendency for human beings to turn the aggression against themselves. A historian documents the tendency among a suppressed group to teach their children to deny or control anger (Genovese, 1974). This denial has sometimes resulted in difficulties with real self-assertion that can lead to apathy. Sometimes obstinacy, or performing a task very slowly as if bored, or "forgetting" to do something are symptoms of such feelings. Apathy holds the threat of culminating in explosive violence.

POSITIVE ASSERTIVENESS

However, aggression has positive aspects that need recognition. To assert oneself is to risk action. May (1972) clearly distinguishes between aggression and assertion and makes the case that there are times when each is necessary. For the young child, assertion may involve testing limits. Aggression may be a way in which young children assert their growing independence and may be a message that legitimate self-assertion has been blocked.

The problem for the teacher is one of accepting the feelings that children bring, and helping them to direct their anger into forms that are supportable within group life. Handling aggression is a particularly subtle issue in early education since most teachers of young children have been women. As women, they are the repository of society's constraints upon women's assertiveness, currently in a beginning process of change. At the same time, research has found that boys are more aggressive than girls and receive more scolding and restraints from teachers in nursery school (Maccoby and Jacklin, 1974). They also receive more positive attention than girls. These are attitudes about which teachers need to become more conscious.

In any case, when it comes to aggression, it is fruitless to fight fire with fire. If you want to put out fire, you need to remove the fueling source or add water. The calm surface may hide an underlying storm. If you look at the source of fuel for hostility, you find that dependency and overly controlled situations make their contribution. Instead, children need to develop their independence through legitimate responsibilities. When children feel secure enough to *take risks,* to *try* new activities, they are using their "power-to-be." It is the teacher's role to provide the setting of materials and activities, and to bring together persons in ways that help children to be *challenged* and to feel successful.

When children are involved in legitimate activities, they do not have the time or need the opportunity for mischief. At most, they may use humor as a way of showing their power, as when a child knowingly matches pictures or objects or words incorrectly in jest. It shows that she knows what she is doing, and feels competent enough to play with her acquisition. Surely, her behavior is a clue that the teacher needs to help her move to additional challenges after appreciating her humor.

The teacher can plan positive activities that directly respond to the form in which a child's problem presents itself. If a child has tried to cut his own hair or somebody else's, then various substitutions seem to follow. Perhaps the child could be given newspaper, or could fold and cut paper in "snowflake" patterns, or create paper bag puppets with yarn or paper fringes for hair that would need trimming. Such activities suggest that the teacher interpreted the child's meaning as either aesthetic (the feeling of the hair) or in terms of the adult model of the barbering act.

Gardening, where possible, or window box plantings offer another way to provide legitimate, responsible activity. In effect, when children can grow their own vegetables or flowers, or help another child, or give a gift to somebody, or act on their own behalf, they build a sense of power.

Activities that require mutual effort are useful also. Some suggestions are offered in other sections. In addition, the Patty Smith Hill type blocks that bolt together are one such piece of equipment that young children can use cooperatively. Murals, planned together and executed together, can bring children together, beginning in nursery school. However, the four- and five-year-olds can be expected to have an egocentric notion of which side is up. This makes a tablecloth created for parent meetings with felt-tipped pens an ideal free-form mural project.

In the primary grades, children can construct a wooden play building together with intermittent adult supervision. Such a specialized structure can also serve as the site for subsequent sociodramatic play or special creative dramatics projects. Dramatic play activities can take on infinite forms for nursery as well as primary children. In addition, the children can create puppetry productions together, showing some of their productions and self-made puppets to other groups of children. In this way, they can receive additional recognition for their focussed work. Animal and plant exhibits with attendant illustrated and/or written commentary can be still another focus for children's cooperative efforts.

When the teacher tries to bring children together, she might ask them directly to make suggestions during an individual conference time, rather than to make all decisions by herself. It is also interesting to hear children's reasons for selecting associates. In a suburban kindergarten, George, the "messenger of the day," had selected Alma to accompany him. When they returned, the kindergarten teacher assumed that he had selected her because all of the children had paid her a great deal of attention that day. When the teacher said,

"I bet I know why you selected Alma—because of her costume . . . ," George answered, "No, because I have a new allergy and she's the only other person I know who has one."

LOOKING FOR THE CHILD'S MEANING

It is useful to find out why a child behaves in a particular way or asks a particular question. The general literature concerning work with human beings—and common sense—underscores the need for "active" listening. It is best to answer a child's question when it is clear what he means, answering what it is the child asks rather than elaborating. When children ask about basic issues such as birth, death, and imaginable disasters, it is important to answer children accurately and honestly. Teachers frequently ask, "Why do you ask?" in order to be clearer about what response to make.

A child might be asking because she needs clarification, or confirmation, or new information, or permission, or absolution, or reassurance. It follows that children who receive direct responses will have their curiosity satisfied or will feel comfortable enough to seek further clarification. Children frequently reveal their own misconceptions when the teacher asks for the child's ideas.

For example, some young children imagine that *death* means a return to "mommy's stomach" (Isaacs, 1933). Others have concluded from films and television that the dead person "will sleep in the coffin and then get up and walk around." Adults clearly and simply explain the facts. A young child's curiosity or actual grief are important feelings for them to experience and to accept.

Children are also understandably curious about the *birth* process. In both instances, prurient interests are averted when children's concerns are directly addressed in reasonably general terms. Children will be direct if they do not understand clearly. When five-year-old Evan's teacher was expecting a child, and was told that a baby was growing inside her, he lifted her blouse to better see the baby. His teacher explained that nobody would know what the baby looked like until it was ready to be born.

Children's own bodies and functions may serve as a brake or accelerator to the growth of self-concept. When a child's acquisition of bladder or bowel control is incomplete, other children might tease him. Since control is a recent acquisition for three- and four-year-olds, teachers expect that children will have an occasional loss of control. Sometimes this results from tension and daydreaming, or from forgetfulness while playing, or before a child is becoming ill. Since children may not want to miss anything, the youngest need a regular time each morning and afternoon, and around lunch time, when the teacher builds the reminder into the program as a scheduled routine. Even five- and six-year-olds need to be scheduled to use the toilets before a trip.

In addition, it helps if children are appropriately active and are not overly pressured to maintain a high standard of performance. If you suspect that expectations at home or in school are too high, it is important to be sure that children can choose their activities. It is also helpful to appreciate their efforts as well as their accomplishments.

It has been generally accepted nursery school practice that three- and four-year-old boys and girls are provided with common toilet facilities. In this way, curiosity can be satisfied. Some psychiatrists, however, regard this practice as overstimulating. Whatever your persuasion, there is general agreement that the kindergarten and primary years mark the beginning of privacy. There is also agreement that adults should use standard terms such as "urinate," "defecate," or "bowel movement," "penis," and "vagina," rather than euphemisms. This practice is consistent with the position that direct information and a standard model of language should be provided by the teacher.

"Cheating" is another issue that calls for a look at the meaning of the behavior for the child. Usually, the responsibility for "cheating" is placed on the child. The "perpetrator" may be trying to avoid a sense of failure. However, if he is working at his own rate, there is likely to be less tendency to look at some other source for "the" answer. In addition, if activities are structured so that knowledge is used rather than formally tested, such activity may be avoided. In this sense, the elimination of cheating, or lying, or tattletaling lies with the teacher's avoidance of conditions that foster their growth.

When children can see their own progress in relation to their own pace, and can see that the teacher sees it, the competitive outlook is undermined. When children are worried about their standing in relation to others, competitive feelings grow. It is contradictory when the teacher urges helpfulness, cooperation, and sharing, but operates a chart with stars or a point system. It is the teacher's attitude of sharing, rather than separating responsibilities, that serves as an important prototype for children.

If the teacher trains the child to think getting a good mark is an absolute good, she must consider what nonarbitrary basis the child might have for thinking cheating is bad. (Kohlberg, 1964, p. 427)

However, when the teacher's efforts to plan and participate in an environment that supports sharing, honesty, caring, success, and joy are unsuccessful, there are real problems that must be solved. When problem questions are raised by a teacher or a child, a discussion of alternative solutions is useful. It is important that those individuals who are concerned be the persons who help to resolve the trouble. In addition to problem solving discussions, behavior modification techniques and the role of modelled behavior are considered in the following sections.

PROBLEM-SOLVING DISCUSSIONS

The French philosopher Pascal (1941) makes the general point that a person's position can be swayed if he feels that the other person understands his viewpoint. From "his" viewpoint he was not mistaken but only needed to see the issue from another viewpoint. His feelings, as well as his thinking, influence the modification of his thinking.

Piaget's (1947) concept of decentration reflects this interaction of affect and cognition, and supports the notion that "logical thought is necessarily social" (p. 164). Through social interaction, thinking becomes more flexible.

Simulation Forms. The simulation experience of metaphoric extension is a lever that might provide a way for solutions to surface. The synectics techniques discussed in the preceding chapter can be extended through the "Juggler Flowsheet."

The discussion leader's role is "to form questions, keep the group within the process, and record the group's responses . . ." (Synectics Education Systems, n.d.). The first, especially difficult phase, is to establish clearly what the problem is. The discussants and the discussion leader, or "juggler," need to agree about what they understand the problem to be. It is recommended that the participants "keep the Problem as Understood to ten words."

Once the problem is identified and agreed upon, the discussion leader solicits direct analogies of the problem, favoring "living" analogies, for example, "What animal acts like that?" When there is agreement that a direct analogy is sufficiently distant from the problem, the group can imagine that they "are" the direct analogy and use the personal analogy, being the thing. "What does the animal do? Say? Feel?" "How does the animal feel when his friend brings him a treat? Takes away the toy? Wins the race? Breaks his sand castle?"

The personal analogy phase can be a sort of role-playing situation in which children can suggest how they feel or what they can do in their analogous role. The synectics methodology then suggests continuing with the "compressed conflict" phase and other steps. It may be that for children under the age of seven years, the demands for concentration and written records will limit the possibilities of a total excursion. However, they can certainly move through the first personal analogy level and explore alternative solutions in fantasy and reality.

This limited format is similar to the Shaftel and Shaftel (1967) values-role-playing materials that do not require writing or reading. Also, the Shaftel and Shaftel set of large, interracial photographs provides the analogues with which children are to identify. They depict ethical problems. First, the children and teacher discuss each of several possible interpretations of the illustrated problem. Selecting one interpretation, they discuss a range of alternative solutions and consequences.

Then, the children take turns playing out each of several solutions from the perspective of different persons in the photograph. These varied roles need a series of meetings in order to be explored. Beginning with small groups of children, the teacher can start the role playing process by taking one of the parts and using evocative questions, as she might do during the personal analogy phase of the "Juggler Flowsheet."

The discussion process needs enough time. If the participants feel pressured or rushed, it is reasonable to postpone the resolution of the problem. There is a great deal of self-reliance and important observation of positive models that is at stake, as well as the resolution of a problem. Teachers who share problems with a child or group of children find that the children's solutions are useful, and a powerful basis for action.

Direct Forms. The "Teacher Effectiveness Training" (T.E.T.) system recommends that problems be solved through a parallel process (Gordon, 1974). The authors similarly recommend that a series of sessions may be needed but that at least one phase of a problem be dealt with in a given session.

Crediting Dewey, the T.E.T. approach also calls for a clear, mutually agreed upon statement of the problem. The second phase involves the consideration of alternative solutions, evaluating each one, and then deciding which one the group favors. The third phase explores how best to implement the solution. The final phase involves assessing how well the problem was solved.

The T.E.T. approach cautions that consensus is important if action is to follow and that the group needs to imagine what would or would not happen in each circumstance. A group decision is then arrived at with a tentative outlook. It is also important to establish "who does what by when," after the agreed upon behavior is clearly defined and understood by the group.

Ginott (1965), also a psychologist, also recommends that children take responsibility for choosing solutions to problems that are within their ability. Parallel with the techniques mentioned above, he recommends that the adult be an active listener who states ideas and feelings without attacking the child: "No, walls are not for drawing. Paper is. Here are three sheets of paper. The blocks are for playing, not for throwing. If you are angry, tell it to me in words."

The teacher of young children tries to keep open many possibilities for connection-making. When he is a sympathetic listener who understands children's development, children are more likely to risk divergent actions. While the teacher needs to limit behaviors that can be destructive to others as well as to the child, himself, his basic attitude is to accept the child's feelings.

Consistency and clarity are important. Gordon (1974) recommends the framework of the "I-message" when there is a problem: "When _____ happens, I feel _____." In this sense, the adult's feelings are also legitimate. The teacher is a model who expresses feelings with words. Children need limits placed on them when they are out of control: "It's hard to stop but it's needed for safety." Afterward, the teacher suggests a positive alternative action, activity, or other distraction.

However, the finest intentions and techniques may not be enough to avert collisions. Human relations seem smoother on paper. There will be times when the helpful environment, activities, rational approaches, and positive teacher attitude do not help. There may be ultimate differences in tensions, trust, and values that are beyond the influence of a classic rendition of acceptance-and-problem-solving-discussion. At best, teachers try to help the child build a sense of competence and responsibility.

If threats and restrictions and anger have not worked with some children, then more of the same is not an answer, in the same sense that the traditional look–say basal reader is not an answer for the child who has failed to learn to read by this method. To persist in continued application of the same obstructive remedy is to invite "coping and defending" behavior (Bruner, 1966). There is no instant pill or recipe in human relations situations.

Personal relationships consist of much more than a stock set of questions, however effective, positive, or carefully worded. Love with clenched teeth is a sham. Children can intuit attitudes and feelings that underlie accepting words. Consistent teacher behavior is influenced at the level of the teacher's feelings and values. The ways in which adults were treated when they were children will surface from time to time, against their better judgment or designs. Rather than hesitate to act for fear of oneself, it is important for the teacher to work at each day as a new day, with a fresh start.

BEHAVIOR MODIFICATION IN PERSPECTIVE

Having just finished saying that there are no easy recipes or pills, I propose to discuss one kind of recipe because consciousness needs to be heightened about what one does. Systematic behavior modification techniques, or shaping, have been used as a way to circumvent the problems that exist in human imperfections. The teacher lists the procedures and ingredients, making objectivity easier.

At the outset, it is important to affirm that whatever you do or do not do will shape children's behavior. The least you can do is to be more conscious of how you affect children. It is then that you have a chance to compare your own actions with what you value and see what level of "cognitive dissonance" (Festinger, 1957) sets in. It is relatively easy to modify young children's behavior because they are likely to be dependent upon adult approval and their ability to be consciously critical is limited. External rewards work best in a dependent relationship. At the same time, external rewards extend dependency and can confirm a sense of powerlessness.

Systematic shaping procedures are intriguing and the results impressive. For example, there are reports of major control of tantrums, flightiness, and other asocial behavior patterns of three- and four-year-old children in barely two weeks (Baer and Wolf, 1968).

The basic procedure involves obtaining a *baseline*. In effect, what does the teacher do when the child engages in the unacceptable behavior? Findings show that the adult usually notices the child more when he is engaged in unacceptable behavior. When the positive counterparts, and benchmarks, of acceptable behavior are identified, the shaping process can begin. Thus, the teacher would develop a triptych "recipe," consisting of a column each for behaviors that will be positively reinforced, behaviors that will be ignored, and behaviors that are "nonnegotiable" (adapted from Spaulding, 1971). See the work of researcher Robert Spaulding for a well-integrated system of diagnosis and treatment.

The *positive column* attempts to deal with motives as well as behavior. For example, the self-motivated achiever may be appreciated when he shows some divergent thinking. The "flitter" who attends for ninety seconds receives attention when he is sitting rather than flitting. The child who throws tantrums and whines is given attention when he asks for help with words: "I noticed that when Lee knocked over the clay, you told him with words how frustrated you were." A kind word, a look of attention, a hug, a smile, are positive reinforcers.

Problems arise when teachers are not conscious of their own values that underlie their positive responses. Are the *efforts* of the child approved as well as productions? Is the child's *competence* as well as her performance appreciated? The key to positive reinforcement lies in the assumption that the child views the teacher as a significant person in the first place. The technique is effective when it addresses the child's need for positive attention. There is a chance for the child to build a sense of competence. It can be both benevolent and/or manipulative. There is a danger that the teacher who labels a child "good" or "kind" or "gentle" places a burden on that child to live up to his billing. Rather than simply to rate a child's work, it probably makes sense for the teacher to share her reasons, why she feels the work was well-done: "That was hard to do, and you did it." "You really thought about what you were doing."

The *ignore column* lists as many behaviors as possible that the teacher could ignore such as flitting, chair rocking, minimal physical forms of communication, and speaking out of turn. The "ignore" activity is the most difficult for many teachers. For reinforcement theory, it is important in order to extinguish the unwanted behavior.

It is dangerous to be complacent about ignoring children's behavior. While the teacher might decide not to communicate with the child, the responsibility to consider the meaning of the child's behavior remains. The modification format presumes that there is value in extinguishing the behavior. However, it may be that to ignore is not enough of a valuing of the child's perceptions. It may be that the teacher needs to notice the behavior internally because the problem may lie with the teacher. That is, the level of activity may be inappropriate or the substance irrelevant. The teacher may need to find more effective ways to involve children rather than to condemn them with the implicit self-righteousness of the listed format. It is still important for the teacher to differentiate between which behaviors grow from the child's self-esteem, and which ones are caused by curricular needs.

The *nonnegotiable column* includes a list of those behaviors that are simply not acceptable, such as hurting others or damaging equipment. The unique form that each child's behavior takes would be stated. Presumably, this list would be the shortest. Consequences, such as separation from the group for five minutes, would be clear ahead of time.

When the unacceptable behavior is eradicated, a *reduced reinforcement* schedule is applied. The teacher can intermittently provide positive reinforcement since it is assumed that the child is becoming self-motivated in the desired areas. Since he is spending more time being social, or attending to activities, or asking for what he wants, he is finding that these new behaviors are intrinsically pleasurable and self-sustaining.

However, the development of values requires more than external reinforcement. Ethical behavior must be performed beyond the sphere of external controls.

One other major problem with a reinforcement schedule is that the teacher cannot modify the behavior before she sees the child use it. In addition, many teachers find that it is difficult to manage the research elements of obtaining a baseline and administering reinforcement consistently while trying to work with an entire group. Behavior modification procedure is an attempt to deal with feelings objectively. The interspersed reservations relate to some of the issues of independence, responsibility, and competence with which this chapter deals.

HUMAN MODELS INFLUENCE BEHAVIOR

By contrast, *behavior that is modelled* by adults and other children is a potent influence upon a child's behavior. Studies agree on several important points (Bandura, 1973; Bronfenbrenner, 1970; Maccoby, 1968; Kohlberg, 1966). When children observe an adult model or a child model they are likely to imitate the expressed or suppressed behavior, as the case may be. Moreover, this imitation has occurred even when the child was told what another person had done in similar circumstances. Sometimes the imitation was a symbolic equivalent rather than a direct mimicry. Aggression, delayed gratification, helpfulness, roles, and generosity are among those behaviors that were studied.

First, children must be developmentally capable of the behavior in question before they can be expected to imitate a model. Then, they must feel that it is meaningful for themselves.

The motivation to act is stronger when children can predict a competent outcome. When children achieve small successes through carefully planned activities, they may be more inclined to participate. Induction is a powerful means for building such successes, and induction is the means by which a model can be influential.

The teacher can see the process of peer group modelling take place, beginning with the earliest parallel play experiences of the toddler and continuing into the nursery school years. Children try out play ideas that they have seen others use. They try out elements of roles about which they have heard in stories, seen in plays, films, or on television. The irony of these times is that films about loving are more restrictively rated than are those that deal with glorified violence and sadism. But it is the individual child's own self-esteem that guides his behavior, rather than a film or observed incident.

As mentioned earlier, when children observe the teacher's behavior toward other children, they can induce ways to approach another child. They also learn by observing other children. Older children represent attainable levels of performance that might serve to encourage a younger child's efforts. In addition, when the child sees others obtaining approval and satisfactions for their achievements, she may be stimulated to engage in similar behavior. In a sense, an older child's behavior may be perceivable to the younger child as a "figure" induced from a more complex "background."

A sense of power that comes with imitating a model can become more complex beyond seven and eight years of age when the peer group begins to gain importance in value development and behavior. Affiliation with other children, by conforming to the peer group standard of expectations, can help to support one's self-esteem. Linguists have found that young children's syntax as well as that of adults can be affected by peer group influences (Labov, 1972).

Social behavior can be influenced by a variety of sources—the peer group, adults, and the self-esteem derived from successful participation in activities. The varied influences can be observed further in the following section, which deals with sociodramatic play, and the teaching functions involved.

SOCIODRAMATIC ACTIVITY

The "here and now" of the young child has changed and continues to change since Lucy Sprague Mitchell (1921) coined the term. However, there has been only the barest recognition given to this phenomenon if one were to judge by the provisions that many teachers of young children have been making. The housekeeping corner and the block corner, when they are present in kindergartens and nursery schools, are relatively stable. The primary age child usually has even less opportunity for sociodramatic activity.

However, it is time to ask many "whys" about the presence of these areas and look at what function they can serve or might serve for today's child. It might be a useful practice for each teacher each year to look at each material element in the school and ask "why?" Sociodramatic play has been traditionally invested with the major task of supporting the incidental learnings of young children. Some adults have defined these kinds of learning in terms of bits of factual accretions and conversational skills. However, there appear to be farther-reaching implications to be drawn from sociodramatic play.

LEGITIMIZING SOCIODRAMATIC ACTIVITY

When children engage in sociodramatic activity they are increasingly living through a decentering process. By representing themselves, however incompletely, in other roles, children are mapping relationships and dealing with personal moves and alternatives for which mathematical sociologists could produce matrices. This kind of activity is ideally suited to the iconic level of imagery common in early childhood. It is yet another manifestation of the *experiencing* of perceptual models.

As in all human interaction, reversibility needs to grow when one decenters and begins to recognize the power of other persons' views and feelings. In this respect, fantasy and imagination play important parts in extending cognitive development. Fantasy and imagery are early forms of symbolic representation. These early forms are tied to the later ability of children to interpret and use humanity's range of symbolic forms, such as written language, mathematics, and the arts.

When teachers talk about starting to provide instruction for children at their developmental level, there is a tendency to unquestioningly refer to the here-and-now of the home—hence, the housekeeping corner. All children surely have a base of experience in some sort of home. While part of learning involves playing out this experience, it is not the only source material that children bring to school. And even if it were, it would be the teacher's job to *extend* children's experiences by introducing tangential activities, new "figures."

Look at the housekeeping corner and block corner play of children. It is apparent that four- and five-year-olds have already broken into groupings where boys play mainly with blocks and girls play mainly at housekeeping. While there will be visiting between areas from time to time as part of the play, or an occasional girl will venture into building, or an occasional boy into parenting, the larger picture remains separated. The very furnishings appear to sustain traditional images and close off one of the major purposes of early education—the maintenance of openness to new connections and alternative possibilities.

With the changing roles of men and women in relations with each other and their work, in the larger community as well as at home, the existing housekeeping corner and block corner appear to be a contradiction at the least, and a repressive tutor in the extreme. A study by Greenberg and Peck shows that occupational role stereotypes already exist by the age of three years. They also found a ceiling on children's aspirations of those jobs with which they were familiar. However, when asked about work roles with which the children were unfamiliar, there was no difference in the choices made by boys or girls. It was similarly interesting that they found girls prepared to build with blocks whereas boys rejected cooking and sewing tasks. Traditionally female roles have already been categorized as less desirable in these early years. This finding is sustained by other researchers (Maccoby and Jacklin, 1974).

This is not a surprising finding when one considers the popular culture image—strongly communicated by television, books, and adults who are the repository of generations of shaping—of women who have passive, convergent, and trivial pastimes, and men who have active and creatively adventurous pastimes. Very early, teachers need to participate in avoiding the subtle ceilings that are placed on the aspirations of girls as well as members of other groups who have been historically mistreated. To talk about aspiration levels is to address the very marrow of an individual's self-concept and general feelings of success, guilt, and anxiety.

A growing concern about helping children to develop career aspirations by providing exposure to many possibilities, beginning in the earliest years, considers the importance of self-concept. In addition, acquaintance with many resource people as models, and on-site visits to work settings, can help children to gain information about occupations (Gysbers, Miller, and Moore, 1973).

There is a growing redefinition of the role of women in the family and the larger community. There is a commitment to the ethical issues of preventing a caste system within a democratically intended milieu. Therefore, the large investment in a separate housekeeping center is unjustified. And this is said seconds after the benefits of sociodramatic play have been advertised. An alternate proposal to a doll corner is a drama corner. There would be a place for dolls and at-home symbols *alongside* rich possibilities beyond that limited piece of here-and-now experience. However, the emphasis would be on the *alongside* activities and the *integration* of sociodramatic substance. A much broader provision of a "socialization center" is presented below, along with some intervention techniques that the teacher can employ. By extending dramatic play beyond housekeeping, all children may comfortably participate.

In addition, I propose that a significant dimension of the socialization center would include "cooperative mathematics." Young children learn best through concrete activities. Many appropriate activities from which children can learn quantitative concepts are embodied in active, social occupations. Varied forms may help children to learn skills and concepts, and children can select from among these forms with the teacher's assistance. When individual work is needed, as it will be, then children can work in a writing center or an "Alone Area" that is reserved for individual use in another part of the room.

THE SOCIALIZATION CENTER

At different times in different classrooms, children have engaged in a range of sociodramatic play other than housekeeping. A look at these varied activities suggests several sorts of provisions for socialization. Children have played:

Going for an automobile trip, a bus trip, a truck trip, a railroad trip, or a covered wagon trip, and traveling to many places for vacation, business, or curiosity

Going to move, using a moving van

Going to an airport, and flying in or piloting an airplane

Going for a space trip in general or to the moon or other planets

Going on a boat trip and engaging in harbor play, oil rig work, and fishing fleet activity

Going to an emergency on a fire engine, in an ambulance, on a boat under flood conditions, in a police car, or on a horse

Going to visit the hospital, the police station, the jail, the fire station, the post office, the telephone company, the ranch, the farm, or the desert

Going to a bank, a stock exchange, a library, the movies, a theater, a garage and fixit shop, or a construction site

Going to a printing shop, a factory, a restaurant, a toy store, a candy store, a bakery, a supermarket, a shoe store, a department store, or a bicycle shop

Children have not only played at going and coming—they have also played at arriving and participating in the milieu that they have created.

Props. Sometimes a puppet frame, or a wood screen, or a two-dimensional facade of a wheeled vehicle, or floor blocks, or a cut out cardboard television screen, or wooden cartons, or ropes and string have served as props. The furnishings for any number of different interiors or outdoor settings have been constructed from hollow blocks and accessories. A picture symbol or a sign have labelled the domain on occasion. One five-year-old was happy to wear a dust mop on her back, representing a tail, and a sign that read "Rabbit." A disembodied wheel from a broken toy or shopping cart, or a circle of cardboard, or a commercial toy have served as steering wheels.

A stick or twig or broom handle or rubber piping has been used as a magic wand, a fire hose, an orchestra conductor's baton, a fishing pole, a sword, a saw, an axe, or a stethoscope. A carton box has served as vehicle, hospital bed, coffin, lake, valise, and tray. Blocks have served as dishes, foods, measures, microphones, tickets, weapons, splints, gems, and furniture.

A variety of caps, hats, belts, badges, buttons, ropes, ribbons, vests, boots, scarves, and other articles of clothing have served as costumes. Miniature animals, people, dolls, furniture, stuffed toys, vehicles, and commercial props have become part of the play. Toy or real telephones have been used. A pulley system with ropes and boxes or baskets that extend across a section of the room reflects still another variant.

Sources.   Ideas for the play arise from all of the child's observations and experiences, as well as from secondary sources such as stories, poems, phonograph records, and television. The activity is usually *episodic* in that there may or may not be a clearly defined beginning or ending. For example, children who enjoy the phonograph record "Building a City" (Young People's Records) may excerpt a part of it in their play, as they might with the "Free to be You and Me" (Bell Records) phonograph recording. The same feeling may occur with a section of the cheerful book, *Caps for Sale* (Slobodkina, 1947) with the younger children, or *Tales of a Fourth Grade Nothing* (Blume, 1972), about the antics and problems of having a younger sibling, for the primary age group. The craze, beginning with kindergarten and primary children, for posters and stickers has stimulated humorous displays of power as children act out television commercials and substitute their own frequently uncomplimentary words and phrases. In addition to playing with the sounds of the words themselves, children are displaying skepticism about propaganda and advertisements that seems to grow more readily when they have contacts with older children, beyond eight years of age.

Puppet Play.   Provision for puppet play is a very important element of a socialization center. It is a route by which more reticent individuals can enter the stream of social interaction, hidden behind the puppet character. Puppets that children make, depending upon age and ability, from paper bags, oaktag stapled on a stick, styrofoam balls and buttons with pins, stuffed toys with capes, balloon heads, wood, or papier-mâché, can be used alongside or instead of commercial puppets.

As children feel the security of hiding behind the puppet, they can save face when the puppet is reprimanded. Their voices can change. Stutterers will occasionally speak more fluently, and children can identify comfortably with the character.

However, puppets alone do not cause dialogue. They are only a vehicle for dialogue. Ideas, and a positive focus, are also needed. While ideas will come from the child's experience, children will need adult help from time to time if puppetry is to develop beyond a punching show or peek-a-boo humor. Many three-, four-, and five-year old children will frequently be more interested in speaking *to* the puppet, whether they hold it or it is held by somebody else, than participating in dialogue between puppets. Five-year-olds who provide *individual* puppetry "shows" may be more common than groups who do shows.

In effect, brief, episodic puppetry events in the early years are reasonable expectations. However, many more six-, seven-, and eight-year-old children are capable of extended puppetry play in which dialogue keeps developing as the same children repeatedly meet. Whichever children use puppets, the teacher supports and stimulates dialogue by addressing the puppet rather than the children behind it.

Flannel Board.   A flannel board with felt forms to manipulate is a variant of puppet play. Children can act out their fantasies or reproduce parts of stories that they have heard. *Ask Mr. Bear* (Flack, 1958), in which a child asks each animal to suggest a birthday present for his mother, and other simple cumulative tales, are easily adapted and seem "made" for this medium. There could be some uncut felt from which children might construct their own characters and props. Inasmuch as a certain amount of cutting, gluing, and sewing would be part of these activities, a crafts shelf should be nearby.

Blocks.   Large floor blocks are stored in the socialization center as *part* of the more specific substantive occupations in which children engage. In that way, various props and costumes can be integrated with the block play. Such integration adds the potential for increased verbal interaction among the children. This is particularly important when you notice that block building, when isolated from other sociodramatic concerns, becomes verbal only after an enormous amount of physical activity, frequently of a parallel sort, takes place.

Dramatic activity may grow from block building, or it may remain merely actions upon objects. Exploration with this material may yield a sense of accomplishment that is visually validated.

Dramatic activity with or without props such as blocks may create a product that is less tangible but has strong potential for self-involvement. This, too, is an experience of competence. Children need both sorts of experience.

The mixing of boys and girls can be encouraged by a more integrated setting. Since the block play helps children to build spatial relationships that are part of mathematical development, all children can have closer contacts and stimulation.

Cooperative Mathematics.   *Measuring and comparing* activities that require large-muscle activity can be part of the socialization center. A balance scale and varied materials for comparison are available for children from three years of age onward. Materials for liquid measure may also be used in this area, depending upon facilities. Teachers of five-year-olds begin to add standard measures to the range of nonstandard materials, some of which are described in earlier parts of this book. Many kinds of surveys are possible.

"Skittle Ball" (Aurora Products) types of games, beginning with five-year-olds, and extending to pendulum activities in other forms as children seem ready, are valuable for this area. Equipment such as Cuisenaire rods or Dienes blocks, detailed later in this chapter, could be used at a nearby table. In addition, for those five-year-olds onward who seem ready, paper and pencil should be at hand.

Multiple Toys   Such materials as Lego, Tinker Toys, and Erector Sets should be nearby, stored with a cloth upon which they can be contained while in use. Although younger children prefer to use materials on the floor, some primary age children may prefer to use Lego materials at a table.

These kinds of materials may be used individually as well as by two or three children at a time, and children may want to use materials in conjunction with floor blocks or miniature animals, or as animals with miniature furniture. As long as the purposes have a constructive focus, the children's new associations should be encouraged and appreciated.

From time to time, children will want to include the class guinea pig in the socialization center. They may also find use for electric circuitry to light the puppetry area or another project or social interest. When those materials usually associated with physical explorations of the world are nearby, they may become relevant parts of socialized activity. In this way, children may come to see new relationships and find divergent ways to use materials.

Symbolic Representation.   Many reasons for *writing* and other *expressive forms* will grow out of the socialization center. For example, the large muscle activities of cooperative mathematics represent a beginning phase of new mathematical understandings that eventuate in written representations and drawings. Episodic play can become ritualized through children's self-propelled repetitions, and lends itself to written records, audiotaping, and photographed records. An elaborate, cooperative construction can be "saved" by photography and hand drawings.

Primary age children begin to have an interest in duplicating a construction from a drawing, or photograph, or even a story. While these duplications supplement but do not supplant original constructions, they serve as yet another step in the developing use of symbols. Mapping and construction skills are encouraged. In turn, children's aesthetic appreciation of engineering and architectural work may grow.

When writing and drawing require extended individual concentration, or when concrete materials are no longer needed in order to write or draw, then these activities have no place in the socialization center. A more sedentary setting, free from interruptions, is needed. These are times when the teacher needs to redirect children to an atmosphere that is more supportive of their concentrated, individual activity.

Outdoors-Indoors. It would be too bad if the concept of the socialization center were limited to the indoors. When an outdoor area is available and when outdoor play equipment or an indoor gymnasium room and equipment is available, many of these kinds of activities can continue. It is too bad when teachers let children out-of-doors and then ignore them except for physical safety. In the short time that a child spends in school, the outdoors can be used as an important socialization resource.

Children transform climbing apparatus into buildings, vehicles, mountains, and caverns. Rope ladders can extend the imagination. Sand boxes and corners can be the source of new worlds. When packing crates, real discarded boats, or tires, hollow blocks, and wagons are available, the social activities are further supported. Most important, they can be much louder and larger in scope. Facilities vary but an easy flow between the indoors and the outdoors is helpful.

THE TEACHER'S ROLE IN THE SOCIALIZATION CENTER

It is clear that a single teacher in a single year will not provide as many topics as mentioned here or that could be conceived. One group of children would be unlikely to generate this much variety in any significant depth. Also, children of different ages and in different locales would be inclined toward different commitments.

However, resources and imagination will limit the specific large equipment and props that the teacher makes available. If anything, one should be cautious about overstocking to the point of inhibiting activity and movement.

One kind of screen or frame can accommodate retail store activity or a ticket booth or a cashier. You may find puppetry and a supermarket too much to handle in the same time period or you may find that both activities can co-exist in your space with your children. How may options and when you make them available are important administrative decisions that can be discussed with the children.

ADD A MATERIAL

When an activity has been well-developed, perhaps repeated, it may be useful for the teacher to *add a material*. One teacher saw four-year-olds using large blocks as a train. The children had developed cars, seating, an entry point, a front and rear, a conductor, and a driver. They had returned to the activity, while developing it, over a period of several days.

The teacher brought some slips of paper to the alternating group of three to seven children, and suggested a ticket system, thinking to expand their symbol learning. Within a few minutes, the children had dispersed, apparently overtaxed by the tickets. Their behavior revealed that they were not yet ready to deal with the symbols. A similar intervention with a similar population one year older proved to be much more successful.

Teachers have also added signs that say "Stop," "No Parking," or "Gas Station." They have supplied play money, bags, boxes, string, and a box marked "cash register." They have also added pencils, crayons, and paper when these have been relevant.

REMOVE A MATERIAL

Occasionally, it makes sense to *remove a material*. When children ignore the presence of a thermometer or have had access to the cardboard television screen for more than a month, the teacher has removed them. If it is relevant to bring back a material after a few weeks or months, the children may perceive it in a fresh light and create new adventures.

Sometimes the removal of a *particular* doll or truck or box of Lincoln Logs can be synonymous with the removal of a conflict. Removal of one or more items may create needed space into which other activities can expand, or in which still other equipment can acquire fresh relevance. When the number of children permitted in a given area is altered, the activity may improve because there may be more opportunities available to the participants.

REDIRECT OR ADD AN IDEA

The teacher might *redirect or add an idea* by a direct suggestion such as, "Try to find out what happens if you added more beans to the bag." "Can you make a train of people on the slide?"

A new direction can be found by a well-timed question, "What other way could you go?" or "How could they solve their problem without hitting?" "What things about a person make you want to be her friend?"

When six-year-old Gail declined to join the space travel play, saying, "Oh, going to the moon is just for boys, not girls," the teacher saw a chance to ask:

"What are some reasons that people would want to go to the moon?" Others?"
"What are some qualities a person would need in order to travel in space?"
"What does a space traveler need to know?"
"Monkeys and dogs have travelled in space. Has a woman ever travelled in a space vehicle?"
"Could a woman want to go to the moon?"
"What would she need to do in order to become an astronaut?"

Such an issue could extend into other situations. For example, the teacher could set up situations that might invert the children's sense of reality by providing stories, filmstrips, films, visits, resource people, and pictures, of women in nontraditional roles. Examples might include a woman who is a truck dispatcher, a farmer on a tractor, a sea captain, a fruit picker, a dentist, a house painter, a money manager, a mail deliverer, and a judge.

STEP INTO A ROLE

The teacher can also elect to *step into a role* during sociodramatic activity in order *to extend* the action or to expand children's language possibilities. Cazden (1971) corroborated the findings of other researchers when she observed that the peer-group conversation in a housekeeping corner was severely restricted. It may be that the rituals and routines are sufficiently repetitious and limit expanded possibilities, especially when the same children meet one another.

The teacher who helps to bridge activities in a socialization center may avoid some of the restricted syntactic patterns and minimal variety of concepts in such settings. She can add a problem to be resolved, such as shown in the following.

"Uh-oh, I see a truck coming."
"Look out, the hose is about to break."
"Now, let's see what size shoe you wear!"
"How many inches is that? How many centimeters is that?"
"That dog looks so ill that he might need hospitalization."
"The giraffe just whispered in my ear (holding the rubber toy to his ear) that she needs to find taller trees because the other animals have eaten all the greens from these shorter ones."

"I just lost my watch and it's floating all over our space vehicle. How can we retrieve it?"

In addition, the teacher can take a role in order to avoid stereotypical actions.

BRING CHILDREN TOGETHER

Another significant way in which teachers intervene in children's social activity is to *bring children together*. A teacher might encourage a child to join an activity by focussing on a task to be done: "They need your help in order to attach the hook." He might suggest that a group invite another player: "This store seems to need a cashier as well as sales persons and stock clerks. George looks as if he's just about finished. Perhaps he would want to make change." He might see that three children are ready for more stimulation after some individual, sedentary activity, and directly suggest that they work together at the flannel board, or with the puppets they had made.

The teacher also *helps to resolve conflicts*. The various questioning techniques and problem-solving procedures mentioned in earlier sections of this writing are useful. The best help includes careful listening to both viewpoints, avoiding hasty decisions, and asking children to suggest positive alternatives when they have calmed down.

While the teacher can be anxious to enrich children's experiences through social activity, it is also important to respect children's rights to privacy as well as to recognize individual styles of working. In addition, some activities are best pursued in an "Alone Area," a reflection of the intrinsic structure of the activities.

Three-year-olds are likely to be socially oriented for briefer spans of time than when they grow older. Often, they will use materials side-by-side with other children. This parallel play will be true of their style to some lesser degree when they are five years of age and beyond.

The adult who observes young children respects this parallel activity as developmentally significant. Not only do children have a chance to concentrate, focus their energies, pace themselves, and extend their scholarly skills—they also have a chance to observe others as models of alternate behaviors and ways of working. Therefore, it is only when the same child persists in this exclusive pattern day after day that the teacher needs to intervene.

She might bring other children to sit near him and share the materials, or develop activities that require cooperative effort. Rocking boats, extra-long play dough rollers that need more than one person, games with balls, "pairs," and some of the kinds of games in Chapter 5 lend themselves to joint efforts with three- and four-year-olds.

Five-year-olds, in addition, can play checkers, and some chess with predictably bendable rules. Children can take turns jumping rope. Mathematics surveys particularly lend themselves to dyads or pairs of dyads who can work on a problem and compare their findings.

Spelling help can be mutual in the primary grades when children select an established number of words from among those on a reasonable teacher supervised list. An isolated child can become the focus of planning a party or a fair: "Mark is working on plans for a poetry fair. Would you work with him on the illustrations?" Two children may wish to use a xylophone and Chinese gong to explore and compose music together. In short, the teacher can find many ways to bring children together when it is needed to balance their experiences and further their development.

Smilansky's (1968) work with disadvantaged children in Israel successfully used teacher intervention in sociodramatic play to extend and elaborate it rather than to influence its content. A combination of the teacher's help in learning play techniques and the children's direct school-enriched experiences was more effective than one or the other exposure alone.

However, when a story, rather than the children's direct experiences, served as the source for sociodramatic play, children's interaction with each other was least spontaneous. When a story becomes the basis of play for young children, it requires the kind of monitoring that becomes "creative dramatics." This form can develop after some experience in less formal sociodramatic play.

Before moving on to consider creative dramatics forms, it is worthwhile to elaborate on one of Smilansky's observations of early childhood teachers' initial resistance to intervention in children's sociodramatic play. Although the same teachers felt comfortable in stimulating their own offsprings' play, their philosophical preparation for teaching inhibited such activity with the children in their classes. They felt that they should only foster assimilative activity rather than to stimulate accommodative activity in *any* occupation that was creative. However, Piaget (1951) has also taken the position that "creative imagination" improves with stimulation and experience (p. 289).

The interaction of sociodramatic activity and cognitive development is underscored. Again, a balanced view of humane, human interaction rather than the training of children in verbalisms or a laissez-faire atmosphere is indicated.

CREATIVE DRAMATICS

Since it involves more structure and the guidance of an adult, creative dramatics can grow from children's rich backgrounds of experiences in sociodramatic play. Creative dramatics also grows from children's music and movement activities. It is at once social, substantive, verbal, and aesthetic activity.

In *sociodramatic activity,* children's favored, repeated plays may become more formalized as creative dramatics. However, the drama can continue to retain an evolving, episodic format around this kernel of common experience and interaction. These plays express actions, feelings, and problem issues. It is a group authorship in flux, as it were. It may never be written down, or it may evolve into written form with children of primary age.

The collaborative efforts of children as they explore space through *rhythmic movement activities* and experiment with the sounds and the interplay of music can also become creative dramatics. In one group of five-year-olds, a teacher noticed that a few children's rhythmic movements complemented one another. When the remainder of the group observed with her, several other children developed partner and trio and quartet movements. As they enjoyed this cooperative effort of using space together, they began to develop pantomimes. They explored ways in which tempo and dynamics further supported their pantomime activities. As the activity became increasingly elaborate, they added squeaks, squeals, and grunts until dialogue emerged—creative dramatics. These explorations spanned a period of five months during which three or four sessions each week endured anywhere from ten to twenty-five minutes.

Outside-In Sources.   Another group of five-year-olds was able to explore the use of their bodies in space alone, and with partners.

Angles.   When your feet stay in the same place without moving, your body can lean. . . . That's very special.
Now try a different way to lean.
Take a partner, and try leaning with him or with her.
Moving.   Move toward somebody.
Move away from that person in a new way.
Meet somebody else in a new way. (repeated) (Adapted from P. Press, Bellmore, N.Y., 1974)
Directions.   With your partner, try moving together toward the labels on our wall—first toward the North, holding hands.
Hold your partner by the elbow and move in a very tall way toward the West. Oh, Alan has found an interesting way to hold Jan's elbow. Betty is

making a new line with her head. Charlie is showing us the West side with his ear also. It's beautiful to see so many different ways.

Move toward the South with your partner in a very low way, as if there is a tunnel for dogs. Find a new way to move together. . . . You're leaving that tunnel in so many different ways. Danny, that's a new way that you never tried before—very clever idea. Evan, how original. Gloria looks so relaxed and comfortable. Hal looks as if he's done a great deal of hard work.

Mirrors. Next, with your partner—whoever is nearest the East side of the room, move very slowly as you hear the drum begin. Partners, try to copy that person. What nice new movements. Slowly, carefully, now. Ian and Lil, move over there so you have more space.

Now, the lead partner, change, and be the mirror to your partner.

Personal Analogy. Everybody go to the end of the room. Now, come to me in a new way. That's fine, so many different ways—some high, some low, somebody sideways. Oh, it's good to see you.

Try a new way now, and move backward to where you started.

Try a new way to come sideways.

Find a new way to return sideways. So many new ideas. Martin was really following his neck. Nora, what an original way to use your shoulder. Let's rest for a minute and talk. Were you thinking of something that can move sideways? What else can move sideways? Four children (*pointing*), try to be that thing. (*repeats procedure*) Let's think together about some things that can move backwards. Yes, Uh-huh. Interesting . . . What a fine idea. The objects can bend or stretch? Let's try (*pointing to a small group of children*) to move backwards as those things do. Become those things.

When children have had many opportunities to explore moving through space, and to isolate varied directions and body parts, they can begin to move into elaborations, alternating with movement activities. Young children have engaged in pantomimes and charade movements that grew from such experiences. They have pantomimed and guessed parts of trips that they have taken to the zoo, the bakery, and a bottling factory. They have "become" parts of cooking processes and electrical experiments, and have pantomimed volcanic eruptions. Some of the pantomime activity presses itself into sounds and dialogue.

The teacher functions to highlight elements, variable forms, original efforts, and growing skills and sensitivities. He notices when children's movements become more spontaneous and authentic as well as when they are contrived and restrained. He conveys that all movement is acceptable in order to help children to become as spontaneous and authentic as they are able. Each child is recognized and appreciated in relation to his or her own progress.

For the most part, teachers *accompany* children's movements on a drum. With more experience, children try to adapt to teacher-initiated rhythms. When teachers can play other instruments such as the piano, guitar, recorder, or autoharp, these can serve to *follow* the movements that children create.

These practices extend and lend support to children's imagery processes. Body movement is a medium that is a primary source for symbolic expression. With careful development, such movement can become an important additional way in which children's expressions are legitimized and developed.

A contrasting *source* for children's creative dramatics comes from the out-side–in as compared with these more evolutionary forms. The folk song-game "Up On the Mountain" is a partners song-game in which children swing each other to become "frozen" into statues (Landeck, 1950, pp. 110–111). The "frozen" statue can be used to emphasize variety, originality, and specific elements.

Some poems and cumulative types of folk tales lend themselves to dramatization. *The Three Billy Goats Gruff* is an all-time folk favorite. Children enjoy taking turns at playing different characters and watching them being played by others. Four-, five-, and six-year-old children find high drama, suspense, and glee with this sort of manageable threat. Lindsay's poem "The Little Turtle" (1961) is the sort of very brief poem that young three-year-olds enjoy playing out. At first, the teacher might take the role of the turtle as a way of helping the children get started.

Children increasingly elaborate their play, adding simple costumes and props. Cleary's *Ramona the Pest,* a mischief-maker with whom to identify and laugh, and *The Pied Piper* (Jacobs, 1968) are the sorts of stories that kindergarten and primary age children have dramatized. Everyone can have a role in *The Pied Piper*. Siks (1958), Ward (1960), and McCaslin (1974) are among the sources for specialized techniques and source materials.

SOCIALIZATION AND SUBSTANTIVE LEARNING

The human medium in which perceptual models grow needs to be emphasized as one continues to bracket the ineffable phenomenon of integration. Selected, generally accepted knowledge is "socialized" and integrated in the following section.

Mathematics in early childhood can become social through its use as a research tool in science and social science. Motor experience is an initial means for perceptual and conceptual learnings in mathematics as well as concerns beyond mathematics. From whichever avenue one enters the discussion, it is essential that matters of meaning remain the destination.

School practices have frequently obscured meanings through labels. Perhaps the prime culprit has been the term, "unit," a study that begins and ends at times that are preordained by an adult. Many teachers have interpreted the unit as a teacher fact-stating and child memory-stuffing process. In this way, a teacher might use the same set of plans with any group of children within a finite, preestablished unit of time.

It has been the contention throughout this book that a stronger base for the development of facts, labels, and memory arises from children's involvement with activities in an environment that interacts responsively and adaptively. Both the children and teachers are active participants with the power to alter interaction.

THE STUDY OF SOCIAL EXPERIENCE

To reiterate, many teachers of young children have been satisfied that social study has taken place when they have, in fact, provided ritualized pagan calendar worship. Each week's unit adheres closely to the calendar that directs one holiday to end as another begins. The flaccid symbols of these holidays proliferate meaningless frills. While many holidays arose as responses to human struggles for safety, sustenance, freedom, and opportunities for ethical interaction, these roots are largely missed. Rather, children are asked to cut out paper pumpkins, turkeys, and fir trees as the calendar directs. The social has been deveined from such social studies.

Through such practices, schools do more than bore children or separate them from meanings. They widen the schism between the after-school reality, rich with meanings, however painful or inspiring, and the school reality. When teachers maintain the social dimension in children's studies of their world, they help children to approach new situations with a more appropriately tentative attitude.

Not only do teachers need to understand that knowledge is a human creation but that "To be biased is as human as to err" (Commager, 1965, p. 5). Historians agree that a tentative attitude is basic to their interpretations of events (Meyerhoff, 1959; Genovese, 1974).

The attitude that alternatives must be considered is a valuable one, and an important learning. As young children grow in their ability to decenter themselves, it becomes increasingly possible for them to appreciate shifting perspectives. Whenever possible, it is important that children use original sources in order that they might make their own interpretations. Through discussions, other independent views, whether of animals, or events, or processes, can be shared and contrasted.

There are several biographies written about the same person that can bear comparison. Six-year-olds may be able to create autobiographies and compare them. Teachers can create games with pictures or puppets or flannel boards that allow varied interpretations. Motion pictures that show varied human patterns of living are still another source for preliterate children as well as a way to show data that could not be known more directly. The best films that can be used with young children are brief. They communicate material without active propagandizing. As with other learnings for young children, inductive attainments are significant.

The synectics strategies support varied outcomes and invite contrasts. Maps that were created at different times may be compared by primary age children. Lavatelli (1970) offers materials that involve reversibility and changing perspectives for younger children, in the form of a diorama and a figure that moves in relation to it. Whatever referents are used, children need to build imagery first. Driftwood, art forms, mystery boxes, and incomplete data may contribute in diverse ways toward a sense of multiple interpretations and possibilities.

A variant technique may be adapted for seven- and eight-year-olds from suggestions made for older children (Robinson and Thomas, 1972, p. 93). Children consider what questions they need to ask about a valley into which a small group enters and settles. After having elicited information about the time, locale, climate, members, natural resources, terrain, and tools, children may make some projections. They consider what problems these people face and what solutions these people might apply. Many answers might be obtained through reading. Thus, children's motives to read arise from a need to utilize their readings.

Just as humans can make changes to their physical environments, in the sense of "human" geography (Broek, 1965), so can humans alter the ways in which the world is perceived by aesthetic means, such as works of fiction and drama productions. In short, there are a multitude of ways in which human experience can be ordered, and social interaction is influenced by these constructions.

INTEGRATING SUBSTANTIVE AND SOCIAL CONCERNS

In a suburban school, the integration of substantive and social concerns may become apparent. The primary teacher asked a parent of one of the six-year-olds to be a resource for the group. Inasmuch as he was a real estate executive and the children needed exposure to large numbers, she asked him to visit and share some of his experiences. The children were accustomed to resource people because, in the past, a professional artist grandmother, a dentist, and a stock broker parent had visited.

Following a fire drill, the teacher asked Deb to introduce her father. She turned to the group, said firmly, "This is my father." and rejoined the group.

Mr. F. began by asking, "You all go to school in Neville and you all live in Neville now but can anyone remember a time when you didn't live in Neville?" About a dozen hands shot up.

JEREMY: I lived in Manhattan and before that I lived in Utah. (*Children take turns.*)

CHILD 1:   We lived in an apartment house and it was very crowded and there was a lot of traffic on the street and Bobby almost got hit by a truck one day.

MR. F: We also lived in an apartment house, near downtown and when Deb was about to be born we decided that we needed another bedroom for her and we decided to look for a house in Neville. What do you think are some of the things that we considered when we were looking? What would be some of the things that you would be interested in if you were looking for a house?

(*A rash of hands shot up.*)

CHILD 2:   A house that was big enough for you.

CHILD 3:   A house that didn't have a lot of cars going back and forth so that I could play in the street.

CHILD 4:   Children on the block to play with.

CHILD 5:   A place where they had good schools.

Mr. F: Yes, these are all things that we considered. Does anybody have any idea how much houses cost in Neville?

CHILD 6:   Two hundred and fifty-six dollars.

CHILD 7:   Sixty hundred dollars.

CHILD 8:   A thousand dollars.

CHILD 9:   My house cost forty thousand dollars.

CHILD 10:   My house cost eighty thousand dollars.

CHILD 11:   We live in a large apartment house and every month we pay some money, about five hundred and twenty-six dollars.

CHILD 8:   We agreed to buy a house and we signed a paper but before we moved into the house the people changed their mind and wouldn't sell it to us.

Mr. F: By the way does anyone know what $40,000 looks like? I know that you all know how to write 4 and 40 (writing it on the chalkboard) but do you know how to write 400?

CHILDREN: Add a zero.

MR. F: That's right. (*Writing*)

CHILD 1:   Three zeros.

CHILD 2:   No, it's four, comma, and then the zeros.

MR. F: Good! Now, 40,000?

(*Many different simultaneous responses as he wrote until he stopped.*)

MR. F: Now, how about $400,000? (*Repetition of preceding*)

CHILD 6:   A dash.

CHILD 2:   No, a comma.

MR. F: Do you think that you would want to live next door to a large factory with a big smokestack and with large, noisy trucks coming in and out of it all day long?

CHILDREN: No. It's too noisy. It's dangerous.

MR. F: A car wash?

CHILDREN: No. (*brief interchange and anecdotes*)

MR. F: Well, I didn't want to either. So we chose a house on a quiet block. We had an idea that younger families might be moving onto our block soon and they did. It's nice in our town because there are some areas where there are houses and apartment houses and some areas where there are shopping centers and some small factories. Now, what would happen after you bought the house, if someone next door to you wanted to sell their house to a person who wanted to build a large, loud, smelly factory?

CHILDREN: (*Many statements of protest*)

MR. F: One of the things people did in Neville was to make laws that make certain areas for houses, another area for a park, a school, shops, and even small factories.

CHILDREN: (*Buzzing and discussion. One child voice used the word, "zone."*)

MR. F: Yes! And the laws that they made that designate the various areas are called zoning laws or zoning ordinances. We can design our own community in ways that reflect some of the things we discussed here today. We can decide where we want to put the houses for people to live in, where we'll put the factories for people to work in and to build the things we use, for example, furniture for schools. We can decide where we want to put the parks for children to play in. We can design our own community and develop our own zoning laws. One way we can do this is to build a model. (*Takes out Elementary Science Study box of colored cubes and colored loops of braided cord.*) (*Shakes box*) What do you think I've got in here?

CHILDREN: (*Several children guessing simultaneously*)

MR. F: Now I was going to tell you that I have a whole city full of houses, factory buildings, trees, and stores in here but I know that no one would believe that so I'm not going to tell you that.

CHILD 1: Blocks.

CHILD 2: A lot of blocks.

CHILD 3: Little colored wooden blocks.

MR. F: You're right. But, you know, we could take these blocks and just to make it easy for us to remember what they are, we can decide that every green block is a tree, then what could every blue block be?

CHILDREN: (*agree on colors for houses, factories, school*)

MR. F: (*Explains that the area within each of the four colored loops can be a zone, and some zones can overlap. Demonstrates some possibilities for houses within the red loop.*)
Now, where do you think you would like to have the park?

CHILDREN: (*Several suggestions. Agree on a park near the houses.*)

MR. F: Then how about the factories. Should we put them near the park or near the houses?

CHILDREN: Oh, No. No. No. We don't want any pollution.

MR. F: But you know people will need jobs and a place to work.

CHILDREN: (*Suggest locale for factory in a zone not adjacent to or within the residential zone.*)

MR. F: That's pretty far away. How will the people get to the factory?

CHILDREN: They can ride on a bus.

MR. F: That's a good idea. Now, more people may like the way we've designed our community and more people will want to live here (*adds cubes*). It's getting pretty crowded here. There's no space for a new house. Frequently when this happens someone in the community gets the idea that he and his neighbor will sell their houses to somebody who will build an apartment house in which many hundreds of families can live. (*Discuss locations and consequences.*) (*Distributes materials so that subgroups of four or five children share a complete set of cubes and loops. The teacher and guest circulate and help children to ask questions and consider consequences.*)

MR. F: (*With a small group*) We need to remember to build a school. How do you suppose we can get the money to build it?

CHILDREN: (*Various responses*)
We can have a book fair . . . School taxes . . .

MR. F: We need a lot of money. We'll have to do it by collecting taxes from all the people who live in our community and from all the people who own factories and stores.

CHILD: You also need money to build a shopping center.

TEACHER: A shopping center is a private thing and somebody who has enough money can build it. What are the public things that everybody in the community needs or can enjoy using?

CHILD 6:   A school.

CHILD 7:   A shopping center.

TEACHER: No, that's private.

CHILD 8:   A museum.

TEACHER: Good idea.

CHILD 9:   A medical school.

CHILD 10:   A hospital.

MR. F: Yes, and things like building roads and sidewalks and fixing the roads and hiring people to take away the garbage. We have to find out the total value of all of the houses and factories. Then we'll decide how much each home owner or factory owner will have to pay in tax. (*Teacher and guest help as children assign values. Teacher suggested tax be one dollar out of every five dollars of valuation. Some children were able to compute after initial modeling. While some were computing tax, others were adding values, and still others were building.*)

MR. F: I noticed that when you were building your communities some of you wanted one way to do it and some of you wanted another way. It was hard to decide because there is no one way to do it. There are many ways to do it.

Here in Neville we have the same kinds of discussions and arguments among adults. Sometimes it's very difficult for the adults in Neville to decide how our city should be run. For example, every year we vote on a school budget and we vote for members of a school board. They decide very important things like how many schools we have, whether we should build another school, or we should use one school less than a year before and how many teachers we should have in the schools. We also vote for Park Commissioners who buy land and design parks for everyone to enjoy. And when you grow up you can vote for these people or you can decide that you want to help do this job yourself. Now you know some of the problems you have.

This interchange represents one way in which cooperative mathematics, social study, and social science were integrated. A lay person trod where teachers sometimes fear to tread. However, the entire episode grew from a teacher's recognition that children were ready for a particular skill in mathematics—acquaintance with large numerals. The teacher's thinking grew from a criterially referenced framework of mathematical skills.

While an extended look at some of these mathematical skills is important, and is considered later in this section, the preceding episode points to other implications. Assumptions about an economic order, and a political structure, also surfaced. Mr. F. alluded in an accepting tone to some difficulties that the children were having in sharing materials and working cooperatively. A clearer development of the varied purposes that were planned, and of the needs that emerged, might be aided by a series of similar and related activities. Teachers also need to be conscious of values that are embedded in purposes and priorities.

Stated objectives are eclipsed by the human interaction and temperature of the moment. Therefore, not only knowledge objectives, but values and feelings operate in any interaction. Values, reflecting cognitive development as well as social experiences are discussed in the next chapter as part of a consideration of critical consciousness. Now, the mathematics dimension is considered further.

MATHEMATICS, COOPERATIVE ACTIVITIES, AND OTHER ACTIVITIES

Reviewing extensive research studies about the differences between males and females, Maccoby and Jacklin (1974) conclude that boys' mathematical achievements exceed those of girls after the elementary school years. There is a general acceptance that boys' visual and spatial aptitudes are largely responsible for this difference, whereas girls generally appear to perform with greater proficiency at verbal processes.

They also find, contrary to popular belief, that boys seem to be at least as social as girls in a somewhat different way. That is, boys will congregate in larger peer groups, beginning in nursery school, while girls tend to retain one or two social contacts at a time and are found in smaller social groups.

These are general research trends, summarizing an immense number of studies, and subject to some exceptions. However, it can be useful to plan for counterbalancing factors that may avoid handicaps later in school. Maccoby and Jacklin propose that:

There are special remedial classes for poor readers, and boys are considerably over-represented in such classes. However, special remedial instruction in visual-spatial skills is not normally offered in the schools. If such skills do prove to be important in higher education or adult occupations, it might well be the case that many students, especially girls, would profit from such remedial instruction. (pp. 366–367)

In addition to providing activities that support the development of visual-spatial skills, it may be that varying the sizes and constituents of groups in which children work would be helpful. Children need motor experiences as a foundation for more abstract operations whether they are called mathematics or science or social science experiences.

Foundations in Motor Activity.   Various perceptual models that support the development of the visual-spatial dimension are inherent in movement and music activities, and in motor activities generally. For three- and four-year-old children, gross motor activities can be made available. Playground ball games and bean bag toss games can be developed around a focus of large shapes that are taped or chalked on the ground. Cratty (n.d.) recommends that children work together and duplicate large playground patterns, or patterns drawn on an easel, in a sandbox. Then they try to identify the original pattern from the sandbox footprints.

He also recommends using ropes for shaping patterns on the ground. Children can move through or around the ropes in creative and agile ways. Children can set tasks for each other as well as duplicate one another's patterns. Very simple ball games can develop into bases placed fifteen feet to thirty feet apart. Children can "change," using varied instructions and directions that they set for one another as they maintain their balance. Children can create more complexity by increasing the number of movement patterns to be followed in series. They can create more variety by setting problems that require divergent ways to move within shapes, without repetition.

Motor activities are inherent in children's use of concrete materials. Place values and the concept of base are readily acquired by five-year-olds when they have concrete referents. For example, the Dienes multibase arithmetic blocks (McGraw-Hill) and a home-made die or dice can easily become a place value game using bases between two and ten. The original Dienes blocks are calibrated pieces of natural wood in which the cubic centimeter unit block has the value of, x^0; the long block, x^1; the flat block, x^2; and the "block" block, x^3. In base two, the wooden blocks have the following relation:

Block	Flat	Long	Unit
2^3	2^2	2^1	2^0

Thus, the long block in base three is equal to three units, or three cubic centimeters, and the long block in base ten is equal to ten units. If I have collected ten units in throwing my dice, then I trade for a long block in base ten. However, if I were playing with a die using base three, I would have traded up to one flat and one unit: $\boxplus$ + $\square$.

It is a delight to see five-year-olds' enthusiastic absorption as they trade two units for a long when they play in base two, or three units for a long when they play in base three, and four longs for a flat when they play in base four, and five flats for a block when they play in base five. In base ten, ten units (ones column) can be traded for a long, ten longs (tens column) can be traded for a flat, and ten flats (hundreds column) can be traded for a block (thousands column). Adults who thought they understood bases in adulthood have found their authentic understanding after playing with the Dienes blocks.

The use of United States coins is a helpful concrete introduction to the notion of place value for six- and seven-year-olds as they use numerals for computation. It is important that children have the opportunity to use real or artificial coins that they can move around and regroup.

Foundations in Rules.   Simple ball games can also serve to begin the codification of rules, somewhat reminiscent of the Elementary Science Study's cubes and loops. That is, some rules retain a position either inside or outside, or neither inside nor adjacent to, a specified region.

Holt and Dienes suggest a similar game of "Sand-Castles," a maze game that can be played on snow or sand. The object of the game is for children to take a most efficient route to avoid "tolls" at the vertices. This is reminiscent of the African children's game of "networks," in which children attempt to duplicate a pattern in the sand without lifting one's finger or repeating one's path (Zaslavsky, 1973). In these networks activities, it is possible to develop a simple sequence in order that younger children can participate. In addition, any activities with simple mazes are helpful in the development of these skills. The perceptual model of indirect progress is represented in these activities.

Such activities also sharpen visual-spatial skills in ways that challenge children.

Older children can play out and create "magic squares," where, for example, all the numbers in a three-by-three square along the vertical, horizontal, or diagonal axis add up to the same sum. The participant needs to be able to imagine reversals, rotations, and "bending" of the two-dimensional result. These are complex spatial demands. For young children, activities such as using cubes to form color matrices can be a helpful preliminary activity. Three-year-olds play at guessing which cube is missing. In addition, with the reversal of two cubes, children can attempt to locate the change. Scanning skills that have broader use are an ancillary experience.

When children play with mirrors and pattern duplication and when they play with parquetry blocks, some of the rotational and reversal skills are built. In this context, the use of decorative stencils made by five-year-olds, or their own potato prints, that they rotate and with which they make patterns, also contribute to the development of this spatial sense. The earliest activities require plenty of time for exploration and repetition.

The teacher's function is to see that girls receive many opportunities to participate in such activities on a regular basis. In addition, since mathematics is a rule-bound occupation, children need to have opportunities to explore and codify and test rules in many games that they play. It may also be helpful if girls participated in the primary grades, and, in later years, in more rule-bound games with larger groups of children.

Piaget's (1965) studies of children's understandings of rules indicate that there are developmental changes that reflect cognitive growth. He finds that children between the ages of three and five years imitate rules in games, but they incompletely apply these rules with confidence. He also finds that children seven and eight years of age are more strictly social about rules, yet their adherence is sometimes approximate rather than precise. It is only through repeated social interaction and feedback from one's peers that consistent rule-bound behavior and morality develop. Children need repeated opportunities to test the rules, to see how they work, and to see how their actions affect other people.

The parallel between the rules of children's games and the rules of mathematics is too tempting to set aside. Particularly with respect to boys, it seems that their traditionally greater involvements with group sports, building with large blocks, and woodworking, tend to support their visual-spatial development. Although girls in early childhood appear to engage in activities more interchangeably and communally with boys, their activities and associations do appear to diverge from boys during the primary years in school.

Special effort should be extended to plan for girls as well as boys to build with large blocks, to engage in sports, and to continue their woodworking activities in the primary years as well as earlier. The socialization center, cooperative mathematics, and regular individual teacher and child planning conferences can contribute to these considerations.

Foundations in Relationships. One might infer that mathematics is to discursive forms what music is to nondiscursive forms. As an expressive form, each is a kind of unique abstract symbol. While music can be directly and concretely knowable, mathematics is a more general kind of knowledge, the application of generalizations.

In the education of young children, there is general agreement that mathematics involves the developing understanding of relationships and the developing ability to represent these relationships through symbols. It is more than the acquisition of a rapid command over "number facts" and basic arithmetic computation. Machines will be able to do that better than people. Rather, education should help children to understand how to use the tool that mathematics is, as well as to apply computation skills where they are relevant. As in the field of teaching reading, it would be unfortunate to get bogged down by either–or controversies. Meanings as well as skills are needed. *Skills function to serve meanings.*

First, young children need a variety, that changes, of relevant experiences that they can explore in active ways (Nuffield, 1967; Hawkins, 1965). Second, they need adult help in order to clarify relationships, and to compare and contrast observations and findings. Finally, they need adult help in order to build skills, to record their findings, and to interpret and use symbols.

Concrete objects and task cards and books together, and in and of themselves, do not ensure that children will learn. The teacher needs to juxtapose elements at the proper times, with adequate preparation, and appropriate follow-up activities. This supports the saturation of the child's environment with perceptual models. In this way, the tool of mathematics helps children to have an enriched sense of the world. The Nuffield Mathematics Program, developed with children, offers a framework that is useful with young children, and is integrated in this section.

Children learn about *relationships* of space, of shape, and of size. This means that size is a *relative* concept. Therefore, children require *contrastive experiences* in order to grasp this relativity notion. Schlein's book for nursery and kindergarten children, *Heavy is a Hippopotamus*, conveys some of this relativity in a way that children can perceive. However, it is important that concrete experiences *precede* the use of a book in order to deepen children's understandings. Relative relationships also exist in social dealings.

As children have experiences in focussed observation, as they match and compare phenomena, as they measure phenomena, and as they transform phenomena, they develop increasing intuitions, inductions, and understandings.

The materials with which they work may be continuous materials such as liquids and gasses. Time is also a continuous kind of experience, at once concrete and exquisitely abstract. The materials with which children work may be discontinuous, such as discs, beads, and building materials. However, when beads are bagged or poured for weighing, they may be viewed as continuous. The section that follows details some activities and relationships that have been selected to convey a sense of children's involvements, supplementing activities mentioned in other sections.

Space.   Children can explore *space* in a variety of ways. Visual and plastic arts, block building, and construction activities provide data. When toddlers and young children try to fit into boxes, tunnels, toys, last year's coat, father's shoes, or an area near the teacher, they learn about space.

The shapes of markings made on a deflated balloon will change when the balloon is inflated, but the topological relations—the relative ordinal positions among any set of points on the markings—remain the same. Children learn this kind of order through repeated actions, just as they learn to recognize a particular person intuitively on the basis of a profile view (Copeland, 1974; Piaget and Inhelder, 1956; and Sauvy, 1974).

Activities with clay, yarn, rubber bands, and other malleable materials that children can mold, tie, weave, stretch, and compress can help to extend the sense of continuity as well as the notions of enclosures and boundaries. While enclosure and boundary learning comes through such activities as those mentioned above, from puzzling mazes, and from various mapping activities detailed in Chapter 4, children learn about proximity and continuity through countless daily activities. Children acquire these topological understandings inductively. They represent early geometric developments upon which projective and Euclidian geometry can develop.

While a three-year-old is likely to accurately interpret his observations by retaining topological relationships, his sense of relative length and number of surfaces or angles will be casual. Sometime during the nursery school years, children begin the transition to Euclidian geometry by becoming more aware of these elements. This transition parallels the development of conservation of length and quantity.

The teacher helps to extend and deepen children's learning by providing materials and activities in which contrasting and transforming are central, and by helping children to talk about what they are observing. For example, yarn or raffia that has two adjacent colors can help to sharpen a child's sense of continuity in twisting, tying, or weaving. The types of activities that can help children to perceive contrasts are the following.

Cooperative pattern building with a friend using blocks or beads or stickers
Touching an unseen object and matching it with corresponding pictures
Games with dioramas
Using varied media for art work
Large muscle creative movement activities with props such as hoops, ropes, discs, and cloth
The use of Elementary Science Study loops and cubes.

As they draw and paint with their own beginning plans, four-year-olds learn to adjust their starting points more accurately in order to avoid running off the paper, a necessary experience. When young children pour water, sand, or beans through funnels, sieves, and tubes into containers of varying sizes and shapes as well as a series of containers of standard size gradations, they learn still more about volume.

It is especially important for the teacher to provide children with containers of varied shapes and sizes as well as standard measures. Children acquire the concept of conservation of quantities only after many experiences in which they have observed and created transformations of shape that are reversible.

It is the manipulation by the children, tied with their readiness to imagine relationships, that helps their perception to develop. Therefore, teachers are careful to avoid glib verbalisms and deductive expectations in favor of many manipulative experiences that are rich in contrastive, inductive possibilities. They are also aware that different children can acquire equivalent learnings when they engage in different activities.

Shape.   Children can explore *shapes* in a variety of other ways. Activities that require children to match and compare similar and different shapes, and series of shapes whose size varies, contribute to discrimination skills. Toddlers who fit different shapes into holes develop skills that help children solve two-dimensional, and later, three-dimensional puzzles. The sequenced Tangrams have already been mentioned, as have seriation activities. The peg boards of the nursery school become elaborated with rubber bands and evolve into geo-board activities.

Geoboards have been circular and triangular as well as square. Wherever possible, it is useful for two or more children to work together when children are independent from the teacher. Using the same sequence of teacher-made task cards, they can work on parallel, equivalent geoboards or boards that have different proportions. Then, the children can compare their findings, an experience in concrete topology. Children have found how many different three-, four-, five-, or six-sided figures they could create on the geoboard. They have replicated street signs, such as the hexagonal stop sign.

In addition, beginning with seven- and eight-year-olds who are experienced with geoboards, children can work out their own rubber band patterns, create instructions, and set problems for one another or for the teacher. The commercial game "Chutes and Ladders," that many five-year-olds can use, reinforces children's scanning skills as do other similar board games. In "Chutes and Ladders," each child takes a turn to spin on a card numbered to six, and then moves his marker along a grid of one hundred spaces toward the last space.

Pairs of seven- and eight-year-olds have cooperated, doing lattice computations that they have then translated to a grid of numerals. The grid of numerals—whether a "hundred frame" or a combined number and letter grid—can become a game. As children locate and connect by lines, B-2, A-1, F-4 and other points, they complete a picture. The motive becomes the completion of the picture, or the spelling of a riddle answer, or a riddle numeral. The grid becomes a self-checking device.

For those children who are able, the clues to connecting points might be found through simple computations, best done by pairs of children. Such activity can be an adjunct of map activities and related "treasure hunts." Through comparing shapes and sizes, geoboards also lend themselves to the beginning study of perimeter and area concepts during the kindergarten and primary years.

Size.   Relative *size* and absolute size, or standard measures, form still another dimension for study. Children become involved with such phenomena as the size of a group of children, the size of a portion of strawberries, the length of their own feet, their height and weight, the length of a truck, the height of a building, and enough money for ice cream.

Nonstandard measures and approximations are early forms for observing and measuring size. The child's foot, his span (the spread between outstretched thumb end and pinky finger end), his cubit (the distance between fingertip and elbow), his digit, or his stride have been used. A length of string or a block or stick or crayon or favorite doll also have been used by children. Flotation in water and balance scales have served as other ways to compare size with density.

The teacher's role is to gradually introduce each new variable and help children with the needed language. Gross observations and approximations become refined through repeated guessing and testing.

Young children need opportunities to observe carefully, along with verbal aid. One three-year-old boy, faced with a balance scale for the first time, produced an anthropomorphic interpretation: "Heavier things go higher. Lighter things go lower." He was not yet able to move away from a social interpretation of the material world.

A teacher and four- and five-year-old children sorted heavy and light objects by touch (Biggs, 1971). They observed the scale's movements. The teacher asked them to guess between a small metal object and a large piece of styrofoam. When *contrasts* take place between appearance and performance, children notice, and are stimulated to raise questions.

The same kinds of contrasts were evident when children used magnets, described in Chapter 4. Similarly, flotation in fresh and in salted water is another way for children to perceive these contrasts. In addition, these activities contribute to the growth of concepts relating to density, discussed earlier. Soap bubbles and soap flake sculpting add to the sensorial aspects of learning about density, beginning with nursery age.

Relative density can also become the subject of seriation activities whether in comparisons of foods or materials within centrifugal tops. In turn, the level of density can be a transformed state that children can notice as they engage in cooking activities. Small groups of primary children have melted old crayons, with adult help at the heating source, in order to make candles with layers of different colors. The nursery teacher brings a variety of materials for children to compare such as alcohol, oil, glycerine, maple syrup, and honey. Balsa wood, pine wood, and oak wood add to these contrastive experiences as do contrasts between aluminum, copper, and steel.

As children classify materials, and have many experiences with one-to-one correspondence, their seriation skills grow. Three- and four-year-olds have opportunities to set out a napkin and a chair for each child. They have opportunities to match baby and parent animals. They have opportunities to classify living things and objects. As they match keys to padlocks, and the number of items grows, the teacher can encourage the children to seriate, beginning at first with three locks, and adding materials as children seem ready.

Four- and five-year-olds are similarly able to classify ages of people, creating a baby-child-teenager-young adult-elderly adult series to which they can add pictures. The varying levels of mercury in a thermometer on different days can be retained by cutting a paper straw length (Sandra Petrek, Personal Communication, 1974). Besides seriating lengths to see which were the warmest and coolest days of a week or two, children are exposed to another transformational experience. This is a type of survey that is useful with young children.

Still other *survey ideas* are interspersed in preceding sections. The "survey" is useful because children can be active, work cooperatively, use nonstandard as well as standard measures, and have reasons to develop and use counting skills. Children as young as three years of age have surveyed the number of trucks passing their window for a specified time by placing pegs from one box into another.

Survey of the girth and length of growing pets and plants have been mentioned. Nonstandard measures such as yarn are useful with children through five years. Older children can use such standard measures as inches, centimeters, ounces, and grams when they are ready.

Bed times, family size, mail surveys, height and girth of children, a monthly weather survey, an evaporation survey, automotive colors, the number of birthdays within the group in any given month, favorite foods, television shows, and baseball results are a sampling of other surveys. Different children can learn similar concepts and receive practice through variant forms. In addition, the survey begs to be represented symbolically.

Symbolic Representations.   The earliest representations have a direct relationship between each variant and symbol. For example, each child's bed time would be represented by a separate paper plate clock face with the hands set. The girth of a guinea pig, represented by yarn, could be hung on a chart and dated. Every two weeks a newly measured length and date could be added. For weight, a glued disc could be added to the chart for each block that the animal needed in order for the scale to balance. Height might be represented by a one-to-one seriation. That is, a listing of children in order of height, could be made.

Favorite desserts or family size might be represented by a bar graph, a more abstract representation. Eventually, a coordinate graphing system can develop. Many seven-year-olds have been able to employ such a representation when surveying traffic on a series of occasions.

These representations can be written or dictated. They can be illustrated on a chart or graphed on a felt board. As long as the form is appropriate for the children, the results should be recorded. Children have an added sense of accomplishment and a record of the many things that they have done together. In addition, their ability to use symbols will grow as they engage in repeated functional practice. It is significant that real experiences, numerals, and counting become related in the children's experience.

Numerals and *standard measures* also develop in other direct ways. The simplest color mixing and cooking activities can be recorded and posted beginning with the three-year-olds. Any cooking activitiy should involve children actively. (There are too many cooking sessions as well as "experiments" when children look on as the teacher does all of the touching and doing. In addition, it is recommended that ingredients be natural rather than packaged. Prepackaged mixes may reinforce magical explanations.) The hands-on recipe of one cup of natural peanut butter, two cups of dry milk powder and one cup of honey is a great mess when hand mixed, rolled into balls, and rolled in ground nuts that the children have pounded by themselves. The ratio of $2:1:1/2$ can be charted with illustrations as a simple first exposure. Similarly, how much salt added to how much water in order for flotation to occur is another kind of recipe, using standard measures.

Another direct way for standard measures to be used cooperatively is the measuring wheel. Also, children can measure the distances that frogs or grasshoppers or "tiddley winks" or other children jump, using yardsticks and meter sticks. Standard size measuring spoons of varying size can be compared with cup size, quarter liter size, ounce, and deciliter size. Children can estimate the length created by the contents of a mystery jar. The children can take turns measuring the contents, laid end to end, using inches or centimeters. Results can be charted; differences between estimates and findings can also be charted and compared. The contents of the jar are changed periodically.

Task cards, sequenced for difficulty by the teacher, serve as ways to provide children with varied forms of practice in the use of standard measures and computation skills. It is especially appropriate for the socialization corner that task cards involve children in cooperative activities. Each task card should provide opportunities, for those children who are able, to record their findings. Tape-recorded or pictorial tasks have been used with limited success in working with preliterate children. However, interage grouping extends the preliterate child's possibilities.

While children are exposed to numerals, ordinal numbers, and counting quite early outside of school, their school setting needs to provide repeated opportunities for focussed practice. Many experiences with different groups of objects consisting of the same number, and larger and smaller sets, need to be part of the child's experience. In this way, the concept of "any" can grow.

Five-year-olds frequently need help with counting, and need to begin all over again if interrupted. Using fingers, they often cannot hold up one hand and begin to count at six onwards with the second hand, but begin again from "one." A six-year-old was observed as he kissed each finger in turn as an aid in computation. A seven-year-old's teacher noticed that he had been able to conserve quantity in several Piagetian tasks that she set him. However, when he used a ruler, he needed the skill of aligning the end of the ruler with the end of the wood he was measuring.

If you look only at outcomes, young children may appear to be able to count and compute adequately. However, adults need to keep in mind that they may have developed these skills unevenly. Concrete referents should be made available to help children check their own computations themselves. Calibrated balance scales, Cuisenaire rods, and Dienes' blocks, as well as non-standard multiple materials, are valuable accessories.

A world famous ancient game, commercially available as "Kalah," calls upon counting skills in order for children to transfer beans from hole to hole until they reach a bowl at each end for each player. One-to-one correspondence is used by the players. Addition and subtraction skills grow naturally out of repeated play. The simplest game board can be made out of a two-by-six egg carton with an attached "bowl" or box at either end, made from two halves of the upper part of the egg carton. The game begins with four beans, or three beans for younger children, in each of the twelve depressions. African children use pebbles and holes on the ground in order to play (Zaslavsky, 1973).

As you face your side of six pots, "your box" is at your right. The object of the game is to empty the beans from your six pots into your box. Moving in a counterclockwise direction, you empty the beans from any one of your pots, one at a time, into succeeding pots. If the last bean of the pot lands in your box, you take another turn. If any beans remain as you pass your box, you drop one each in each of your partner's pots. If your partner drops any beans in your pots, you become responsible for moving them.

Other teacher-made games are also useful means to help provide computation practice that primary age children find involving. A number grid that is large enough to walk on can be a popular material. The teacher can create different sets of task cards with a self-checking system on the reverse side of each card or in an envelope. Children can also make up problems for other children to solve with the grid.

"Slapjack," "Paris" games, other card games, "Twister" games, and other teacher-adapted board games can also contain controlled variables in a form that interests children. Task cards that call for computation with coins are interesting also. Some six-year-olds and most children, beginning at seven years of age, can use a game such as "Monopoly." It contains a reasonably limited range of computation skills and serves as a stimulating form of practice. It is an excellent game for use by a group of mixed age.

Shop keeping and other dramatizations lend themselves to a functional use of computation. Valuable activities are those in which children can use their skills and vocabulary functionally. There need to be many ways in which skills can be used, related to the child's accomplishments. The teacher can alter the complexity by altering the price structure, or by removing or adding materials. Any environment, whether commercially prepared at great expense, or the raw materials of nature, can serve as useful resources most effectively when teachers customize tasks for their children.

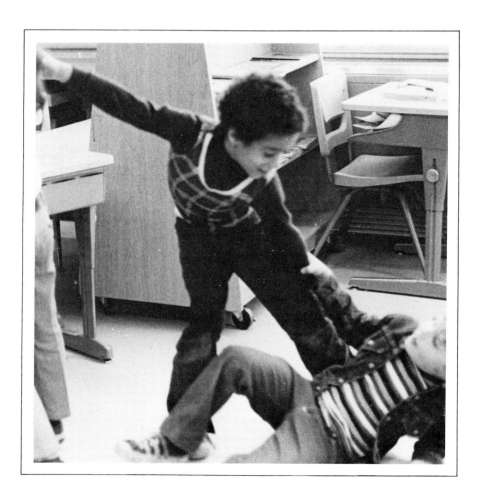

CHAPTER 8
THE POTENCY OF
EARLY CHILDHOOD

INTRODUCTION

In this unpredictably changing world, people need to be flexible enough to make new connections. In the face of technology, there is a need for people who can keep a human balance in the future, who can see a parallel need to "give back seed grain to the earth in exchange for clay." In the future, people will need to be capable of entertaining alternative possibilities for ordering the world. They will need to make ethical, reasonable decisions that can sustain humane living.

A major thrust of this writing has been to underscore the potency of the early childhood years as a rich source of *processes* that are pivotal in humanity's survival as human beings. More than a foundation or precursor of later forms, early imagery contains important processes, possibilities, and flexibilities that human beings need to retain throughout life as this imagery blends with continuously extended and deepened experience.

The purpose of this chapter is to indicate some ways in which these perspectives fit the larger system of human interaction. Critical awareness, an outgrowth of the integrated processes that have been discussed, is related to values and the political development of children. The concluding discussion focuses briefly on the relation of early education to forces beyond the classroom.

CRITICAL EDUCATION

Critical education is a multifaceted subject for teachers to consider. It is a long-term purpose of education. It eventuates in citizenship and political

CHILDREN GAIN SELF-AWARENESS AS THEY COOPERATIVELY CREATE NEW WAYS TO USE THEIR BODIES IN SPACE.

responsibility and action. It involves ethical behavior. It entails knowledge of concepts as a by-product of action and participation. It concerns the heightening of aesthetic experience. It furthers the enrichment of self-perception. It is at once rational, emotional, social, aesthetic, and active—a synthesizing and clarifying experience.

Each of the facets is discussed in turn although they are interconnected. Language offers little choice in the matter. A discussion of the parallel developments of morality and cognition will lead to a focus on the political socialization of children. Then, the critical aspects of aesthetic experience can be considered. The enrichment of self-perception can be seen throughout these discussions.

DIALOGUE

Freire has proposed an education for "critical consciousness" that reflects consistency with Piaget's and Kohlberg's findings concerning children's moral development (Freire, 1970a, b, c, 1973; Piaget, 1965; Kohlberg, 1964; Kohlberg and Mayer, 1972). To be critically conscious is to act with awareness and rational clarity. It is to perceive one's own humanness and possibilities for becoming more human.

The fullness of being human in this sense grows from mutual relationships with others. The experience of being-human develops from an interactive relationship and dialogue with others. Both Freire and Piaget criticize the image of a "vertical" interaction, in which an authority figure dominates, directs, and doses the dependent learner. Rather than constraint they advocate cooperation, disagreements, and the active involvement in dialogical relations with other children and adults to serve the development of mature thinking and action.

People have been concerned about violence and competitiveness in society and in schools. Many educators have accepted the inevitability of growing acts of violence in schools. While it is all too easy for teachers of young children to manipulate them into dependent acquiescence, and to transmit humanity's fund of knowledge in a variety of ways, the inside-outside issue of education surfaces. As children grow older, they need the power of internal controls if one may consider a humane future for human beings. This kind of morality can be supported when it is *consistently* present in the experience of the early years.

Many educators are not at all sure that schooling as it is currently practiced can create a new humanistic morality. But it is *one* important influential institution. Each new generation of teachers implicitly accepts responsibility for contributing toward such a goal. However, problems arise in the space between willingness and action. The "Yes, but . . ." games of existing institutional structures and the vertical authority of administrative practices have confused the issue.

While young children need the teacher's protection and advocacy because they are not yet capable of self-awareness, adults are presumed to be capable of reflective activity. And reflective activity involves criticism, an ability to experience one's situation clearly and with reason. In effect, to be a teacher means to take responsibility for supporting children as they develop the intrinsic motives that are needed in order for critical awareness to occur. Similarly, a futurist thinker suggests that "education occurs when the individual learns to question the assumptions which lie behind existing classifications of information" (Theobald, 1972, p. 171).

As discussed in the preceding chapter, cooperative behavior becomes possible when one feels a sufficient sense of competence and effective power. These feelings grow from having responsibility for making choices and decisions, and dealing with the consequences of one's actions. The teacher of young children helps children to make competent choices by helping them raise the kinds of questions that they are able to pursue and through which they can be challenged and extended. In this way, teachers and children can participate together in the pursuit of what Freire calls, "generative themes." Such action reflects a balance between advance and emergent planning.

This process grows when the teacher canvasses children by means of observation, discussion, and conversation, a kind of "reverberation," to find out their perceptions of the world. The teacher tunes into the child's-eye view of the world. In this sense, Kohlberg and Mayer explicitly integrate the views of Dewey, Piaget, and implicitly Freire, when they suggest that educational intervention should follow the child's ways of working, to encourage the "arousal, among children, of genuine cognitive and social conflict and disagreement about problematical situations" (p. 459). Freire might extend the language usage, "among children," to include the interaction of the teacher whom he sees as an active, "horizontal" participant in problem development and solution. In turn, the teacher can also develop greater insight into the children.

When children can act in accordance with their capacities and feel competent, their self-awareness grows and their experience of reciprocal relationships with others can grow stronger.

However, such development is not linear. It is fraught with struggle, conflict, and dissonant dialogue. Such contrasting experiences are to be welcomed by the teacher as the substance of development, rather than denied or suppressed. In this sense, critical education is not the same as criticism for its own sake. It is a heightened awareness of one's real self in relation with others and the world of institutions and objects. It receives nourishment from a "horizontal communication" at the child's-eye level rather than a "vertical transmission" from above. Critical education integrates the many dimensions for knowing through the use of tools drawn from many ways of knowing. The values component, political-activist component, and aesthetic component of critical education are considered in turn.

VALUES AND YOUNG CHILDREN

Every educational practice implies a concept of man and the world. (Freire, 1970b, p. 205)

Therefore, if you are to try to support children's critical education, it is important to explore your own values as well as to help children deal with theirs. It is important to recognize that values are *voluntary* decisions to act. While these decisions are drawn from feelings and attitudes, they also grow from knowledge. In early childhood education, perceptual models form an integrated knowledge base. The techniques that have been discussed in this connection emerge from a framework in which children are perceived as *active* participants in their own learning experiences.

Alternative Choices.   Although young children are building an internal sense of what they ought to do, and a sense of the difference between intent and action, they can begin to deal with some of these issues on a *competent* level. What they need is a setting in which they have opportunities to make choices, to imagine choices, and to simulate choices. It is helpful when the teacher assists children in exposing alternative interpretations and actions.

What do you think about this ending?
What are other ways you have seen people act when that happened to them?
What are some other things that he might have done?
What else could he do?
What might happen?

   The role playing activities and synectics activities discussed in prior chapters are useful, systematic ways to help children become aware of alternatives. The daily contrasting of their views with those of other children and adults is another source through which children learn about alternatives. The teacher's appreciation of varied ways of working, and varied products, is still another source. Sometimes, the teacher plays "devil's advocate" in order to extend the range of alternatives: When/Whom/How/What could that solution hurt/help?

Commitments. Teachers' own awareness of their sense of commitment can support children's valuation activity. The scholars who specialize in "values education" use the term "prizing" that addresses the following questions.

What do you get aroused about?
Under what circumstances would you try . . .?
What is more important to do?
Why is that important for you?
Does this suggest anything different you would want to do in your life?
What would you like to do?
If you were there, how would you have voted?
Have you ever tried any of these ways?
What would you do if this happened to you some time?
If you could talk to _____, what would you say to her or him?" (Harmin,
    Kirschenbaum, and Simon, 1973)
Which character is most like you?
What did he do which you would like to do some day?
What did he need to do to get ready?
What will you need to do?" (Raths, Harmin, and Simon, 1966)

The teacher serves as a responsive listener. He helps children to focus on the variable elements that create commitments about which they feel justified. Again, there are occasions for the teacher to take the contrasting viewpoint: Why would this *not* be important? What are some reasons that you (or they) would not want to do this?

Actions. Action grows out of a consideration of alternatives that leads to the *free selection* of a commitment to a particular position. However, some children may feel inhibited to speak in a group situation. One child may say something that closes off another child's thinking. Since the specialists remind teachers that values need free choices if they are to be meaningful, there are times when it is useful for children to work individually before sharing their concerns with others.

When teachers work with young children, such sharing is limited to small groups. Each child can have more opportunities to contribute. The teacher has a better chance of diagnosing what is needed next. In addition, spontaneous opportunities may arise for helping children to extend their questioning to larger social issues as well as to deal with individual concerns (Harmin et al., 1973).

Larger social issues become inevitable subjects for discussion because they deal with children's ongoing concerns with, and growing knowledge of rules, authority, and power. The ultimate development of critical faculties lies in the capacity to perceive the dynamics of power and control in life experiences. These experiences may be primarily political matters or the arts. The next section deals first with political development and then with the actions in which young children can engage.

POLITICAL DEVELOPMENT

Political action is, after all, an outgrowth of values. There is agreement among educators, psychologists, and political scientists, that political awareness grows with self-awareness through the socialization process and cognitive development (Hess, 1968; Hess and Torney, 1967; Peters, 1967; May, 1972; Sorauf, 1965; Lasswell, 1958).

Political attitudes and awareness, and the ability to deal with the conceptual load involved, develops most evidently in the ten- and eleven-year-old child according to the psychologists Hess and Torney (1967). They found that the public school in the United States was "the most important and effective instrument in political socialization" (p. 110). On the other hand, their colleague Niemi (1973) contends that the school is *one* influence among many socializing influences that have a variable impact on different individuals. He and an associate agree though that the impact of experiences in the early years "are not only formative but for the most part enduring" (Jennings and Niemi, 1968, p. 467).

Thus, while political awareness becomes measurable beyond the early childhood years, it hardly surfaces full-grown and rootless. Younger children have responded to queries about political figures and institutions at the *recognition* level of: Yes, I've heard of it but I don't know what, how, or why about it. As with other learnings in the early years, "recognition" rather than "recall" would be a predictable expectation.

The core of political considerations is power and its use. Laws and rules; authority figures and political leaders; and governmental institutions are the forms through which children may perceive the use of power. Their own peer group, family, school, and community relations serve as initial exposures.

Political Socialization.   It is the social forms that precede the cognitive forms in these relations. Therefore, children directly experience rules and limitations as "given" and behavior as "good" or "bad" as it conforms. It is only in the primary years that they begin to raise "whys." Protection can then be sought from institutions rather than individuals, and the individual authority figure becomes seen as separate from his or her institutional role (Hess and Torney, 1967). The idealization of adult political figures may give way to the notion of fallibility. It is in this very distinction that adults can be pivotal in helping children perceive reality from the early years.

The "double bind" perceptual model, in which appearance and reality contravene one another, includes politics and takes many forms outside of politics *per se*. Discussions in which the teacher welcomes different views, activities in which first appearances prove to be inadequate, and an atmosphere in which varied suggestions are aired and attempted—all serve to expose this image. Specific activities are discussed in preceding chapters. In addition, a book about feelings, with which many five-year-olds onward can identify, touches the sense of what you see, what you feel, and what you show, as a reflection of the double bind perceptual model: *T. A. for Tots* (Freed, 1974). Through many concrete experiences and verbal accompaniment, children participate in the long process of distinguishing between intent and action.

It helps children to have words for their experiences. When the teacher comments on children's intentions and expresses appreciation for their motives, this adds to such learning.

When the teacher asks children for their opinions and asks them to make choices, their consciousness of themselves is addressed at the level of: I am expected to have an opinion. I am considered capable of making a choice. It certainly helps if the teacher does not play a double-bind-act to the children. Whether or not a child expresses his perception, it is useful for adults to remember that it was a young child who clearly saw that the emperor wore no clothes. By these different routes, early concerns on the aesthetic and personal level grow toward conceptual and universal issues.

The young child may transfer his dependency needs to political figures, and "attribute benevolence to authority" (Hess and Torney, p. 221). The rituals of the Pledge of Allegiance or the emotional symbolism of the flag are extensions of the acceptance of authority. When teachers are conscious of these tendencies, there may be fewer instances in which political concepts are built around a focus in authority and a system of compliance and rules alone. For it is *action* that *is the purpose of political education* rather than knowledge, emotional attachments, or attitudes for their own sake.

Activities. It is in the realm of activity that young children are particularly adaptable. On one level, simple activities such as taking turns at being class president, vice-president, senator, and so forth can help build vocabulary and a sense of power. These officers may be given responsibilities, that the group and the teacher work out together—and respect. Voting for the kinds of material to order, the place to visit first on a trip, or what theme will dominate a party may be a way for children to develop a further sense of what "majority rule" means in less competitive situations.

On another level, teachers have discussed "What would happen if there were no police or governor or judge or _____, in a particular situation?" "What would happen if we selected a president in a different way?" This sort of dialectical line of questioning can provide contrasts to sharpen children's understandings of conditions as they exist. The same question frameworks can be translated to intragroup procedures for younger children. The inversion of reality generally takes on a humorous cast while sharpening children's awareness of reality, for example, discussing a newborn baby brushing his teeth, or the Soviet poet Chukovsky (1963) who supplied an example of the four-year-old who could not read to the older folks because he could not find his reading glasses.

One seven-year-old who visited New York City felt assaulted by the intrusion of graffiti to which she was unaccustomed. Since she had not yet learned to tune it out, she attempted to influence the government by means of its most visible symbol, the mayor.

Dear Mr. Mayor:

I am Jane Doe talking about the graffiti that is going around. I think the people that are doing the graffiti i think they should have a sertain place to do it. Like a ript down building or some walls to right on. Do you think so too? I do. Jane Doe 11 Country road, Phone number 123-4567 zip code 91011. Family John father mary mother Iris sister and me Jane.

Her teacher suggested that she might write and offered the spelling for "graffiti" and "building." The mayor of the city answered her letter and included his photograph, which now hangs in her room. For this child and her peers there was a concrete sense in which a government figure was responsive. Perhaps with more such encounters, these children can develop a sense of efficacy vis-a-vis government. Meanwhile, they send petitions to the school nurse to obtain permission to wear outlawed wedge-heeled shoes to school.

To develop this sense of efficacy further, the teacher can help children to become aware of ways in which they have used their influence to sway her to change a decision. This is important when framed by May's (1972) definition of power as "the ability to cause or prevent change" (p. 99). Perhaps if children have some experiences through which they have been able to influence visible political or authority symbols, they may feel encouraged to extend their participation in political matters.

It is important to consider the way such influence takes place. Cooperative, reasonable influence would be preferable to manipulative or menacing influence. Cooperative activities, beginning in the nursery school, can serve to support the development of later, more complex group influences. In addition, the perceptual model of synergy, where the whole exceeds the sum of its parts, reflects the advantages of cooperative involvement through many other forms. Related activities have been integrated in other parts of the book. These activities serve to reinforce the concept of cooperative activity. In a similar sense, the "Prisoner's Dilemma" matrix, used in the research of cooperative attitudes, may be adaptable (Maccoby and Jacklin, 1974). In effect, by giving up some gains—whether peanuts or marbles—to another, you can succeed, but competition is maladaptive.

The use of simulation through board games is another kind of learning activity. There is a challenge to early childhood educators to adapt such commercial games as "Landslide" (Parker), an electoral vote game that uses the United States as a base. This particular game has been used with enthusiastic seven- and eight-year-olds as have similar games, such as "The Game of the States" (Milton Bradley) that helps children develop a geographic sense of the nation.

Children can also learn about adult political processes in quite direct ways. Adult elections are apparent to young children as they walk down the street, look at the television, and hear others speak about candidates. It is part of a quantity of unclassified data that they bring to school. While it is isolated information, it becomes part of the gradual mapping process by which children juxtapose bits of data until they merge into concepts.

Therefore, it is a useful excursion for young children to accompany their parents to polling places each year and to watch them vote. It is also useful for the teacher to help children talk about the names of candidates, political parties, and the kinds of issues about which they hear. One parent reported her four-year-old asking why the president wanted more "warring." They proceeded to discuss a range of concerns, including the notion of electing government officials.

CRITICAL AWARENESS

Much of the quality of children's experiences resides in the realm of imagery, on the level of storytelling mythology. It is worthwhile to consider "that in a modern democracy a citizen participates in society mainly through his imagination" (Frye, 1970, p. 104). Part of developing a sense of what is real and what is propaganda or mythology is to have been exposed to a *variety* of humanly *authentic* imagery. In this sense, earlier mention of the need for children to hear different singers render the same songs, to hear different authors, to read biographies of the same people, to see more than one edition of a particular story, to see different photographs of the same subject, and similar experiences—all serve to develop a relevant outlook.

Beginning with four-year-olds, children can begin to discuss minority group roles, sex roles, and aspirations that they find in stories, television, and in their community. It is a pretty grim social outlook when a little girl whose mother is a physician aspires to be a nurse because "girls can't be doctors." While there is a growing body of literature for children that attempts to reverse such stereotypes, there remains a need to discuss such issues.

Some insights into thinking critically are found in the fields of art criticism. Some aspects were dealt with implicitly in Chapter 6. There are many parallels between political consciousness and artistic criticism. Both perspectives deal with values, the sorting of alternatives, and the evaluation of outcomes. Both seek an understanding of the sources of power and control, matters of style in this sense, with respect to effective communication. It is at the point of communication that *contextual* differences make a difference (Richards, 1924, pp. 55, 221; Lasswell, 1958, p. 187).

Different practices, organizational forms, or products, are more and less acceptable in different contexts of time and community. Yet the valuing of human beings, the ethical stance toward what Peters (1967) calls "worthwhile," that answers the questions, "What ought I to do?" or "Why do this rather than that?" presses teachers to attempt a decision that is paradoxical.

On the one hand, the same treatment of different children may be seen as rigid rather than equal, because the children are different. They need different kinds of help or activities. This kind of decision is made in the context of each child. On the other hand, the cultural surroundings and climate of a particular time or movement in education—no less than politics or the arts—may restrict the openness to seeing the work of children, or artists, or political figures, as relevant.

This is a problem of relative thinking and critical awareness in the teacher's work. It is also a human problem for which young children need to be prepared. Inasmuch as relative thinking is needed for contextual valuation, activities are relevant when they help children develop relative thinking. As the perceptual model of dialectical activity becomes perceived through varied activities, suggested in earlier sections, relative thinking can develop. In addition, peer-mediated instruction is a valuable opportunity for children to gain insights into reciprocal roles.

As teachers consider how to keep open young children's possibilities for critical awareness, it is worth noting that it is very hard to see one's own social reality. For a professional teacher, it is an essential competence. One commentator observed that the teachers and administrator who resisted self-examination and change of sex-stereotyped behavior did so because they already viewed themselves as providers of an open and liberated setting (Harrison, 1974).

Inasmuch as schools in this country are locally controlled, and administrative authority tends toward vertical forms of communication, early childhood teachers bear a heavy responsibility to educate administrators and the lay public about early childhood education.

THE LOOK OF LEARNING IN EARLY CHILDHOOD EDUCATION IS A PUBLIC RELATIONS NIGHTMARE

The education of administrators and the lay public is unique for early childhood education, the sight of which can be a public relations nightmare. The naive observer's first impression of a group of normally active young children is often an undifferentiated blur. Guidelines are needed in order to understand the significance of what strikes the sensorium.

The task is not an easy one because many non-early childhood educators, including other educators, approach the matter with inaccurate assumptions.

She wasn't able to handle fifth-graders so let's see how she does in kindergarten.
When you get more experience, will you be able to teach high school?
Oh, you teach in a nursery school. Do you wear a white uniform?
Kindergarten prepares children for first grade.
They play all day.
Well, you don't have to cover any subject matter.

The education of young children need not be viewed as a preparation for "first grade"—as if life were less significant beforehand. Rather, each moment needs to be lived more fully. In this sense, adults probably expect too little of six-year-olds rather than too much of three- and four-year-olds. Such a restricted view of young children occurs when the 3 R's generally—and especially in programs for disadvantaged children—are the exclusive emphasis. The public relations nightmare rests directly with adults who see teaching as telling and learning as listening and repeating.

I am not sure that you can foresee a major change in these perceptions— unfortunately. Nor am I sure that you can expect the lay public to *understand* a dialogical conception of education that they, themselves, have not *experienced*. Understanding and experiencing are different, related processes. However, it may be possible for teachers to help *this* generation of children to break the pattern. If, in some modest ways, teachers can help other adults to appreciate the relevance of an active, open, human education, it may be by helping them to redefine knowing. At the simple level of technique, there are some things that teachers have done.

When children leave the classroom, many parents greet them with, "What did you do/learn in school today?" Often, there is no response from the child since he or she has not the self-awareness to deal with this inquiry. Some teachers have used the moment before departure to provide a verbal description for the children of some of the activities/learnings that took place that day. The child who emerges hatless or unbuttoned on a cold day is a small distraction to a waiting parent. Any substantive information becomes secondary. It is a small, reasonable thing to consider the weather when sending out the children.

You may have noticed the clash between the levels of thinking to which the early childhood teacher becomes subject in a matter of seconds. The swings between considering how to foster young children's critical faculties and how to respect their parents' concern with details are real swings. Simply, the distance between humanity's fund of knowledge and the physical beginnings of knowledge is vast. However, this is what makes consistency between these phases all the more challenging and exciting.

PARENTS

The teacher interprets to parents the long-range significance of visible activity. One way to communicate this relationship is by labelling the children's works that have been displayed with respect, attractively. Another way to communicate this relationship is by using appropriate vocabulary in contexts that encourage children to acquire impressive words. It is just as easy to discuss "opaque" materials as it is to talk about materials that "you cannot see through." In turn, the various benchmarks that define developing skills can be interpreted during parent conferences, group meetings, and in the one-line notes that parents receive on a regular basis. And, across all this, the strongest support will come when parents feel that you know who their child is, that you notice what he or she does, and that you have specific ideas for his or her future activity.

A regularly scheduled individual meeting with a parent is important if such communication is to occur—even if it is by telephone. Most teachers can manage anywhere from two to four conferences a year, with informal conversations interspersed. (Montessori organized weekly parent meetings.) An important facet of working with parents is that the teacher needs to consider the parent's self-concept. A parent who feels threatened or guilty will be less helpful to the teacher or to the child. It is useful to plan such conferences to include several features.

Open with a positive statement or anecdote about what the child has done that communicates something you appreciate about his or her being a child.

Listen to the parent's concerns as you accept feelings, and clarify statements. Some parents hesitate to speak. You might ask, "Do you have any questions about your child's work at school?" or "Is there something you think I should know about him?" or "How does she spend her time at home?" "What does he like to do at home?" Relate the responses to what you have observed at school. You might indicate a way that you are planning to balance or extend the child's experiences at school.

Relationships with other children can be discussed with a similar emphasis upon hearing out the parent's views, *waiting* for the parent to comment, rather than breathlessly "reporting."

One area in which you would particularly like to see a child grow should be planned ahead. Sometimes, your perception of the need may be clarified by the parent's comments. This is the place to deal with a problem you perceive and what you could plan to do in order to help. The problem is stated in positive terms rather than in negative terms of what is wrong with this parent's "production." It is important to pause frequently to give the parent an opportunity to comment, question, and offer suggestions for coping and planning. Should your perception be challenged, it makes for a calmer interchange when you ask the parent to clarify his concerns, and to define his use of terms, "What does that look like?" "What do you mean when you say . . .?," and the reasons for his thinking. In a tight spot, should you feel threatened, it is useful to *postpone* a decision until you can think about it more carefully.

It is useful to *end with a positive comment* about the child's activity as well as the conference.

The individual conference is a time for teacher and parent to share their observations of the child in order for *both* to be of more help to the child. Parents have problems with, and goals for, their children and these concerns need to be appreciated and respected. The parent conference is also a time for teachers to share some of their thinking about the "look of learning" in early education, and to share some of their ways of interacting with children.

Such communication can also occur when parents spend time in the classroom. They may take turns assisting the teacher, or come with a specialized skill to share, or for a particular activity, or a trip. At these times, the teacher behavior becomes an alternative model for parents to see. It is a chance for parents to absorb techniques for handling their own child by observing a more objective adult. In addition, the classroom becomes a reservoir of ideas for activities to do at home. It is also an occasion when parents may feel competent and self-satisfied enough to share a positive approach with their children.

It is all too easy to overlook that a significant part of the teacher's job is working with adults. When the same dialogical approach that teachers use with children is extended, it is likely to be an effective form of communication. Part of being a professional educator is to acquire some critical awareness of one's own conditions, and to take responsibility for being a children's advocate with administrators and other colleagues.

The same format can continue. Problems are raised. Alternative implications, concerns, and actions are explored. Decisions are made. Actions are attempted and assessed, and new problems raised.

BEYOND PARENTS AND SCHOOL

Yet, the within-school and parent involvements of the early childhood educator have taken on a broader perspective in recent years. Educating babies, parent education about babies and toddlers, and parenting education for adolescents and expectant parents, are growing concerns. Honig (1975) and Lane (1975) are two sources that touch on these matters. It can be expected that the next decade will see an expansion of such activities in an attempt to consider the larger systemic influences upon young children. It is the ethical responsibility of early childhood educators to see that human beings will be treated in humane ways and that children retain their right to be educated.

As outlined within the scope of this book, "to be educated" means something quite different from babysitting. The "family day care" concept is better than a laissez-faire conception when educational facilities are unavailable, and when "day care mothers" are prepared, even for a minimal number of hours. However, it is a far cry from what is possible in a professional milieu. It may be that as future parent roles change, a hybrid variety of professional parent may emerge (Toffler, 1970). Perhaps the movement of some three- and four-year-olds and their teachers into high schools, for pre-parent education of adolescents, is prophetic.

Perhaps early childhood classes, in a period of declining population, will be extended to a longer day. This would be preferable to the electronic babysitting service afforded by television in many homes. It might also provide the time that teachers feel they need in order to expose children to a broad range of activities and materials. However, if the longer day is to make a difference, the time needs to be used differently.

There has been little issue with the notion that an ounce of prevention is worth a ton of cure. Individual regions have begun to attempt such an extended involvement with children. "Experimental" pre-kindergartens in New York State, the addition of kindergartens to public schools in parts of the South, and California's extension of educational opportunities for four- through eight-year-olds are examples.

Intervention services in the past have supported largely poverty programs. While such a priority is reasonable, there is a danger present when any single stratum or group is the recipient of particular services. It tends to institutionalize racism. Rather, early childhood services should be made available to youngsters in general, including the handicapped. In addition, a systemic view of parent–child–teacher dialogue—and truly *joint* learning—is needed.

You might well imagine a time when the notion of institutional education will be quite different from what it is now. Schools may be composed of vastly larger units or vastly smaller units. If comparative educational systems suggest anything, it is that smaller administrative units can create more deeply human possibilities and individualization. If children were taught tool skills such as writing and reading by efficient, short-session means, individually or in small groups, the role of early education and later elementary education might become a more richly idea-focussed and experience-focussed phenomenon. A cooperatively organized teaching relationship would help. Such organizational variants and alternative possibilities could be ways to provide a better match for parents, children, and teachers.

The voucher system, a kind of entrepreneurial public education, may not be as futuristic a possibility as one might imagine. It does, however, raise the issue of pluralism vs. unity in our society—the world? Some of the basically unquestioned institutions may be questioned in the future. There are many things that have always been taken for granted about the ways teachers work with children in institutions, within regional and national boundaries, that may change unpredictably. If *The New York Times* (July 11, 1972 dateline) reports that "Films From Moon Cast Doubt on Role of Photosynthesis," how can we be sure of mere institutionalized conventions? The very significance of the early childhood years as basic to education is actually questioned from time to time.

Part of the extended public relations work of the educator is best accomplished through engagement in professional organizations. Part of the task lies in following through with letters to elected officials who may influence legislation for young children. This is the least an educator can do who wishes to be involved with young lives in an imaginative, personal way.

There is much work to be done and many challenges to meet in early childhood education. Not the least source of problems lies with other educators. There are those who know better, yet develop "teacher-proof" materials and question humane education because they do not trust teachers to be sufficiently able or professionally minded. These practices reinforce the fragmentation and faddish pendulum swings to which education has been heir. There is sometimes a fine line between stimulation and manipulation. Perhaps it is less evasive to suggest that only good teachers could support a balanced education for young children. And only good teachers or those capable of becoming good teachers, in this sense, should become educators.

The competent early childhood educator can recognize the point when repetition becomes perseveration, where exploration approaches diffusion, when concrete materials grow static, where enthusiasm becomes overstimulation, where facts become reified, and where cognitive growth has lost its passion. He or she can appreciate the beauty of "authentic innocence" in the young child and enjoy children's raw, primitive efforts at organizing their experiences in unique ways. The competent educator can respond to their reaching out, with a sense of balanced intervention in their lives rather than a neglect or pollution of their experience.

Clearly, it is time to end the self-deprecating chauvinism of early childhood teachers or their would-be protectors. Neither affective development nor cognitive development is a deity to be set upon a pedestal and worshipped, but more like part of a very earthbound system. For children to live in the world, education for young children must be part of the world, not an artificial reproduction or extension of the world, not a glamorized perpetual birthday party, not just an escapist fantasy, and not just a recreational camp-type program.

The issue for early childhood educators need no longer revolve around more-or-less, sooner-or-later, for young children. Rather, there is a moral obligation to let children be, and become. If the guise of a more carefully balanced, integrated education for young children fits, then it should be worn.

REFERENCES

Abe, Kobo (script). *Woman of the dunes*. Direction: Hiroshi Teshigahara. Japan: Teshigahara Productions. 1965. Film.

Adams, E. Merle, Jr. "New viewpoints in sociology," *New Viewpoints in the Social Sciences*. Washington, D.C.: National Council for the Social Studies, 1958.

Allport, Floyd H. *Theories of perception and the concept of structure*. New York: John Wiley and Sons, Inc., 1955.

Allport, Gordon. *Becoming*. New Haven, Conn.: Yale University Press, 1955.

Anderson, Verna Dieckman. *Reading and young children*. New York: The Macmillan Co., 1968.

Aschner, Mary Jane McCue. "The analysis of verbal interaction in the classroom," in *Theory and Research in Teaching*. Edited by Arno A. Bellack. New York: Bureau of Publications, Teachers College, Columbia University, 1963, pp. 53–78.

Baer, Donald M., and Wolf, Montrose M. "The reinforcement contingency in pre-school and remedial education," in *Early Education*. Edited by Robert D. Hess and Roberta Meyer Bear. Chicago: Aldine, 1968, Chapter x, pp. 119–129.

Bandura, Albert. *Aggression. A social learning analysis*. Englewood Cliffs, N.J.: Prentice-Hall, Inc., 1973.

Bellack, Arno A., Kliebard, Herbert M., Hyman, Ronald T., and Smith, Frank L., Jr. *The language of the classroom*. New York: Teachers College Press, 1966.

Bereiter, Carl, and Engelmann, Siegfried. *Teaching disadvantaged children in the preschool*. Englewood Cliffs, N.J.: Prentice-Hall, Inc., 1967.

Bertalanffy, Ludwig von. *Problems of life*. New York: Harper & Row, 1960.

Biggs, Edith. *Mathematics for younger children*. New York: Citation Press, 1971.

Binswanger, Ludwig. "The existential analysis school of thought," trans. by Ernest Angel in May, Rollo, Angel, Ernest, and Ellenberger, Henri F. (ed.), *Existence*. New York: Basic Books, Inc., 1958, pp. 191–213.

Blakeslee, Sandra. "School for blacks offers money-back guarantee," *The New York Times*, June 4, 1975.

Bloom, Benjamin S. (ed.), *Taxonomy of educational objectives*. New York: David McKay Co., Inc., 1956.

Bloomfield, Leonard and Barnhart, Clarence L. *Let's read*. Detroit, Mich.: Wayne State University Press, 1961.

Broek, Jan O. M. *Geography—its scope and spirit*. Columbus, Ohio: Charles E. Merrill Publishing Co., 1965.

Bronfenbrenner, Urie. Introduction to Chauncey, Henry (ed.), *Soviet preschool education*. Volume II. New York: Holt, Rinehart and Winston, Inc., 1969.

Bronfenbrenner, Urie. *Two worlds of childhood: U.S. and U.S.S.R.* New York: Russell Sage Foundation, 1970.

Brown, Roger and Bellugi, Ursula. "Three processes in the child's acquisition of syntax," in Eric H. Lenneberg (ed.), *New Directions in the Study of Language*. Cambridge, Mass.: M.I.T. Press, 1964, pp. 131–161.

Browning, Sherry and Ingham, Susan. *Aesthetic education: a social and individual need*. St. Louis, Mo.: CEMREL, Inc., 1973.

Bruner, Jerome S. *The process of education*. Cambridge, Mass.: Harvard University Press, 1961.

Bruner, Jerome S. *Toward a theory of instruction*. Cambridge, Mass.: Harvard University Press, 1966.

Bruner, Jerome S., Goodnow, Jacqueline J., and Austin, George A. *A study of thinking*. New York: Science Editions, Inc., 1962 (1956).

Buber, Martin. *Between man and man*. Translated by Ronald Gregor Smith. Boston: Beacon Press, 1955 (1947).

Buber, Martin. *I and thou*. Second Edition. Translated by Ronald Gregor Smith. New York: Charles Scribner's Sons, 1958 (1923).

Burrows, Alvina Treut, Jackson, Doris C., and Saunders, Dorothy O. *They all want to write*. Third Edition. New York: Holt, Rinehart and Winston, Inc., 1964.

Butts, R. Freeman and Cremin, Lawrence. *A history of education in American culture*. New York: Holt, Rinehart and Winston, Inc., 1953.

Calitri, Charles. "A structure for teaching the language arts," *Harvard Educational Review*, 35, No. 4 (Fall 1965), pp. 481–491.

Cazden, Courtney. *Child language and education*. New York: Holt, Rinehart and Winston, Inc., 1972.

Cazden, Courtney B. "Language programs for young children: notes from England and Wales," in *Language Training in Early Childhood Education*. Edited by Celia Stendler Lavatelli. Urbana, Ill.: ERIC, 1971, pp. 119–153.

Chall, Jeanne. *Learning to read: the great debate*. New York: McGraw-Hill Book Co., 1967.

Chase, Stuart. *The proper study of mankind*. Revised Edition. New York: Harper & Row, 1956.

Chomsky, Carol. "Stages in language development and reading exposure," *Harvard Educational Review*, 42, No. 1 (February 1972), pp. 1–33.

Chomsky, Carol. "Write now, read later." *Childhood Education*, 47, No. 6, 1971, pp. 296–299.

Chomsky, Noam. *Aspects of a theory of syntax*. Cambridge, Mass.: M.I.T. Press, 1965.

Chomsky, Noam. *Language and mind*. Enlarged Edition. New York: Harcourt, Brace Jovanovich, 1972 (1968).

Chukovsky, Kornei. *From two to five*. Translated and Edited by Miriam Morton. Berkeley: University of California Press, 1963.

Church, Joseph. *Language and the discovery of reality.* New York: Random House, 1961.

Clark, Kenneth and Clark, Mamie. "The development of consciousness of self and the emergence of racial identity in negro preschool children," *Journal of Social Psychology,* 10 (1939), pp. 591–599.

Combs, Arthur (ed.). *Perceiving, behaving, becoming.* Washington, D.C.: Association for Supervision and Curriculum Development, 1962.

Commager, Henry Steele. *The nature and study of history.* Columbus, Ohio: Charles E. Merrill Books, Inc., 1965.

Copeland, Richard W. *How children learn mathematics.* Second Edition. New York: The Macmillan Co., 1974.

Craig, Gerald S. *Science for the elementary school teacher.* New York: Ginn & Co., 1958.

Cratty, Bryant J. *Intelligence in action.* Englewood Cliffs, N.J.: Prentice-Hall, Inc., 1973.

Cratty, Bryant J. *Learning and playing.* Fifty vigorous activities for the atypical child. Freeport, New York: Educational Activities, Inc. n.d. (post 1968).

Curti, Merle. *The social ideas of American educators.* Paterson, N.J.: Littlefield, Adams and Co., 1959.

Davis, Allison and Dollard, John. *Children of bondage.* Washington, D.C.: American Council on Education, 1940.

DeBoer, John J. and Dallman, Martha. *The teaching of reading.* New York: Holt, Rinehart and Winston, Inc. 1970.

Dewey, J. *Art as experience.* New York: Capricorn Books, 1958 (1934).

Dewey, J. *Experience and education.* New York: The Macmillan Co., 1959 (1938).

Dewey, J. *How we think.* Boston: D. C. Heath & Co., 1933.

Dienes, Zoltan P. *Concept formation and personality.* England: Leicester University Press, 1959.

Disney, Walter Productions. *Dumbo.* Adapted for screen by Joe Grant and Dick Huemer. 1941. Film.

Dorn, Miriam Selchen. *A study of the questions asked by kindergarten children.* New York: Teachers College, Columbia University, doctoral dissertation, 1966.

Downing, John, and Thackray, Derek V. *Reading readiness.* England: University of London Press, Ltd., 1971.

Durkin, Dolores. *Children who read early.* New York: Teachers College Press, 1966.

Ellul, Jacques. *The technological society.* Translated by John Wilkinson. New York: Alfred A. Knopf, 1965.

Ervin, Susan M. "Imitation and structural change in children's language," in Eric H. Lenneberg (ed.), *New Directions in the Study of Language.* Cambridge, Mass.: M.I.T. Press, 1964, pp. 163–189.

Fader, D. and McNeil, E. *Hooked on books.* New York: Berkley Medallion Books, 1968.

Feingold, Benjamin. *Why your child is hyperactive.* New York: Random House, 1975.

Festinger, Leon. *A theory of cognitive dissonance.* New York: Harper & Row, 1957.

Freire, Paolo. *Pedagogy of the oppressed.* New York: The Seabury Press, 1970. (a)

Freire, Paolo. "The adult literacy process as cultural action for freedom," *Harvard Educational Review,* 40, No. 2 (May 1970), pp. 205–225. (b)

Freire, Paolo. "Cultural action and conscientization," *Harvard Educational Review,* 40, No. 2 (August 1970), pp. 452–477. (c)

Freire, Paolo. *Education for critical consciousness.* New York: The Seabury Press, 1973.

Freud, Sigmund. *The interpretation of dreams.* Translated and edited by James Strachey. New York: Basic Books, Inc., 1965 (1932).

Fries, Charles Carpenter. *The structure of English.* New York: Harcourt Brace Jovanovich, 1952.

Fromberg, Doris Pronin. *The reactions of kindergarten children to intellectual challenge.* New York: Teachers College, Columbia University: doctoral dissertation, 1965.

Fromm, Erich. *Escape from freedom.* New York: Holt, Rinehart and Winston, Inc., 1941.

Frye, Northrop. *The stubborn structure.* Ithaca: Cornell University Press, 1970.

Gattegno, Caleb. *Reading with words in color.* Reading, England: Educational Explorers, 1969.

Gattegno, Caleb. *Teaching reading with words in color.* New York: Educational Solutions, Inc., 1968.

Genovese, Eugene D. *Roll, Jordan, roll: the world the slaves made.* New York: Pantheon Books, 1974.

Ginnott, Haim G. *Between parent and child.* New York: The Macmillan Co., 1965.

Gleason, H. A., Jr. *Linguistics and English grammar.* New York: Holt, Rinehart and Winston, Inc., 1965.

Goldstein, Kurt. *Human nature in the light of psychopathology.* New York: Schocken Books, 1963.

Gombrich, E. H. *The story of art.* New York: Phaidon Publishers, Inc., 1957.

Goodman, Kenneth S. "Analysis of oral reading miscues: applied psycholinguistics," *Reading Research Quarterly,* 5 (Fall 1969), pp. 9–30.

Goodman, Mary Ellen. *Race awareness in young children.* New York: Collier Books, 1964.

Gordon, Thomas, with Burch, Noel. *T.E.T. Teacher Effectiveness Training.* New York: Peter H. Wyden, 1974.

Gordon, William J. J., and Poze, Tony. *The metaphorical way of learning and knowing.* Cambridge, Mass.: Porpoise Books, 1973.

Gordon, William J. J. *Synectics.* The development of creative capacity. New York: Collier Books, 1961.

Gotshalk, D. W. *Art and the social order.* Chicago: The University of Chicago Press, 1947.

Greenberg, Selma and Peck, Lucy. Untitled manuscript. Hempstead, N.Y.: Hofstra University, n.d.

Gysbers, Norman C., Miller, Wilbur, and Moore, Earl J. (editors). *Developing careers in the elementary school.* Columbus, Ohio: Charles E. Merrill Publishing Co., 1973.

Hainsworth, Peter K. and Siqueland, Marian L. *Early identification of children with learning disabilities: The meeting street school screening test.* Providence: Crippled Children and Adults of Rhode Island, Inc., 1969.

Hall, Calvin S., and Lindzey, Gardner. *Theories of personality.* New York: John Wiley and Sons, Inc., 1957.

Hanson, Norwood Russell. *Observation and explanation.* New York: Harper & Row, 1971.

Harmin, Merrill, Kirschenbaum, Howard, and Simon, Sidney B. *Clarifying values through subject matter.* Minneapolis, Minn.: Winston Press, Inc., 1973.

Harrison, Barbara Grizzuti. *Unlearning the lie: sexism in school.* New York: William Morrow and Co., Inc., 1974.

Hawkins, David. "I, Thou, It," in Charles E. Silberman, Editor. *The Open Classroom Reader.* New York: Vintage Books, 1973, pp. 365–373.

Hawkins, David. "Messing about in science," *Science and Children,* 2 (February 1965), pp. 5–9.

Hayakawa, Sessue Ichiwa. *Language in thought and action.* New York: Harcourt Brace Jovanovich, 1949.

Heidegger, Martin. *Being and time.* Translated by John Macquarrie and Eward Robinson. New York: Harper & Row, 1962.

Henry, Jules. *Pathways to madness.* New York: Vintage Books, 1973 (1965).

Hess, Robert D. "Political socialization in the schools," *Harvard Educational Review,* 38, No. 3 (Summer 1968), pp. 528–536.

Hess, Robert D., and Torney, Judith V. *The development of political attitudes in children.* Chicago: Aldine Publishing Co., 1967.

Hildreth, Gertrude. "Early writing as an aid to reading," in *New Perspectives in Reading Instruction,* edited by Albert J. Mazurkiewicz. New York: Pitman Publishing Corp., 1964, pp. 155–163.

Holt, John. *How children learn.* New York: Pitman Publishing Corp., 1967.

Holt, Michael, and Dienes, Zoltan. *Let's play math.* New York: Walker and Co., 1973.

Honig, Alice S. *Parent involvement in early childhood education.* Washington, D.C.: National Association for the Education of Young Children, 1975.

Horney, Karen. *New ways in psychoanalysis.* New York: W. W. Norton and Co., Inc., 1939.

Hunt, J. McV. *Intelligence and experience.* New York: The Ronald Press Co., 1961.

Husserl, Edmund. *Experience and judgment.* Translated by James A. Churchill and Karl Ameriks. Evanston, Ill.: Northwestern University Press, 1973.

Hyman, Ronald T. (ed.), *Approaches in curriculum.* Englewood Cliffs, N.J.: Prentice-Hall, Inc., 1973.

Hyman, Ronald T. "Means-end reasoning and the curriculum," *Teachers College Record,* 73, No. 3 (February 1972), pp. 393–401.

Imhoff, Myrtle M. *Early elementary education.* New York: Appleton-Century-Crofts, Inc., 1959.

Isaacs, Nathan. "Children's "why" questions," in Isaacs, Susan. *Intellectual growth in young children.* London: Routledge and Kegan Paul Ltd., 1930, pp. 291–349. (a)

Isaacs, Susan. *Intellectual growth in young children.* London: Routledge and Kegan Paul Ltd., 1930. (b)

Isaacs, Susan. *Social development in young children.* New York: Schocken Books, Inc., 1972 (1933).

Jacobs, Leland (ed.), *Using literature with young children.* New York: Teachers College Press, 1965.

Jaspers, Karl. *Reason and existenz.* Translated by William Earle. New York: The Noonday Press, Inc., 1955.

Jastrow, Robert and Thompson, Malcolm H. *Astronomy: fundamentals and frontiers.* Second Edition. New York: John Wiley and Sons, Inc., 1974.

Jennings, M. Kent, and Niemi, Richard G. "Patterns of political learning," *Harvard Educational Review,* 38, No. 3 (Summer 1968), pp. 443–467.

Jersild, Arthur T., and Tasch, Ruth J. *Children's interests and what they suggest for education.* New York: Teachers College Bureau of Publications, 1949.

Johnson, Jean, and Tamburrini, Joan. *Informal reading and writing.* New York: Citation Press, 1972.

Joyce, Bruce. *New strategies for social education.* Chicago: Science Research Associates, Inc., 1972.

Jung, Carl Gustav. *Analytical psychology.* New York: Vintage Books, 1970 (1968).

Karplus, Robert, and Thier, Herbert D. *A new look at elementary school science: science curriculum improvement study.* Chicago: Rand McNally and Co., 1967.

Kazantzakis, Nikos. *Report from Greco.* Translated by P. A. Bien. New York: Simon and Schuster, 1965.

Koestler, Arthur. *The act of creation.* New York: The Macmillan Co., 1964.

Koestler, Arthur. *The call girls.* New York: Random House, 1973. (A novel)

Kohlberg, Lawrence. "A cognitive-developmental analysis of children's sex-role concepts and attitudes," in *The Development of Sex Differences.* Edited by Eleanor E. Maccoby. Stanford, Cal.: Stanford University Press, 1966, pp. 82–173.

Kohlberg, Lawrence. "Development of moral character and moral ideology," in *Review of Child Development.* Edited by Martin L. Hoffman and Lois Wladis Hoffman. New York: Russell Sage Foundation, 1964, pp. 383–431.

Kohlberg, Lawrence and Mayer, Rochelle. "Development as the aim of education," *Harvard Educational Review,* 42, No. 4 (November 1972), pp. 449–496.

Kounin, Jacob and Gump, Paul. "The ripple effect in discipline." *The Elementary School Journal,* 30 (1958), 158–162.

Labov, William. *Sociolinguistic patterns.* Philadelphia: University of Pennsylvania Press, 1972.

Lane, May B. *Education for parenting.* Washington, D.C.: National Association for the Education of Young Children, 1975.

Langer, Suzanne K. *Feeling and form.* New York: Charles Scribner's Sons, 1953.

Langer, Suzanne K. *Philosophy in a new key.* New York: A Mentor Book, 1948 (1942).

Langer, Suzanne K. *Problems of art.* New York: Charles Scribner's Sons, 1957.

Lasswell, Harold D. *Politics: who gets what, when, how.* New York: Meridian Books, Inc., 1958.

Lavatelli, Celia Stendler. *Piaget's theory applied to an early childhood curriculum.* Cambridge: American Science and Engineering, Inc., 1970.

Leach, Edmund. *Levi-Strauss.* London, England: Fontana, 1970.

Leacock, Eleanor Burke. "Abstract versus concrete speech: a false dichotomy," in *Functions of Language in the Classroom.* Edited by Courtney B. Cazden, Vera P. John, and Dell Hymes. New York: Teachers College Press, 1972, pp. 111–134.

Lecky, Prescott. *Self-consistency.* Garden City, N.Y.: Anchor Books, 1969.

Levi-Strauss, Claude. *The elementary structures of kinship.* Translated by James Harle Bell, John Richard von Sturmer and Rodney Needham, Editor. Boston: Beacon Press, 1969 (1949).

Levi-Strauss, Claude. *The raw and the cooked.* Translated by John and Doreen Weightman. New York: Harper Torchbooks, 1969 (1964).

Lewis, M. M. *Language thought and personality in infancy and childhood.* New York: Basic Books, Inc., 1963.

Lorenz, Konrad. *On aggression.* Translated by Marjorie Kerr Wilson. New York: Bantam Books, 1970.

Luria, A. R. *The mind of a mnemonist.* Translated by Lynn Solotaroff. New York: Basic Books, Inc., 1968.

McCaslin, Nellie. *Creative dramatics in the classroom.* New York: David McKay Inc., 1974.

Maccoby, Eleanor E. "Early learning and personality: summary and commentary." in *Early Education.* Edited by Robert D. Hess and Roberta Meyer Bear. Chicago: Aldine, 1968, Chapter XIV, pp. 191–202.

Maccoby, Eleanor Emmons and Jacklin, Carol Nagy. *The psychology of sex differences.* Stanford, Cal.: Stanford University Press, 1974.

MacKay, David, Schaub, Pamela, and Thompson, Brian. *Breakthrough to literacy.* London: Longmans, 1970.

McClelland, David C., Atkinson, John W., Clark, Russell A., and Lowell, Edgar L. *The achievement motive.* New York: Appleton-Century-Crofts, Inc., 1953.

McGinn, Joyce and Rudnick, Fredda. *Primerrily.* New York: Hewlett Public Schools, 1973.

McLuhan, Marshall. *Understanding media: the extensions of man.* New York: Signet Books, 1964.

McLuhan, Marshall. "We need a new picture of knowledge," *New Insights and the Curriculum.* Edited by Alexander Frazier. Washington, D.C.: Association for Supervision and Curriculum Development, 1963, pp. 57–70.

McNeill, David. *The acquisition of language.* New York: Harper & Row, 1970.

Mann, Horace in *The republic and the school.* Edited by Lawrence A. Cremin. New York: Teachers College, Columbia University Bureau of Publications, 1957.

Marcuse, Herbert. *Eros and civilization.* London: Sphere Books Ltd., 1970.

Martin, Lyn S. "What does research say about open education" in *Open Education: Critique and Assessment.* Edited by Vincent R. Rogers and Bud Church. Washington, D.C.: Association for Supervision and Curriculum Development, 1975. Pp. 83–98.

May, Rollo. *Power and innocence.* New York: W. W. Norton & Co., Inc., 1972.

May, Rollo, Angel, Ernest, and Ellenberger, Henri F. (editors). *Existence.* New York: Basic Books, Inc., 1958.

Mazurkiewicz, Albert J. *New perspectives in reading instruction.* New York: Pitman Publishing Corp., 1964.

Mead, George Herbert. *Mind, self, and society.* Chicago: The University of Chicago Press, 1934.

Merleau-Ponty, Maurice. *The primacy of perception.* Edited by James M. Edie. Evanston, Ill.: Northwestern University Press, 1964.

Meyerhoff, Hans (ed.). *The philosophy of history in our time.* Garden City, N.Y.: Doubleday Anchor Books, 1959.

Mills, C. Wright. *The sociological imagination.* New York: Oxford University Press, 1959.

Minnesota, University of. *Project social studies.* United States Office of Education, 1966–1968.

Minsky, Marvin. *Computation: finite and infinite machines.* Englewood Cliffs, N.J.: Prentice-Hall, Inc., 1967.

Mitchell, Lucy Sprague. *Here and now story book.* Revised edition. New York: E. P. Dutton & Co., 1948.

Mitchell, Lucy Sprague. *Young geographers.* New York: John Day Co., 1934.

Moffett, James. *A student-centered language arts curriculum, Grades K-6: A handbook for teachers.* Boston: Houghton Mifflin Co., 1968.

Montessori, Maria. *The Montessori method.* Translated by Anne E. George. New York: Schocken Books, 1965 (1912).

Moore, Omar K. and Anderson, Alan Ross. "The responsive environments project," *Early Education.* Edited by Robert D. Hess and Roberta Meyer Bear. Chicago: Aldine Publishing Co., 1968, pp. 171–189.

Morphett, Mabel V., and Washburne, Carleton. "When should children begin to read?" *Elementary School Journal,* 31 (March 1931), pp. 496–503.

Nagel, Ernest. *The structure of science.* New York: Harcourt Brace Jovanovich, 1961.

Navarra, John Gabriel. *The development of scientific concepts in a young child.* New York: Teachers College Press, 1955.

Niemi, Richard G. "Political socialization," in *Handbook of Political Psychology.* Edited by Jeanne N. Knutson. San Francisco: Jossey-Bass, 1973, Pp. 117–138.

Northrop, F. S. C. *The meeting of east and west.* New York: The Macmillan Co., 1946.

Nuffield Mathematics Project. New York: John Wiley and Sons, Inc., 1967 (Series)

Page, David A. "University of Illinois arithmetic project," *Science Education News* (December 1962), 11.

Pascal, Blaise. *Pensée and the provincial letters.* New York: The Modern Library, 1941.

Peters, Richard S. *Authority, responsibility and education.* New York: Atherton Press, 1966.

Peters, Richard S. *Ethics and education.* Glenview, Ill.: Scott, Foresman and Co., 1967.

Pfeiffer, John. *The thinking machine.* Philadelphia: J. B. Lippincott Co., 1962.

Phenix, Philip H. *Realms of meaning.* New York: McGraw-Hill Book Co., 1964.

Piaget, Jean. *Logic and psychology.* Translated by Dr. Mays and Dr. Whitehead. New York: Basic Books Inc., 1957 (1953).

Piaget, Jean. *The mechanisms of perception.* Translated by G. N. Seagrim. New York: Basic Books, Inc., 1969 (1961).

Piaget, Jean. *Play, dreams and imitation in childhood.* Translated by C. Gattegno and F. M. Hodgson. New York: W. W. Norton and Co., Inc., 1962 (1951).

Piaget, Jean. *The psychology of intelligence.* Translated by Malcolm Piercy and D. E. Berlyne. London: Routledge and Kegan Paul, Ltd., 1950 (1947).

Piaget, Jean, and Inhelder, Bärbel. *The child's conception of space.* Translated by F. J. Langdon and J. L. Lunzer. London: Routledge and Kegan Paul, Ltd., 1956.

Piaget, Jean, and Inhelder, Bärbel. *The early growth of logic in the child.* Translated by E. A. Lunzer and D. Papert. New York: Harper & Row, 1964.

Piaget, Jean, and Inhelder, Bärbel. "The gaps in empiricism." In Koestler, Arthur and Smythies, J. R. *Beyond reductionism.* The Alpbach Symposium 1968. New Perspectives in the Life Sciences. New York: The Macmillan Co., 1969, pp. 118–160.

Piaget, Jean, and Inhelder, Bärbel. *The psychology of the child.* Translated by Helen Weaver. New York: Basic Books, Inc., 1969 (1966).

Piaget, Jean, et al. *The moral judgment of the child.* Translated by Marjorie Gabain. New York: The Free Press, 1965.

Polanyi, Michael. *The study of man.* Chicago: The University of Chicago Press, 1963.

Porter, Judith D. R. *Black child, white child.* Cambridge, Mass.: Harvard University Press, 1971.

Pulaski, Mary Ann Spencer. "The rich rewards of make believe." *Psychology Today* (January 1974), pp. 68–74.

Raths, Louis E., Harmin, Merrill, and Simon, Sidney B. *Values and teaching.* Columbus, Ohio: Charles E. Merrill Publishing Co., 1966.

Renshaw, Domeena C. *The hyperactive child.* Chicago: Nelson-Hall Co., 1974.

Reinhold, Robert. "Sign language offers clues to primeval gift of gab," *The New York Times* (September 30, 1972), 33.

Richards, I. A. *Principles of literary criticism.* New York: Harcourt Brace Jovanovich, 1924.

Robinson, H. Alan, and Thomas, Ellen Lamar. *Improving reading in every class: A source book for teachers.* Boston: Allyn and Bacon, 1972.

Rosenthal, Robert and Jacobson, Lenore. *Pygmalion in the classroom.* New York: Holt, Rinehart and Winston, Inc., 1968.

Rugg, Harold. *Imagination.* New York: Harper & Row, 1963.

Russell, David H. *Children's thinking.* Boston: Ginn and Co., 1956.

Sartre, Jean-Paul. *Being and nothingness.* New York: Philosophical Library, 1956.

Sauvy, Jean and Simonne. *The child's discovery of space.* Translated by Pam Wells. Baltimore: Penguin Books, Inc., 1974.

Shaftel, Fannie R. and Shaftel, George. *Role-playing for social values.* Englewood Cliffs, N.J.: Prentice-Hall, Inc., 1967.

Sheehy, Emma Dickson. *The fives and sixes go to school.* New York: Holt Rinehart and Winston, Inc., 1954.

Siks, Geraldine Brain. *Creative dramatics.* New York: Harper & Row, 1958.

Siu, R. G. H. *The tao of science.* Cambridge: The M.I.T. Press, 1957.

Slobin, Daniel I., and Welsh, Charles A. "Elicited imitation as a research tool in developmental psycholinguistics," in *Studies of Child Language Development.* Edited by Charles A. Ferguson and Dan Isaac Slobin. New York: Holt, Rinehart and Winston, Inc., 1973, pp. 485–497.

Smedslund, Jan. "The circular relation between understanding and logic" (Manuscript. Revised version of paper presented at the XIX International Congress of Psychology, London, 1969), p. 5.

Smilansky, Sara. *The effects of sociodramatic play on disadvantaged preschool children.* New York: John Wiley and Sons, Inc., 1968.

Smith, H. and Dechant, E. *Psychology in teaching reading.* Englewood Cliffs, N.J.: Prentice-Hall, Inc., 1961.

Snygg, Donald and Combs, Arthur N. *Individual behavior.* Revised. New York: Harper & Row, 1959.

Sorauf, Francis J. *Political Science.* Columbus, Ohio: Charles E. Merrill Publishing Co., 1965.

Spalding, Ramolda Bishop with Walter T. Spalding. *The writing road to reading.* Second revised edition. New York: William Morrow & Co., Inc., 1969.

Spaulding, Robert L. *Durham education improvement program: educational intervention in early childhood.* Volume I. Durham, N.C.: Ford Foundation, 1971.

Spodek, Bernard. *Developing social science concepts in the kindergarten.* New York: Teachers College, Columbia University: doctoral dissertation, 1962.

Spodek, Bernard. *Early childhood education.* Englewood Cliffs, N.J.: Prentice-Hall, Inc., 1973.

Steiner, George. *Language and silence.* New York: Atheneum, 1970.

Stephens, Lillian. *The teacher's guide to open education.* New York: Holt, Rinehart and Winston, Inc., 1974.

Stern, Catherine and Gould, Toni. *Children discover reading.* New York: Random House, 1965.

Sullivan, Harry Stack. *The interpersonal theory of psychiatry.* New York: W. W. Norton and Co., Inc., 1953.

Sullivan, Walter. "The Einstein papers: a flash of insight came after long reflection on relativity," *The New York Times,* (March 28, 1972), pp. 1ff.

Sullivan, Walter. "A hole in the sky." *The New York Times,* July 14, 1974, pp. 11ff.

Swensen, Charles Thomas. *An epistemology and the curriculum.* New York: Teachers College, Columbia University: doctoral dissertation, 1975.

Synectics Education Systems. "Aesthetic flowsheet"; "Juggler flowsheet"; "Learning flowsheet" n.d.

Tauber, Edward S., and Green, Maurice R. *Prelogical experience.* New York: Basic Books, 1959.

Theobald, Robert. *Habit and habitat.* Englewood Cliffs, N.J.: Prentice-Hall, Inc., 1972.

Thomas, Alexander, Chess, Stella, and Birch, Herbert G. *Temperament and behavior disorders in children.* New York: New York University Press, 1968.

Tillich, Paul. *The courage to be.* New Haven, Conn.: Yale University Press, 1952.

Toffler, A. *Future shock.* New York: Random House, Inc., 1970.

Torrance, E. Paul, and Myers, R. E. *Creative learning and teaching.* New York: Dodd, Mead and Company, 1970.

Tudor-Hart, Beatrix. "Reading and the acquisition of speech," in *The First International Reading Symposium.* New York: The John Day Co., 1966, pp. 24–33.

Vygotsky, Lev S. *Thought and language.* Translated by E. Hanfmann and G. Vakar. New York: John Wiley and Sons, Inc., 1962.

Walter, Deborah Klein. *Socioemotional measures for preschool and kindergarten children.* San Francisco: Jossey-Bass, 1973.

Walter, Nina Willis. *Let them write poetry.* New York: Holt, Rinehart and Winston, 1962.

Wann, Kenneth, Dorn, Miriam Selchen, and Liddle, Elizabeth Ann. *Fostering intellectual development in young children.* New York: Teachers College, Columbia University Bureau of Publications, 1962.

Ward, Winifred. *Drama with and for children.* Washington, D.C.: Superintendent of Documents, 1960.

Waters, Barbara. *Science can be elementary.* New York: Citation Press, 1973.

Weikart, David, Rogers, Linda, Adcock, Carolyn, and McLelland, Donna. *The cognitively oriented preschool.* Washington, D.C.: National Association for the Education of Young Children, 1971.

Wellek, René and Warren, Austin. *Theory of literature.* New York: Harcourt Brace Jovanovich, 1962.

White, Robert W. "Motivation reconsidered: the concept of competence," *Psychological Review,* 65 (September 1959), 297–333.

Whitehead, Alfred North. *The aims of education.* New York: A Mentor Book, 1929.

Wiener, Norbert. *Cybernetics.* Second Edition. Cambridge, Mass.: The M.I.T. Press, 1961.

Wiener, Robert Behr. *An investigation into open classroom practices in Nassau and Suffolk counties, Long Island, New York, and the types of reading programs implemented in the open classroom.* Hofstra University: doctoral dissertation, 1973.

Wittgenstein, Ludwig von. *Philosophical investigations.* Third Edition. Translated by G. E. M. Anscombe. New York: The Macmillan Co., 1968.

Wolfe, Tom. *The electric kool-aid acid test.* London: Weidenfeld and Nicolson, 1969.

Wolfe, Tom. *The kandy-kolored tangerine-flake streamline baby.* New York: Farrar, Straus and Giroux, 1965.

Wolsch, Robert A. *Poetic composition through the grades.* New York: Teachers College Press, 1970.

Wright, Richard. *Black power.* New York: Harper & Row, 1954.

Yonemura, Margaret. *Developing language programs for young disadvantaged children.* New York: Teachers College Press, 1969.

Yutang, Lin. *The importance of living.* New York: The John Day Co., Inc., 1937.

Zaslavsky, Claudia. *Africa counts.* Boston: Prindle, Weber and Schmidt, Inc., 1973.

BIBLIOGRAPHY FOR USE WITH CHILDREN

Adoff, Arnold. (Editor). *My black me.* New York: E. P. Dutton & Co., Inc., 1974.

Beim, Jerrold. *Eric on the desert.* New York: William Morrow & Co., 1953.

Beim, Jerrold, and Beim, Lorraine. *Two is a team.* Illustrated by Ernest Crichlow. New York: Harcourt Brace Jovanovich, 1945.

Bendick, Jeanne. *The first book of automobiles.* Second Revised Edition. Illustrated by Jeanne Bendick. New York: Franklin Watts, Inc., 1971.

Blume, Judy. *Tales of a fourth grade nothing.* Illustrated by Roy Doty. New York: E. P. Dutton & Co., Inc., 1972.

Brewster, Benjamin [pseud.]. *The first book of baseball.* By Mary Elting. Illustrated by Jeanne Bendick. New York: Franklin Watts, Inc., 1963.

Brown, Marcia, retold by. *Three billy goats gruff.* Illustrated by Marcia Brown. New York: Harcourt Brace Jovanovich, 1972.

Brown, Margaret Wise. *The dead bird.* Reading, Mass.: Addison-Wesley Publishing Co., Inc., 1958.

Brown, Margaret Wise. *The noisy book.* Illustrated by Ross Thomson. New York: Scroll Press, 1973.

Burchard, S. H. *Walt Frazier.* Illustrated by Paul Frame. New York: Harcourt Brace Jovanovich, 1975.

Burton, Virginia. *The little house.* Illustrated by Virginia L. Burton. Boston: Houghton Mifflin Co., 1942.

Chapman, Victoria. *Let's go to a service station.* Illustrated by Paul Frame. New York: G. P. Putnam's Sons, 1974.

Cleary, Beverly. *Ramona the pest.* Illustrated by Louis Darling. New York: William Morrow & Co., Inc., 1968.

Credle, Ellis. *Down down the mountain.* Illustrated by Ellis Credle. Nashville, Tenn.: Thomas Nelson, Inc., 1934.

de Regniers, Beatrice Schenk. *The giant story.* Illustrated by Maurice Sendak. New York: Harper & Row, 1953.

Felt, Sue. *Rosa-too-little.* Illustrated by Sue Felt. Garden City, N.Y.: Doubleday & Co., Inc., 1950.

Flack, Marjorie. *Ask Mr. Bear.* Illustrated by Marjorie Flack. New York: The Macmillan Co., 1958.

Freed, Alvyn M. *T. A. for tots.* Sacramento, Cal.: Jalmar Press Inc., 1974.

Gag, Wanda. *Millions of cats.* Illustrated by Wanda Gag. New York: Coward, McCann, & Geoghegan, Inc., 1938.

Gerger, Dawn. *Word find puzzles #1.* New York: Grosset and Dunlap, Inc., 1973.

Giovanni, Nikki. "Winter poem," in *My black me.* Edited by Arnold Adoff. New York: E. P. Dutton Co., Inc., 1974, p. 27.

Guthrie, Woody. "Put your finger in the air"; "Wake up"; *Songs to grow on.* Volume One. New York: Folkways Record and Service Corp., 1958. (FC 7005)

Henriod, Lorraine. *Marie Curie.* Illustrated by Lorraine Henriod. New York: G. P. Putnam's Sons, 1970.

Henry, Joanne Landers. *Marie Curie, discoverer of radium.* Illustrated by John Martinez. New York: The Macmillan Co., 1966.

Hughes, Langston. *First book of rhythms.* Illustrated by Robin King. New York: Franklin Watts, 1954.

Jacobs, Joseph. (Editor). *Pied piper and other fairy tales.* Illustrated by James Hill. New York: The Macmillan Co., 1968.

Johnson, Crockett [pseud.]. *Harold and the purple crayon.* By David Johnson Leisk. New York: Harper & Row, 1958.

Keats, Ezra Jack. *Peter's chair.* New York: Harper & Row, 1967.

Kesselman, Wendy. *Angelita.* Photos by Norma Holt. New York: Hill and Wang, 1970.

Kettelkamp, Larry. *Magic made easy.* Illustrated by Larry Kettelkamp. New York: William Morrow & Co., 1954.

Krauss, Ruth. *The carrot seed.* Illustrated by Crockett Johnson. New York: Scholastic, 1971.

Krauss, Ruth. *The growing story.* Illustrated by Phyllis Rowand. New York: Harper & Row, 1947.

Lamorisse, Albert. *The red balloon.* Garden City, N.Y.: Doubleday and Co., Inc., 1956.

Landeck, Beatrice. *Songs to grow on.* New York: Edward B. Marks Music Corp., 1950.

Lexau, Joan M. *Benjie on his own.* Illustrated by Don Bolognese. New York: The Dial Press, 1970.

Lindsay, Vachel. "The little turtle," in *Johnny appleseed and other poems.* Illustrated by George Richards. New York: The Macmillan Co., 1961, p. 4.

Lipkind, William, and Mordvinoff, Nicholas. *Russet and the two reds.* New York: Harcourt Brace Jovanovich, 1962.

Lundgren, Max. *Matt's grandfather.* Illustrated by Max Lundgren. New York: G. P. Putnam's Sons, 1972.

MacDonald, Golden [pseud.]. *The little island* by Margaret Wise Brown. Illustrated by Leonard Weisgard. New York: Doubleday & Co., Inc., 1971.

McCloskey, Robert. *Blueberries for Sal.* Illustrated by Robert McCloskey. New York: Viking Press, 1968 (1948).

McCloskey, Robert. *One morning in Maine.* Illustrated by Robert McCloskey. New York: Viking Press, 1952.

McKown, Robin. *Marie Curie*. Illustrated by Robin McKown. New York: G. P. Putnam's Sons, 1971.

Manton, Jo. *Elizabeth Garrett, M.D.* New York: Abelard-Schuman, 1960.

Meyer, Jerome S. *Engines*. Illustrated by John Teppich. Cleveland: The World Publishing Co., 1962.

Miles, Miska. *Annie and the old one*. Illustrated by Peter Parnall. Boston: Little, Brown & Co., 1971.

Milne, A. A. *Now we are six*. Illustrated by E. H. Shepard. New York: E. P. Dutton & Co., Inc., 1958.

Milne, A. A. *When we were very young*. Illustrated by E. H. Shepard. New York: E. P. Dutton & Co., Inc., 1958.

Milne, A. A. *Winnie-the-pooh*. Illustrated by E. H. Shepard. New York: E. P. Dutton & Co., Inc., 1957.

Minarik, Else H. *Little bear*. Illustrated by Maurice Sendak. New York: Harper & Row, 1957.

Olsen, James T. *Joe Namath, the king of football*. Illustrated by Montie Salmela. Chicago: Children's Press, 1974.

Rey, Hans A. *Curious George*. Illustrated by H. A. Rey. New York: Houghton Mifflin Co., 1973.

Schlein, Miriam. *Heavy is a hippopotamus*. Reading, Mass.: Addison-Wesley Publishing Co., Inc., 1954.

Schlein, Miriam. *My family*. Illustrated by Harvey Weiss. New York: Abelard-Schuman, 1960.

Schlein, Miriam. *The way mothers are*. Illustrated by Joe Lasker. Chicago: Albert Whitman & Co., 1963.

Schneider, Herman and Nina. *Follow the sunset*. Pictures by Lucille Corcos. New York: Doubleday & Co., Inc., 1952.

Segal, Edith. "Be my friend," *Be my friend*. New York: The Citadel Press, 1952, p. 9.

Selsam, Millicent. *All about eggs*. Reading, Mass.: Addison-Wesley Publishing Co., Inc., 1952.

Slobodkina, Esphyr. *Caps for sale*. Reading, Mass.: Addison-Wesley Publishing Co., Inc., 1947.

Southgate, Vera, retold by. *The enormous turnip*. Illustrated by Robert Lumley. Loughborough, England. Wills and Hepworth, Ltd., 1970.

Steinbeck, John. *The grapes of wrath*. New York: Viking Press, 1939.

Stevenson, Robert Louis. "My Shadow," *The child's garden of verses*. New York: Platt and Munk, 1961, p. 38.

Sullivan, George. *Pass to win*. Illustrated by Pers Crowell. Chicago: Garrard Publishing Co., 1968.

Tresselt, Alvin. *I saw the sea come in*. Illustrated by Roger Duvoisin. New York: Lothrop, Lee & Shepard Co., 1968.

Tworkov, Jack. *The camel who took a walk*. Illustrated by Roger Duvoisin. New York: E. P. Dutton & Co., Inc., 1974.

White, E. B. *Charlotte's web*. Illustrated by Garth Williams. New York: Dell, 1968.

Wilder, Laura Ingalls. *The little house on the prairie*. Revised edition. Illustrated by Garth Williams. New York: Harper & Row, 1975.

Wilder, Laura Ingalls. *The long winter*. New York: Harper & Row, 1940.

Yashima, Taro. *The umbrella.* Illustrated by Taro Yashima. New York: Viking Press, 1970.

Zim, Herbert S. *What's inside of engines?* Illustrated by Raymond Perlman. New York: William Morrow and Co., 1953.

Zim, Herbert S., and Skelly, James R. *Hoists, cranes, and derricks.* Illustrated by Gary Ruse. New York: William Morrow & Co., 1969.

INDEX